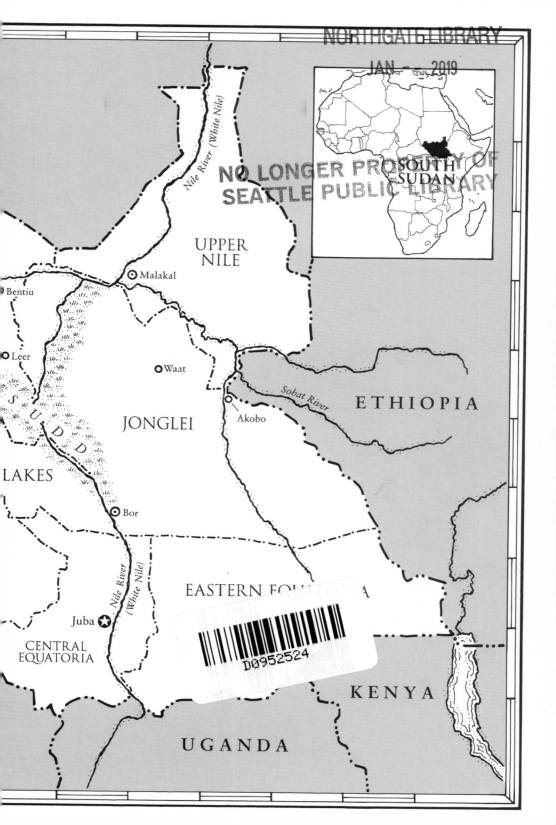

SOUTH
SUDAN

UPPER
NILE

Nile River (White Nile)

Malakal

Bentiu

Leer

Waat

S U D D

JONGLEI

LAKES

Sobat River

ETHIOPIA

Akobo

Bor

Nile River (White Nile)

EASTERN EQUATORIA

Juba

CENTRAL
EQUATORIA

KENYA

UGANDA

A ROPE
FROM THE SKY

A ROPE FROM THE SKY

The Making and Unmaking
of the World's Newest State

ZACH VERTIN

PEGASUS BOOKS
NEW YORK LONDON

A ROPE FROM THE SKY

Pegasus Books Ltd.
148 W 37th Street, 13th Floor
New York, NY 10018

First Pegasus Books edition January 2019

Library of Congress Cataloging-in-Publication Data is available.

ISBN: 978-1-64313-051-4

10 9 8 7 6 5 4 3 2 1

Printed in the United States of America
Distributed by W. W. Norton & Company, Inc.
www.pegasusbooks.us

For Princeton Lyman

a rope from the sky

In the Nilotic folktales of South Sudan, the earth and sky were once linked by a rope. This rope gave the people direct access to God, the heavens, and eternal life. But the rope was severed, tragically, on account of human action. And forever since, the fate of the people has been bound to the earth and to the difficulties, suffering, and mortality that constrain the human condition. This book, too, is a story of paradise lost.

CONTENTS

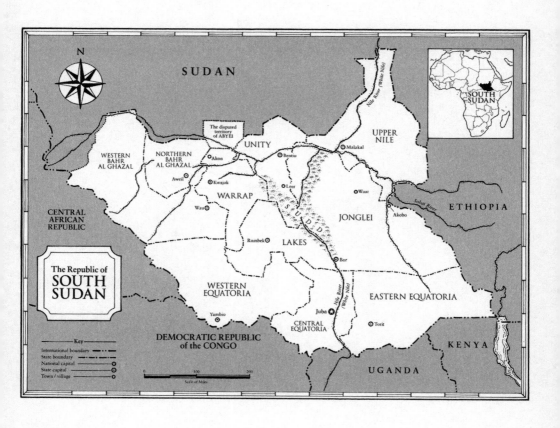

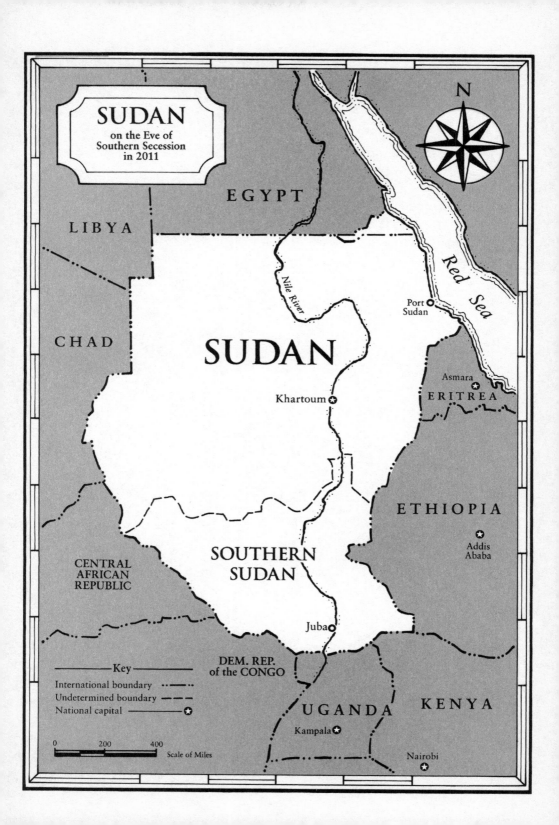

TIMELINE

1983–2005   Second Sudanese Civil War

1991   SPLA "split" fractures the Southern rebellion, igniting a decade of fighting between Southern Sudanese factions and, by extension, between ethnic Dinka and Nuer

2003   Conflict in Sudan's western region of Darfur begins

2005   Sudan's North and South sign the Comprehensive Peace Agreement, ending the Civil War

2005–2011   "Interim Period"—Sudan's North and South attempt continued union for a six-year trial period; at the end of the period, South Sudan can vote to remain part of Sudan or to become an independent state

2011 (January)   South Sudan votes to secede in referendum on self-determination

2011 (July)   The Republic of South Sudan achieves independence

2013   Civil War erupts in the new Republic of South Sudan

2014   South Sudan is ranked No. 1 on list of world's most fragile states

2014–2016   An internationally-backed peace process attempts to end the civil war and salvage the promise of the world's newest state

AUTHOR'S NOTE

Sudan is a faraway place, but its extraordinary stories register widely in popular consciousness. For some, Sudan is the devastating war in Darfur, and the popular Western campaign to stop it. For others, the first words that come to mind are "George Clooney," the celebrity activist who introduced millions of Americans to a righteous cause. Many know of the "Lost Boys" from popular books and film, the refugee children who walked thousands of miles to escape war, famine, and wild animals before assimilating in towns across Europe and North America. Others simply know that many Sudanese are tall, and that a select few have achieved success at the highest levels of American professional basketball.

But most do not know the extraordinary story that led Sudan—Africa's largest country—to be split in two. On July 9, 2011, the Republic of South Sudan declared its independence from Sudan, marking an end to generations of repression and neglect. The euphoric birth of the world's newest nation was celebrated the world round, a triumph for global justice and a signal that one of the world's ugliest wars was finally over. "A proud flag flies over Juba," read a declaration from President Barack Obama, "and the map of the world has been redrawn."

But the honeymoon did not last long. South Sudan came undone just two years later, when its liberation heroes turned their guns on each other, plunging their new nation back into war. The shocking events that followed shattered the promise of freedom that had won the hearts and minds of so many champions around the globe.

What went so horribly wrong?

This book tells the story of the making and unmaking of the world's newest state. It is the story of a people who rally around a common idea and achieve the unthinkable. Driven by conscience, righteousness, or religion, it is also the story of an unprecedented Congressional coalition, three U.S. presidents, and legions of ordinary Americans mobilizing on their behalf. Finally, it is a story of picking up the pieces and starting over, an uncertain quest to salvage a republic from the shards of a shattered dream.

A Rope from the Sky is first a story of hope, loss, power, greed, and compassion. But it is also a story of America's attempt to help forge a nation amid a deeply divided society. Washington's intervention in South Sudan reflects both the best and worst of America—its big-hearted ideals and its reckoning with the limits of U.S. influence amid a changing global order.

This book is not another "B" movie script about savage African warlords, nor another tale of faceless depravity from a mysterious continent. More nuanced narratives from Africa don't fit the persistent inclination for black-and-white explanations, bite-sized moral judgments, and romantic constructs of good guys and bad guys. When it comes to journalism and discourse on Africa, we continue to accept a lower bar. The truth is more complicated, and we lose it, to our detriment, in every reductionist tale from the "dark continent."

At dinner parties back home in the United States, I am sometimes asked the question: "They just seem so destined to kill each other; is there really any hope?" Indeed, it is easy for any of us to forget our own struggles in nation-building, and to expect that other countries—aided by the tools of modernity—should simply get their act together. But it wasn't so long ago that Americans fought their own civil war, to the tune of 750,000 deaths, over identity, economy, and the nature of their state.

South Sudan's formative first years presented a challenge no less complex. Its leaders confronted a task far greater than themselves, and the consequences of their failure have been devastating. But South Sudan's turbulent arrival cannot simply be explained by "bad men" who are "inherently violent." It is a confluence of ideas and interests, personalities and systems, tradition and modernity. Its protagonists are both inspired and ordinary; their aspirations are matched by insecurities, their sins by courage and kindness. The story, and the voices that help tell it here, are rich, complicated, hopeful, sad, beautiful, messy, and human.

South Sudan's independence was not a mistake. And nor are its foreign supporters to blame for what ensued, as the nation's destiny does not ultimately belong to outsiders. But having adopted the underdog's cause, leaned on the scales, and then moved on too soon, the role of the West warrants critical reflection. This book considers how America became so deeply invested, and why it matters for Americans amid a world in disarray.

The troubled birth of South Sudan is a unique episode in global history—an unprecedented experiment in state-building, and a cautionary tale. It is a political story, and a human one—about perseverance, liberation, survival, and the line dividing good and evil, as Alexsandr Solzhenitsyn wrote, that cuts through each of our hearts.

This book is the product of eight years living in, traveling to, and working on Sudan and South Sudan between 2009 and 2017. I first went to Sudan as an analyst for the International Crisis Group—a non-profit organization that conducts research and analysis on the prevention and resolution of armed conflict. I arrived two years before South Sudan's independence, and was fortunate to travel widely, talking with Southern citizens, political leaders, military officers, chiefs, youth leaders, refugees, cattle keepers, cleaning ladies, fishermen, and motorcycle taxi drivers. They taught me a great deal about their country-in-waiting, one with as many rich, fascinating, and confusing layers as my own.

I followed political, social, and economic trends in the emergent region as it closed in on independence—a goal more than five decades in the making. Those were heady days: from the brinkmanship that defined the period before independence, to the wider political chess match in which the separation of the country occurred, to the new nation's attempts to find its footing.

My reporting was informed by hundreds of conversations—in government offices, and rebel strongholds, and under mango trees on the banks of the River Nile. It was also shaped by conversations in African capitals, and in Washington, London, Oslo, Brussels, Beijing, and the halls of the African Union and the United Nations—each of which played a role in the making of South Sudan.

On a sweltering day in July 2011, hundreds of thousands gathered to declare, at long last, an independent Republic of South Sudan. It was an unforgettable moment—an exercise of political self-determination after decades of marginalization and violence in the "old" Sudan. I continued writing about the young country in its first year after independence—the good, bad, ugly, ominous, and exciting, until returning to the United States in the summer of 2012.

I joined the U.S. government in the fall of 2013, serving for three years as Director of Policy in the Office of the Special Envoy for Sudan and South Sudan, which spearheads American diplomacy on behalf of the White House and the Department of State.

The majority of my time as an American diplomat was spent at the center of the South Sudan peace process, working closely with the warring parties, international mediators, and African governments who sought to end a senseless war. This included days, then weeks, then months of dialogue with South Sudan's leading men—and they were mostly men—many of whom I had come to know during my years in their country. Fortunately, my history and relationships afforded me a degree of credibility that allowed for frank and open dialogue.

I left the Obama administration in 2016 to begin writing this book, though I thought long and hard before doing so. I knew that I had been present—often with insider access—during the country's most formative years, and in some sense I sat astride the unique relationship between South Sudan and America. Nonetheless, I wondered whether I was an appropriate narrator. After soliciting advice from confidants in both countries, I decided to proceed.

A Rope from the Sky is the untold story of the making and unmaking of South Sudan. It is one narrative, and one set of reflections, from an observer who became enthralled by the place, its people, and its rhythms.

The pages that follow draw on hundreds of interviews, many conducted specifically for the book, others that were done during years of prior research. In addition to my own tattered notebooks, files, photos, and memories, I relied on a network of South Sudanese individuals who shared with me their lives—their ideas, opinions, emotions, hopes and predictions. Some of them were new to me, others I had known for years. Some were political big shots, others were ordinary citizens. Each brought unique perspectives and helped piece together this incredible puzzle of a story.

And so I am forever grateful to the many Southern Sudanese who taught me about their country, and who shared their stories for this book.

NOTES FOR THE READER

- The terms "Southern Sudan" and "South Sudan" are used at different stages in this book. The former is used to refer to the geographic (and semi-autonomous) region of Sudan prior to independence. The latter refers to the independent Republic after July 2011.

- The guerrilla army known as the Sudan People's Liberation Army, "SPLA," was founded together with the Sudan People's Liberation Movement, "SPLM," its political wing, though the line between the two was often indistinguishable. The SPLM went on to become South Sudan's ruling party at independence, and the SPLA became its national army.

- At the time of South Sudan's independence in 2011, the country was divided into ten states. These administrative units will be referenced herein for political and geographical purposes. (A new system of states was introduced in 2015, albeit amid some controversy.)

- The names of some individuals who appear in this book have been changed to protect their identity. This does not include public figures. Most interviews were conducted in English, though some were conducted (whether in indigenous languages or Arabic) with the assistance of a translator.

A ROPE
FROM THE SKY

PROLOGUE

JUBA, DECEMBER 15, 2013

Just before midnight, the crack-crack of an AK-47 disturbed the quiet. For a city long awash in eastern bloc rifles, the familiar staccato wasn't out of the ordinary—but it drew heightened attention on this already tense evening in Juba.

Crack-crack.

These were not the errant shots of a foot soldier who had downed one too many beers. The rounds had been fired inside the headquarters of the presidential guard, the so-called Tiger Division, in the south central part of the city. Seconds later, a barrage of gunfire erupted.

Rival factions within the guard, from South Sudan's two dominant ethnic groups—Dinka and Nuer—had turned their guns on each other. Tracer bullets streaked through the darkness. The chatter of small-arms fire intensified. Fighting spread like brushfire to military facilities across Juba as each side sought control of ammunition depots and rallied more units to action.

Gun battles spilled into residential neighborhoods, sending scores of frantic civilians into flight. Thatched-roof homes were set alight, dotting the darkened horizon with flares of incandescent orange and thick plumes of smoke. Small-arms fire soon gave way to the thud of heavy machine guns and the blasts of mortar shells. Hundreds of terrified civilians swarmed to the United Nations base in the Tomping neighborhood, pleading for the gates to be opened.

In a matter of hours, the military chain of command collapsed, replaced by dueling ethnic authorities. Those now trading fire were elements loyal to the country's president, Salva Kiir, a Dinka, and to its deposed vice president, Riek Machar, a Nuer.

Hours earlier, a long-simmering dispute inside the country's ruling party, the Sudan People's Liberation Movement, had reached a boil. After fighting Africa's longest civil war against dominant regimes in the North, the SPLM had assumed power in the newly independent Republic of South Sudan in 2011. But a growing struggle between the party's leading figures had sparked the night's violence—and now threatened the young nation's collapse. Riek *(Ree-ack)* and other would-be challengers wanted the president to step down. But Salva wasn't about to be pushed aside.

Their dispute was about power, not ethnicity. But while a state had been born in South Sudan, a nation was still in the making. Tribal allegiance remained paramount in the new Republic, and the two men were scions of rival ethnic communities with a troubled history. Together they personified the unreconciled sins of a war era that had sometimes pitted their tribes against each other. And so in the ensuing days, each man would mobilize his ethnic base by summoning the ghosts of the past.

After a decades-long liberation struggle, a return to war seemed unthinkable. Now, just two years since the triumph of independence, South Sudan's guerillas-turned-governors seemed set on throwing it all away. It was not supposed to go this way.

Two years earlier, on July 9, 2011, cries of "South Sudan *Oyyyyy-aaayyh!*" rang out from atop a ceremonial balcony. "South Sudan *Oyyyyy-aaayyh!*" the master of ceremonies belted out again,

"Jenub Sudan Oyyyyy-aaayyh!" The crowd below—the largest ever in Juba—responded exuberantly, *"South Sudan Oyyyyyy-aaayyh!"* The call-and-response would be repeated frequently on this most historic of occasions, as a sea of giddy nationals readied to taste freedom for the first time. Today was Independence Day.

Tens of thousands had arrived at the newly christened Freedom Square to celebrate their nation's birth. Many had been standing in the blazing sun since dawn, and they stood elbow to elbow for as far as the eye could see. They sang songs, waved miniature flags, and boogied to the pulsing beats of their homeland. Some dressed in their Sunday best, while others sported sashes, feathered headdresses, and strings of colorful beads. Some came with painted shields, others with painted faces. Many carried framed portraits of their liberation icon, the late Dr. John Garang, and his successor, Salva Kiir.

Dignitaries and invited guests packed a concrete grandstand stretching several hundred feet down one side of a wide avenue. The grandstand was topped by a balcony draped in the nation's colors and a canopied section for "VVIP"—very, very important guests.

Like an eager host rushing to prepare for a housewarming bash, the South Sudanese had spent the preceding weeks readying their city for its moment in the spotlight. Streets had been paved, fences painted, and thoroughfares lined with freshly planted trees and rose bushes. Young boys cut grass with machetes, and elderly ladies collected rubbish and swept dusty roads with hand brooms. Youth groups previewed vibrant new costumes and rehearsed traditional songs for the people's parade that would dance its way to the party.

It was hot, white hot. Guests in the grandstand shimmied to the music as sweat poured down their cheeks and onto soaked shirt collars. Soldiers in dress uniform stood at attention for the duration of the ceremony, dozens of whom would collapse from heat stroke and be carried away on stretchers. Even so, it was hard to distract from the excitement.

Military units marched in formation down the broad avenue wearing green, blue, and red dress uniforms and matching berets. Tall, thin, and exceptionally dark, these young men and women enjoyed the most distinct of honors, representing not only their communities and their country, but the millions of heroes who had fought and died over decades of liberation struggle. The cheers crested as one special unit—the war-wounded veterans—hobbled down the avenue on crutches, their dark green fatigues wrapped around the stumps of missing limbs.

Meanwhile, bands and fireworks marked parallel celebrations in state capitals and county seats across the country, and the excitement did not stop there. Because so many war-era refugees had resettled abroad, Southerners gathered to celebrate at school gymnasiums as far away as Omaha, Nebraska, and Portland, Maine. Sons and daughters of the struggle became choked up at ceremonies in London, Toronto, and Sioux Falls, South Dakota.

Back at Freedom Square, the atmosphere was electric. Shivers ran through the bodies of the country's inaugural citizens, the crowd infused with a palpable energy. Hundreds of cameramen, photographers, and journalists from around the globe perched precariously on elevated platforms rising from within the crowd, each filing live updates as the big moment approached. On this one day, the whole world was watching Juba. And on this day, it seemed, there were no Nuer, no Dinka, no Anyuak, and no Shilluk. There were only South Sudanese.

Exactly six months earlier, in January 2011, millions of Southerners had waited in long lines to cast their votes for independence. Yellow signs hung from government offices and mud huts, from corrugated tin schools and under designated groves of trees, each one of the thousands of polling stations opened nationwide. In a country more than 70 percent illiterate, the ballots were made simple. One box depicted two hands clasped—a representation of "unity" with Sudan. In the other box, a single free hand raised alone—a representation of "separation" from Sudan. A purple-inked fingerprint would mark the spot.

Adorned in white dress, tiara, and a wreath of native flowers, Mama Rebecca Kadi was carried in her wheelchair up the steps of a polling station in Juba. Thought to be South Sudan's oldest woman—reportedly 115 years—Mama Rebecca had seen everything. Upon inking her vote for independence, she exclaimed, "This is the best day ever in my life!" Mama Rebecca could now die happy, she said; the liberation struggle was finally over.

Southern Sudan was among the most marginalized and underdeveloped places on earth, and had been embroiled in wars with repressive governments in Khartoum for half a century. Its people had battled not only racial and cultural subjugation, but decades of hunger, disease, and displacement. They had lost more than two million sons and daughters to war, and those who survived continued to be denied services, opportunity, or any real voice in their own government. They had been treated as outsiders, trapped inside an arbitrary colonial border with scant hopes of improving their lot.

And so John Garang had once famously asked his people, "When the time comes to vote at the referendum, it is your golden choice to determine your fate. Would you like to be second-class citizens in your own country?" In the end, the answer to that question was overwhelming. Four million Southern Sudanese cast votes in the referendum—99 percent of them for independence.

As the independence ceremony was about to begin, sirens blared and red-and-blue lights flashed as convoy after convoy delivered foreign diplomats and VIP guests to the huge new grandstand. Thirty heads of state and dignitaries from around the world had descended upon Juba for the festivities. The American delegation settled in to their seats, headed by former Secretary of State Colin Powell, who had signed the historic 2005 peace agreement affording Southerners the right to self-determination. Sitting beside him were Susan Rice, then President Obama's ambassador to the UN, and Congressman Donald Payne of New Jersey—two of South Sudan's most ardent champions.

All eyes fixed on two flag poles as the afternoon ceremony approached its climax. For ten precious seconds, the cheers and ululations reached an ear-splitting crescendo as the Sudanese flag was lowered, and the new South Sudanese flag simultaneously raised. Independence, at last. Tears streamed down the faces of elderly women, strangers hugged one another, and triumphant fists thrust into the air.

Donning his trademark black cowboy hat, the president rose to the podium. "I, General Salva Kiir, do hereby swear by the almighty

God ..." When he finished his oath, Salva clutched the new constitution with both hands and waved it to a crowd in full fervor.

The often underwhelming president then rose to the occasion, delivering a magnanimous inaugural address. He spoke of duty, sacrifice, and the tall tasks ahead. "The eyes of the world are on us," he said, and rising to the challenge of statehood would require South Sudanese to overcome the divisions of the past. "May this day mark a new beginning of tolerance, unity and love for one another," the president concluded. "Let our cultural and ethnic diversity be a source of pride and strength, not parochialism and conflict."

Vice President Riek Machar followed suit. Salva and Riek had always been uncomfortable bedfellows, but their complicated history was set aside today as Riek extolled Salva's courageous leadership. As the new Republic's citizens listened to the words of their leaders, expectations swelled.

Remarks were delivered by African heads of state, the UN Secretary-General, the Crown Prince of Norway, and a Chinese presidential envoy—each one taking the opportunity to formally recognize the Republic of South Sudan. Susan Rice was next. Climbing atop a milk crate to reach the podium, she hailed a "day of triumph" for the people of South Sudan. Their story, she said, had reminded the world that "few forces on Earth are more powerful than a citizenry tempered by struggle and united in sacrifice." Emphasizing the special relationship between the United States and South Sudan, she declared: "My country too was born amid struggle and strife on a July day. On this day, the world's oldest democracy welcomes the world's newest state."

All urged the South Sudanese to be mindful of the huge challenges ahead. But it was hard to give tomorrow's task much thought; today was for celebrating. After two civil wars and two million lives lost, their tumultuous history with Sudan was now behind them. The 9th of July meant overcoming the legacies of exclusion, racism, and subjugation. The people of South Sudan were finally free to be themselves in their own land. The slate was clean, and the future theirs for the taking.

Simon huddled alone in his shack, listening nervously as the fighting drew closer. His chest tightened with fear. Earlier on the afternoon of December 15, in a local market, he had overheard a couple of Dinka boys talking surreptitiously about impending violence. He wondered, now, if this was what they had been discussing.

After a late-night lull in the fighting, Simon settled down on his sleeping mat for a few hours of restless shuteye. But as the sun rose on Monday, December 16, he knew he was not yet safe. "The violence started again," he recalls, and it was about to get much worse. "PKMs, AKs, anti-tank guns"—he rattles off the soundtrack of the escalating conflict, his ability to identify such an arsenal by ear revealing much about his homeland.

Two years have passed since those terrifying hours, but Simon remembers them vividly. He and I sit alone at a quiet patio table in the back of a Juba restaurant. I met Simon earlier in the afternoon while walking around Manga Ten, a predominantly Nuer neighborhood on Juba's north side. He's in his early twenties—tall and skinny, with relaxed shoulders and a distinctive scar over his left eyebrow. A native of Akobo, some 200 miles northeast of the capital, he was just eighteen months away from completing his studies at a Juba secondary school when the fighting erupted. He is the first of many who will recount to me their experience of that awful night.

He emerged cautiously, he recalls, to consult neighbors in Manga Ten, but the jumble of rumors then circulating confused him. What was not in doubt, he says, was the ethnic dimension of the unfolding conflict.

Simon had returned to South Sudan in 2009 after nearly a decade in Kakuma Refugee Camp, in neighboring Kenya. The dusty supercamp has hosted those fleeing Sudan's wars for a quarter-century, and was a transit point for many of the "Lost Boys" later resettled in Europe and North America. Despite the upheaval that once drove Simon and millions of others across international borders, the education he received at Kakuma—one he would not have gotten at home—was a silver lining.

To complement his native Nuer, he learned Swahili and English, which set him apart from many of his peers in the village. So did his outlook. Back home he would have grown up in an isolated enclave, separated from most of Sudan's 60 other ethnic groups by great distance and sometimes impenetrable terrain. But at Kakuma, Simon learned, ate, and chased about the camp's dusty alleyways with boys from many of those groups. He was particularly close to a few Dinka boys, and even learned to speak a bit of their language—a skill that would later save his life.

On the morning of December 16, bands of Dinka soldiers fanned out across known Nuer neighborhoods—Mia Saba, New Site, and Gudele. Clad in Tiger Division fatigues and dark maroon berets, amped-up soldiers hopped out of crowded pickup trucks with their weapons cocked. They roamed from house to house, kicking in doors and forcibly entering homes to intimidate, beat, detain, and kill. Some Nuer men were dragged into the street and shot in the head in front of their families. Others were forced to run before being shot in the back.

Soldiers entered family huts and ordered their inhabitants to speak, thereby determining their ethnicity—and their fates—on the basis of language. *"Mah-lay,"* an assailant might say, mimicking a common Nuer greeting; an affirmative reply would invite an immediate spray of gunfire. Those who could not converse in Dinka met the same terrible end. Young men were also identified, and executed, on the basis of facial scarring—a traditional practice that leaves permanent markings on the forehead, the patterns of which can denote ethnic origin.

Some victims were tied up and bludgeoned to death. Others were barricaded inside their homes, which were then set on fire. One man's hands and feet were bound behind his back before he was shot in the chest and put on display at the entrance of a Nuer community. Victims and their families reported disappearances, torture, and brutal gang rapes. Men and women in one neighborhood described being forced to drink the blood of slaughtered family members, others to eat the burned flesh of decaying corpses.

As more reports of ethnic killing circulated among Simon's neighbors, he pulled out his cell phone and rang his elder brother Samuel, who was staying in a rented shanty nearby. Samuel had been in Juba for medical treatment, and was preparing for the journey home to his wife and three young children in Akobo. "Do not move anywhere," Simon insisted, "you stay inside that house."

That afternoon, President Salva appeared on television from the presidential palace. He had traded his customary suit and tie for military fatigues, and the ominous symbolism was impossible to ignore. Speaking from a podium and flanked by a group of hardline cabinet ministers, the commander-in-chief began his address to the nation with a shocking claim. Riek Machar, he said, had attempted a *coup d'état*. Forces loyal to the deposed vice president were responsible for a series of "criminal attacks" and for the fighting that had enveloped Juba overnight. "The culprits," he added, "will answer for their crimes."

Seeking to project a sense of authority, the president then claimed his government was in "full control" of the security situation and doing all it could to "ensure the citizens of Juba are secure and safe." But Salva's assurances belied the reality unfolding outside the pressroom, where his own forces were hunting members of Simon's tribe.

The optics of the event, the military fatigues, and the implied threats laid plain that things were about to get worse. Calling Riek a "prophet of doom," the president declared that he would not allow "1991 to happen again." Though lost on foreign ears, the evocative reference to 1991—when Riek's attempt to oust a Dinka leader had prompted a decade of ethnic violence—was unmistakable for every South Sudanese. This was a declaration of war.

Roadblocks sprang up, tanks roared down capital streets, and loyal army elements flushed remaining Nuer forces from the city. National Security operatives rounded up high-profile members of the ruling SPLM, alleged conspirators in Riek's supposed *coup*. Only the prophet of doom himself remained at large.

As day gave way to dusk on December 16, the attacks on Nuer civilians continued. At a police compound on Juba's west side, more than two hundred Nuer men were forced into a small holding facility. The doors were locked, and soon congestion, heat, and darkness prompted panicked gasps for air. Uniformed guards then shoved their rifles into the building's windows—and began firing indiscriminately. Screams emanated from the compound as bullets ricocheted off interior walls and cut down the mass of bodies within. Beneath the heap of corpses, a few terrified survivors lay motionless, pretending to be dead.

Meanwhile Simon, standing outside his tin hut, felt the fighting coming closer. "Bullets were flying everywhere," he says, jabbing a series of repeated fingers in the air, emulating the tracer bullets that crisscrossed the darkening sky. Scampering back inside, he placed another call, this time to an old schoolmate from Kakuma, a Dinka, to find out what was happening. The friend got straight to the point: government forces were targeting Nuer. He urged Simon to seek refuge. "You run *now* to a place where you can save your life."

Simon decided he would try to reach the United Nations base just a few kilometers to the south. He redialed his brother Samuel, who was unfamiliar with Juba's sprawling neighborhoods, to inform him that they had to flee immediately. No answer. He rang twice more, but still no answer. With death squads descending on his neighborhood, and the window to run closing fast, Simon made a dash for it. He tore out of the house, made a hard right, and sprinted down a rust-colored dirt path lined by piles of burning rubbish and patrolled by stray dogs. Then he took a left, weaving through a hundred yards of waist-high grass, and arrived, panting, at the entrance to his brother's rented hut.

Samuel was gone. At his feet, Simon noticed a trail of blood darkening the dirt floor, and a single bullet shell casing. "Samuel! Samuel!" he screamed, wheeling around to follow the trail outside. There in the tall grass opposite the entryway lay his brother, flat on his back, white undershirt soaked in blood. Simon dove to the ground and lifted his brother's head and shoulders. "There was so much blood," he remembers, slowing his words and fixing his gaze as he recalls the moment. Simon found an exit wound under his brother's right shoulder blade. Samuel's body was still warm, but the life had drained out of him.

"Then I just cried," Simon says, "I cried so hard."

Samuel had last visited Juba on South Sudan's Independence Day, in 2011, when he'd bought Simon a new black suit and necktie to wear to the historic day's festivities. Now he was dead.

Choking back tears, Simon wiped his face and hands, kicked off his sandals—they would only slow him down—and began running in the direction of the UN camp. Zigzagging through back alleys and ditches, he tried to avoid the main roads, where soldiers were patrolling. As he neared areas where people were moving about, he tamed his speeding legs and slowed to a deliberate walk, trying to harness his sense of alarm.

Simon was shocked by the bodies lying about the streets. "I tried not to look at them for long," he explains, as he believed it would draw attention to himself. He kept his head down and did not speak his mother tongue. Luckily, he points out, he does not bear the Nuer facial markings—six parallel lines across the forehead—that made so many others easy targets that night.

As he rounded another corner, he spotted three soldiers directly in front of him, not 20 yards away. His heart was suddenly in his throat. "On your knees!" one of them shouted. Clad in green, brown, and black camouflage, with berets molded hard to their right temples, the young men trained their rifles on him and approached. "*Yin lo noh?*" one asked in the Dinka language—"where are you going?"

Simon knew his life now depended on this language test. "I tightened my heart," he says, steeling his torso muscles. "So I could be confident." He promptly replied to the soldiers, also speaking Dinka. "I told them, 'I'm going to join our brothers in town.'" They told him to get up and waved him by.

When he arrived at the UN base, Simon found thousands of other Nuers already inside. "People were screaming," he recalls. "This one lady, she described her children being murdered." Others inside the crowded sanctuary were nervously moving about, phoning contacts on the outside, assuming the worst for their unaccounted-for kin.

Over the next 24 hours, the number of civilians seeking refuge at the UN compound would swell to 30,000. Six times that many would ultimately flee to UN bases countrywide. While these impromptu safe havens saved many lives, the huge and ethnically homogenous groups now crowded inside them were sitting ducks. UN officials dreaded the thought of a direct attack on the sites, which peacekeepers would be unable to repel.

Rumors of tribal kill lists and secret infiltrators fueled anxiety and polarization inside the camps. Abductions, rapes, and fights increased as the number of people swelled. The camps would later become desperately overcrowded and overwhelmed by disease and malnutrition. A stew of water, mud, and sewage exhaled an awful stink, as rains and poor drainage compounded already abysmal circumstances.

But for Simon and thousands of others, the relative security of the camps was preferable to the terror outside the fence. Simon thought of his mother, and of Samuel's wife, back in the town of Akobo. They were unaware of the chaos unfolding in Juba. When he finally reached them by phone, he broke the news about Samuel. The women wailed uncontrollably. "Come home to the village immediately," his mother begged between sobs, but he had no choice but to stay put.

Riek Machar was the government's most wanted man, but by the third day of the crisis, he was still nowhere to be found. His state-issued vehicles and more than a hundred personal guards remained at his official residence, but rumors put the fugitive in any number of hiding places around town—including, some said, at the American embassy. As government agents hunted him, Riek was secretly ferried to a nondescript mud hut in Mia Saba, another Nuer neighborhood. Only a handful of trusted aides knew his true location, and to divert attention, they had planted the rumor about his taking refuge at the American embassy. The deposed vice president would remain hidden there, amid the fighting and confusion, for two days.

At 11am the following morning, December 17, the president's men ordered elite security forces to surround Riek's house. They were accompanied by a pair of T-72 Russian-built army tanks, which rumbled slowly toward the compound's front and rear gates. Moments after they came to a rest, a thunderous boom rocked the capital.

Unaware of the siege unfolding just a few miles away, staffers at the American embassy were stunned. "You could feel the vibration everywhere," one reported. "It was the loudest explosion I had ever heard." A tank had breached the wall and fired artillery shells into Riek's two-story stone house. Government soldiers stormed the premises, and a bloody firefight with Riek's guards ensued, killing scores on both sides. But when survivors picked through the rubble, Riek was not among them.

Horrifying accounts of ethnic targeting in Juba began spreading north and east to Nuer communities, traveling up the Nile to Leer and Fangak, then to Bentiu and Malakal, and across swampland to Ayod, Waat, and Akobo. Unable to help their kin under siege in the capital, their shock and fear quickly morphed into a desire for revenge. Huge numbers of armed young men began mobilizing.

The following afternoon, Riek fled his secret Juba hideout, speeding north in a convoy of vehicles toward a crossing on the Nile River. Across the formidable waterway lay the gateway to the Nuer heartland, where he could find refuge and take stock. Upon reaching the crossing, Riek and his entourage abandoned their vehicles, commandeered a barge, and headed for the eastern bank.

They landed in the elephant grasses just south of Bor, the capital of Jonglei state, where a feared Nuer army commander awaited them. Peter Gadet had already defected with his Nuer forces and would soon seize control of the state capital. Joining forces with rag-tag bands of armed Nuer youth, some wearing plastic flip-flops and carrying rocket-propelled grenades, they would exact revenge upon the Dinka citizens of Bor town, committing crimes as horrible as those they sought to avenge.

Torching homes and ransacking markets, the marauding forces unleashed their weapons on government workers and ordinary residents. Scores of bodies—including women, children, and the elderly—soon lay decomposing in the streets. Teenage militia boys, sporting red headbands, later slaughtered a group of women sheltering in the compound of a local church. Others burst into a hospital, shooting patients in their beds. Because Bor was the site of an infamous 1991 massacre of the Dinka, the revenge attacks further cemented a narrative of ethnically motivated violence.

Meanwhile, what had begun as a reaction was about to be christened a rebellion. Riek, his whereabouts now known, spoke to reporters from his new headquarters in the bush. "I have attempted no *coup*," he asserted vehemently. Firing accusations back at President

Salva, he then announced, "I have appealed to the SPLM and the army to remove Salva Kiir from the leadership of the country." The statement erased any doubt that, no matter its spark, a new war for the soul of South Sudan had begun.

PART I

THE MAKING OF
SOUTH SUDAN

1

BOOMTOWN

*"Cities, like dreams, are made of desires and fears . . .
their rules are absurd, their perspectives deceitful, and
everything conceals something else."*
— Italo Calvino, *Invisible Cities*

JUBA, 2016

A*sante sana,"* the pilot announces over the intercom in Swahili. "Thank you for flying with Kenya Airways, and we hope you enjoy your stay in Juba." Flight #352 from Nairobi begins its initial descent into the capital of neighboring South Sudan, and as the silver bird dips below the cloud line toward Juba, a familiar landscape reveals itself below.

A vast scrubland plain stretches into the horizon—greens, tans, and golds dotted with thorny trees and short round bushes. East and west of the city are lone mountains, or *jebels*, as they are known in Arabic. They are not ranges, but rather free-standing rock outcroppings, huge, coffee-colored giants that rise abruptly and mysteriously from the otherwise flat terrain. The Nile River meanders through the eastern part of the city, the towering mango trees and elephant grasses on its banks bathed in a pleasant yellow. Men maneuver in wooden fishing canoes, and lime-green tufts of water hyacinth bob and turn frivolously in the river's swirling currents, deceiving the uninitiated of its immense and silent power.

The first signs of town appear at the front edge of the oval window, conical huts of mud and thatch, small clusters of them surrounded by rudimentary fences, worn patches of earth, and of course, cattle. First a half dozen homesteads spaced far apart, then a dozen more, the space between them shrinking fast. Finally the crescendo breaks into the dense residential neighborhoods of what is now a sprawling capital city.

It's a steamy afternoon in June 2016. Having finished my stint as a U.S. diplomat, I'm back in a personal capacity to meet with familiar faces, and new ones, to reflect on all that has happened in this Republic's short but turbulent history. Though I've made this descent many dozens of times, I remember vividly the first time I set down on the tarmac at Juba Airport, seven years ago, in what was then a united Sudan. The descent—or plunge—that day was aboard a flight operated by *JetLink,* one of the only commercial airlines then flying to Juba. Its pilots had a penchant for the kind of free fall descents that elicit weapons-grade anxiety. Out the left side of the aircraft I'd caught an unsettling glimpse of a downed MiG fighter jet just off the runway. On the seat-back in front of me, the embroidered words "*No Fumar*" had been scratched out, a hint that the regional carrier's aging fleet had been acquired mostly from second-hand planes originating in, oh, say, Venezuela.

Back then, most days at the airport were slow days. The UN peace-keeping mission operated fixed-wing planes and large transport helicopters, and humanitarian aid agencies supplied their rural outposts every week or two using a gaggle of small rotary prop planes. Just one or two commercial flights touched down daily, such that when the roar of jet engines could first be heard in the distance, a local might say, "there's the afternoon *Jetlink* now."

But just two years later, in the wake of independence, Juba's sweltering tarmac was a crowded parking lot. And today, five years after independence, the traffic on the expanded apron seems even more congested. I count a half dozen commercial airliners, and a host of hulking *Antonovs*—the Soviet-era flying beasts commonplace in this part of the world—which tower over a field of planes of all shapes and sizes. As I descend the mobile stairway, I'm instantly blinded by the 3:00pm sun. The color is washed out of everything. Beads of sweat materialize on my forehead, and a taxiing aircraft sends a wave of hot exhaust across the concrete, blowing dust into my eyes.

It's right around 100 degrees, and I wish I weren't wearing a suit jacket. As Juba was preparing to become a true capital city in 2011, business had suddenly gotten formal; suits, ties, and wingtips became the norm. But in the preceding six years of limited self-rule, Juba had still been something of a small and informal town. It had few paved roads and foreign visitors often put up in tented camps. Like many others, I used to meet senior government officials in a button-down shirt (sometimes short-sleeves) and a sturdy pair of boots—critical even in town when it rained. I never wore a tie and only put on a jacket for formal functions or meetings with the president or vice president.

Head down and squinting, I see the deputy minister, who disembarked ahead of me, being received by a line of well wishers in business suits and flowered dresses, their toothy-white smiles and exuberant long-armed waves suggesting they are quite happy to see him. Behind them, a company of lackadaisical-looking UN peacekeepers from India unload racks of supplies and equipment from their trucks as they prepare to rotate out of the country. Up ahead is the new glass-walled terminal that was the subject of considerable excitement in 2011, though it was not completed in time for independence day as planned, and it remains unfinished now—a glittering reminder of all that might have been. The nearby VIP terminal for government fat cats and foreign diplomats has twice been upgraded, but the rest of us make our way into the familiar old one-story, one-room arrival "terminal" to await passport stamps and retrieve luggage.

It is dark inside, and a veritable hotbox. As my eyes re-adjust, I notice the blades of two wall-mounted desk fans sitting idle, signaling no electricity at the terminal this afternoon. Fading signs in Arabic advertise charter services for long-defunct companies, and silver and green Christmas tinsel decorations hang by wires from the ceiling. Men dressed in short-sleeve plainclothes watch the arrivees, their occupation—national security grunt—given away by conspicuously interested eyes and airs of self-importance. The heavy emphasis on security is a product of the government's militarized pedigree, but even more so it is an emulation of former overlords in Khartoum—the capital of Sudan's bona fide police-state, where paranoid intelligence and security organs are immensely powerful.

A rusting red tractor pulls a wooden luggage cart to an opening in the ramshackle terminal, and lean young teenagers—all bone and muscle—heave backpacks and overstuffed roller bags inside. After passing through an unmanned X-ray machine with a broken monitor, bags are tossed and inspected haphazardly, underwear and toiletries quickly scoured by tired customs officials in sweat-saturated blue uniforms, who then scrawl chalk marks on the bags to authorize entry. A third of those waiting for their luggage are South Sudanese, the remainder are foreigners: European aid workers, Lebanese businessmen, East African clergymen, development experts from the World Bank. Their body language reveals their respective experience; some are relaxed and familiar, while first-timers nervously try to make sense of the protocol, which defies intuition. Some are wondering just what the hell they were thinking in coming here.

Muscling my way through the logjam of sweaty commuters, I step outside again into the over-exposed light and hop into a hired vehicle. Traffic is a zoo. Cars, SUVs, UN vehicles, *tuk tuks*, and motorized cargo carts fight for advantage on the road, making up traffic rules as they go. Tottering trucks spew a black exhaust so acrid you can taste it. Horns are generously honked. Teenage boys in reflective sunglasses sit slack on *boda bodas*—the East African term for motorcycle taxis—speeding through narrow gaps in traffic at cringe-worthy speed. Many of them end up at Juba hospital. Two cars make U-turns in the middle of busy thoroughfares, causing a truck driver to shake a frustrated open palm out his window. An aging and top-heavy bus swerves to evade a flock of aimless goats. Creativity trumps order. One driver, whose maroon SUV succumbs to the record-setting fuel shortages now choking the city, gets out of the vehicle and leaves it, door open, in the middle of a busy intersection.

It's good to be back.

On the next corner is a gas station, but long lines suggest its underground tanks are empty. Stretching for several blocks, then snaking around a corner, and another, two rows of cars are parked awaiting the next fuel delivery. As we pass by, I count upwards of 200 thirsty vehicles. The fuel shortage is staggering, and reflective of a collapsed economy, the lack of infrastructure, and a continuing dependence on petrol products delivered by truck from neighboring Uganda.

"I will come here and park tonight, around 11pm," James, my Kenyan driver, says, pointing with raised eyebrows to the end of the line of cars. "And leave it parked in the street?" I ask. "Yes. I'll lock the doors, and come back—maybe 5am," he says, when he hopes the line will be moving. Whatever he gets at the pump, he will siphon a portion of it out with a rubber hose and save in empty soda bottles— either for later use or sale on the black market.

In 2009, there were just two or three paved roads in Juba. Today the still-expanding city center is almost entirely paved. Back then I hired a 4x4 vehicle and driver to take me around town to meetings day and night, and I regularly had to haggle with Peter, my Ugandan driver, to bring him down from $150 per day. When the air conditioner didn't work in his silver and blue Nissan Patrol, I negotiated harder. The price was standard fare for a sufficiently robust vehicle in Juba those days, in part because regular cars weren't common—they would bottom out or suffer flat tires on Juba's notoriously bumpy network of dirt paths. Some roads were so bumpy—a sea of earthen waves—that I sometimes wished I had a helmet, and regularly kept a firm grip of the leather handle above my window.

When Peter slowed to rock the 4x4 over huge dips and swells in the dirt road, I would sometimes crack my head, *hard*, right temple on the passenger side window. "Sorry boss," Peter would say, genuinely, before cracking into a smile and cackling at both my folly and the absurdity of Juba's road network, and all that it represented. I occasionally took *boda bodas* as more and more materialized in town, as they were cheap and their young drivers sometimes a good source of local gossip, if not smooth gear-shifters. But the motorbikes weren't always convenient for conducting professional business, and the more trips you logged with the accident-prone speed-junkies, the more you were tempting fate.

Late one evening I was riding home from a meeting on a main thoroughfare in Peter's Nissan Patrol, when one such speeding *boda boda* careened down a sloping side street to our right. I caught a peripheral glimpse of its single head light just before it crashed head-on into the side of our vehicle. After Peter hit the brakes, I jumped out and found the twenty-something driver, bloodied, lying on the ground in a spray of shattered glass and motorbike parts. There was a sizable dent in our vehicle, and the young man appeared unconscious, maybe dead.

I stopped a passing truck, got help loading the limp body into its bed, and asked the driver to speed us to Juba hospital. When we arrived, the night-shift doctors were none too urgent. Not only was the electricity out, but there appeared to be half a dozen other injured *boda* drivers already on site. The docs had seen this movie before. In the end, the young man left the following morning with minimal injuries. He had been profoundly drunk, his body most likely relaxed as he smashed into the chassis, which, ironically, may have saved his life.

While solid statistics are hard to come by, estimates put Juba's 2009 population at a few hundred thousand. Just seven years later, credible guesses had doubled and tripled that figure, but its hard to say for sure. I had been back numerous times between 2013 and 2015 as a U.S. diplomat, though all were short visits with tightly scripted schedules. Today we drive around at a more leisurely pace than I've been able to in years, and I notice landmarks that used to be miles out of town but today are enveloped by urbanization. The city pushes outward by the day, in haphazard fashion. Considering the economy is in total free fall, I'm stunned at the continuing construction. The growth might otherwise be a signal of a healthy and developing nation, except that I know it is confined to the relative calm of the capital city.

Disparities between national capitals and the hinterland are common in emerging African economies, but here, in the world's most underdeveloped plot of land, the chasm is particularly wide. Driving out of Juba on almost any gravel road is like traveling back in time; a decade seems to slip away with each passing mile. As the bustle and boom grow smaller in the rear-view mirror, one begins to understand that Juba is not the norm, but a bubble foreign to most Southern Sudanese. Radios and cell phones have been game-changers, and the creep of modernity is underway. But by some basic measures, from the outside looking in, daily life for the majority of people is not unlike it was for their ancestors four or five generations before.

As Juba grew rapidly in the oil-fueled years before independence, the rest of the country remained at a virtual standstill. What you wouldn't know from a spin around the bustling city today is just how badly the rest of the country has been left behind, or how ravaged it has been by two years of civil war since independence. More than two million people have been displaced—enough to fill 25 professional football stadiums—and a steady stream are still leaving. An additional 50 stadiums full of people, or one-third of the country's entire population—are facing a potential famine.

⸺⸎⸻

I'm planning a trip outside Juba next week, and I'll need a mosquito net. So I ask James to take me to Konyo Konyo market, one of the largest open-air markets in the city. Konyo Konyo is located on the south-east side of town, just before the lone bridge crossing the Nile River, and it is a rocking place. I used to pick up the occasional item here—a pair of cheap sunglasses, some shoe laces—but I haven't been back in years and it, like Juba, has grown exponentially since independence. I'm shocked. Thousands of people move in ordered chaos, bartering for goods of all kinds, chattering about the day's gossip, and pressing wads of filthy and devalued pound notes—each graced with John Garang's likeness—into the sweating palms of hustling traders. There is a tempo and a hum about this place, one that can you can become transfixed by.

The unmistakable smell of smoking charcoal wafts from a make-shift stove that rests between an elderly woman's weathered bare feet. Overhead, a maze of electric wires convenes from all directions into a knotted mess, begging to spark a fire, except that they carry no power. The afternoon heat is furnace-like, and the air is filled with sand, diesel fumes, and the smell of men fixing *bodas*, shirtless and up to their elbows in grease.

Giant red bags of potatoes and purple bags of onions lean against wood shacks and metal shanties that form long meandering rows of commercial bustle. Inside the shacks are packages of powdered milk and flavored drinks, tubs of durum wheat and cooking oil stacked to the ceiling in precarious towers. The shade of a corrugated tin awning saves one veteran shopkeeper from the solar onslaught. He is measuring dry goods in metal coffee mugs, before him a sea of round wash basins filled with orange lentils, purple beans, two-tone brown dates, sparkling sugar and spices, and bleach-white flour packed into conical, temple-like mounds.

At the next stall are brightly-colored dresses and second-hand clothing—T-shirts emblazoned with logos of American Rotary clubs and high school lacrosse teams. At the next, a smooth-talking trader nods and stretches an open hand toward stacks of woven mats, mosquito nets, cell phone batteries, flashlights, soccer balls, foam mattresses, aluminum buckets, and bars of soap. Like everything else here, his wares are imported. "A good price for you, my friend," he says, switching from Arabic to English. Despite the country's rich ethnic and cultural diversity, successive governments in Khartoum had tried to impose an Arab and Islamic identity on the whole of Sudan. Though their project ultimately failed, some elements endured. Arabic thus remains the most common lingua franca in South Sudan, although the new Republic, eager to distance itself from that troubled past, adopted English as its official language in 2011.

Konyo Konyo's perimeter is framed by long yellow buildings—remnants from the period of Sudanese control—their rusting roofs, peeling yellow paint, and blue metal doors resembling the market stalls in Khartoum's *souks*. Here, more traders, most of them from the Darfur region in western Sudan, sell used shoes, backpacks, cigarettes, motor bike parts, spare tires, and sim cards. Dried fish and sides of beef and goat hang on display out front. If you are discreet, and know whom to consult, you can also exchange dollars for South Sudanese pounds here at the black market rate. I remember when the rate was 3 pounds to the dollar. Today, the illicit banker in fraying jean shorts tells me, "40 to 1." By the end of the year that ratio will rise to more than 100 to 1.

Out front is a sea of umbrellas—orange, gold, blue, and rainbow-colored, most splashed with cell phone advertisements. Spread beneath them are blankets and rickety wooden tables topped with grain, rice, sweet potatoes, avocados, bananas, pineapples, mangoes, tomatoes, cucumbers, wild greens, ground nuts, and golf ball-sized plastic bags of peanut butter. An infant lies face down in an afternoon siesta between two pyramids of tiny green peppers.

The women running these miniature produce stands are third or fourth in the retail chain, as foodstuffs are also trucked in—mostly from neighboring Uganda. Despite the abundance of rich soil, water, and sunshine in this vast country, startlingly little food is grown for commercial sale. And what is grown here is hard to get to market. South Sudan's Western Equatoria region, its most tropical, is known for quality produce. But, as an old friend from the area laments, the lack of reliable roads and infrastructure means "it costs much more to truck in a pineapple from Yambio," the state's capital, "than it does from Uganda."

Idling aside the arched dirt road between the rows of shanties is a queue of black and yellow *tuk-tuks*, the three-wheeled passenger rickshaws first popularized in Asia. One driver naps on his handlebars while he waits for passengers to materialize and cram themselves into the back of his honking buzzard of a vehicle. Two women in long dresses and head scarves cross the road, each carrying bulging sacks of charcoal tied with red and green twine. Another, ferrying a plastic tub of purple tea on her head, scurries to avoid two *boda* bikes that rip past, engines growling.

Unfazed by the chaos, three aging men sit with hands on knees under a metal awning, the line between sun and shade cutting just across their chins. They are taking tea and comfortably passing the hours. Tea has long been a fixture of Sudanese life, a hangover from the British colonial period. As has become the norm in the South, these men fill their small glasses with as much powdered milk and sugar as tea and hot water.

At one end of Konyo Konyo is an aging mosque, at the other a two-story bank of new brick and mortar shops occupied by airlines, mobile phone providers, and a computer parts supplier—the creep of pleasures familiar across East Africa that have now made their way to Juba. In recent years tens of thousands of war-era refugees have poured back into South Sudan from elsewhere in East Africa. Like Simon, the 20-year-old student from Manga Ten, they are among the generation who walked to refugee camps in neighboring Kenya, Uganda, and Ethiopia, and eventually received some level of education. They face a particular set of challenges reintegrating in South Sudan, but their connections, tastes, and familiarity with these more advanced economies have also accelerated the changes in Juba.

On the corner, men assemble wooden bed frames, chairs, and tables, each stained a deep reddish brown. Such locally made furniture is a staple in the region, but it too is a recent addition to Juba, and the local timber, says James, my driver, "is the best... *swear*, it is the best you can get anywhere." James regularly comments about the potential of this country and its resources, though such mentions are always shaded by a tone of opportunity wasted.

As in most major markets, many of the traders here are not South Sudanese, nor are those up the supply chain. Darfuri traders bring goods from Sudan, while the huge trucks packed with food and rumbling up the main supply road are owned by Ugandan and Kenyan firms. It isn't the only sector dominated by foreigners. As we pass a group of listless young South Sudanese men sitting on a pile of empty barrels, James makes a dismissive *theth* clicking sound, tongue against the back of front teeth. "Yes, what's that for?" I ask. "They don't like to work," he scoffs, summing up the view shared by many of his East African peers who drive cars for hire and work in Juba's service industry. "It's just their culture," he says in a breath of condescension.

It's an assessment I've heard for years, but again I am not convinced. Others here have offered more nuanced and credible explanations for the comparatively apathetic working culture—no history of a formal economy, decades of instability, and the dependency resulting from a generation of food aid. Add to that the absence of formal education, the dislocating changes of refugee migration, and the social status associated with a career in the military—which has a way of deterring private sector initiative.

Whatever the contributing factors, the reality is that many unexploited niches in this still expanding capital have been, and continue to be, seized by enterprising foreigners. It is why James and many of his friends have been driving cars-for-hire in Juba for years.

"We thought these guys would learn from us, copy the things we are doing, and then we'd soon have to go home." He shakes his head, now striking a more sympathetic tone. "But they don't." He shrugs his shoulders. "So we are still here."

I first arrived in Southern Sudan as an analyst for the International Crisis Group during the so-called "interim period"—the six years between the signing of the 2005 peace agreement that ended the North-South war, and a referendum on Southern independence planned for 2011. It was a volatile period, shaped by a dizzying mix of political dynamics and competing interests that felt then—and still feel—like a roller coaster ride: the peace agreement's "one country, two systems" model of government, the rush of billions of dollars of new oil money, a dangerous arms race, rampant corruption, the brinkmanship of larger-than-life personalities, a humanitarian disaster, and an international debate about self-determination.

The risk of war between North and South was present throughout, fueled by deep mistrust, provocative military posturing, and credible concerns that Southern independence might be denied by Khartoum. This tale of two capitals, spun over six tumultuous years, was a truly unique experiment, unprecedented in post-colonial Africa and unlikely to be repeated again.

When I arrived in Juba, half way through the interim period, the writing was on the wall—Southerners were going to vote for independence, come hell or high water. Despite the talk of preserving a union with Sudan, as envisioned in the peace deal, most Southerners were simply counting the days until they could bid their Northern oppressors farewell. The challenges of building their own nation from scratch were obvious, and stark, but they would not be deterred.

Preparing for that first visit in 2009, I sought all the names and numbers I could get my hands on, eager to begin research but equipped with no contacts or resources beyond my own curiosity. A colleague gave me the name of an SPLA handler who could facilitate a meeting with a senior army general, one who had drawn undue attention after recent disobedience, no less. Perfect; if I was to develop a network of contacts that could really teach me about the emerging capital's politics, its power structures, and the transition now underway, this sounded like as good a place as any to start.

On one of my first days in the country, I arranged to meet the handler at the Juba Grand Hotel, then the most prestigious hotel address in town, though the "grand" establishment was no more than a series of free-standing metal containers and concrete courtyards dotted with cheap plastic chairs. Making my way around to one of the farthest containers, I gave a hesitant knock. A thirty-something SPLA officer in a stained white tank-top and wrinkled army trousers interrupted his television show to answer the door. As he asked a series of spontaneous and seemingly confused questions about who I was and what I wanted with the general, I wondered whether this vetting was really necessary, or an exercise in self-importance for an otherwise unoccupied mid-level officer.

He vaguely OK'd my visit, and walked me through a series of complicated directions to the general's home in the Tomping neighborhood—there were no street signs in Juba, only landmarks from which one could triangulate. When I attempted to relay the roundabout route to my driver, Peter, he kindly interrupted and said he knew the place. As dusk gave way to darkness, we tic-tac-toed our way through a maze of dirt roads toward what was then the outskirts of town, where the general was completing a new home for himself and his wife.

Peter pulled up to a nondescript iron gate hung between two cinder-block walls and honked his horn. A pair of Kalashnikov-toting shadows in army fatigues emerged. As they came to inquire about our business and inspect the vehicle, I guessed their age at no more than 19. Satisfied with our response and our lack of an arsenal, they casually retreated through the gate, opened it, and waved us into the compound.

Inside, another thirty-odd armed teenagers, and a number of muscular dogs, perked up, turning to size up the visiting *khawaja* (white man). Some of the young soldiers were perched atop army "technicals"—camouflage-painted pickup trucks usually mounted with 12.7 millimeter heavy machine guns. Others attended to one of the two brand new gleaming H2 "Hummers" parked inside. The price tag on these monster SUVs—with their standard leather upholstery and Bose premium sound systems—was north of $50,000, triple the annual salary of an SPLA general.

I hopped out of my vehicle and began making my way toward the square cinderblock house, framed by a front porch and a single light fixture swinging from a chain above. The compound was suddenly silent, save for the gravel crunching beneath my boots. The uncomfortable focus on me was soon interrupted as a man emerged from the front door. Clad in green army beret, wrap around sunglasses, a cinched belt, and short-sleeve fatigues rolled up over biceps, the towering general stepped onto the porch wearing a huge grin. Lit dramatically by the spotlight above, he shouted to the dogs and raised two giant racks of raw meat into the air. Converging on the porch in nanoseconds, the animals leaped and growled and ripped furiously at the meat, trying to tear it from his grasp. Not letting go, the spotlight reflecting in his sunglasses, the general let out a sinister, high-pitched laugh reminiscent of *Batman*'s "Joker."

Was this really happening? I felt as if I were on the set of some low-budget exploitation movie featuring a stereotypical African warlord. I could feel Peter behind me in the car, surely muffling his laughter at the whole scene and the absurdity that had just enveloped his rookie *khawaja* client.

The general was projecting an image. Did it come naturally, or was it an adopted caricature? The raw machismo, the flashy vehicles, the unsolicited tumbler of Johnny Walker whiskey he later poured me—was this stylized persona on display for me, I wondered, or for the coterie of armed and impressionable teenagers outside? Was it a projection of authority in a long-militarized society, part of cultivating the loyalty of a youthful personal guard—themselves eager to "become men" and experience power?

The 2005 peace agreement had elevated the Southern rebel movement—the SPLA—to the status of a national army, one in desperate need of professionalization, particularly if it was to secure and defend an independent country in just a few years' time. At the moment, it was an ill-disciplined guerrilla movement, paling in comparison to the established armies of the region. Perhaps the general's performance was his way of joining the club—a member of the newly minted military brass asserting himself as an equal.

Whether a product of conscious deliberation or not, the image was a powerful one—for me and for the men under the general's tutelage. What this kind of relationship and role-modeling meant for the future of this nation-in-waiting, I wasn't yet sure, but it seemed important to understand in a place where advancement had long come through the barrel of a gun.

⁓

The general and I spoke for two hours, during which time we discussed the state of the SPLA, the personalities driving politics in the emergent South, and threats to the forthcoming referendum—a matter over which the general left no doubt about his readiness to return to war. After our discussion, I thanked the general for his time and walked back up the gravel path to my vehicle, keeping an eye out for the dogs. It was late.

As we backed out of the compound gate, I nodded at the same solemn-faced teenage soldier who had let us in earlier. He sauntered back inside. As a young SPLA recruit, he was surely drawing some kind of salary, even if it was irregular, or if a cut was taken by his superior. An army salary had been the single most tangible dividend of the peace agreement, essentially a vast welfare program for war veterans and the families who had given up their sons to "the struggle." In a country with little or no other economic opportunity, this teenager's choice to enlist was a no brainer.

What's more, he was part of a social structure, and carried a gun. I thought about the parallel to disenfranchised young men in America, joining a gang as a means to belong, to attain some status or identity, and to survive in an otherwise unforgiving environment.

As we bounced back to my camp near the Nile River, I contemplated the fact that my interviewee was one of a reported 700 generals in the SPLA. It was a staggering figure, especially when compared with the 200 generals commanding the American military—which was ten times the size of the SPLA. I also noted to Peter my surprise at the size of the man's personal guard. Peter had passed the time mostly napping in the back of the vehicle, but had stepped out once to stretch his legs and chat with some of the soldiers. "They're all from one area," he said. "What do you mean?" I asked. He said that most of them were from the same region, and same tribe, as the general who had been pouring me whiskey.

Though many SPLA members had fought their entire adult lives as guerrillas, their army was anything but unified, and anything but professional. On the eve of independence it remained a hodgepodge of ethnically homogenous units, occasionally rebellious commanders, and parallel chains of command. In a moment of crisis, a soldier might heed unofficial orders from a war-era commander from his own tribe before he listened to his new platoon superior. More worryingly, many of those war-era commanders were now occupying senior party positions and leading government ministries, and sometimes used these parallel chains of command to advance personal objectives. Whether the allegations were well founded or not, the general I visited that night had once been kept under house arrest on suspicion of mobilizing a force to overthrow the president.

When the war with Khartoum ended in 2005, collective opposition to the North—and for many, the shared goal of Southern independence—had bound disparate Southern constituencies together. But it was a fragile coalition, comprising communities and armed groups that had not yet reconciled their own historical animosities. Though a 2006 order had welcomed 60,000 war-era Southern militia fighters under the SPLA umbrella, by 2009 this integration of the South's armed forces was still far from a reality. Many mainstream SPLA leaders still resented the absorption of old enemies, even if they were fellow Southerners. They scuttled integration and denied promotions on account of ethnicity or past allegiances, and the ill-treatment did not go down well.

One military veteran later summed up the SPLA's fractious character: "A general wearing stars on his collar walks by a foot soldier, and if the soldier does not know him, he will not even get up to salute him!" Even in Southern Sudan's one quasi-national institution, regional and ethnic identities remained stronger than any national or institutional allegiance. It was hard not to wonder what this would mean when it came to building other national institutions.

The images of that night's visit would stick with me for years, and the more time I spent in Southern Sudan, the more I realized just how many of its challenges had been on display during my evening with the general: a militarized society, a bloated and unprofessional army, deep ethnic fault lines, economic torpor, financial corruption, a dangerous focus on "big man" politics, and the absence of any unifying national identity.

2

A DAMP HELL

"The dark-skinned races that live in the land vary widely. Some are war-like, cattle-owning nomads; some till the soil and live in thatched huts shaped like beehives; Some are ape-like naked savages, who dwell in the woods and prey on creatures not much wilder or lower than themselves."

—President Theodore Roosevelt;
Sudan, Spring 1910

"If we visit the corridors of history from the Biblical Kush to the present, you will find that the Sudan, and we the Sudanese, have always been there. Let us affirm and remind ourselves that we are a historical people because there are concerted efforts to push us off the rails of history."

—John Garang

More than a thousand miles down river from the general's cinderblock house stand the ancient pyramids of Nubia. Though dwarfed in size and reputation by the better-known Egyptian pyramids, the pyramids that rise from the shifting sands of Meroe are a point of pride for modern Sudanese, and a lasting reminder of the rich and diverse history of their homeland. The magnificent landmarks were built by ancient rulers who established kingdoms in the Nile Valley, and who for centuries were influenced by, or subject to, powerful Egyptian pharaohs to the North. Trade routes later led Arabs from the Middle East to settle and integrate northern Sudan's arid deserts, and Africa's broader Sahel belt, beginning in the early Middle Ages. Islam followed.

To the south, the *Sudd*, a rain-fed swamp the size of England, formed a formidable geographical barrier, limiting external influence for centuries in the progressively greener and more fertile Southern Sudan. "It is a fever-stricken wilderness," wrote British explorer Samuel Baker as his expedition headed south by boat in 1862. "We are thoroughly among the negroes now," he noted in his journal, "the country one vast and apparently interminable marsh." Baker thought it "not surprising that the ancients gave up the exploration of the Nile" when he found himself stymied by the difficult swampland. The *Sudd*, he wrote, was, "a heaven for mosquitoes and a damp hell for man."

Most of Southern Sudan's indigenous black Africans did not establish formal systems of central government in their vast territory, but instead ordered themselves loosely by family and tribe. Though their horizontal organization had long proven functional, in time it also made them vulnerable to organized outsiders with big appetites. And so generations of black Africans in the South were targeted as part of a massive slave trade, first by Egyptian and Nubian rulers, and later by their Arab successors.

The modern nation-state of Sudan eventually took form in the early 19th century. Neighboring Egypt was then under control of the Ottoman Empire, and its expansionist governor Muhammad Ali Pasha sent 4,000 troops south to seize control of Sudanese territory in 1820. His conquest swallowed up existing kingdoms and a diverse set of peoples under one territorial authority. Political, economic, and military interests under Turco-Egyptian rule drove new—and accentuated existing—divisions between Sudan's North and South. The Pasha centralized power in the North's central Nile valley, where

34

an Arab-Islamic identity prevailed, and established a capital in Khartoum. Powerful kingpins oversaw waves of new slave raids into the Southern hinterland, gobbling up able bodies as well as ivory and other resources. And so racial and cultural subjugation of Southern black Africans also became more pronounced, just as the modern state was forged.

The most enduring tale in Sudan's modern history came six decades later, in 1885, when a charismatic agitator and religious mystic known simply as "the Mahdi"—an Islamic messiah—laid siege to Khartoum. The religious warrior and his 50,000 *Ansar* forces, dressed in white cotton robes adorned with beads and colorful patches, attacked and defeated the occupying Egyptian army. Their stunning victory was the culmination of a four-year revolt against Turco-Egyptian rule, and they marked the occasion by cutting off the head of the man hired to lead the occupiers—imperial Britain's General Charles Gordon.

Gordon had served as governor-general of Sudan a decade earlier, and during that tenure he had made it his mission to crush the slave trade, an objective born of Christian moral conviction and spurred by a formidable anti-slavery movement then gathering steam in Britain. But when British and Egyptian interests came under siege by the daring *Mahdi*, the British reappointed Gordon—by then a famed officer in Her Majesty's Armed Forces—and sent him back to defend the city.

Hollywood mega-stars Charlton Heston (as Gordon) and Laurence Olivier (as the *Mahdi*) captured this formative moment on the silver screen in 1966, together portraying the infamous battle for the film's namesake city, *Khartoum*. The 40-year-old Mahdi subsequently established the country's first national and Islamic rule, but died soon thereafter of an infectious illness, and a joint British-Egyptian force recaptured the territory just before the onset of the 20th century. It was a spectacular series of events, but as with most affairs of political consequence since Sudan's inception, it was all happening hundreds of miles away, at considerable remove from the lives of most Southern Sudanese.

Under subsequent British rule, Sudan's north and south continued to be administered separately. Like their predecessors, Queen Victoria's colonial administrators focused their energies on the northern half of the country and its capital—designing institutions, building political alliances, and pursuing ambitious infrastructure schemes. The southern frontier, meanwhile, was a backwater, quite literally, that figured little in their designs. And so the South, like Sudan's other outlying regions, remained isolated, under-developed, and poorly understood.

In addition to its sheer size, the defining characteristic of the Sudanese state was its diversity—in cultural, religious, ethnic, linguistic, and political terms. But colonizers, early governments, and later academics nonetheless maintained a disproportionate focus on the country's Arab-African and Muslim center, while the rest of the country remained, in the words of one notable historian, "relegated to an exotic periphery." British authorities initially sought only to pacify Southern populations and establish dominion over the remote territory, edging out French and Belgian competitors in the great scramble for Africa.

Then in 1930, Britain's administrators first articulated a "Southern Policy," whereby Southern Sudan would be developed and administered along "African" lines. Some believe they intended to assimilate the Southern backwater instead with the colonial states of British East Africa (Kenya, Uganda, and Tanzania). Interaction and movement between North and South were thus heavily restricted. Slavery and the southward spread of Islam was curtailed, in what some interpreted as a policy of protection. But for those in the isolated South, the experience of comparative neglect and racial prejudice continued.

While an educated class of civil servants, businessmen, and trade professionals emerged in the North, education was neglected, or outright discouraged, in the South. Not only were there no roads and no services; there were also no schools. Christian missionaries took up some of the slack, and their pupils would ultimately form the small core of educated Southerners active in politics on the eve of Sudan's eventual independence from Britain and Egypt.

Born in Yei River district in 1928, Aggrey Jaden was one of the few to see the inside of a classroom, and later one of the first Southerners to be admitted to Khartoum University. A bright and promising young mind, Jaden became involved in student politics and later took up a post as a low-ranking government administrator. But too few and too foreign to the systems in the faraway capital, Jaden and the disadvantaged Southerners would have little say in shaping the character of the state that was about to emerge in their name.

When Western colonial powers receded from the continent in the 1950s and 60s, Sudan was the first of the British-administered colonies to be granted independence, as London hastily sought to extricate itself. But as colonial authorities prepared to hand over the reins, tensions mounted between North and South. Jaden and the few Southerners in government raised questions about regional autonomy or independence for the South. He worried, quite rightly, that a unified and independent Sudan would be dominated by Northern Muslims in the center. Though huge chasms existed as a result of decades of "administrative segregation," the British merged the two increasingly disparate territories and left Northern elites in charge. Southern Sudan was largely an afterthought in the high politics of the transition, and so too were its leading voices.

Jaden and his colleagues were none too pleased. On Sudan's official day of independence, Jaden, then a district commissioner, was fired by his Khartoum bosses after he refused to play the new national anthem in his district or hoist the country's new flag. The defiant politico returned to Juba and then fled across the border and into exile, where he became active in Southern Sudan's earliest resistance movements.

In short order, the British were gone from Sudan, but as it looked to Jaden and his fellow Southerners, a new foreign overlord had simply taken their place. Jaden and thirteen colleagues later penned a 23-page petition to the United Nations detailing systematic discrimination against Southerners. "Of the 800 posts taken over from British Administration, only 4 junior posts were offered to Southerners," it read. "It therefore became clear... that we in the South were going simply to exchange masters." And so Sudan was born in conflict, as subordinated Southerners were locked in a struggle against a new Northern hegemon.

A period of internal wars would follow, characterized by marginalization, extreme violence, and attempts to forcibly assimilate the country's diverse population. Those ruling in Khartoum—who in many ways were a hybrid of "Arab" and "African" identities, but identified as Arab—sought to Arabize and Islamize the whole of the country. This problematic North-South dichotomy, and the power dynamics infused therein, had begun centuries earlier. It was reinforced during periods of foreign conquest, solidified during 20th-century colonial rule, and then enshrined in national institutions.

This "North-South" theme is necessary in understanding Sudan's turbulent history, a Southern identity forged mainly through resistance, and the eventual separation of South Sudan. But it is by no means sufficient. Fifty years of conflicts large and small would illustrate a more complex sickness ailing the entire Sudanese body politic: a fundamental imbalance between the country's center and its peripheries.

Extreme inequality was the national ill. The concentration of power and resources in the hands of a small and privileged Arab class in the center came at the expense of the country's diverse and marginalized regional peripheries—most recognizably in the South, but also in the Nuba Mountains, Darfur, the East, and beyond. This structural flaw would drive decades of instability, and the Arab and Islamic character of the dominant elite would infuse Sudan's conflicts with complicated notions of power and identity. Stir in racism, complex social hierarchies, ethnic and linguistic differences, a diverse and formidable geography, competing livelihoods, and large-scale displacement, and Sudan's wars, as one historian noted, would be difficult not only to resolve, but even to explain.

Despite their dominance of the center, Sudan's post-independence governments were never strong enough to project state authority on a national scale. After all, Sudan was huge—equal to all of the United States' territory east of the Mississippi River. The attempts of these governments to achieve unity by imposing a singularly Arab and Islamic identity on the whole of Sudan backfired, intensifying the very centrifugal forces they had initially set out to subdue.

So they resorted to crude and repressive measures to hold sway over already disadvantaged peripheries. They controlled local elites, manipulated short-term economic interests, and outsourced heavy-handed security to regional militias. They used ethnicity and identity to divide populations and turn them against one another, and employed violence wherever necessary. While the South and other parts of the country suffered, a bubble of economic and political superiority was preserved at the center, in Khartoum.

But it was hardly a sustainable enterprise; these governments would not only fail to build national cohesion, they would one day lose the battle to maintain the territorial integrity of Africa's largest state.

~~~

Sudan's first civil war (1955–1972) began even before Britain's flag was lowered. Southern mutineers waged a low-intensity guerrilla conflict, with the goal of Southern secession, until *"Anyanya"* (snake venom) rebels emerged in the 1960s, and intensified the war. "It is now clear beyond any reasonable doubt that the war between the Southern Sudan and the Northern Sudan can never be won by your country," wrote Aggrey Jaden in a 1965 letter to Sudan's prime minister. By then a leading voice of the *Anyanya* political arm, he summed up the separatists' view, concluding, "I wish, therefore, to avail myself of this opportunity to request you to pay heed to the sacred demand of our people: IMMEDIATE INDEPENDENCE."

Neither could the Southern rebels win the war. And though hobbled by internal divisions over both tactics and objectives, the Southern resistance reached a political accommodation with Sudanese President Jafaar Nimeri in 1972. The "Addis Ababa Agreement" did not yield independence, but rather vested limited powers of self-rule in a new Southern "regional government." But the deal did not satiate the separatists, who wanted more, and nor did it convince those who distrusted Khartoum. Soon thereafter, the powers delegated to the South were watered down, and Khartoum's commitment to the deal bottomed out. *Anyanya* fighters returned to the bush, and Southern officers active in the national army conspired to join them. A new Southern resistance was in the making.

Two major developments were meanwhile underway that would hasten a return to conflict and frame Sudanese politics for decades. First, oil was discovered by American oil giant Chevron in the late 1970s, intoxicating both President Nimeri's government and enterprising American businessmen. Former U.S. President George H.W. Bush—then President Nixon's ambassador to the UN, and an accomplished oil man—had visited Khartoum to alert the Sudanese to oil deposits and facilitate introductions to American companies, at a time when relations between the two countries were cordial. Rich oil basins were eventually discovered near the border between North and South, in areas settled by Dinka and Nuer communities. Shortly thereafter, Nimeri's government attempted to re-draw borders along the North-South frontier, so as to keep the newly discovered oilfields "away from any Southern regional government and firmly under Khartoum's control." The surreptitious move was rebuffed, but it gave Southerners a good hint of what was to come.

Secondly, Sudanese politics in the North were undergoing a tectonic shift, as a new brand of political Islam had arrived from Egypt in the form of the Muslim Brotherhood—a religious, political, and social movement first launched in the late 1920s. President Nimeri, then a Cold War ally of the United States, came under pressure from Brotherhood fundamentalists who opposed Southern autonomy and advocated a more overtly Islamic state. This group, which had already infiltrated Nimeri's government in the form of a charismatic and controversial Islamist named Hassan Turabi, would force the president's capitulation on both counts. After dissolving the Southern regional government, he sent a second shockwave throughout Sudan in September 1983, introducing *sharia* law and declaring Sudan an Islamic Republic. Sudan's second civil war, already in the making, had its spark.

Meanwhile, a group of Southern commanders defected from Sudan's national army and crossed the border into neighboring Ethiopia, with the consent of its then Soviet-allied regime. An ambitious colonel named John Garang, then a 39-year-old officer with an American education, consolidated command of the fledgling rebellion, and the Sudan People's Liberation Movement/Army (SPLM/SPLA) was born.

"Because of the oneness of the Sudanese people," Garang proclaimed in his first major speech in the spring of 1984, "the armed struggle in the South must of necessity engulf the whole Sudan." Garang's vision—and what distinguished his new movement from its unequivocally separatist predecessors—was his stated commitment to the "liberation of the whole Sudan, the unity of its people, and its territorial integrity." Unlike those who had gone before, Garang was *not* demanding independence for the south. Rather, his vision of a "New Sudan" was that of a free, democratic, and inclusive national polity. Most Southern dissidents preferred simply to opt out of Sudan, but Garang was intent on liberating the entire Sudanese state and reforming the structural inequality at its center. His "New Sudan" idea would thus carry appeal beyond the South, as other marginalized populations would rally around his aspiring "national" movement.

In the coming years, Garang's SPLA waged a guerrilla campaign against government installations, oil companies, and the national army, while Khartoum was in political disarray. The new movement grew with military successes, but also faced fierce opposition from Southern opponents and waves of Arab militiamen—each of them backed by Khartoum. An increasingly barbarous war proved devastating for millions of Southern civilians who were subjected to ruthless violence, displacement, famine, and disease.

By 1988 the ferocity of Sudan's war and a catastrophic drought had combined to induce an unprecedented famine in parts of the south. It was considered by many the worst famine in modern African history, more so even than those in Ethiopia and Biafra which had been etched in Western consciousness. Images of skeletal Southerners and their dreadfully emaciated children trickled out over the ensuing period, they but a few of the hundreds of thousands that would die from hunger and the knock-on effects of war. The international community eventually established Operation Lifeline Sudan in 1989, an ad hoc collaboration of UN and humanitarian agencies tasked to deliver an emergency influx of food and life-saving assistance. But the temporary operation would continue for sixteen years.

In 1989, things took a turn for the even worse. President Nimeri's recently elected successor was ousted from office by a cabal of northern army officers. Though their ringleader was a largely unknown briga-dier general named Omar al-Bashir, it soon became clear that Islamist Hassan Turabi was the political mastermind. The Brotherhood's frontman had orchestrated the *coup d'état* and was now calling the shots.

The two men, under the banner of Turabi's National Islamic Front, intensified the military campaign against Garang's Southern rebels. They also accelerated an Islamist revolution in a country known for its decidedly moderate brand of Islam, while dismantling institutions and cracking down on anyone who stood in their way. In doing so they had put John Garang's hopes of a secular, democratic Sudan further out of reach. The ascension of the hardline regime and its increasingly iron-fisted rule would also raise eyebrows in the United States, and mark the beginning of a decades-long feud between Washington and Khartoum.

Though the war had a prevailing North-South character as well as strong religious currents, the oft-cited characterization of "Arab, Muslim North against African and Christian South" didn't do it justice. Southerners fought on both sides of the war, as did Muslims, and "Africans," and "Arabs." Much of the most intense fighting took place in borderlands which were not technically part of the South but were home nonetheless to huge and influential SPLA constituencies. Intent on keeping the war far away from Khartoum, the government employed Arab proxy militias on the frontlines who terrorized, killed, abducted, and sold women and children into slavery. The regime exploited local dynamics and resource interests, and pitted Southern militias against each other in a campaign of divide-and-rule.

More Southerners ultimately died fighting against one another than they did fighting against Northern forces. Garang's SPLA was the dominant, but by no means the only fighting force in South Sudan. A series of other regional and ethnic militias were significant players—some had national aims, others merely protected local interests, but many were on Khartoum's payroll and took the fight to the SPLA.

South-on-South violence was particularly devastating for civilians, as fighters preyed on local populations, used food as a weapon of war, and targeted villages on the basis of ethnicity. Even Garang's movement would not remain whole over the course of the war, split by differences in vision, style, and ethnicity. Though Southerners would ultimately unite to achieve independence in 2011, these painful war-time divisions remained largely unreconciled, and would one day come back to haunt the new nation.

The Khartoum government and the SPLA fought and talked sporadically for years until slow-burning peace negotiations finally gathered momentum in 2002. The new impetus was a result of changes on the battlefield and the opening of another war front in Sudan's Darfur region. But it was also catalyzed by a new diplomatic push from Washington and new Sudanese trepidation about America. The 9/11 attacks had taken place only a year earlier, and the emergent American war on terror was cause for concern in Khartoum's Islamist circles. Forged through a dynamic partnership between two of Sudan's most effective minds—Garang and Sudanese Vice President Ali Osman Taha—the Comprehensive Peace Agreement (CPA) was eventually signed in January 2005.

Of all the long and terrible wars on the continent, its longest and most terrible was finally over—at least for the time being. More than two million lives are believed to have been lost in the space of a generation—nearly double the number of Americans who died in all wars, from the Revolutionary War to Iraq, in the nation's more than two hundred years of existence.

Baked into the historic accord were two visions for the future of the South—Garang's "New Sudan" and the option favored by most Southern leaders—independence. The accord's aspirational principle was to "make unity attractive"—especially to Southerners. A six-year trial period would attempt to bridge chasms between North and

South by transforming the government, devolving power, developing marginalized areas, and sharing the country's abundant oil wealth. The goal of the "CPA" was to retain a united Sudan, but the deal also offered Southerners an opt-out clause. If a more perfect union could not be forged during this peace period, the South would be entitled to a referendum on independence in 2011.

Sudan would never be the same again. The end of the war and the unique political arrangement fashioned in its stead had deferred the inevitable North-South reckoning. But it would not preserve a unified state. The stage was set for a turbulent union, a messy divorce, and ultimately South Sudan's secession.

3

WAR, PEACE, AND
THE AMERICANS

*"It is important to this administration, it's important to
the world, to bring some sanity to the Sudan."*
—President George W. Bush, White House
Rose Garden, September 6, 2001

White walls, speckled blue-gray carpet, and cracked blue leather chairs frame the third-floor office reception area. A water fountain hums rhythmically, and two earnest young female staffers offer coffee and keep the trains running on time. As I prepare notes for the afternoon's interview, I notice three items on a coffee table that offer a concise summary of my interviewee's worldview: one, *World*, an evangelical biweekly—"Today's News, Christian Views"; two, the establishment monthly *Foreign Affairs*; and three, a King James Holy Bible.

It's approaching 100 degrees on a sticky August day in Falls Church, Virginia, a well-to-do suburban enclave just across the Potomac River from Washington, D.C. For 34 years, the adjoining Congressional district, Virginia's 10th, was represented by Republican Frank Rudolph Wolf. The former congressman has occupied this suite, in a three-story brick office complex, labeled "Baptist World Alliance," since he retired from Capitol Hill in 2015.

A conference room door opens and I hear Wolf finish a conversation with a priest and two activists about Yazidis and other religious minorities under siege amid the continuing war in Syria. A self-described "follower of Jesus," the Congressman has stated that his personal mission, even as a retiree, is to protect "human rights and religious freedom—both domestic and international." Wolf spent a considerable portion of his three decades in Congress pursuing these issues, from human rights in former Soviet states to religious liberties in Tibet and Iraq, and now runs a nonprofit alliance of Christian churches advocating these causes worldwide. But few issues captured his attention as wholly and as viscerally as Sudan, where his voice was among the loudest in shaping American policy.

"I was interested because of my faith," Wolf tells me, as we take seats across a wide conference table. He turns to Bible verses as guiding principles. "Matthew 25—'when I was hungry you fed me, when I was naked you clothed me, when I was in prison you visited me,'" he recites. "Well, there were a lot of Matthew 25s in South Sudan."

Wolf has snow-white hair, parted neatly on the left. His features are long and narrow, his nose and ears larger than average, like those of many in their late seventies (he is 77). He leans back in his chair across the conference table, his soft blue Oxford shirt buttoned neatly over a red tie and tucked into Dockers khakis. "I fell in love with the people," he explains, asked about the origins of his enduring commitment to South Sudan.

Wolf tells me about traveling to dark corners of the globe to pursue righteous causes. Such journeys, he explains with an air of experience, are best undertaken in small groups and low-maintenance style. "Also, I think you gotta stay the night." Asserting his bona fides, he reels off a list of rough-and-tumble locations he visited during his Congressional tenure, and it is impressive. He then squirms, and a sour expression emerges as he recounts various unpleasantries along the way—sleeping in a hut, stomaching the local food, navigating various health hazards.

"In every generation," the foreword to Wolf's memoir, *Prisoner of Conscience*, begins, "God chooses a handful of courageous leaders to defend the truth and promote righteousness—often against the prevailing currents. Frank Wolf is such a man of our times." The words were written by Charles Colson, a top Nixon aide who was indicted in the Watergate scandal and later became an outspoken Evangelical Christian. Before arriving, I'd skimmed a copy of the book, subtitled "One Man's Crusade for Global Human and Religious Rights." The memoir chronicles the Congressman's religiously inspired exploits across nearly a dozen countries. Colson describes Wolf as a "hero" for his pursuit of virtuous causes, for daring "to go where few members of Congress have gone before." Wolf "measures himself by his faithfulness," Colson writes, and is part of a group in Congress who "pray for one another as they fight great humanitarian battles." It is not hard to see why John Garang and his American advisers would identify the crusader from Virginia's 10th as one of their champions.

"Why Sudan?" I ask Wolf. "What made you interested in this part of the world?"

Wolf pinpoints a trip to Ethiopia during the 1984 famine as a "life-changing event" that soon thereafter spurred him to get involved in the war in neighboring Sudan. In 1989, when Wolf was a fifth-term congressman, a pilot from Norwegian Peoples' Aid invited him along on an impromptu trip into Southern Sudan. Wolf recounts hopping aboard a small twin-prop Caravan at Wilson Air Field in Nairobi and touching down—during a firefight—just across the border in SPLA-held Eastern Equatoria. Wolf fondly revisits the memorable scenes like most any wide-eyed Westerner on a first trip to the developing world—the unfamiliar geography, difficult terrain, strange cultural practices, and exotic wildlife.

He'd come to meet the man everyone had been talking about—John Garang—but was unable to track Garang down until his third visit. Settling in to a story he's clearly told many times, the congressman tells of the long distances he traversed to find the rebel leader. "I was getting really upset," he says. Finally, after an extended goose chase, his SPLA minders informed him Garang was waiting "atop that hill, just across this stream."

"I'm not going to walk in the damn water!" Wolf fussed, concerned about water-borne parasites. The men stretched a log across the stream for him, but as soon as he attempted to cross—Wolf slaps his hands together—he fell face-first into the stream. Sopping wet and tired of the chase, an angry Wolf charged up the hill and found Garang. "I just... I... I really *gave* it to him." But diffusing the congressman's frustration, Garang "just laughed and laughed... and we became friends." Wolf speaks proudly of the personal connection he developed with this "very, *very* charismatic guy," and of his lasting investment in the rebel leader. "Then, every time Garang came to Washington he would come by to see me, and every time I went out there I would see him."

On these initial visits to SPLA-controlled territory, Wolf witnessed the brutality of the civil war up close. Soon thereafter he became one of America's most vehement critics of the Sudanese government in Khartoum. "I had seen what they did... I saw what Bashir's people were doing," Wolf tells me twice during the interview. He frames the conflict in racial and religious terms, and makes no bones about choosing sides. This was a moral imperative, and in time the energy of the SPLM's foreign supporters was defined as much by a personal and visceral contempt for President Bashir's regime in Khartoum as it was by their allegiance to the South. For Wolf and many others, this was a battle of good versus evil.

And in battle, the congressman was as prolific as he was unequivocal: he wrote letters to U.S. presidents and top diplomats, proposed hard-nosed legislation, and rained rhetorical bombs on the floor of the U.S. House of Representatives. He demanded action and reserved excoriating commentary for anyone not on board. During one speech on the House floor, he derided President Obama for his policy choices, calling his administration "morally bankrupt" and arguing that his "abdication of leadership" would yield more misery and suffering. In another hearing, an animated Wolf spewed relentless criticism and shouted incredulously from the bench, "This is a *fundamentally evil* government... evil... *evil*!"

He yelled, gesturing wildly, "You hafta *remove* Bashir... regime change!... these are evil people!"

Wolf's energy and outrage were of the kind that can be necessary to drive change, if harnessed with savvy. But his remarks occasionally framed Sudan's conflicts as a simple morality play, and his solutions sometimes glossed over complex issues. One veteran U.S. official familiar with Wolf's work over three decades chuckled as he lauded the congressman's activist credentials, "Frank was often the first guy to jump on a plane and go to a place, and then come back and say 'we gotta do something.'" Commenting on his foreign policy acumen, the official continued, "his heart was always in the right place, but when it came to solutions, well, let's say he did not always have the best judgement."

<hr />

Without America, simply put, there would be no Republic of South Sudan. Frank Wolf was an early advocate, and a loud one, but he was far from alone. American officials in Congress and three White Houses, together with a vocal activist community, developed a special relationship with the South's underdog guerrillas, cultivated over years of what is known simply as "the struggle." Those ties helped deliver aid to war-ravaged communities and put Garang's liberation fighters on the map. Together with allies in Africa, the Americans helped isolate the South's enemies in Khartoum, end the civil war, and guarantee the region a right to self-determination. In the end, American efforts safeguarded the vote for independence and its result. Thus was a country born in the heart of Africa, after a half-century of turmoil and suffering, and Washington was its midwife.

Washington's contempt for a brutal regime in Sudan was justifiable, as was its determination to aid the beleaguered South Sudanese people. But in time America's posture skewed too far from a constructive and balanced center. The ideological fervor of its anti-Khartoum lobby failed to produce desired changes in the North and yielded unintended consequences in the South. A simplified narrative, an unqualified belief in the rightness of the cause, and a compulsion to act together distorted U.S. policy and blinded Wolf and fellow American supporters to the flaws of their chosen heroes.

Neither Washington nor Juba's other international supporters are principally to blame for South Sudan's unraveling, as the nation's leaders squandered an opportunity that most liberation movements could only dream of. The "gotcha" accounts by critics and journalists that point the finger solely at the West are simplistic and cheap, overlooking both the considerable achievements in making peace and saving lives, and the hard policy decisions that accompanied every stage of South Sudan's political evolution. But because America and its partners so heavily influenced the events that led to the country's birth, and then moved on too soon, the role of the West deserves careful scrutiny. Born of moral outrage and advanced with righteous zeal, this partnership with South Sudan's underdogs helped to achieve lofty goals, but it also helped nurture the seeds of the new Republic's collapse.

In the 1980s and into the 1990s, Cold War dynamics framed American foreign policy in East Africa. Washington had Sudanese President Nimeri onside, his government one of the largest recipients of U.S. foreign aid and a bulwark against Soviet proxies in the region. To the east, Ethiopia's Colonel Mengistu Haile Mariam was a Communist foe, and by extension, so too were the Southern Sudanese rebels he was backing. John Garang's Marxist rhetoric of revolution and "national liberation" marked a break from past southern rebellions, and was born of both strategic and tactical motivations. His articulation of a "New Sudan" was necessary to secure the political and military support of the Soviet-allied regime in Ethiopia—the SPLA's initial patron. Garang's commitment to a unified Sudan would also be necessary to curry favor elsewhere on the continent, as African leaders—many battling their own breakaway minorities—did not look kindly on separatism.

But Garang's affiliation with the Eastern bloc garnered him no support in Washington, where many distrusted his new movement as "a bunch of Marxists." The Americans were meanwhile rallying behind Ethiopian rebels, who eventually toppled Ethiopia's communist junta in 1991 as the Iron Curtain receded worldwide.

The tectonic geopolitical changes underway in 1989–1991 provoked tumult for the young SPLA. Not only were its training camps and supply channels compromised with the fall of the Ethiopian regime; it was suddenly without a patron and seemingly on the wrong side of history. Aides say Garang announced soon thereafter that the "times were changing, and we must change with them." And so he set out to forge a new relationship with the Cold War victors. Garang would travel back to the U.S.—where he had spent the better part of a decade as an undergraduate, Ph.D. student, and army trainee—to begin building a new coalition of supporters.

Still viewed with skepticism by the American government, Garang had little entrée with the U.S. administration, so he focused his efforts elsewhere. Deftly tailoring his message to different interest groups, Garang sold religious persecution to Evangelical Christians, racism and marginalization to African-American constituencies, human rights violations and slavery to advocacy groups. (By the mid-1990s, the SPLM would add Khartoum's support for Islamic terrorism to its selling points in Washington and capitals across sub-Saharan Africa.)

Conscious, however, of the staying power of Congress and its ability to shape the environment in which presidential administrations made policy, Garang saved the best of his legendary charisma for Capitol Hill. He cultivated lasting personal relationships with both Republicans and Democrats, and importantly, their staffers. Chief among them were Wolf and the late Donald Payne, a twelve-term Democrat from New Jersey and chairman of the Congressional Black Caucus.

Remarking on the success of Garang's sales pitch, one of Garang's disciples told me, "In time, Frank Wolf was no longer doing it for Garang; it was now *his* cause." Wolf and Payne visited liberated areas in Southern Sudan together, and remarked two decades later on the extraordinary bipartisanship that sustained their odd-couple coalition's influence all the way through independence. Wolf, supported by Republican Senators Bill Frist and Sam Brownback, represented a white, Southern, conservative component of the caucus. Payne represented a liberal, black, Democratic contingent. But they weren't alone.

Black church leaders had visited Sudan in the early years, as had the nation's most famous televangelist, the Reverend Billy Graham. Graham and his son Franklin, and their humanitarian aid organization, Samaritan's Purse, were drawing America's Bible belt to the plight of Southern Sudanese Christians. They provided clean water and medical supplies to war-afflicted villages, but their work didn't stop there. The younger Graham, who once called Islam "evil and wicked," met several times with Bashir, Sudan's Islamist president, to discuss the war and the plight of Christian Southerners. Once Franklin even tried to convert him to Christianity.

When South Sudan finally achieved independence, Franklin wrote again to American supporters asking for their prayers and dollars—not only to continue supplying aid, but to help him lay a spiritual foundation. "They know that the only hope for their nation is the Lord Jesus Christ," Graham wrote, announcing plans to convene tens of thousands of Southern converts in Juba for an "evangelistic Crusade."

Garang did not limit his U.S. visits to Washington, but took his show on the road across a country he had once called home—to schools in Ames, Iowa, and community centers in Phoenix, Arizona. One Sunday in Midland, Texas, Garang asked for support at two churches—one Evangelical, the other liberal. "He tailored his remarks and the Bible verses he quoted" to match the respective congregations, one of Garang's American friends told me. "They were hanging on his every word."

Major television spots also helped draw attention to the Southern cause, including a 1991 special report by *60 Minutes*' Ed Bradley that provoked shock over starvation in Southern Sudan. The Soviet Union's demise was meanwhile re-orienting power dynamics in the region, also to the SPLA's advantage.

But Garang's vision, personal charm, and familiarity with American culture were at the center of the SPLM's new political image and its swelling band of supporters. With the exception of the anti-apartheid movement, African countries didn't enjoy this kind of attention anywhere. Africa was still a sideshow in world affairs, the lowest rung on the geopolitical ladder. For Garang to come from the wrong side of the Cold War divide and build a multi-sector constituency in the space of a few years was nothing short of astonishing.

By the mid-1990s, South Sudan and its SPLM leader had cultivated an army of true believers, and their influence and commitment would only increase with time. But Garang hadn't achieved this sea change on his own. Nearly a decade earlier, Garang had begun liaising with a small group of committed and well-positioned American friends, each of whom—like Wolf—had been won over by his vision and charisma. The quiet, informal advisory club would later become known as "the Council," and effectively served as the SPLM lobby in Washington.

Drawing on government experience and personal connections on Capitol Hill, the group was instrumental in mobilizing popular support, shaping views across Washington, and engineering legislation that aided the Southern cause—sometimes backing policies opposed by the White House and State Department. They facilitated SPLM delegations to Washington, gathering privately in hotel suites with Garang and other SPLA spokesmen to shape messaging and plot objectives. As members of the Council later boasted in a 2012 article, "The Wonks who Sold Washington on South Sudan," the group met for discreet strategy sessions over lunch in the back of a Washington restaurant and even gave themselves nicknames: the "Emperor," the "Spear Carrier," and the like. Like Frank Wolf and the others they cultivated, the group's support for the South was unequivocal, and their assessment—at least outwardly—appeared simple. As founding member Roger Winter once summarized it, in Sudan, "there's a good guy and a bad guy."

A longtime official for the United States Agency for International Development (USAID) and other humanitarian groups, Winter had spent an impressive amount of time in Southern Sudan in the early years and would later serve as a State Department adviser to the peace negotiations between North and South. He was close to Garang and arguably the best-known American in Southern Sudan; they loved him and his hard-charging commitment to their cause. The white-haired Winter made no bones about his allegiance to the South. In a 2008 *New York Times Magazine* profile, "The Man for a New Sudan," Winter suggested he wasn't interested in engagement with Khartoum, and thought neutrality "morally bankrupt." "I'm an evangelist," he told the reporter, "I preach the gospel of Sudan."

Given some remarkable advancements Winter had engineered on their behalf, Southerners often had huge expectations about what their dogged advocate could deliver. But his outsize role wasn't welcomed by everyone, in South Sudan or in Washington. Some found his presence unhelpfully polarizing. Winter caused a stir after leaving the U.S. government, when he took up a formal position advising the SPLM, which reinforced opponents' suspicions that the SPLM was simply an American proxy in an ideological battle against the North.

Ted Dagne, a one-time Ethiopian refugee who became a U.S. citizen, was arguably the most pivotal, and controversial, member of the Council. Then working for a congressional research arm, Dagne was seconded to the Africa subcommittee in the House of Representatives, where he cultivated a following, molding the views of leading congressmen, organizing bi-partisan delegations to Southern Sudan, and penning pro-SPLM legislation.

Dagne maintained an intensely personal relationship with Garang. The two reportedly spoke almost daily by phone, and some say "Uncle" Garang reportedly referred to Dagne as his "nephew." When I asked Wolf's former aides about his Sudan policy—whether legislation, statements, or positions on the issues—they regularly referred to Council members, and to Dagne in particular. "He was the driver," one of them said, echoing a sentiment I had heard from many others.

"He was all over it... nothing happened in Congress without Ted, and without checking with Ted."

John Prendergast, the Council's youngest member, would go on to build an activist organization and series of high-profile campaigns against the Sudanese government, harnessing celebrities, youth groups, and popular media in support of the cause. Eric Reeves, an English professor at a small Massachusetts college, joined the Council years later. Though he had spent little time in Sudan, he quickly became one of its most public and outspoken voices, infusing the effort with moral outrage in opinion articles and blog posts for major news outlets. Several members of the Council were involved in the CPA negotiations, and like Winter, several later advised the SPLM government in various capacities—sometimes volunteering, sometimes paid.

Council members testified regularly before Congress, helped establish a "Sudan Caucus" in the House and Senate, and positioned themselves as the go-to experts for the emerging popular Sudan constituencies. But they also developed strong ties with key State Department and White House officials. Most notably, Dagne and Prendergast linked up in the early nineties with an emerging star in U.S. Africa policy named Susan Rice.

Then a 31-year-old Senior Director for Africa on Bill Clinton's national security council, and later the youngest ever Assistant Secretary of State for Africa, Rice would soon be confronted by the 1994 genocide in Rwanda. Among the many torn by guilt over inaction as hundreds of thousands were slaughtered, she would later say, "I swore to myself that if I ever faced such a crisis again, I would come down on the side of dramatic action, going down in flames if that was required."

Rice too developed hardline anti-Khartoum views, liaised closely with allies from the Council, and even hired Prendergast to join her staff. She would help position the Clinton administration firmly in the SPLM's corner, and go on to shape American policy on Sudan more than any other single figure, and not without controversy. She later served as UN Ambassador and National Security Adviser for President Obama, where her visceral contempt for Sudan's government was coupled by close relationships with South Sudan's leaders—until its collapse in 2013.

⁑

After their first visits to rebel-held territory, Wolf and Payne—representing the unique alliance between evangelical Christians and the Congressional Black Caucus—helped put Southern Sudan on the agenda through a flurry of action on Capitol Hill. They started with a 1993 resolution—drafted by Dagne—recognizing a right to self-determination for Southern Sudan, a move that sent a clear signal of support to the liberation fighters and put Congress well out in front of the Clinton administration.

Additional bills, resolutions, and hearings pummeled the Sudanese government for its prosecution of the war and its gross human rights abuses, the continued practice of slavery, alleged crimes against humanity and genocide. They also called on the Clinton administration to ratchet up pressures against the North and provide political and material support, as well as food and humanitarian assistance, directly to the SPLA and its allies.

Meanwhile, Hassan Turabi and his new brand of Islamist hardliners in Khartoum had piqued a different kind of interest in Washington, given his grand visions of a pan-Islamic revolution. Though it ultimately proved a hollow affair, Turabi's government once played eager host and benefactor to a who's who of fundamentalists, militant radicals, and unsavory characters from across the Muslim world, chief among them Osama bin Laden. These associations, together with alleged links to the 1993 bombing at the World Trade Center in New York, led President Clinton to designate Sudan a "State Sponsor of Terror."

Later, following the 1998 Al Qaeda bombings of American embassies in Kenya and Tanzania, Clinton responded by firing thirteen cruise missiles at a suspected chemical weapons facility in Khartoum, which faulty intelligence had tied to bin Laden. (Intense criticism followed, when it was established that the pharmaceutical factory destroyed had no link to Al Qaeda and was manufacturing only medicines, not VX nerve gas).

Concerns about radicalism in Sudan indirectly reinforced support for the Southern rebels, and the Americans weren't the only ones getting close. Regional countries—particularly Ethiopia, Eritrea and Uganda—began offering greater support and cementing personal ties with the SPLM vanguard. The threat of revolutionary Islamist expansionism then emanating from Khartoum was deeply unsettling to these neighbors, and they saw the SPLM as the principal instrument to check this threat. Garang's New Sudan vision also appealed to them, as he wanted not to leave Sudan, but to reform it in a manner amenable to black, non-Islamist Africa. And so the movement was reinforced, its legitimacy again bolstered by external, rather than domestic, sources.

With the Cold War relegated to the history books, the rise of a new group of African leaders, and emerging concerns about the regime in Khartoum, Washington began to re-frame its posture in the region. Ethiopia's Meles Zenawi and Eritrea's Isaias Afwerki "helped to shift that view," recalls one veteran African diplomat, "working on Susan [Rice] and others to see Sudan from an African perspective." Then steering U.S. policy, Rice championed an effort to elevate this new generation of "African renaissance leaders"—including Meles and Isaias, as well as Uganda's Yoweri Museveni and later Paul Kagame of Rwanda. Most of them turned out to be autocrats, or worse.

At the time, some State Department staffers scoffed at the new mantra. "Sweet lord. New leaders of Africa?" one recalls, slapping his forehead in mock disbelief. "Unbelievable... none of these scalawags were democrats." America's friends in the region urged Washington to see the emergent Garang as part of the African renaissance club. What followed erased any doubts that the U.S. had chosen sides in Sudan. The Clinton administration began providing millions of dollars in weapons and surplus military equipment to the SPLA by way of Uganda, Ethiopia, and Eritrea. All three "frontline states" hosted opposition forces, procured weapons, and sent their own soldiers across the border directly in support of SPLA offensives, sometimes even donning SPLA uniforms.

By 1997, Frank Wolf had introduced legislation on the House floor calling for sanctions against Sudan. Five months later President Clinton, by some accounts seeking to pre-empt even stricter measures from Wolf and the SPLM lobby, imposed a range of economic sanctions. The hawks in Washington were cementing a policy of isolation and aggression, while those expressing concern were ignored. "There was no logic to our policy," the American ambassador in Khartoum later lamented, no logic "beyond punishing Khartoum and supporting the rebellion in South Sudan."

By the end of the 1990s, Washington was providing covert support to the SPLA and regional adversaries, imposing sweeping economic sanctions, and had already rained a torrent of tomahawk missiles into the heart of Khartoum; taken together, there was little doubt in Sudanese government circles that the Americans were intensifying a policy of regime change.

A small group of like-minded individuals had assembled a coalition that would grow to have an outsized, and arguably unprecedented, impact in shaping American foreign policy. Bite-sized messages had helped solidify a narrative—North versus South, Arabs versus Africans. Slavery, racism, and the domination of helpless and hungry victims. The themes were based in reality, as no one could deny the horrors being perpetrated against Sudan's marginalized people. But the complexities of the war and Sudan's turbulent post-colonial experience were being smudged out.

With a Washington consensus established, the SPLM lobby was fashioning solutions with little resistance. Scores of Congress members, advocates, and journalists piled on. It was easy to score points, and there were essentially no consequences to joining the righteous chorus. After all, they were excoriating an oppressive Islamist government and extolling the virtues of a freedom-loving Christian underdog.

This phenomenon was possible precisely because Sudan was not China, or Russia, or Iran, or the Middle East—there was little if any U.S. national security interest in Sudan. This was Africa, and it was far away. Concerns about Khartoum's links to terrorism had once roused national security interest, but attention dissipated after bin Laden was chased away and Khartoum became a counter-terrorism partner. Beyond that, Sudan didn't concern energy, or nuclear weapons, or strategic defense. Had the stakes been higher, if matters of geopolitical import were at hand, one can imagine American policy being shaped by a more diverse and rigorous debate, with competing ideas that reflected the complexity of Sudan's crisis and its range of political constituencies. But it simply didn't matter enough.

Led by Representatives Wolf and Payne, and those shaping their talking points, members of Congress lent their names to letters, issued statements, offered testimony, and drafted resolutions. Wolf's chief of staff also emphasized how Wolf and Payne, working with the material provided by members of the so-called Council and allied advocacy groups, came to own Sudan policy. "You couldn't criticize them," he said. "It was *their* issue."

Another Congressional staffer, registering no reservations about the way things worked, explained, "It was easy; when things were black-and-white, you could lay out a clear-cut case... and members of Congress would just sign on." When I asked how many members had a reasonable understanding of the situation in Sudan, she hesitated, then twisted her mouth and discreetly admitted that number could be counted on one hand. "Often members just signed on out of respect for Wolf and Payne, and their command of the issue." She described the limited bandwidth in Congress when it came to matters of foreign affairs, and said that it was "harder to sustain interest" after South Sudan's collapse in 2013, when the situation became, "murkier... when it wasn't so black-and-white, or so easy in terms of solutions."

The increasingly hardline posture against Sudan's regime meant, in turn, that few questioned the close relationship with the SPLM or its lionized leader. Few sought counter-arguments, confronted the reality of South Sudan's deep internal divisions, or held the idealized rebels to account for their own egregious acts at home. The SPLM was well aware of this dynamic, and became increasingly adept at lobbying American interest groups.

With the arrival of George Bush in the White House, American support for the SPLM would intensify. The uniquely bi-partisan and increasingly powerful Sudan coalition—no longer limited to Washington—had congealed by 2000. At its heart were Christian conservatives, a huge and nationwide constituency that had also been essential in Bush's narrow election win. If Sudan mattered to them, it mattered to Bush. Republican evangelicals like Wolf, together with super-evangelist Franklin Graham, were their voices in Washington, and infused Bush's embrace of the issue with religious overtones and moral idealism.

Wolf, together with Republican and Democratic colleagues, had meanwhile introduced another piece of legislation on the House and Senate floor, which would become the Sudan Peace Act. Reflecting the gathering steam of the activist movement, the legislation formally fingered Khartoum for genocide, appropriated an eye-popping $300 million of new support for rebel-held territories in the South, and demanded the U.S. government throw its full weight into ending the war, including using "all means of pressure" necessary.

On September 6, 2001, just five days before the terrible event that would define the Bush presidency and reshape American foreign policy, Bush appointed retired Senator Jack Danforth as his "Special Envoy to Sudan." The presidential appointment was a clear signal of the importance the White House attached to the file, and so was Bush's personnel choice; Danforth was a three-term Senator and had been on the short list to become Bush's vice president. He was also an ordained Episcopal priest. Standing in the White House Rose Garden for Danforth's appointment ceremony were members of the congressional Sudan caucus, including a proud Frank Wolf. "I was there," Wolf says. "I had been the one that asked for the Special Envoy, over and over and over."

Bush tasked Danforth with reinvigorating a flagging peace process. The president emphasized that he was under no illusions about the difficulty of the job, but resolved that his administration was "committed to bringing stability to the Sudan, so that many loving Americans, non-governmental organizations, will be able to perform their duties of love and compassion within that country." Danforth tempered expectations, noting that peace in Sudan was up to the combatants, "not to even the best-intentioned of outsiders, including the United States." But the "best-intentioned" of the Americans didn't share his view, and would intervene forcefully on behalf of the Southern cause.

Days later, the 9/11 attacks would forever change the world and re-frame American foreign policy in simple, binary terms. "Either you're with us, or you're with the terrorists," Bush famously proclaimed in a speech seen around the world. Launching the War on Terror, he went on, "Our enemy is a radical network of terrorists, and *any government that supports them.*" Having recently hosted bin Laden, and been hit once already with American cruise missiles on account of alleged Al Qaeda connections, Khartoum's politicians and securocrats sat up straight in their chairs. American ground troops and B-52 bombers would soon invade Afghanistan, and according to one senior U.S. diplomat, "the Sudanese thought Bush was nuts. They were absolutely convinced they would be next."

With Bush and the bi-partisan coalition now expecting results, American diplomats approached their Sudanese counterparts to set the table for Danforth. In a quiet rendezvous at a luxurious Nairobi golf club, the Americans conveyed their seriousness about reinvigorating the defunct peace process. The men spoke over tea in a dark wood-paneled corridor, outlining their views of a negotiated end to the war, as well as what it would take for Washington to restore normal rela-tions with Sudan's regime. One of the American diplomats also cau-tioned Khartoum's representatives to tread carefully, hinting bluntly at the fundamentally different character of the man now occupying the Oval Office. "Clinton may have bombed an aspirin factory... try Bush," he recalls telling them. "They got the message."

Shuttling between Sudan's warring parties and consulting counter-parts in regional capitals, Danforth and his team of diplomats helped catalyze the peace process and bring international partners around a common goal. Eight months later, in July 2002, the "Machakos

Protocol"—which provided a framework for an eventual political settlement—was signed by government and SPLM negotiators in Machakos, Kenya. The breakthrough breathed new life into the talks. The deal also embraced Garang's New Sudan vision—unity between North and South—while also re-affirming the South's right to self-determination. If unity was not made attractive, the Southerners could choose to go their own way.

The blunt American diplomat, now retired, says Washington had "chosen sides from the beginning," but remained pragmatic about the objectives nonetheless. "We were clear with the Sudanese that they didn't have to capitulate, but that we saw the South as the aggrieved party." Yet as talks evolved over the ensuing two years, he and other career diplomats complained that more Bush officials with "ties to the 'Sudan bad, Garang good'" constituency asserted an increasingly partisan agenda. These American hardliners, he explained, together with congressional action "led by a fanatical Frank Wolf," had several times "made negotiations more difficult."

He wasn't alone. Some Southern Sudanese, as well as more neutral foreign observers, also worried that the SPLM lobby had become "more Catholic than the Pope," and that their posture and advice was making SPLM negotiators more bellicose in negotiations with Khartoum. "They wanted to free the South… and that was going to be their big claim to fame," the retired diplomat says derisively. And when it came to Khartoum, "they were in full punishment mode from the beginning."

Council members, and the growing circles around them, pursued their goal with religious fervor. And it was this group that would help train Washington's crosshairs on the regime in Khartoum. While the SPLM's friends working in government were careful not to betray their true colors, the regime change agenda was always thinly veiled. Congressional advocates spoke about it openly, and Council member Eric Reeves penned a 2004 opinion in the *Washington Post*, titled simply "Regime Change in Sudan."

The growing cast of American friends had helped cement a singularly pro-South and pro-SPLM narrative in Washington's policy community, and those who proposed policies that involved anything but isolation and punishment for Sudan were fingered as apologists or traitors, or met with charges of moral equivocation. One long-time observer described the "vindictive" manner in which some Council members "went after anyone who questioned the narrative" or attempted to advance alternative solutions.

In January 2005, with support from the region and the United States, the warring parties signed the Comprehensive Peace Agreement, which established a regional government in Juba and slated a referendum on Southern independence for 2011. In addition to the diplomatic push and the backdrop of the war on terror, Bush himself had worked the phones, calling the leaders of North and South to nudge them over the line. Some observers argue that domestic realities and a dynamic partnership between Garang and his Sudanese counterpart were far more important than U.S. interventions. But there could be no doubt about Washington's responsibility for turning a defunct peace process into a serious negotiation and forcing Khartoum to the table.

South Sudanese perceptions of America were sky-high, especially atop the SPLM. Washington had helped end a war the rebels could not win on their own, establish a Southern regional government, and pave a path to independence. In the ensuing years, the Americans would commit billions of dollars of additional foreign aid. The SPLM had an indispensable ally, and henceforth its leadership would look to friends in Washington to deliver what they could not, or chose not, attain on their own.

Though the guns had fallen silent, and the South had been afforded temporary autonomy, the SPLM's battle with its senior partners in Khartoum was far from over.

4

"SAVING" DARFUR

"A good intention, with a bad approach, often leads to a poor result."

—Thomas Edison

In 2003, as North-South talks continued, a second but related crisis erupted in Sudan's western region: Darfur. Instability was not new to Darfur, another periphery where many people had been subject to the kinds of marginalization and political violence familiar to Southerners. As the peace talks hinted at a deal for Southern Sudan, rebels in Darfur took up arms, seeking to rectify their own long history of neglect. The ensuing events would both reshape the environment in which a "North-South" peace was eventually concluded and alter ideas about peacemaking and political transformation in Sudan.

After the Darfur rebels achieved early military successes against the government, and articulated a national agenda, Khartoum responded with an unprecedented campaign of violence. Garang's SPLA, keen to squeeze the embattled government, sent weapons and trainers to help the insurgents. More political and military pressure, he hoped, would improve the South's hand both before and after the peace deal was done. Garang also encouraged his American friends to shine a spotlight on Darfur.

Over the next seven years, the Darfur crisis—and the unprecedented activist campaign it prompted—would eclipse popular attention on South Sudan, embedding "Darfur" in the American psyche and hardening Washington's posture toward Khartoum. Though international attention shifted away from the South once the CPA was signed, the unprecedented new pressure on Khartoum would ultimately reinforce American support for the regime's opponents, chief among them the SPLM. But in time, the popular campaign for Darfur would also bring the hazards of mass mobilization into stark relief.

The conflicts in Sudan were often characterized in binary terms: North-South, Arab-Black, Islamic-Christian. Yet the complicated situation in Darfur would challenge these prevailing explanations and blur the lines of identity as seen from outside. The 2003 insurgency prompted a brutal reaction from Khartoum. In the eyes of the regime's politicians, the wars in the South and now in Darfur were deeply connected and threatened their very survival. And so they responded with an unforgiving counter-insurgency.

Manipulating the politics of race, tribe, and resources in Darfur, Khartoum enlisted predominantly Arab militias to spearhead the violence, much of it directed at civilian populations. Antonov jets dropped barrel bombs from the sky while military forces and camel-mounted *janjaweed* militias waged a scorched-earth campaign on the ground. They raided villages and burned whole settlements to the ground, massacring civilians in huge numbers and driving hundreds of thousands more from their homes. They employed rape as a weapon of war while systematically destroying food stocks and water sources. By 2004, the United Nations said the ongoing events amounted to "ethnic cleansing."

In response to the emerging crisis and its shocking death toll, Sudan advocates—including members of the so-called "Council," joined by faith-based and human rights organizations—built one of the largest and most vocal activist campaigns in modern history, one not seen since the international movement to end apartheid in South Africa. In July 2004, in an effort spearheaded by Council member John Prendergast, actress Mia Farrow, and other prominent advocates, the "Save Darfur" movement was officially launched.

The stated mission of Save Darfur was to "raise public awareness and mobilize a massive response to the atrocities." The movement would come to epitomize a new kind of popular human rights advocacy, buoyed by the rise of the internet and social media, celebrity activism, and an expanding discourse about universal human rights and a global "responsibility to protect" those in grave danger. Harnessing the star power of Hollywood's biggest names—Farrow, and later the likes of George Clooney, Angelina Jolie, and Stephen Spielberg—Western media was soon abuzz with the story of Darfur, its marauding devils on horseback, and the new coalition of crusaders out to stop them.

Popular mobilization drove media coverage, and media coverage drove further mobilization. Congress followed suit, ramping up the rhetoric while adopting resolutions and tightening sanctions at the behest of the campaign. Successive U.S. administrations were also compelled to act. In September 2004, after contentious battles over the nature of the crimes committed in Darfur, then Secretary of State Colin Powell announced the State Department's conclusion that "genocide had been committed." Years later, the International Criminal Court indicted Sudan's President Bashir on the charge of genocide.

The genocide label—itself the result of a fierce debate over the evidence—elevated the brutal conflict to a new level. It infused "Darfur" with moral and historical consequence and drew even more constituencies to the cause, but it also cemented a binary, good vs. evil, interpretation of events on the ground. The ensuing international outcry far exceeded anything the Sudanese government had confronted to date, and its image went from abysmal to even worse. "Already an 'evil' regime," one experienced Africa watcher explained, "and now they were *genocidaires.*"

The expanding movement for Darfur grew louder. Over the next several years, its multi-faceted campaign was hugely successful in rousing millions of Americans and Europeans, drawing attention to the awful devastation, and getting the crisis onto the foreign policy agenda of Congress and the White House. But to what end?

The power of popular activism was evident. Advocacy campaigns had helped expedite the end of a racist apartheid government in South Africa and drawn early attention to unfolding atrocities in hotspots around the globe. Values-based campaigning had the power to reframe issues on a grand scale, and had also proven an important counterweight against detached policy-making, when cold calculations and realpolitik had taken politicians into troubling moral terrritory. But what happened in Sudan also suggested that, if not carefully harnessed, popular mobilization could complicate matters—and possibly even do more harm than good.

For most of Save Darfur's members, the motivation was pure: the Holocaust, the Rwandan genocide, the massacres of the Balkan wars—these events, and the indifference that accompanied them, were stains on the collective conscience of the world. "Never Again" and "Not on Our Watch" read the campaign's T-shirts and green wristbands. They had shed light on Darfur, a critically important intervention that probably saved lives and prevented the Sudanese government from finishing its campaign of atrocities. But in time, the seemingly irreproachable movement would warrant closer review. Its tactics, message, and prescribed solutions—too often reflecting an inclination to "act before seeking to understand"—would have adverse effects on peacemaking efforts and on the crisis itself. Despite the best of intentions, the Save Darfur movement was skewing America's posture too far from a constructive center, hindering the very cause of peace it purported to champion.

Leaving aside the thorny semantics of Westerners "saving" Africans, the campaign's mass marketing appeal made it prone to oversimplification. As with South Sudan, a deeply complicated conflict was reduced to a simple, sexy, and morally satisfying narrative. Darfur, millions were told, was about government-backed villains on horseback and helpless victims on foot; it was about Arabs killing Africans—a campaign of racial hate. Except that it wasn't quite so simple.

There was a deeply troubling racial component at the center of the violence, and the government's culpability for the worst periods of violence in 2003–2004 was as indisputable as the violence was shocking. But Darfur was also a complex environment—involving local politics and governance, land disputes, migration, competing livelihoods, desertification, national marginalization, and regional security politics (including neighbors Libya and Chad)—and it was by no means static. Its crowded field of players and shifting interests was not easily reduced to good guys and bad, and its solutions were not as straightfoward as the righteous sloganeering sometimes suggested. The *New York Times*'s Nick Kristof and other journalists used their columns to draw important attention to Darfur, but in time, their sometimes simplified narratives and moralizing tenor reduced Darfur to a hellscape of horrors and victims while reinforcing the stridency of the movement and its demands. When compared with more "serious" regions of the world, the framing of Darfur's conflict seemed another instance of simplification in Africa, a continent still subject to both prejudice and romanticism.

Save Darfur's mobilization was impressive. Church groups held vigils, students formed chapters on hundreds of college campuses, youth groups organized fundraisers, and social media exploded with calls to action. The movement, which ultimately claimed nearly a million active members, launched divestment initiatives and postcard campaigns, and enlisted the help of big-name corporations. They set up a genocide hotline and attempted to embarrass China—a Sudanese ally—by branding its 2008 Olympic Games the "genocide Olympics." There was even an online video game, developed with support from MTV and Reebok, that put players in the role of a Darfuri civilian fleeing the infamous *janjaweed* militias.

Demands for aggressive international action appeared on television, on billboards, and in full-page newspaper ads. Mass rallies were convened in New York's Central Park, on Washington's National Mall, and in cities across America, drawing members of Congress, artists, musicians, faith leaders, Olympic athletes, and big-name actors. Rally goers carried signs calling for "boots on the ground" and chanted slogans suggesting the American military should move "Out of Iraq and into Darfur!"

As the campaign gained more attention and more followers, the echo chamber grew louder, as did the rhetoric of righteousness and the calls for intervention. But the activism lacked context, and seemed to prioritize action and moral certitude over all else. In time, the righteous finger-wagging became increasingly disconnected from the realities of Darfur and its people.

One afternoon at a Berlin airport in 2007, a middle-aged, well-educated Sudanese man found a seat at his gate and sat down, dropping his bags on either side of him. Sitting across from him were a young man and woman, twenty-something Germans, one of them wearing a "Save Darfur" T-shirt. They struck up a conversation, and the Sudanese traveler learned that "they were going to a Darfur rally in the U.S." But when he told them that he was from Sudan, the data point didn't register. Confused, it took a few moments to dawn on him, "they didn't know Darfur was in Sudan." His positive impression of the young idealists was surpassed by sadness at their apparent ignorance, not only of the conflict but of the map itself. He could hardly make sense of it, "spending all that money to travel to the United States to rally, but they didn't know that Darfur was in Sudan?" He wondered whether the celebrities, concerts, and zeal had eclipsed the very reason for the rallies themselves.

Aid groups working on the ground in Darfur also began to worry about the activist movement, its celebrity drop-ins, and its "high-decibel" campaigning. They wondered whether its leaders were asking themselves a fundamental question: "Are we doing more good than harm?" Complaining directly to its leaders, one aid representative wrote, "I am deeply concerned by the inability of Save Darfur to be informed by realities on the ground and to understand the consequences of your proposed actions." He fingered the movement for "misstating facts," spending millions on unhelpful activities, and even falsely claiming ties to groups delivering life-saving services. He also expressed concern about unintended consequences, arguing that the movement's ill-informed policies "could easily result in the deaths of hundreds of thousands of individuals." But the warnings didn't seem to matter, or to slow down, those spinning the narrative and recruiting followers.

Darfur, one critic argued, had become "a place without history and without politics." Instead, it had become a cause that offered the average American a chance to feel like a "powerful savior." Another complained of policies "driven, very often, by activists who have never been" to Darfur, and who "perceive the war as a simple morality tale in which the forces of 'evil' can be defeated only by outside saviors." Darfur, she said, had become "not a place with a complex history; it's a moral high ground. Darfurians are no longer real human beings who laugh and love and care for their children; they are one-dimensional images of suffering."

Save Darfur's architects were also grafting specific policy prescriptions onto a campaign built to raise popular awareness. Campaign supporters were often ill-positioned to assess their suitability, but nonetheless joined rallies, signed petitions, and demanded their elected representatives get on board. They even published scorecards grading how vigorously individual Congress members had fought for tough policies on Darfur.

With no incentive to be seen as "soft" on a bad regime, members of Congress and executive branch officials responded, compounding the message and infusing it with moral indignation. Popular media regurgitated the narrative, fawned over the movement's celebrities, and gave a free pass to those selling a story of a modern-day crusade. It wasn't a "serious" national security issue, after all, so why not join in on what one journalist aptly called "culturally hip do-goodism"?

The puritanical posturing left little room for alternatives, however, and circumscribed the difficult gray space where most change is negotiated. Sudan's political system was broken, its governments were brutal, and the ugly wars they waged demanded external intervention of some kind. But the solutions to its problems weren't sexy. They would require not moral absolutism but difficult trade-offs, incremental steps, and nuanced diplomacy. Too often, however, the campaign seemed to tie the hands of diplomats and limit the tools available to leverage the change advocates sought.

One top diplomat from the Obama years scoffed at the campaign's appeals to the simplistic: "It was *easy*... and it was *gratifying* to have such a righteous cause." A top Bush administration diplomat went further, rebuking the movement and explaining that it had chosen to deliberately "mischaracterize the situation in order to keep their followers motivated"—an approach he argued had aided Khartoum and "made it much more difficult" to end the tragedy.

Years later, one thoughtful member of the Darfur movement, Rebecca Hamilton, conducted a thorough examination of the campaign. She concluded that its demand to "do something" had prompted politicians to undertake quick and visible actions over those best suited to resolving the crisis. That desire for "quick wins," and the inclination to demonstrate the influence of the advocacy campaign, Hamilton wrote, often did not improve the situation for the voiceless people it purported to represent. The Khartoum-bashing rhetoric adopted by political leaders sounded good and made advocates feel relevant, but was increasingly employed simply to appease them, regardless of whether it advanced the goal of resolving the conflict. And it wasn't without consequence.

Such unqualified rhetoric complicated U.S. bilateral engagement with Sudanese government counterparts while warping the calculations of the rebels in Darfur. Much as the SPLM had been, the Darfur rebels were also uncritically embraced as white-hatted heroes by Western advocates, and so saw little reason to compromise with a pariah government. As Richard Cockett rightly observed in a 2010 book on Darfur, the rebels sometimes mistook the moral outrage of Americans—no matter who they were—"for real political and military commitments to topple President Bashir's regime" on their behalf. "The rebels were often left with the impression that a settlement of the conflict in their favor would be imposed on Sudan, by force, from outside."

The increasingly hard line from Washington also distanced diplomatic allies who found adversarial posturing unhelpful and undermined American credibility when bold threats of action and punishment went unfulfilled. Meanwhile, in New York, when the U.S. and the UK eventually demanded robust action at the UN Security Council (and there was certainly a case for a peacekeeping intervention), the atmosphere was polarized. China, Russia, and other skeptics came to Sudan's defense and effectively stymied greater UN action for several years.

The actions demanded by the Darfur lobby—often geared toward pressure, punishment, and confrontation—seemed to reflect the ideological bent of its most influential founders and their associates. These forceful American voices, many shaped by their experience with Southern Sudan, maintained a core belief: "Khartoum will only respond to pressure." But the evidence for their unwavering assertion would grow thinner with time. Their posture—mimicked by legions of advocates—was sometimes absolutist and very often adversarial, a kind that can be particularly loaded when originating in the West. And they sought not only to change behavior; they wanted to topple a government they deemed "too deformed to be reformed." In time, this objective seemed less a clear-eyed calculation of risks and benefits for the people of Sudan, or of U.S. national security interests; it was something visceral. For them, it was a moral vendetta, and the acts of Khartoum's government could only be avenged with its demise.

But as Washington was then learning in Iraq—and would soon confront in other fragile states—regime collapse is a fabulously dangerous event, with unintended and often incalculable consequences. Sudan's National Congress Party (NCP) government was among the world's worst. But agitating for its departure hardly seemed a solution in itself. The NCP permeated most Sudanese institutions and social structures; simply wishing it away was not realistic. And forcing it out—as Washington had recently tried with the Ba'ath party in Iraq—was likely to be equally disastrous. A decade of isolating Sudan meant that outside of an on-again, off-again intelligence relationship, Washington already had precious few relationships with institutions, individuals, or social organizations, the kind necessary to help pick up the pieces in the wake of turbulent political change.

International attention had turned away from North-South tensions during the Darfur years. But when it returned in 2010, the popular Sudan constituency had grown exponentially, and Western governments had doubled down against the regime in Khartoum. Support for the Southern cause would be even stronger.

Those in Washington who questioned the established narrative on Sudan, or proposed alternative solutions, were met with unflinching opposition. When one senior U.S. diplomat advanced an unpopular view, Frank Wolf's staffer recalled fondly, "all hell rained down on him… the advocacy community declared him persona non grata." But he wasn't alone; nearly every U.S. envoy appointed, whether Republican or Democrat, pushed for constructive dialogue with Khartoum. However distasteful, ending conflict and engineering change required talking to Sudan's leaders. But members of congress and advocacy groups—together with allies inside government—mobilized to frustrate such efforts.

Asked about coming under fire for engaging Khartoum, Richard Williamson, one of President George W. Bush's envoys, said, "It's not enough to criticize. It may make you feel better, but people are still suffering." Princeton Lyman, an Obama envoy, reported that advocates blamed him for "betraying the friendship" with South Sudan. When U.S. diplomats considered, or adopted, policy positions deemed at odds with SPLM interests, support groups worked with Southern leaders to force the diplomats to capitulate. By 2010, Lyman says, the SPLM "made no secret of its readiness to mobilize its 'friends' in the United States or threaten to do so" when it disliked Washington's official positions.

"The intimidation factor is a very worrisome thing, it was almost a loyalty test," Lyman says. "And I got the message. It's not open for debate, and I think that hurt us in the end." He says this "kind of advocacy does influence policy people, but it doesn't make for good policy."

The unprecedented activism on Sudan—first in the South and then more notably in Darfur—had been well-intentioned, it had mobilized millions of people, and it had secured an impressive array of legislative and judicial action on both national and international stages. It had influenced multiple administrations, and satisfied the urges of Westerners genuinely inclined to make a difference. But a decade later, U.S. pressure had failed to force President Bashir or his NCP from power, and sanctions were instead mostly hurting ordinary citizens. Darfur remained mired in a complicated web of low-intensity conflicts, and a multi-billion-dollar international peacekeeping mission struggled to have an impact. Meanwhile, South Sudan was in ruins, destroyed by a power struggle among America's old SPLM allies.

It raised the question: How much had all this activism done for the people of Sudan?

5

THE ACCIDENTAL
PRESIDENT

*"If we want to blame anyone, we should blame our-
selves. We're the ones who put him there."*
—Member, SPLM Political Bureau

W e greeted President Salva Kiir solemnly, with formulaic
handshakes. It was our fourth meeting in eight days,
and each side shared a sense of the strained discussion
to come. Standing six feet four inches, the president is tall by most
standards but far from remarkable in the land of the Dinka—where
height only becomes noteworthy north of seven feet. He was of course
wearing his signature black cowboy hat—a gift from President George
W. Bush, and an odd Texan touch in the middle of Africa.

It was New Year's Eve, 2013. In the days following the eruption of
South Sudan's post-independence crisis, U.S. Special Envoy Donald
Booth and I had flown to Juba to deliver a firm message from Washington: 'Stop the fighting, initiate talks, exercise leadership before
the country disintegrates; the people want no part of an elite power
struggle.' Our four meetings with the president were matched by four
hammering phone calls from Secretary of State John Kerry. The scale

of the crisis was then making itself known, as massacres in the new Republic of South Sudan led international news coverage—a good news story gone bad.

Guided to dark leather sofas, we took our seats opposite "Salva," as he's informally known to peer and everyman, in the low-lit office at "J-1"—the Presidential Palace. Behind dark suit, dark hat, and dark beard, yellow-white eyes betrayed the stress of the moment. In them one could see a seemingly harmless character contaminated by years of unforgiving struggle. He looked gaunt, too. Salva's fluctuating weight had long prompted gossip among Juba's chattering classes about his purported health problems and his relationship with Johnnie Walker Blue Label, a favorite among the big men of Juba. As days turned to weeks, and weeks to months, the physical toll exacted by Salva's new war would become increasingly apparent.

The normal air conditioning units that hum in the palace office were idle, making for a thick, stifling atmosphere. Was it a problem with the diesel-fueled power generators, or was it a conscious move—a subtle home field advantage intended to keep this unwelcome meeting short?

"You are welcome," the president said, in an obligatory sort of way, and then waited for us to steer the meeting. Salva has a slow and measured physical manner, his movements often telegraphed in advance. His body language was characteristically muted on this day, sometimes offering drooped shoulders and the bowed head of a victim. A self-styled prisoner of circumstances, the posture of the president would soon reflect reality as the war expanded and the positions of hardliners tightened around him like a noose.

Unlike his decisive predecessor John Garang, this accidental president equivocated. He rarely made decisions on his own, and almost never without consulting the stronger personalities around him. Now he was overwhelmed by extraordinary circumstances that had spiraled beyond his control.

As in our tense meetings on previous days, we discussed measures that might defuse the rapidly unfolding conflict: a ceasefire, safe access for humanitarians to deliver food and services to those affected by fighting, and the release of a group of high-profile political detainees—who many believed might be executed, whether at Salva's direction or that of one of his more entrepreneurial security chiefs. Special Envoy Booth warned that those responsible for recent massacres would be held accountable. But above all, we echoed the message already conveyed by African diplomats in the region: you must initiate direct talks with the leaders of the new rebellion.

Confronted by Booth's repeated appeals, Salva recoiled. "I do not believe Riek will talk," the president blurted, unconvincingly. Revisiting an already tired platitude, Salva then repeated that he, by contrast, was a man "for peace." Though prompted over and over with ideas, Salva appeared frustratingly unable or unwilling to plot a serious way out of the crisis. We grimaced at the endless rounds of rope-a-dope as the horrors continued to unfold outside.

I then took a turn, conveying to Salva the popular perceptions of the crisis as images of dead bodies splashed across news broadcasts the world round (some of them looping on the television screen behind him). "You say you are for peace, but people in Washington do not believe you," I said, suggesting that no one was buying his empty rhetoric. "They see two sides fighting and two sides refusing to talk. You must take action to prove you are serious." We suggested that he send a team to Ethiopia, hold a press conference, and demonstrate that his government was there to talk peace. Salva was no political tactician, and so we noted that by doing so, he could also isolate his warring rival and gain the upper hand.

"Ok, I will do that," Salva uttered after a long pause, "I will send a delegation today, if that is what is needed." Stunned silence. The president almost never took decisions in the moment; I wondered whether my ears had betrayed me. But a quick glance at Booth suggested they had not; his body language likewise suggested surprise. Booth quickly concluded the meeting, and we exited the offices, climbing into our SUV where we could debrief on what had just happened.

As the driver exited the palace grounds and pressed on the gas pedal, the scene whipping by the window was conspicuously abnormal: no bustling alleyways or crowded storefronts, no boys hawking phone credit scratch cards, and no women hauling overstuffed bags of onions to market. There were no smiles or people-watching or jokes being told. The muted life on city streets reflected the collective anxiety in a capital still absorbing the shock of violence, and bracing for a retaliatory assault.

As we made our way across town to rendezvous with other members of the diplomatic corps, we called Riek Machar. Secretary Kerry and others in Washington had been dialing Riek's satellite phone around the clock for days, demanding he too call off his forces. Now we hoped to leverage President Salva's unexpected commitment and lock the rebels in to peace talks as well.

Salva and his nemesis could not be more different. Riek is fiery, a man whose mood and body language can change rapidly; one minute jovial, easygoing, flashing his unmistakable smile, and the next intense and confrontational, jabbing a finger in the air, moving forward in his chair and leaning in to you, a conscious imposition of his presence. No matter the mood, Riek is not one to withhold whatever is on his mind. Having narrowly escaped with his life after being accused of high treason, I knew he would be unrestrained today.

Booth reached Riek by satellite telephone deep in the bush. Channeling Machar's combative exhortations with skill and patience, Booth secured his agreement to talks and hung up. We were stunned again. Amid all that was going wrong, and the labored incrementalism that defines most diplomacy, the rapid succession of commitments that afternoon provided a dose of adrenaline and of hope. Maybe the conflict could be arrested before it got any worse.

Having reneged once on their pledges to negotiate, we thought it wise to get the morning's commitments on the record publicly. Doing so at this moment of heightened media attention might make it harder for the two men to back out. It would also make it more difficult for hardliners—who were numerous on both sides—to talk them out of it.

I hopped out of the car and, juggling a handful of mobile phones, found one that would connect to an old contact and experienced journalist with years on the Sudan beat, the BBC's James Copnall. Copnall answered the familiar double-ring on his London mobile and was quickly explaining that he was about to go live on a television spot, when I interrupted him. "James, you should call Riek," I said. He began to suggest that he was otherwise occupied, but I interrupted, this time with enough tonal import to convey my seriousness. "Trust me, I think it's a good idea to call Riek, and ask him about peace talks." I sensed that he'd understood, and we hung up.

Upon learning we had been granted access to visit the political detainees, we canceled our next meeting, scrambled back into our vehicles and headed toward National Security headquarters, where the eleven high-profile SPLM members were being held. We arrived there and were deposited in a waiting room with cream-colored leather sofas and a giant flat-screen TV, which happened to be tuned to the BBC. Moments later, the news presenter cut to Copnall live, who said something to the effect of: "I'm just off the phone with deposed Vice President Riek Machar, and he has agreed to send representatives to Ethiopia today to engage the government in ceasefire talks."

I left Special Envoy Booth, walked outside into the whitewash of Juba's mid-day sun, and placed a second call to Copnall. Pacing the dusty gravel parking lot out of earshot of the government's security personnel, I connected. "Hi again. Just saw you live; good report." I indicated that I understood Salva had likewise committed to peace talks and urged Copnall to get in touch with the president's office right away. I asked only that he not mention any U.S. involvement in securing these commitments or tipping the information, to which he obliged with a friendly chuckle, "No, don't worry, I'm happy to take the credit."

I returned to the waiting room, and minutes later, the BBC cut to Copnall again. Salva's government, he announced, was also sending a delegation to talk peace.

Salva Kiir and his predecessor, John Garang, were two very different men. Garang, the elder, was an intellectual, intoxicated both by classical economics and by the Marxist-Leninist ideals popular in post-colonial Africa during his formative years. A Dinka from the grassy savannahs of greater Bor in Jonglei state, Garang attended elementary and intermediate schools in South Sudan before leaving for secondary school in Tanzania. The promising young mind then won a scholarship to study economics at Grinnell College in Iowa, and later underwent advanced infantry training at Fort Benning, Georgia, while a young officer in Sudan's peace-time national army. Garang convinced his superiors to let him return to the U.S. again, in 1977, to pursue a doctorate in agricultural economics, this time at Iowa State University.

In between his American stints, the aspiring intellectual returned to Tanzania for further study at the University of Dar es Salaam, a hotbed for the revolutionary ideas and pan-African ideology then sweeping the continent. In those heady days of African independence, Garang became active in student politics and was introduced to revolutionary peers from across the region. The most significant friendship forged was with Yoweri Museveni, the future rebel-cum-president of Uganda, who would one day become an indispensable patron of the SPLA. Garang left Dar es Salaam to join the Southern resistance in 1971, serving at the side of several *Anyanya* leaders, before 1972 brought a temporary peace between Sudan's North and South.

Each stop on Garang's tour would shape his political outlook, and each stop offered a lesson that he would file away for later use. In Tanzania, he learned the language and mores of African liberation, credentials that would shape his views of Sudan's problems and gain him entrée with revolutionary thinkers across the region. While an apprentice in the *Anyanya* rebellion, he kept quiet and studied organizational flaws—the divisions that plagued the movement and the feuds between members of its separate political and military high commands. (Perhaps over-learning the lesson, Garang would later fuse the SPLA military and political hierarchies and appoint himself head of both.)

Most formative, though, was Garang's time in Iowa and Georgia. These nine years would teach the aspiring leader much about the United States, a cultural curriculum that would come in handy when he eventually returned to win American support for his cause. One American friend and confidant told me that "this African military officer from a faraway land" was not only "brilliant," but that people in Ames, Iowa, had quickly "thought him one of us." Garang's years in America would also plant the seed of his grand vision for a "New Sudan." Garang would ask himself, "If the United States could fashion a free, secular, democratic, and united society" from its own multi-ethnic, multi-religious, multi-cultural society, "why not Sudan?"

With his transformational vision crystallizing, Garang went home to Sudan and would put his economic, political, and military training to work toward the cause of national liberation. In the early days of the SPLA, "Dr. John" translated his new ideas into party manifestos, rallied supporters in radio addresses, and coined memorable turns-of-phrase that would convert many to his cause. His new articulation of Sudan's fundamental problem was a game changer, inspiring supporters not only in the South but across Sudan's marginalized regions—and even among progressive circles in Khartoum.

Today, Garang's earliest disciples speak of "New Sudan" with both reverence and the inescapable pang of opportunity lost. In the summer of 2016, I sat with one such disciple, now graying, in his office, a damp metal shipping container, in central Juba. Breaking into a nostalgic grin, the former aide begins by recalling Garang's heady presentations, in which he regularly employed Venn diagrams—the overlapping circles he used so frequently that they became synonymous with his ideas. With little prompting, he's initiated a conversation I have had dozens of times with Garang acolytes.

Extolling "the virtues of Dr. John's orienting principle," and painting its core tenets with fingers in the air, he momentarily detaches from reality. He is enjoying a walk down the political road not taken, and his obvious attachment to the idea and its author means I'm not about to interrupt him. His eyes light up and his mind whirs with excitement as he explains the "intellectual genius" of New Sudan, and the promise of the revolution that might have been.

Garang was on a pedestal while he lived, and in death, he would be lionized in a manner that is hard to over-state. One statue of Dr. John presides over Freedom Square, the fallen hero in Western suit and tie, clutching a book in one hand and staff in the other. Another presides over Juba's military headquarters—this time as fatigue-clad general, Kalashnikov strapped on his back, an outstretched finger pointing the way to legions of foot soldiers. As in many African states, the presidential portrait is displayed prominently in government offices, hotel lobbies, restaurants, and local businesses—a not-so-subtle reminder of who is in charge. In South Sudan, Salva's gold-framed headshot is almost always accompanied by one of the late Dr. John.

The country's first currency was unveiled on Independence Day, and Southerners eagerly examined the crisp green, blue, and pink notes, each depicting the icon's ubiquitous image—bald head, bearded chin, and penetrating eyes. Independence celebrations unfolded along John Garang Mausoleum Avenue, and the festivities began with a visit to his resting place at Freedom Square—a landmark known to every resident of Juba. His widow, "Mama Rebecca," is the country's most recognized and revered woman, and her voice carries considerable weight in national politics. His acolytes speak of "Garangism" and "Garangnomics," while his most celebrated maxims today adorn T-shirts and billboards and remain widely cited in political discourse. The lionization of John Garang reveals much about the nation's short history and its current disaster. It is at once a historical reflection, and a dangerous contemporary driver, of the hyper-centralization of leadership in South Sudan. It is also a product of the SPLM's control of the state and a predominantly favorable narrative that has carried the day since his death.

Despite the hero-worship one might encounter on a cursory visit to Juba, Garang was far from universally popular. Though his capacity to represent Southern Sudan's interests was unsurpassed, Garang was also a deeply polarizing figure. And it wasn't only that Southern secessionists found his "New Sudan" politics dubious. Garang's audacity, authoritarian style, and lack of transparency alienated important leaders inside and outside the SPLA, as well as considerable sections of the Southern population. For all the talk of Dr. John's charisma, there was also a reservoir of contempt.

The strong man from Bor—SPLA code name "THUNDER"—maintained absolute control of his movement. He sat squarely atop a

militaristic hierarchy, and dealt brutally with dissent. But he meanwhile neglected both the political development of the movement and
the population more broadly. Instead of cultivating ordinary civilians, the SPLA often preyed on them. Deep resentment and internal
feuds sometimes broke out along ethnic fault lines, more than once
threatening to destroy the rebel organization. Though the SPLA would
achieve important successes on the battlefield and later in leveraging a
peace deal, Garang's domineering style and the ethos of the movement
he built would have consequences for South Sudan that extended well
beyond his death.

Love him or hate him, Dr. John was a force of nature. The ambitious and hard-charging visionary was often mentioned in the same
breath as the revolutionary peers of his era, the class of emergent
African leaders that spoke in Marxist dialects and advanced bold
visions of Pan-Africanism—the new ideology of African solidarity,
self-reliance, and empowerment. They were to lead a new African
renaissance, and Garang was set to join them. Salva Kiir, by contrast,
did not belong to this genre; he was no such giant. The accidental successor was neither as educated, nor as enlightened, as Garang. In both
literal and figurative senses, Garang starred in the role of visionary
general, and Salva that of the good soldier.

———

Six years Garang's junior, Salva Kiir Mayardit was born in 1951
in the village of Akon, atop the clay plains of Bahr al Ghazal cattle
country. His Gogrial sub-clan is part of the largest and most influential ethno-regional bloc in South Sudan. While the Dinka of Bahr al
Ghazal (those of Salva) and the Dinka of Bor (those of Garang) aligned
when it suited them, they also competed for preeminence in matters of
government and the military, and thus for the leadership of the South.

Salva first took up arms with the separatist *Anyanya* rebels in
the 1960s, and was integrated into the national army following the
1972 peace agreement with Khartoum. As a middle-ranking officer,
he served in the Sudan Armed Forces' military intelligence division

before defecting in 1983 to join Garang and the latest generation of Southern rebellion. Wearing green fatigues, military cap, and red-and-gold insignia, the lean and bearded commander led SPLA recruits in war songs before leading them into battle. He ascended the ranks of the SPLA precisely because he was a quintessential good soldier: Salva took orders, executed them, and did not present a threat to Garang. He was a capable commander, and his practical skills helped the SPLA win early military successes.

Garang soon named Salva and four others to the SPLA's joint political-military high command. Though none shared Dr. John's grand visions or ideological capacity, several members of the high command had ideas and ambitions of their own, and so posed a threat to Garang. Fallouts with each of them ensued, and Garang had them either punished or killed. By most accounts, Garang's authoritarian grip on the fledgling SPLA was intended to prevent the divisions that beset rebellions past. He would not allow focus to stray from the larger objective. But his ruthlessness generated anger and a near constant strain of conspiratorial suspicions among the senior ranks. The comparatively non-threatening Salva, meanwhile, rose in the void. By the early 1990s, Salva, code-named "HAMMER," was No. 2 of the SPLA.

Garang, the unyielding locomotive, squashed dissent mercilessly and dominated the decision-making process. His even-keeled deputy, by contrast, was reserved and inclined toward consensus. Salva was a respected military man but possessed neither the political stature nor agenda of his highly educated boss. Salva would prove more concilia-tory than Garang, but also more passive—even deferential. When it came to politics, Salva was anything but a "HAMMER." Some saw this as an opportunity.

In December 2004, with peace talks between North and South nearly complete and the end of Sudan's civil war near, an open rift emerged between Salva and Garang. Following rumors about lead-ership changes and a plan to remove Salva, a tense standoff ensued. The "Yei incident," as this row would later be known, nearly split the movement again—this time on the eve of peace. An emergency

SPLA summit was convened, at which Salva and others voiced growing complaints about Garang's heavy-handed leadership, lack of transparency, and circumvention of formal SPLA structures.

The uproar was no doubt grounded in widely held grievances, but skeptics also doubted that Salva would mount such a challenge on his own. Instead they saw the hand of Garang's enemies, secretly cultivating the impressionable Salva Kiir and using him to advance their agenda. The group mixed regional interests and personal ambitions but was dominated by the Dinka elites of Bahr al Ghazal. Salva was their native son, and thus the ticket to asserting the power and influence of the Bahr al Ghazal Dinka. Garang maneuvered to defuse the eleventh-hour crisis and maintain control, but the acrimonious affair would prove a seminal moment. Neither Garang's loyalists, nor his challengers, would forget what had been said, and who stood where.

The competition between rival SPLA camps was warming up, just as they were about to begin governing. For some, the 2004 Yei incident was the first attempt to co-opt Salva and through him usurp control of the SPLM, but it would not be the last. Unbeknownst to anyone at the summit, Salva's covert backers would soon get a second chance.

⸻

"It is one of those events, like the Kennedy assassination, that becomes a historical enigma," recounts Pagan (pronounced *puh-GAWN*) Amum, once a member of the SPLA leader's inner circle. On July 30, 2005, Sudanese history would be changed forever. John Garang, the South's most powerful man, was killed in a helicopter crash.

Just three weeks earlier, the former rebel had been inaugurated as First Vice President of Sudan, and president of the regional government of the South, in keeping with the terms of the peace deal between North and South. He had strode triumphantly into Khartoum, cheered by a crowd so large that it shocked and unsettled his Northern adversaries. After decades of preparation, John Garang was primed to begin his campaign to transform the government and engineer a New Sudan—North and South unified in a multi-ethnic, multi-religious, and democratic state. But now, in a shocking twist of fate, he was dead.

On the morning of July 30, a Saturday, Garang and a handful of aides climbed aboard a charter plane en route to visit his friend and ally, Uganda's President Museveni. The wheels of their dual-prop aircraft lifted off the dusty red soil of a remote airstrip and touched down a short while later at Entebbe airport in neighboring Uganda. From there, they boarded one of President Museveni's helicopters, which flew them to his private farm another hundred miles to the west.

According to aides, Garang and his trusted Ugandan ally were to discuss joint efforts to combat the Lord's Resistance Army—a notorious Ugandan rebel group wreaking havoc in the region—as well the matter of Paulino Matiep, a powerful Southern Sudanese commander whose sizable Nuer militias had fought against the SPLA during the war. Following the meeting, Garang's coterie flew back to Entebbe, where they boarded another of Museveni's Russian-made military helicopters, used to transport VIPs. The chopper pilots were instructed to deliver them back to "New Site," an SPLA outpost just across the border in South Sudan.

SPLA guards walked out on the dirt airstrip at New Site around 5:30pm on schedule to receive their commander-in-chief. But the skies were empty. When the chopper did not arrive as planned, alarm spread quickly through SPLA networks. Pagan Amum was then in Rumbek preparing to receive an American delegation when he got the call, but information was scarce. "We knew there was an incident," he says with a heavy sigh, "but we were not sure if he was alive."

Pagan dialed Salva Kiir, who was preparing to leave for a meeting in Europe, and suggested he hold in place. Anxious hours ticked by as search teams scoured the surrounding environs. "By mid-day on the 31st, dread set in," Pagan remembers. Later that afternoon, the wreckage of Garang's helicopter was found amid the bamboo thickets of the densely wooded Imatong Mountains, just inside South Sudan. An SPLA recovery team collected the bodies of their beloved chairman and twelve others and returned to New Site. There, Salva and the rest of the SPLA command convened for an emergency meeting.

"I was in shock, I felt a loss of hope," Pagan recalls, re-living a vivid mix of emotions from the 24-hour period. "Of course we thought it was an assassination." Pagan was a trusted aide whose life and political career would be impacted as much as any by the death of Garang. He would later rise to become the party's secretary-general and attempt to fashion himself as the late leader's standard bearer.

"Who would do this?" Pagan thought to himself, his mind a jumbled mix of personal grief and political calculation. Darting around a map of Africa in his head, he wondered who could conceivably gain from Garang's demise. He inevitably zeroed in on Khartoum and assumed their enemies were out to undermine the peace deal. "But there was no time for speculation," he remembers. The SPLA was in a state of emergency but decided against making any immediate public announcement, conscious of their own vulnerability in the throes of such a disaster.

It was an existential moment; the movement had to anoint a successor to the inimitable Garang, and quickly. With the ink on the potentially transformative peace agreement barely dry, and the SPLM due to join a unity government in Khartoum, the high command's decision would forever shape the direction of the movement and the fate of South Sudan.

⁂

"Nothing could be more precious than our unity," recalls one senior military man at the heart of the impromptu deliberations. It's a windy summer day in 2016, eleven years after the crash, and I've come to the Crown Hotel, Juba's newest and best, to revisit that fateful moment with one of its central figures.

I'm sharing an outdoor patio table with the ex-general, to whom I promised anonymity. A straight-faced waitress delivers a box of fruit juice, while I strain to hear my soft-spoken tablemate over the cacophony of construction equipment just beyond the patio walls. A decade has passed since the pivotal hours after Garang's death, and I can see the general replaying them in his mind, albeit through the filter of his country's now abysmal state of affairs. A blast of dust pummels the patio area, blowing my notes into the swimming pool. The general and I laugh as we retrieve the soggy pages, grab our juice glasses, and make for the enclosed cafeteria.

After he greets a gaggle of eager supporters and friends, as is standard for any "big man" in town, we take our seats and return to the familiar movie replaying in his mind. "Nothing could be more precious than our unity," he says again, picking up the story. With the direction of the movement suddenly in question, that precious commodity hung in the balance. Internal politicking ensued. Comrades moved nervously about the camp, eyed one another with suspicion, and huddled to speculate about would-be challengers.

Most of the SPLA brass believed succession should follow the military hierarchy—Salva was No. 2, so he should be immediately ordained chairman and commander-in-chief. Opening the leadership issue to a contest risked fracturing the movement, they argued, and those of questionable loyalty to Garang might attempt to seize the throne. Worse yet, they worried the NCP would smell blood and attempt the divide-and-conquer tactics it had perfected through years of practice.

But not everyone was convinced. Riek Machar and Garang's widow, Rebecca, were among those cited as possible alternatives to Salva. Southern secessionists, who had always doubted Garang's New Sudan vision, saw an opportunity to restore the simpler, purer objective of Southern independence. Still others believed Salva was too weak-willed for the job—he lacked the requisite leadership skills and would be prone to manipulation by narrow interests. The Yei incident was fresh in their memories.

These concerned skeptics thought it best "to go for the nuclear option," the general explains—supplant Salva now, and save the movement from vultures. It would be a dangerous gamble, but "better to endure turbulence now," they argued, then an even larger problem later.

Stretching long legs across the floor, and clasping his hands behind his head, the general pauses again. He's conscious that the "larger problem later" is the one in which South Sudan now finds itself. And it's bleak: Garang's vision is long gone and so is the SPLM, destroyed by factionalism, narrow self-interest, and a lack of direction.

Some of the players the general held in suspicion ten years ago are now in Salva's inner circle. A controversial group of Dinka elders from Salva's home region are also heavily influencing the beleaguered president, again bent on preserving Bahr al Ghazal dominance at any cost. A peace deal has halted South Sudan's civil war for now, but it is on the ropes. And then, of course, there is the unimaginable suffering. Tens of thousands are dead, and a million more have been driven from their homes.

The general finishes his juice and stands to greet another gaggle of eager hand-shakers, speaking a standard mix of Arabic and Dinka, before returning once more to 2005 to conclude the story. It isn't easy for him to get through.

Rather than leap-frog Salva, the conservative approach prevailed, and Salva was appointed successor. "He *assured* us," the general recalls with a note of bitter regret, "of his commitment to Garang's agenda, and of his independence from those of Bahr al Ghazal." While Salva may then have been genuine in his convictions, the malleable man would soon become the subject of intense courtship, the centerpiece of a vicious fight for control of Garang's SPLM.

In addition to a major shift in personality, the leadership change included an equally momentous policy implication; Salva was neither cut out to advance Garang's vision of a wholly transformed "New Sudan," nor did he believe in it. Though he had faithfully sung Garang's tune, Salva was, like the majority of Southerners, in favor of independence.

The following morning, news of Garang's death rocked Sudan and the entire region. At the White House, mouths hung open. "Cataclysmic," says Cameron Hudson, then a director in President Bush's National Security Council, offering a one-word summary of the sentiment at 1600 Pennsylvania Avenue. "It was an '*oh shit*' moment," not least because the Americans had been so invested in Garang himself. "The truth is, we didn't know anyone else."

The news sparked protests and street violence in Khartoum, Juba, and elsewhere across the country. Roger Winter and the State Department's top Africa diplomat hopped a plane for Sudan. They were keen to salvage the peace deal they'd just helped push across the finish line, and to consult their shell-shocked SPLA friends.

As SPLA cadres tried to make sense of their new reality, Pagan Amum bristled at the thought that someone had targeted his boss. He told comrades it was now more critical than ever that they "honor Garang by overcoming whoever was aiming to defeat us." In the end, an investigation involving experts from America's National Transportation and Safety Board uncovered no evidence of foul play. The Bush White House also scoured intelligence reporting but found nothing that implicated Khartoum. The lack of evidence has never put the issue to rest, however, as many South Sudanese are convinced their liberation icon was murdered.

"I accept that God has come to collect him," Garang's widow, Rebecca, told reporters, as South Sudan prepared to inter its larger-than-life leader. "It is just my husband who has died. His vision is still alive." But her comment was aspirational; while the cause of freedom would outlast Garang, his political project would not.

Back at the Crown Hotel, the cafeteria's fluorescent lights buzz to life as dusk envelops the horizon behind the general. More hotel guests meander into the cafeteria, chattering as they note the score of the European soccer match playing on wall-mounted televisions. Punctuating the end of our talk, the disillusioned general utters the words now synonymous with this pivotal moment in Sudan's history: "New Sudan died with John Garang."

The impact of Garang's death on South Sudan's tilt toward separation was as monumental as his life had been in waging the war and shaping the peace. It's an accepted reality, one analyzed in South Sudanese circles for a decade. But what is evident now is just how far Garang's shadow extended, beyond independence, to the young nation's implosion in 2013.

Garang's untimely death would ignite an eight-year factional battle inside an ethnically, ideologically, and professionally heterogeneous

SPLM. Without the all-powerful linchpin at its center, competing camps would fight for control of the highly-centralized movement and ultimately tear it—and the new country—apart.

South Sudan's post-independence collapse exposed not only the bankruptcy of the SPLM leaders who survived him, but an inconvenient truth about their beloved icon. Despite his many successes, and his intoxicating ideas, John Garang never built the SPLM into a genuine political organization. On the eve of the peace agreement, he issued a new "Framework for War-to-Peace Transition," that articulated his aspirations to transition from a "guerrilla environment" to "formal institutions of democratic governance." But it was too little too late. Getting a rebel movement to suddenly change character after two decades wasn't going to be easy.

"We never had a democratic culture," argues one prominent Southern Sudanese critic of Garang. "Democracy is a process, you know? It doesn't just fall from the heavens into your lap." In the end, the SPLM was not the kind of political organization that could outlast Garang, or define itself beyond its militarism and opposition to Khartoum. "And that," says the critic, was South Sudan's "original sin."

⌖

While Garang was defined by his legendary charisma, Salva Kiir was defined by his lack of it. Thrust into the presidency, Salva was a gentle man with little taste for politics or the spotlight. Neither inspiring nor a gifted communicator, the good soldier would slowly grow into the role, but he never felt at home.

The accidental president lacked resolve, and his underwhelming presence would soon earn him an array of unflattering adjectives: "reactive," "docile," "weak." Many thought Salva a good man, and well-intentioned, but one whose anxiety, self-doubt, and desire to please led him down less worthy paths, succumbing to the manipulative forces around him. Simply put, this was a president in over his head. And in a highly centralized system, it meant South Sudan was without an anchor, a country adrift.

Whether in cabinet meetings, at official dinners, or at the press podium, Salva was not without his big, black cowboy hat. Whether on a state visit to China or an international summit at the United Nations, it made him easy to spot. President Bush had gifted Salva the ten-gallon Stetson during their first Oval Office meeting in 2006, and soon it was Salva's unmistakeable trademark. The prized accessory would become a symbol of friendship between the two men and their two countries.

Sunday morning was the one time the president surrendered his hat. A devout Catholic, Salva regularly occupied the front row at St. Theresa's Cathedral on Juba's south side, where he sometimes delivered sermons to large congregations. Salva truly thought himself a man of God, and so had more in common with "those of Bush" than just Texan headwear. When things fell apart in 2013, and Salva presided over a brutal war, this Christian identity would prompt moral appeals not only from local church leaders, but from Pope Francis himself.

While once blasphemous to admit openly in South Sudan, some believe there was a silver lining in Garang's death. The same hard-nosed qualities that made Garang a powerful and visionary leader also made him intolerant and divisive. Many wondered, in retrospect, whether resulting tensions would have caused the South to crack before independence.

Salva, by contrast, gained a reputation as a unifier. When the war with Sudan ended in 2005, the SPLA would be legitimized as an official national army. But tens of thousands of Southern militia fighters were left outside the peace deal. They had locked horns with the SPLA throughout the war, often preserving their own communities' interests by doing Khartoum's bidding. Most of them were Nuer. To avoid further disenfranchisement, Salva decided in 2006 to bring these groups into the fold. Many believe it was the most consequential decision of the interim period, creating political, financial, social, and military ripples for a decade to follow.

Against the advice of some in the SPLA command, Salva absorbed the constellation of largely Nuer forces under Paulino Matiep into the SPLA. He would erect a big tent and welcome everyone inside. He offered positions and patronage to Matiep and his lieutenants, and salaries to the rank-and-file. Salva had new oil money to use to keep them on side, enough to avoid being outspent by their former patrons in Khartoum. Aversion to the policy persisted in the SPLA high command, and so the planned integration was mostly superficial. Nonetheless, Salva's big tent policy would help to pacify and keep South Sudan together—at least until independence.

Fashioning a climate of conciliation and appeasement more broadly, Salva doled out state and federal jobs and patronage on the basis of ethnicity, and he co-opted the disenfranchised. Though the unintended consequence of the policy would later rear its ugly head, Salva was widely commended for the magnanimous approach, one that may well have been necessary to prevent internal division in the short term.

The accolades, however, would stop there. While his inclination for consensus had well served Salva the unifier, it was also a clue to his greatest weakness: indecision. When it came to making the tough decisions required of any leader, Salva was an empty suit. Amid opposition from subordinates, he folded. Forced to make a difficult policy choice, he demurred. He was deeply affected by criticism, and in time, his insecurities and vacillation would prove crippling. During one 2016 Al Jazeera television interview, Salva the victim complained that he had to follow instructions when it came to addressing the media. Exasperated, the interviewing journalist interrupted him, "Who told you that? You're the *president*!"

"You do this… you do that," Salva responded, "I am now just like a child. Being ordered by everybody."

Salva was often swayed by the last person in his office, which was to say he was swayed by everyone. It was a phenomenon I'd experienced more than a few times in meetings at the presidential palace, as Salva would pledge some concrete new action, only to be talked out of it by an aide just moments after we'd exited. During negotiations with Khartoum, Salva often flip-flopped, persuaded by one group of advisers, then reversed by another. Later, as strongmen fought for Salva's ear during the 2013 crisis, army chief Paul Malong decided his best chance to influence policy was to be the last person in the room, literally. He simply began showing up at Salva's house after business hours and staying put until all other callers had come and gone.

Western diplomats often took "asks" to the president. Salva had to play the game with these important donor countries, but his malleable nature and desire to please was also part of the equation. "Yes, I will do that," he would say, hoping to convey an air of authority, but which instead felt like a need for affirmation. The inquiring diplomat would stride out of J-1 palace bolstered by a sense of achievement, having secured his commitment to this or that reform. But when no follow-up ensued, each would come to treat the president's word as debased currency.

Constantly shifting, agreeing and then reneging—one might think it a deliberate tactic, a teflon politician maintaining control by appearing to please everyone and alienate none. But Salva was not so cunning an actor. The teflon instead reflected his own insecurities, his aversion to confrontation, and his own comparatively limited capacities—a disadvantage of which he was absolutely conscious.

Stronger personalities took advantage of their waffler-in-chief. Aides coaxed his signature onto official memos and took liberties in using the president's name. Cabinet officials sometimes made decisions for him, other times they overwhelmed him with intellectual horse-power and superior nerve. His position afforded him due deference, but Salva was almost always outmatched. And he knew it.

The president was not a coward. Indeed there were times, albeit infrequently, that he took decisions that seemed to defy his need for consensus. Sometimes he summoned the guts to lead. But what drove him on those occasions, what allowed him to transcend his own shortcomings, remains something of a mystery.

Salva is shy and awkward in public settings, particularly around foreigners. More at home among Southern Sudanese, and particularly those of the military class, Salva felt inadequate in conducting foreign affairs. Though more comfortable in Arabic and Dinka, the job meant Salva had to conduct most public business in English. He could surely be forgiven for limitations in a third tongue, but the reality was that his English was not on a par with his more worldly colleagues.

As a public speaker, he was uninspired. His rhetoric was monotone, his delivery slow and disjointed. At one political rally in late 2009, hundreds of supporters, politicians, foreign diplomats, and journalists crammed into a stiflingly hot auditorium in Juba. Fanning themselves and passing around lukewarm bottles of water, they waited for hours for the keynote speaker to arrive. When Salva did enter the hall, a raucous reception was promptly muted by a barely audible president. Standing at the lectern, looking somehow lonely, his voice box emitted a pitch that seemed to fall somewhere between recognizable frequencies. One hoped for a hard clearing of the throat, but it never came. Reciting the words with his head down, he peered through reading glasses which made him appear even less presidential. Every few minutes he paused, pulled a white handkerchief from his breast pocket, and wiped the sweat from his forehead. Midway through, he mixed up the pages of his speech, interrupting an already sleep-inducing address as he shuffled to find his place. It was painful to watch, and hard not to have sympathy for him. This guy was just not cut out for the job.

Salva often turned to drink. Whether genetic disposition or coping mechanism, or both, it affected his performance with cyclical regularity. He sometimes showed up in the afternoon for scheduled morning events, still recovering from a late night. Coupled with persistent health concerns, including secretive retreats abroad for medical care, the president was anything but stable.

As South Sudan's civil war dragged on through 2014 and into 2015, Salva's insecurities became more pronounced. He became increasingly paranoid that the outside world would rather do business with Riek Machar or the party's Garangist intellectuals, whose cosmopolitan ways and Western-speak endeared them to both African elites and Western donors. Whether or not these opponents were more committed to the principled discourse and ideology they traded on—and often they were not—was beside the point.

Six months into the conflict, I walked out of yet another unproductive meeting with the president, expecting to feel as frustrated as I had following contentious meetings past. But instead I felt an awkward mix of pity and disbelief. Salva was presiding over a vicious war that had killed tens of thousands of his own people and displaced nearly a million more. The office afforded Salva more power to end the conflict than anyone, but the man lacked the chutzpah to wield it.

By then, Salva also seemed desperate to be out of the job. If he had the chance to do it all over again, I wondered whether he might have stepped down earlier, just after independence. "He regrets it," one veteran diplomat said without pause when I asked his opinion on the matter. Salva may have enjoyed governing during the prosperous years around independence, the diplomat explains, when Juba boomed and the trappings of high office offered new power and prestige. "But he regrets it, he's a broken man. He wishes desperately that he would have just gone home to the village."

Had Salva stepped down in 2011, he may have enjoyed a legacy of unifying a fragile South against the odds and fathering the nation's independence. Instead, in 2013 he got caught in a political battle for which he was not equipped, waged a war that destroyed his legacy, and earned the visceral contempt of a large number of his fellow South-erners. For them, Salva the unifier had become Salva the "dictator," "butcher," even the "*genocidaire*."

There was sometimes a narrative in Africa that the more nefarious acts of ruling regimes were a product of menacing advisers, that the presidential father figure was surely a character of good standing, his benevolent leadership undermined by the lesser men around him. Such a hopeful disbelief was punctured by more seasoned observers, convinced that highly centralized systems meant the top man had a firm grip on the reins, and was just more skilled at distancing himself from the unpleasantness.

But Salva Kiir was as likely a candidate as any to prove the ratio-nalization could be a reality. Pushed and pulled by men with interests malevolent or parochial, he made poor decisions and allowed for dysfunction during the state's most crucial formative years. Salva's weaknesses do not absolve him of his role in the country's unraveling, but they do help explain it.

Though Salva was initially compared to his predecessor, it was not Garang's long shadow with which he would have to contend. Salva's first decade at the helm—South Sudan's first years—would be defined by intense factionalism inside the SPLM and by a volatile relationship with another very different man. When Salva was thrust into the leading role, Riek Machar had backfilled his No. 2 slot, and the two men would have to find a way to work together.

6

REBEL WITH A PhD

*"History will not forgive them. They will be known
in history as the people who stabbed the movement in
Southern Sudan in the back."*

— Dr. John Garang

Riek Machar stood up. Before him sat a crowd of several hundred, each of them eyeing the vice president, waiting for him to break the silence. It was dusk, and lights had been hung in the trees of the outdoor compound for the occasion. Among the guests was a sizable contingent of chiefs, local dignitaries, and members of parliament from Bor county, the birthplace of the late Dr. John Garang. In the front row sat Mama Rebecca, Garang's widow, who was hosting the night's gathering to commemorate his death. This was not Riek's natural support base, in fact it was something of a lion's den. Until recent years, Riek's presence in her home would have been unthinkable. It was a Tuesday evening, in August 2011, nearly 20 years to the day since Riek's infamous mutiny against Garang.

The 1991 "split," as it is still known, precipitated the infamous Bor massacre—when Riek's Nuer forces launched a withering assault on the citizens of Bor county. Thousands of ordinary men, women, and children were chased into nearby marshlands and murdered, many of them left for the vultures. According to an investigation by Amnesty International, three young boys were found tied to a tree where they had been "clubbed to death." Several more bodies were found "with cords or belts around their necks that had been used to strangle them." Still others had been "bound at their ankles and wrists and then speared to death." Nearly every man and woman in attendance on this night had lost a spouse, a child, a friend, or an elder in those killing fields.

An aide handed Riek the microphone. "I would like to take this opportunity, tonight, to apologize," Riek announced to the captive audience. "I should take squarely the responsibility for the events of 1991." The crowd began to stir, stunned by a moment they thought would never come. "I was shocked!" Rebecca said. For she and many others, hearing the long overdue words jolted in them a mix of emotions—pain, gratitude, confusion, catharsis. Some cried out for lost loved ones, others felt long-dormant anger welling up in them.

After explaining his motivations so many years ago, and admitting to the massacre he had once denied as "propaganda," tears began streaming down Riek's face. One newspaper reported that the vice president "broke down and wept, to the point where he nearly collapsed." His wife, Angelina, rushed to his side, and she was followed by several others. "They were moved… a number of the Bor people, they ran to him, to hold him up," Rebecca said later, "he really became so emotional."

A great deal had transpired in the two decades since the Bor massacre: the war was over, John Garang was gone, and South Sudan was finally independent. It was time to begin a new and brighter chapter. But none had forgotten the events of 1991, or the eleven dark years of inter-ethnic war that ensued. Few had forgiven the traitor now standing in their midst.

Mama Rebecca took the microphone next, flanked by other Bor elders. "It hurts," she said, herself in tears, "you should have done this when Dr. John was still alive." She gave voice to a pain still raw, but also resolved that it was time to absolve Riek of his sins. "As a Christian, no matter how painful, I must swallow this," she said, turning to the crowd. "If God can forgive, who am I not to forgive?" she said, "I forgive you."

When the evening's event broke up, Deng Dau, a ranking parliamentarian from Bor, told reporters the apology had been a watershed moment. "We want Southerners to forget all the bitterness… to forget the past. We want to begin anew so that we build our nation."

But not everyone was so ready to accept, and as news of the "Bor apology" trickled out, Southerners were divided. "We didn't want Dr. Riek to apologize," one Nuer explained, angrily. "We have also been victims of killings for many years before… what about 1986, 87, 89?" he asked, likewise recalling painful episodes. "Riek took responsibility, as a leader, and that was right. But he didn't deserve it alone… it shouldn't have been a one-way thing." Others demanded the repentant sinner go further. Riek "needs not only to apologize to Bor or Jonglei people but to the whole of South Sudan." Still others flat-out refused to accept that Riek had apologized at all, suggesting that accounts of the event had been fabricated.

Given his super-sized ego and a long history of self-promotion, the emotionally-charged event also sparked widespread speculation about Riek's motives. "An insincere stunt," some called it—his tears politically motivated. The old snake, they argued, was simply looking to wipe the slate clean so he could garner support for his long-awaited bid for the presidency.

Indeed, Riek knew many of those assembled in Bor that morning had also tired of Salva Kiir—a man who had hardly filled Garang's shoes. "Let us come together politically," one young SPLM member explained, paraphrasing the perceived motivation of both the apologizer and his audience. "'We will be a political force'… You see, they were just using one another."

Whether genuine remorse or calculated political theater, it was a bold signal. "There was no better place for him to say this," Rebecca recalls, "It was a courageous thing." The man who personified South Sudan's deepest ethnic divide had taken a symbolic first step on the long road to reconciliation.

Riek is arguably the most polarizing figure in South Sudan's modern history, a man about whom everyone harbors strong feelings. Love, hate, respect, or despise him, he is hard to ignore. Whatever their views, supporters and detractors would agree that Riek is charismatic, he is cunning, and he is a survivor.

Dr. Riek Machar Teny Dhurgon, long the standard-bearer of Nuer political interests, is more commonly known as "Riek." As with Salva, many South Sudanese are referred to by their first name—even presidents and vice presidents. The other convention of note is the frequent and proud use of the title "doctor." Given that so few of the nation's sons and daughters had the fortune to pursue Ph.D-level studies abroad, as Riek did, the title is held in unusually high esteem, its cachet not about to be wasted. And so Riek is often "Dr. Riek," just as John Garang is still affectionately known as "Dr. John." Initially born of reverence, the titles have stuck, and are used even by a man's fiercest critics.

A political animal by nature and by self-identification, Riek loved to debate politics, ideas, and people; he is able, direct, engaging, and self-confident. Riek's "honeyed purr of a voice," as one adroit observer called it, is an instrument consciously deployed. His measured cadence and dramatic pauses are designed to hold a room. Skilled in retail politics, he is comfortable in any room and places considerable value on a first impression—your impression of him, that is. Clutching a handshake and sustaining direct eye contact well beyond any normal rules of etiquette, Riek has a way of holding a guest in his gaze, making them feel both slight discomfort and the object of sincere interest. He flashes a mile-wide grin, and his signature front-tooth gap seals the deal. The shtick may be sincere, but it is also the work of a politician who wants to be admired and wants to be on top. If friends and foes were tasked to agree on a single defining characteristic, jury deliberations would be short. The verdict? Ambitious. Throughout three decades at the center of Southern Sudan's political arena, ambition has always been the constant. It is the fulcrum on which Riek's personality pivots.

Riek can also be a jerk, a side of him that emerged under the stress of renewed war in 2013. Cantankerous, moody, and inexhaustibly argumentative, Riek can tire you out. Among Africans and Westerners, descriptions of the man were frequently peppered with a certain class of adjective: selfish, stubborn, egotistical, narcissistic. One minute warm and engaging, the veteran chameleon can turn fiercely combative—equally comfortable in bellicose or benevolent skin. He can be reserved and contemplative, or impose his views through aggressive physical posturing. And he always enjoys the last word.

Today, at 64, Riek is not the lean field commander of yesteryear; his protruding belly has expanded on an annual basis, the goatee is now mostly gray, and his eyes—while still a formidable weapon—have been subjected to multiple surgeries, and it shows. The energy is not quite the same, nor is the political acuity; each has been worn down by time, stress, and the luxuries bestowed upon government fat cats. But the ambition remains, and there is one position he has pursued with reckless abandon for a quarter-century: top dog. Riek Machar wants to be president.

———

Riek was born in 1952 in the town of Leer, in what is today Unity state. A member of the Dok Nuer sub-clan, Riek's father was the traditional chief of the area. Leer's thatched huts face the west bank of the Nile, settlements that expand and contract with seasonal rains. Women pump water from wells into beat-up plastic containers, fishermen launch dugout wooden canoes into the river and navigate floating green beds of water hyacinth. The ambling cattle and squawking birds, the sun-scorched grasses and pungent charcoal fires, the chattering kids and high-pitched church sing-alongs are now as they were in Riek's youth, as Leer has changed little in those six decades.

Seasonal rains make for months of soggy landscape, while the cracked earth of the dry months—when the earth's elements seem particularly unforgiving—symbolize a hardscrabble existence. Amid the normalcy of everyday life in Leer are charred-black foundations, pockmarked buildings, rusting artillery shells, and the occasional town resident with a missing limb—harsh legacies of two generations of war. During the worst of the fratricidal fighting in the 1990s, Riek's hometown fell inside what aid workers called the "death triangle," where countless thousands starved to death while Southern factions battled for territorial control.

Riek was the 26th of 31 children. His mother, Nyadak, was the third of his father's five wives, and by all accounts a woman ahead of her time. Unlike most men his age, Riek does not bear the facial scarring that has been commonplace in South Sudan for generations, a rite of passage and a signifier of tribe. As part of initiation into adulthood, a designated elder uses a blade to cut lines into a young man's forehead, leaving distinct patterns of permanently raised scar tissue. Some ethnic groups have diagonal lines dipping toward the center of the forehead, others have intricate dot-patterns. Six parallel lines resembling a musical staff (each line representing a core value) are common among both the Dinka and the Nuer. Though the practice is today in decline, it was in the 1960s that Riek's mother and father withheld their teenage son—the son of a chief, no less—from the important cultural norm. Nyadak was instead focused on getting him an education—which was then equally rare among the cattle-keeping clans of the Western Nuer.

Nyadak sent the young boy to Atar Intermediate, a missionary school a week's walk to the northeast, where he began a life that would set him apart. Next came Rumbek Secondary School, and Khartoum University, where Riek's political consciousness was born, and where he first met future SPLA leader John Garang. Riek was later afforded a rare opportunity to study abroad and so left for the UK in 1979. After a master's degree in Glasgow came a Ph.D. in mechanical engineering at Bradford University in north central England. By then he was fully switched on to politics and active among Southern Sudanese diaspora circles in the UK.

Unlike Salva, Riek has long been drawn to foreigners, eager to discuss ideas, debate geopolitics, and rhapsodize on philosophy and economic theory. And his interest in foreigners didn't stop with intellectual companionship, as his compulsive flirtations netted him three wives—one British, one American, and one Sudanese.

Emma McCune, a 23-year-old British aid worker, traveled to Sudan in 1987 in search of herself and a purpose. She worked with a variety of humanitarian aid agencies, but after Riek proposed to her—on their second meeting—she became engrossed in the politics of rebellion. Idealistic, single-minded, and sometimes naive, the stylish young expatriate lived with Riek's breakaway faction, helped them procure supplies, and typed his manifestos; not surprisingly, she became a controversial figure among Southern Sudanese rebels and Western aid workers alike. Emma was killed in a car crash in 1993 in Kenya while pregnant with Riek's child, and was later the centerpiece of an excellent book, *Emma's War,* about Sudan's second civil war.

In 2000, Riek married American Becky Lynn Hagmann, a devout Christian from rural Minnesota. Becky was then in her early 40s, and had three children from an earlier marriage to an American pastor, with whom she had first raised money to send to war-torn Sudan. She was a less visible figure than Emma, and spent her time in Juba pursuing Christian-based schooling and agricultural projects. But like his other wives, Becky became active in Riek's politics, advising him when in Juba and appearing at his side when he traveled to the United States for events with South Sudanese diaspora communities.

But the marriage of most significance was Riek's first, to a Southern Sudanese woman. Angelina was a fellow Nuer from a similarly progressive and politically connected Nuer family in Unity state. She left with Riek for the UK when she was eighteen years old, and undertook her own studies alongside him. After giving birth to their four children, Angelina spent the war years in England working for various NGOs and activist organizations. She returned to Sudan to take up a position as state minister of petroleum in 2005, and soon became one of the most prominent women in the SPLM. She fled Juba with her husband in 2013, and the loss of friends and relatives in those first nights of violence had a lasting impact. Angelina would help to build the impromptu resistance movement from the bush, and become one of Riek's most controversial and hardline advisers.

In 1984, Riek returned from England to join the nascent Southern rebellion, and the educated captain—code name SENNAR—quickly ascended the SPLA ranks. He spearheaded a sizable recruitment of Nuer conscripts into what was then a predominantly Dinka SPLA, impressed Garang as an officer, and was named to the SPLA/M High Command.

Shortly thereafter, at the age of 38, Riek would make the audacious move that would come to define his life, his political career, and the fate of Southern Sudan.

In the closing days of August 1991, some eight years into the SPLA's war with the North, Riek and a coterie of disaffected commanders took to the SPLA radio waves. Channeling his Nuer brethren's distaste for centralized power, and wider discontent over SPLA leadership, he railed against "authoritarianism" and "Dinka-domination," complaining that John Garang was a dictator who "carried the movement in his brief-case." Over the crackle of SPLA radio, rebel units then heard Riek's stunning conclusion: "To save the Movement from imminent collapse, it has been decided to relieve John Garang of the leadership of SPLM/A."

In the ensuing days, Riek's faction spoke, however opportunistically, of democracy and human rights, and issued a pamphlet detailing, "Why Garang Must Go Now." Conscious that most Southerners shared his desire for an independent South Sudan, Riek also announced that there would be no more energy wasted on Garang's "New Sudan" adventure. Secession would henceforth be the guiding principle of the rebellion. There were truths in the grievances Riek aired, and the attempted overthrow reflected a confluence of quickening political, ideological, and ethnic undercurrents within the movement. But the move was also about power, and Riek's ambition would never be overlooked again.

Riek's ensuing 1991 attack on Bor was intended to show his strength, draw more SPLA commanders away from Garang, and make his declaration a reality. But it backfired. The wanton slaughter of civilians turned domestic and international opinion against him, rallying support instead to Garang. While Riek did not succeed in ousting Dr. John, his announcement did split the SPLA in two, with devastating consequences for the Southern cause and the South Sudanese people. "The split" reverberated far and wide, as each faction manipulated local grievances and mobilized communities along ethnic lines.

The 1991 Bor massacre was, unfortunately, neither the first nor the last of its kind; Garang, Salva, Riek, and a dozen other warlords would order attacks against civilians in the decades that followed. Nonetheless, the scale and symbolism of that particular event sparked a decade of ethnic recrimination and cemented a legacy of tribal hatred that would prove difficult to undo.

Even more damning for Riek, however, was his collaboration with the enemy regime in Khartoum. To take on Garang, he had procured financial and materiel support from the enemy—the very government that had long been waging war against Southerners and other marginalized citizens. For Riek, it was a tactical alliance. But for Garang, Salva, and all those in the mainstream SPLA, the move was unthinkable—an act of high treason. His betrayal would never be forgiven.

<hr />

Prophecy is deeply embedded in Nuer culture, and Riek's 25 years in the limelight represent a mythical, if unsubstantiated, chapter in this rich history. The predictions and songs of Nuer prophets, passed down and re-interpreted over generations, have been baked together to foretell the ascension of the Nuer people to rule a free South Sudan. Riek's ancestral lineage, his left-handedness, and even his gap-toothed grin each carry some meaning in these prophecies.

It is said that Dr. Riek's grandfather, Teny-Dhurghon, was possessed by spirits which enabled him to speak the language of prophecy. After Teny-Dhurgon traveled to meet with a revered 19th-century Nuer prophet deep in the Nuer heartland, competing stories emerged. In one version, the powerful prophet cursed Teny-Dhurgon and his family; in the other more popular account, the prophet foresaw a descendant of Riek's grandfather becoming a great leader of Southern Sudan. Some of Riek's more aspirational supporters have thus infused his political and military exploits with divine inspiration—Riek the Nuer messiah. He does not claim such prophetic authority, but like any wise politician, neither does he seek to dismiss it.

The Nuer prophets, and their society more broadly, have long been subjects of keen foreign interest, first and foremost in the work of pioneering Oxford anthropologist Sir Edward Evan Evans-Pritchard in the 1930s, and his study *The Nuer*. Prophetic traditions remain an important component of Nuer social, moral, and spiritual life today. A simple search on Facebook or YouTube generates photos and videos of a modern-day Nuer prophet, Dak Kueth—the clash of tradition and modernity evident in his customary leopard skin worn atop a pair of maroon and gold track pants. Though his self-proclaimed authority has stirred controversy, the young prophet garnered attention in 2014 when thousands of armed Nuer youth began marching into battle on his orders.

The South Sudanese have a peculiar tool in their national lexicon, which is to refer to supporters and associates as "Those of Salva" or "Those of Riek." One could refer to "Those of" Deng or Majok or anyone really, but the phrase was normally reserved for the kind of political big men who had a posse, a political faction, or other elite constituency. For someone to have "those of," well, that was a sign of relevance.

It was a flexible and useful term, one seasoned foreigners adopted and used for a laugh or to prove their Juba street cred. It was an especially malleable device in politically tense times, and useful in a country of ever shifting alliances. "Those of" could be employed, and interpreted, in a way that allowed the speaker to maintain some ambiguity. One could badmouth "those of Riek," when they were talking about Riek's immediate political supporters, or the rebels fighting at his direction, or even the Nuer community as a whole. Sometimes it was simply a veiled reference to the man himself.

After the bloody internecine war of the 1990s, an unholy alliance with the enemy, and failed attempts to win wider Southern Sudanese support or match the legitimacy of Garang's SPLA abroad, those of Riek were out of options. Their high-minded pursuit was all but exhausted. After numerous failed efforts to re-unite the SPLA's two warring factions, including a 1993 attempt in Washington, D.C., Riek finally negotiated his return to Garang's mainstream SPLA in 2002.

"Eleven years! *Brother* fighting *brother*," Riek told a packed hall of SPLA supporters and media outlets that January, upon his highly-anticipated return. Appearing arm-in-arm on stage with Garang, he proclaimed to the cheering crowd, "I am happy today this is over... the liberation struggle is united today!"

But by then "those of Riek" were few. The years after "the split" were spent fighting not only Garang, but against Riek's fellow Nuer—a constellation of militias that had sometimes fought with him, and sometimes against. While Riek had failed to sustain a competing force, or to oust Garang, he remained a formidable figure unto himself. And so he would return to the fold within striking distance of Garang's chair. After Salva's succession to the Presidency, Riek would become his vice president—first of the Southern region government, and eventually of the independent Republic. And he would put his skills to work.

During the period of Southern regional government from 2005 to 2011, Riek was more active than his boss in matters of day-to-day governance; he spearheaded administrative processes at home and was dispatched to fix thorny problems abroad. "He was a firefighter," one close observer remarked, "he did everything." Whether negotiating disputes between local communities, asserting himself in regional security matters, or "putting out fires" with the NCP in Khartoum, Riek's superior abilities were evident to anyone paying attention.

But for all Riek's natural talents or leadership skills, the man could not be separated from his treacherous past. Despite his prominent position, the nominal reunification of the SPLM, and the movement's shared pursuit of independence, many retained deep and visceral resentment for Riek. Salva and the party brass would always keep one eye on the opportunist in their midst.

The rivalries between Garang, Salva, Riek, and the SPLM's strongmen were personal, and they were political. But they were also overlaid by a complicated ethnical dimension—one these power-brokers manipulated when they saw fit.

In 2013, 22 years after "the split," Riek would again be at the center of a leadership battle that ripped South Sudan in half and ignited an ethnic war. The eerily familiar circumstances were the stuff of *déjà-vu*. Riek would again accuse a sitting Dinka leader of authoritarianism and mismanagement, voicing complaints that were shared by a growing number in the movement and in society. Again he would mobilize largely Nuer fighters, again he would solicit materiel from old enemies in Khartoum, and again his forces would commit unspeakable atrocities. Again Riek Machar would wage a battle for control of the SPLM, and again he would eventually negotiate his way back into the fold—in the No. 2 position.

But much had changed, too. The South was by then independent, flush with oil revenues, and Riek had until recently been the second-highest ranking official in the land. He shared in the responsibility for the government's shortcomings but had also proved a more capable administrator than Salva. He had publicly apologized for past crimes, and acted in statesman-like fashion when Salva fired him from his post. This time it was the leader who had moved on Riek. He had calmed angry supporters and pursued change through political channels. There was no *coup* attempt this time, as his was a reactionary rebellion. The changed circumstances cast both positive and negative light on Riek. But one unmistakable constant remained, from 1991 to 2016: ambition.

Unlike Salva, Riek's personality was always more akin to that of the region's dominant big men—smart, savvy, self-styled visionaries with big plans and big appetites. If you listen to Riek talk of democracy, modernization, reform, and inclusion, you can be swayed, and he knows it. He does believe in these ideas, it seems, at least until they don't suit him. But he is also a realist, and what drives him is a raw desire for power. He believes that he cannot truly advance his vision—or quench his own thirst—until he is in charge. And he knows the politics, the electoral math, and the lingering legacy of fratricide that stand in his way.

Wrapped in this unyielding ambition is perhaps his greatest evil. Despite Riek's comparatively progressive credentials and lofty rhetoric, he has more than once harnessed ethnic identity and incited fear to achieve political ends. From the Bor massacre in 1991, to the internecine battles that followed, to the targeting of civilians in 2013, ethnic violence and competition between the Dinka and Nuer has long been a central thread of the South Sudan's narrative. There are no clean hands. Sincere or not, the "Bor Apology" was an important first gesture. But the wounds of the past were only beginning to heal when they were suddenly ripped open again in 2013, and then gouged by Salva, Riek, and their respective ethnic warriors.

And so another generation of South Sudanese has endured the kind of violent convulsions and loss that are not easily forgotten. Those who are fed up with tribalism and marginalization argue that Riek's cause is a righteous one, whatever his personal ambitions. Some argue it is the fulfillment of prophecy. Others believe the greatest of leaders might have already stepped aside, conscious that the fate of an embattled nation was bigger than any one man. Riek should relinquish his selfish pursuit of the presidency, they argue—the fact that he keeps trying is more a matter of ego than prophecy.

7

IT ISN'T YET

"We have become not a melting pot but a beautiful mosaic. Different people, different beliefs, different yearnings, different hopes, different dreams."
—U.S. President Jimmy Carter, 1976

"Pan-yang! Pan-yang!" Duop shouts, mimicking himself in a former life, calling out for one of his herd. In the cattle-keeping societies of South Sudan, young men are responsible for the care of dozens, sometimes hundreds, of cows. And given the intimate bonds developed over endless hours grazed, and countless miles covered, each animal is known to his caretaker by sight and by name. "Oh yes, they all have names," Duop says, his expression suggesting it would be silly to think otherwise. "A cow is named for the cattle camp from which it comes, like Panyang."

Duop grew up between the villages and cattle camps of greater Bor near the birthplace of John Garang. He left Southern Sudan in 1987 as a young boy, "something like age seven," he guesses. Fleeing the war on foot, Duop walked hundreds of miles to a refugee camp in Ethiopia before geopolitics forced him and thousands of others back into war-riven Sudan. Like so many of his peers, the so-called Lost Boys, Duop survived aerial bombardment, attacks by wild predators, and deadly river crossings. He spent long nights sleeping out in the open, subject to the unforgiving elements of the bush. His unpredictable years on the move were a drastic change from the familiarity and solace of the cattle camp.

For South Sudan's pastoralists, whether Duop's Dinka or Nuer, or others, the cow is sacred. It is the centerpiece of social, economic, and cultural life. Cows represent a livelihood, a food source, a currency, a measure of social status, and a ticket to marriage. "Without them," Duop explains matter-of-factly, "one's life is wanting." Cattle can be found across much of rural South Sudan, and blocking main intersections in downtown Juba. But in Duop's home and others in the immediate Nile watershed, cattle and their caretakers move with the seasons. The Nile expands into a great swamp during the rains and then contracts, each season assuming a different shape and character, but every season drawing millions of cattle.

When the rains stop, boys and girls in Duop's village leave home and guide huge family herds toward the Nile and other water sources, where they establish seasonal camps. When I ask Duop about his memories of the cattle camps, he perks up with a boyish delight, his motor sparking to life. The cattle camp is hallowed ground.

Duop now lives in Washington, D.C., and I invite him for coffee one afternoon in 2017 to talk about South Sudan, past and present. I spend much of the conversation asking his thoughts about the war and the dire situation in his young country. His demeanor and short answers suggest frustration and an irritated reluctance to talk about what he cannot change. There simply isn't much to say. But the cattle camp is another story. It's been nearly 25 years since he last set foot in one, but the way he gushes about it now, it feels as if he were there just last night.

The cattle camp can be a mystical kind of place, and Duop is excited to hear about my own evening in one near his home in 2009. I'd traveled to Bor to find out more about a wave of violence then rocking Jonglei state. Thousands of lives had been claimed in raids amongst Dinka, Nuer, and Murle communities, and tens of thousands of cattle stolen. On my final evening in the sleepy town, I put up at a modest guesthouse and asked around about local cattle camps. Cattle were often at the center of the fighting, and I wanted to talk to the young men tasked to defend them.

The Kenyan ladies running the guesthouse offered me *Ugali*—the corn-based "African cake"—and I washed it down with bottles of ice-cold Fanta orange soda. As darkness enveloped the tiny capital city and the mosquitoes meandered in from the Nile, white and blue flashes emerged from behind a group of thirty-odd boys sitting in the open-air hall. They sat on the floor and on plastic chairs, each peering over the shoulder in front of them—their eyes fixed on a sixteen-inch television, the aging box connected through a series of gnarled extension cords to the diesel generator humming outside.

English Premier League soccer was on, and Arsenal football club was playing; what aspiring Sudanese star could think of being any-where else? But it was not these city-slicker youths I was here to see. I pried one away from the screen during a break and asked for his help, and he set me up with a cousin who could escort me to a nearby camp.

We set out the following afternoon in a beat-up Honda CRV, and after a few dozen miles of rough riding, a canopy of towering trees gave way to a clearing and a sea of horns opened up before us. Hundreds of the long-horned white beasts were convening on a dirt slope leading down to the river. As the sun descended against an orange and pink sky across the water, more and more of the ubiquitous animals arrived, followed by their young caretakers. The camps are a way to provide col-lective protection to the precious commodity at night, and the number of cows here surely numbered in the thousands.

The boys tethered calves to tree stumps and added dried cow dung to dozens of smoldering fires dotting the camp, their heat and thick white smoke transforming our environs into an eerie volcanic-like atmosphere. As dusk descended, the boys themselves transformed into chalky white ghosts, covering their faces, chests, arms, and legs in the ash of dried cow dung. The ash acts as a repellant to mosquitos and other insects—for the boys and their cattle—and so as I applied some to my own neck and arms, my junior hosts nodded in approval.

Duop reminds me of the systems and rituals that have for genera-tions ordered such camps—places where young men and women "tend to cattle," he says, "and to each other." Young boys mind the calves, while older boys take ever-increasing numbers of mature cattle in search of grass and water during the day. Walking mile after mile in sandals and carrying sticks or guns for protection, they direct their herds with a few simple clicks of the tongue. In addition to assigning them names, the boys brand their cattle by cutting notches in their ears, each shape known to his sub-section of the Dinka.

At night they return to the safety and social life of the camp, where they sing songs and tell stories. It is here that they find both themselves and their place in the wider community. It is also where young men and women flirt and giggle and hope to catch the eyes of the one shooting sheepish glances back at them. Girls have their own space and roles in the camp, including milking cows and ferrying additional food from back in the village.

Cow's milk is the primary source of food. The South Sudanese rarely eat their cattle, except on special occasions—weddings, historical commemorations, or annual sacrifices to the gods. Even in times of hunger, killing a cow is frowned upon. Only under extreme circumstances may a cow may be killed, and then its meat is shared widely among the community.

"Each boy chooses a special ox from the herd," Duop continues, in which "he invests huge value." In Duop's village, it's called a *mioor cien*. He delights in explaining to me that the prized animal's owner then "composes poems and sings songs" in its honor. One of the animal's long horns—and they are very long—is bent forward for aesthetic reasons, so its two horns grow out at different angles. Duop pauses, sits upright and makes the shape of two such horns with his arms, then stretches his head back to admire it, as if it were a piece of fine art. "It's so beautiful," he says, emotion welling up in his face.

"That ox... it is like a bank account," he says, "filled with thousands and thousands of dollars." Though each cow is itself a valuable commodity, his monetary metaphor is meant to convey social and cultural value: "There is just nothing else in the world; you are so rich." When I asked one of Duop's peers about the importance of the prized ox for the adolescent male, he laughed and offered an equivalent: "It's just like a teenager getting a sports car in America."

Some of the social mores around cattle have evolved since Duop left Sudan in the 1980s, but less than one might think. And their actual economic value has only gone up. Today a single cow can fetch $300 in rural areas, and as much as $600 at the market in Juba. The figure is hard to square with the poverty experienced by so many, and can confound anyone who does not appreciate the place of the cow among the Nile river societies.

The high sticker-price has also made cattle a driver of violent conflict. Cattle rustling—in which young men steal herds from a neighboring community—is a rite of passage; but it is not simply for show. By 2009, securing the hand of a suitable wife meant delivering as many as 200 cattle to her family. Though replaced by cash among urban families, cows remain the principal unit of marriage dowry— the bride price—and are given to the bride's family as a gesture of honor and respect.

Duop and his cohort walked out of Sudan again in the early 1990s, this time to Kenya. After another decade in a refugee camp there, Duop was offered the chance to resettle in America. "I was reluctant to be separated, again... from my family," he explains. But they persuaded him to go, and he has since made a new life in Washington.

Not all of Duop's fellow travelers were so fortunate. Duop recalls many who did not make it—roughly half the Lost Boys are believed to have died during their unimaginable trek, succumbing to hunger, dehydration, disease, or violence. "It is my life there, in the camp, that gave me the skills and resilience I needed," Duop says, a matter he's clearly given a great deal of thought. "The cattle camp taught me how to survive."

Duop and his fellow Dinka account for roughly one-third of South Sudan's twelve million people. Historical undercounting by Khartoum, massive displacement, and the lack of reliable data, however, mean that the country's population statistics are little more than an educated guess. Most Southerners live in rural areas like Duop, and when spread over nearly a quarter million square miles, the country's population density is among the lowest in the world. With just a few hundred miles of paved roads in a territory the size of France, its people are also among the least connected.

South Sudan can be broadly, if incompletely, understood in the context of three regions—Bahr al Ghazal, Upper Nile, and Equatoria—blocs which once served as administrative regions. Though South Sudan had been re-organized into states and counties by the time of independence, the three regional blocs remain a fixture of common usage, and are relevant in thinking about both ethnicity and political life.

Bahr al Ghazal, to the north and west, is dominated by the Dinka. The Dinka are the largest ethnic community, comprising more than 35 percent of the population, and they fall under three broad umbrellas. The Bahr al Ghazal Dinka herd their beloved longhorns on the grasslands immediately west of the Nile, and across the ironstone plateau that stretches north through Salva's hometown to the border with Sudan. Move east across the river into the verdant green floodplains of Upper Nile, and you'll find the Bor Dinka of Duop and the late John Garang. Head north on the river to the town of Malakal and you'll find the Padang Dinka stretching along the Nile's eastern banks.

The Dinka—or *Jieng* as they call themselves—have also been the subject of intense interest from social anthropologists, though are perhaps known best for their exceedingly tall and slender frames. There is notable cultural continuity across the Dinka's 25 sub-clans, a point intellectual Francis Deng ascribed to his tribe's intense "pride and ethnocentrism." Francis' second name is important in local mythology—"Deng" is the god of sky and rain—but it is far from unique. Though it's not clear the Dinka descended from a single ancestor, Francis' own father "Deng" was a revered paramount chief who is said to have married some 200 wives and fathered more than a thousand children. Today, it is hard to cross the street in South Sudan without bumping into someone named Deng.

The Dinka, together with their Nuer and Shilluk cousins, are known as "Nilotic" peoples—a term that reflects shared linguistic and cultural characteristics among those indigenous to the Nile River valley. In lifestyle, language, culture, and appearance, there is more that unites these predominant cultures than divides them. At the confluence of their adjacent homelands, inter-marriage is common and it can be hard to even distinguish between them. And yet their recent history is marred by divisions.

The Nuer—or *Naath* in their own language—are South Sudan's second largest ethnic group, comprising roughly 15 percent of the population. Their homeland is an island in the heart of the Upper Nile region; from Riek's village on the western banks of the Nile, Nuer country stretches more than 300 miles east before crossing the Sobat River and continuing into neighboring Ethiopia, itself home to some 200,000 Nuer cousins. The Nuer sub-clans—Lou, Jikany, Bul, and Dok among them—are not organized into a centralized system; each was historically in charge of its own affairs and resistant to hierarchy. Though proud of their diffuse and comparatively democratic structure, Nuer wise men know that at critical junctures in their peoples' history, internal divisions have been deeply damaging to their shared interests.

As anywhere, stereotypes accentuate the divisions between South Sudanese communities, the kind of simplified traits which—real or perceived—can fuel dangerous narratives when leaders resort to playing the ethnic card. Having dominated the new South's governments and the SPLA since its inception, the Dinka are often viewed as power hungry, and charges of "Dinkocracy" are spewed by the resentful.

Fairly or not, the Nuer have a reputation as a martial people, long regarded by feuding tribes and foreigners as violent warriors. Though scholars have since poked holes in such assessments, Evans-Pritchard, the renowned British anthropologist, himself assessed the Nuer to be a "turbulent people," who are "easily roused to violence" and who esteem battlefield skill and courage as among the highest of accomplishments. And so when it comes to contemporary stereotypes, the rap on the Nuer is that they are aggressive. As one South Sudanese social critic lampooned, "they wake up in the morning, they wash their faces, and they go to war."

While the Dinka, Nuer, and their fellow Nilotes represent a two-thirds majority, more than 60 other ethnic groups call South Sudan home. The remaining third is best categorized by their diversity: from farmers in the south who straddle borders with Congo and Uganda, to fishermen with Ethiopian relatives in the east, to the diverse minorities in the austere western borderlands, whose roots can be traced to West Africa.

Equatoria, a horizontal green belt stretching from east to west, is home to a mix of these smaller tribes. The so-called "Equatorians" are not an ethnic group, though the geographic label is used to collectively identify the Bantu peoples—Bari, Mundari, Toposa, Azande, and many others—who live in the country's southernmost territory. The Equatorians are more akin to Bantu cousins in neighboring Uganda, the Democratic Republic of Congo, and elsewhere in Central Africa. They too keep cattle, but rich Equatorian soils and plentiful rains mean they are farmers first. They have the strongest record of civic organization, but not the warrior traditions of their Dinka and Nuer counterparts. "They are cowards," the same South Sudanese social critic says, again caricaturing the stereotype. "They are not nationalists... so when there is trouble, they run to Uganda."

The people of Equatoria have long been frustrated by Southern Sudan's dominant Nilotes—their cyclical fighting, imposition on traditional lands, and subjugation of minorities. Though Equatorians in fact played pivotal roles in the earliest rebellions and the struggle for self-rule, relations with the majority Dinka—including John Garang's predominantly Dinka SPLA—have long been acrimonious. Historical enmities were re-kindled again during South Sudan's post-independence war, when Salva's increasingly polarized army revisited the kind of evictions, occupation, and strong-arming that reminded many Equatorians of a tiresome past.

Many Southerners speak three languages: "Dinka," "Nuer," or another indigenous language; English, a lingua franca and remnant of the British colonial period; and Arabic—a legacy of generations of

Northern influence. "Juba Arabic," to be more precise, is Southern Sudan's unique twist on the language, a dialect at which Northern Sudanese shake their heads derisively.

Despite attempts to dismiss rich Southern religious traditions, and the persistent use of catch-all terms like "animist" to describe them, indigenous religions continue to "inform ideas about ethical behavior, the moral community, and political action" for many in South Sudan, in addition to world religions. Islam is also practiced in Southern Sudan, though most inhabitants now claim Christianity, which arrived with European missionaries in the late nineteenth century. It remains among the few forms of shared identity and practice across South Sudanese society, though the church, too, was divided on regional lines. Catholics worked in Bahr al Ghazal, Presbyterians in Upper Nile, and Anglicans in Equatoria. (American Evangelicals followed, albeit generations later.)

Though weakened by war, the recession of mission work, and competing forces of modernity, the church's networks remain among the strongest in the country. Amid a history of war and division, church leaders have often been voices of reason and reconciliation. But the legacy of divvying up the map between denominations has also complicated the work and perceptions of church leaders, as no institution has remained immune to politics and polarization.

In his introduction to the nation's first anthology of literary fiction, *There Is a Country*, Nyuol Lueth grapples with all this diversity, and an identity forged mostly by war and displacement. "South Sudanese culture," he writes, "is a strikingly hard to define thing." Nyuol's diverse fellow citizens reside together in one large, diffuse, and mostly disconnected homeland. And despite their collective opposition to Northern oppression, and the shared euphoria of independence in 2011, ethnic and regional identities—tribes—remain far stronger than any national consciousness.

"Tribe" is of course a tricky term and a tricky idea. It is at once a crude categorization and a reality on the ground, the most relevant form of identity in a state that is not yet a nation. Historical periods of incursion by Turks, Arabs, and later the British altered inter-tribal dynamics and sometimes drove wedges between peoples. Tribalism was later a polarizing force in the South's internal wars, in the system of governance during the interim period, and in the war that collapsed the independent republic—when an "us or them" mentality held sway.

Reflecting on the complicated matter, the South Sudanese social critic explained in 2016, "It is often said that our diversity is a source of strength." It may turn out to be, he continued, "but it isn't yet."

8

A TURBULENT UNION

"We were only protesting, not governing. Like school boys . . . with big egos."
—Southern Sudanese minister, Government
of National Unity, Khartoum

Opportunities for exercise in Juba were limited, and so I was glad to occasionally hook up with local friends for a game of outdoor basketball. At 6 foot 5 inches, I was nonetheless an average-sized player among this crowd. Some evenings we played on a court opposite Bilpam military headquarters, pick-up games which sometimes included top army officers and so made for distracting security measures. Once, a general's personal guards marched up and down the length of the court while we played, weapons cocked and at the ready. It seemed more a display of "big man" status than a necessary precaution. Even so, I thought twice before committing any hard fouls against those with three stars on their uniform.

Other times we played at a small and crumbling concrete "stadium" in a neighborhood called "Nimra Telata"—Number Three. One hazy afternoon in 2011 we joined a promising group of eighteen-year-olds scrimmaging there. I had played high school ball, and my formal training had yielded solid fundamentals, but my diminishing athletic ability was comically juxtaposed against these youthful prototypes who, simply put, could sky. The oppressive afternoon heat and dry, sandy air didn't make things any easier for me and the other has-beens.

During a break, the man tutoring the young players extended a handshake and a smile. "Bil Duany," he said, introducing himself, and I immediately recognized his surname. "Of *the* Duany family?" I asked, while trying to catch my breath. Bil confirmed that he was the youngest of the Duany siblings, a basketball family of repute in South Sudan. He explained that he was arranging for some of this raw talent to make the leap to a prep school in the United States. Some of them had picked up a basketball only in the last year or two. And to that end, he offered—generously—that he appreciated the chance for his squad of upstarts to play against those of us with formal training.

Bil is one of five children of accomplished and politically active parents, Michael and Julia Duany, each of whom held positions in Southern regional governments both before and after Sudan's civil war. Michael had earned two degrees from Syracuse University, on the same program that had brought John Garang to the United States. In 1984, he then obtained a visa to undertake further study at Indiana University, just as the war had begun. The family remained back home, but when things got dicey, they made a run for it while they could. Julia—then pregnant and due to deliver shortly—boarded a flight out of the country with their four young children. Bil was born just days later.

The Duanys spent much of the war period pursuing higher education and working professionally in Bloomington, Indiana, before returning to Southern Sudan two decades later when the conflict ended. Remarkably, in the interim, all five of their children won scholarships to play Division I basketball in the United States. Kueth captained the 2003 Syracuse NCAA National Championship team, Duany played in the Final Four championship tournament for the Wisconsin Badgers, while Nok, Nyagon, and Bil laced up for Georgetown, Bradley, and Eastern Illinois.

Many in the United States first encountered South Sudan by way of another basketball star, Manute Bol, who played ten seasons in the NBA from 1985 to 1995. A literal "standout" at 7 foot 7 inches, Bol remains one of the tallest players ever to play professional basketball. Bol's impressive stature seemed further amplified when he took the court alongside 5'-3" teammate, Muggsey Bogues, then the shortest player in pro ball. The lanky Dinka from Bahr al Ghazal was cultivated by John Garang, and he became an important source of funding for the SPLA rebellion. Bol reportedly gave most of his career earnings to charitable causes related to his war-torn home.

A handful of other Southern Sudanese hoopsters have since graced the professional ranks, most notably Luol Deng, a two-time NBA all-star who returned home to promote reconciliation in the wake of South Sudan's war, and later took up his country's plight in a 2015 Oval Office meeting with President Obama. Every young man on the court today knew Luol Deng, and everything there was to know about him. National stars of his calibre were greeted like kings upon return, their background, ethnicity, and relationship to war having given way to something larger.

When our game is over, Bil describes his youth in America, and it's evident how lucky he feels to have had the opportunities most of his aspiring mentees, and their families, did not. Instead of basketballs, many young men in the Duanys' home village had picked up guns; they had fought during the war and were now rustling cattle or active in local militias.

But if five out of five of the privileged Duany siblings had reached the highest levels of amateur basketball in America, one had to wonder how much untapped potential remained—both in individual prospects and in what the game itself might do for South Sudanese youth.

"If these guys just started two years ago..." I began wondering aloud, as Bil and I stood at the edge of the concrete court, watching his green but eager players still horsing around under the hoop. "I know," he interrupted politely, nodding in total agreement, "I know."

Michael and Julia Duany returned home in 2005 to take up posts in the new Southern regional government—he a member of parliament, she a senior civil servant—following the signing of the Comprehensive Peace Agreement. It was a formative moment in the making of South Sudan, a period characterized by two sometimes competing realities: one of heady promise and unparalleled growth for a region on the rise, and another, more daunting reality shaped by a hostile counterpart and a menu of state-building challenges that would make mature nations flinch.

Despite its shortcomings, the internationally-backed peace agreement had ended Sudan's civil war and set the stage for important structural changes. Its "one country, two systems" model of governance meant Southerners would enjoy relative autonomy in administering their own territory. But they would also participate in a unity government at the national level in Khartoum. Partnering with the North's National Congress Party (NCP), the two would begin a process of democratic transformation, and, ideally, "make unity attractive."

Sharing power and oil revenues while also pursuing more equitable development—these arrangements were to be the glue that would better bind Sudan's two halves. It was a noble pursuit, but one neither North nor South was committed to. In relatively short order, the landmark peace agreement was on life support.

Such an ambitious peace accord would stand a chance only if accompanied by good faith, capable bureaucracies, and cooperative leaders on both sides. But all three were absent. In Khartoum, the government had signed on reluctantly; it was keen to end a costly war but chafed at the notion of making concessions to the South, sharing power, or submitting to oversight from meddling foreigners. It also worried that compromise would signal weakness to political opponents and threaten their tenuous hold on the state.

The South stood to benefit more from the peace plan, but its commitment also evaporated in the wake of Garang's death. A handful of Garang's disciples sought to carry forward his dream of a united and wholly transformed "New Sudan," but they were fighting a losing battle, and they knew it. The majority of Southerners wanted out of Sudan. Salva, Riek, and the rest of the SPLM had long dreamed of breaking away, and so they would gradually withdraw from the national arena and turn their gaze to 2011. They would go through the motions and pay lip service to unity and national reforms, but they didn't believe in it. The peace agreement was several hundred pages long, but they cared about one clause above all others—Chapter I, Section 2.5: the right to secede and form their own country.

As North-South hostilities subsided in 2005, international attention turned elsewhere. The popular American advocacy movement shifted its focus to Darfur, and Western governments followed. The Bush administration also had far bigger fish to fry—matters of actual national security import, including its ongoing war in Iraq and an expanding war on terror. American oversight alone would not salvage Sudan's lagging peace deal or make the two sides work together. But its absence surely would not help, and caused anxiety inside an SPLM that had come to rely upon Washington.

By late 2007, less than halfway through the interim period, the CPA was on the verge of collapse. The supposed peace partners were spending more time pointing fingers than they were implementing the deal. They had never trusted one another, and the agreement's many checks and balances were not enough to overcome a near complete deficit of trust. The SPLM was fed up at the North's military provocations, its hogging of oil revenues, and a laundry list of other CPA violations.

And so the SPLM staged a dramatic walkout, quitting the unity government in a move that nearly upended the fragile peace. Citing Khartoum's flagrant violations, the SPLM's fiery secretary-general, Pagan Amum, announced to a press conference that his party's representatives would "not report to work until these contentious issues are resolved." The SPLA postured for a military push on Khartoum, and the North's military prepared to counter. Suddenly Africa's longest war seemed ready to begin anew.

The NCP's obstructionism was surely grounds for the disadvantaged SPLM to cry foul, and they possessed little with which to leverage Khartoum. But the walkout was also extraordinarily risky—a kind of nuclear option that jeopardized their agenda. Shutting down the unity government could collapse the CPA altogether, and with it their prized referendum on self-determination.

"Idiotic," recalls one dissenting SPLM figure then serving in the unity government. He was in the minority, but laments the antagonism that continued to be the movement's modus operandi, even after they were in government. "The walkout was mishandled," he says, derisively. "We were just being activist, only protesting, not governing. Like school boys... with big egos."

The SPLM's decision reflected an already deeply adversarial relationship between the Khartoum regime and the SPLM's point-men, chief among them Pagan Amum. It would also foreshadow the deployment of another "nuclear bomb" by SPLM negotiators five years hence. Though unseen at the time, in both cases the bold ultimatums took place amid ongoing stress inside the SPLM, where big personalities and feuding factions were contending over their party's tactics, direction, and leadership.

The walkout accelerated an already dangerous game of North-South brinkmanship: each side hardened their rhetoric, and sporadic fighting in the border regions nearly pushed the antagonists over the edge. But faced with outside pressure and a decision that could well have decimated both the North and the South, the two sides pulled back the reins.

Restraint prevailed, just barely. The parties reformulated a unity government, but the peace deal was now a charade. Any lingering hopes of meaningful reforms or preserving the union had been snuffed out. The race to 2011 was on.

Many Northerners doubted the peace deal would last. They assumed they could manipulate the terms, divide Southerners, and defer Southern self-determination indefinitely. The Southerners, meanwhile, sought to prove them wrong. To reach their long-awaited destination, they had only to keep their own ship on an even keel, and do what they could to deter nefarious plots from Khartoum. They also took out an insurance policy—in the form of a beefed-up army and an arsenal of flashy new toys.

Garang had made a down-payment on that policy during the CPA negotiations, when he fought hard to ensure his SPLA would be officially sanctioned as one of the country's two national armies.

Now, with more than a billion dollars of CPA-guaranteed oil revenue flowing into its coffers each year, the SPLA began bulking up. The more formidable its military arsenal, the thinking went, the less likely Khartoum would risk a new war by scuttling the South's referendum.

In addition to keeping tens of thousands on the army payroll, Salva and company sent cash-wielding emissaries abroad to glad-hand arms dealers in Russia, Ukraine, and other former Soviet states. They came home with T-72 battle tanks and Mi-17 helicopters, 122-millimeter rocket launchers and man-portable surface-to-air missiles. Cargo plane after cargo plane of assault rifles and ammunition followed. The new weapons acquisitions were a violation of the peace agreement, and so were acquired covertly, but not so covertly that Khartoum would miss them.

Sudan held elections in 2010, but they were something of a farce. Designed to be the cherry atop the CPA's agenda of democratic transformation, the polls instead served only to fortify the dominant positions of the NCP in Khartoum and the SPLM in Juba. Salva Kiir did not stand for president of Sudan, and the SPLM withdrew its nominal candidate altogether before the vote. They would concede elections at the national level—the clearest public signal yet that Southern Sudan had no interest in unity. Khartoum and Bashir could have their superficial mandate; the South was packing its bags to depart anyway.

The international community followed suit, as most foreign diplomats had likewise fixed their eyes on the prize—the 2011 referendum. The democratic purpose had been sucked out of elections, which suddenly seemed an inconvenient and potentially destabilizing hazard. It was an uncomfortable trade-off, but one most diplomats and observers could rationalize. The first priority was avoiding a new war and protecting the independence referendum. As Washington's top diplomat at the time wrote, "Transformation would have to wait."

In addition to loading up on conventional weapons, the SPLM would continue to cultivate its most powerful weapon: foreign support. Having waged their war and secured the peace deal with the help of foreign friends, the SPLM would again look abroad—to the Americans, the Europeans, African neighbors, and eventually the Chinese—for help in keeping Khartoum in check.

Salva hit the road. Washington would be a particularly important stop, as the SPLM would keep most of its eggs in America's basket, where they'd been well protected to date. Indeed the relationship between America and South Sudan was at its zenith during the interim period.

Salva gave speeches extolling the decades-long friendship with America, namechecking members of Congress, Susan Rice, and other "brothers and sisters" in the SPLM lobby. Ask a Southerner on the streets of Juba, and he or she would extol the virtues of the United States and speak of President Bush—and later Obama—as if they were personal friends. Successive U.S. ambassadors in Southern Sudan were "treated like rock stars," some of the most recognizable and exalted figures in the country. "Honestly, we could just come and go anytime without an appointment," one U.S. diplomat explained of the privileged relationship with Juba's most senior officials: "No one else had that kind of VIP access."

It was also widely believed that Salva had developed a special relationship with President George W. Bush, underpinned by a strong personal rapport, Christian principles, and a big black hat. The optic was useful—it sent the desired message to Khartoum and satisfied Southern Sudan's American constituencies on the right and left. But it may have been more about appearances than reality. According to one White House official, the first meeting between the two men was "a fucking train wreck."

When Salva arrived in the Oval Office that day, President Bush welcomed him to a set of matching armchairs by the fireplace. Secretary of State Condoleezza Rice, National Security Adviser Stephen Hadley, and their staffers settled in with briefing books on the adjacent couches. After exchanging pleasantries, "Salva said maybe two words during the entire meeting," the White House official explained. While Bush instead talked strategy with his guest's more capable lieutenants, Salva was busy picking his nose. "I mean, it was like nothing I'd ever seen before," says the official, "This guy was up to his knuckle—in the Oval Office!"

Bush had a reputation for being chummy with fellow leaders, but it was tough going with Salva, who "just sat there, silent, and stiff as a rod." When the meeting ended, Bush and his team huddled. Overwhelmed by the contrast between the charismatic Garang and his successor, they asked themselves, "Holy shit, this is our guy?"

Salva would visit Bush several more times before his second term ended, and their relationship gradually improved. "It was an unusual amount of face time for any leader," says the Bush White House official, "much less one from a place that wasn't even a country." Though American engagement had waned in the early years of the interim period, the SPLM continued to rely on friends in Congress, members of the "Council," and the wider advocacy community to ensure their interests were protected, and later to win back White House attention.

Some believe the SPLM's 2007 walkout, and the military posturing that followed, were calibrated in part to get America's attention. "It caught us totally off guard," says the White House official, "It really was a turning point. We thought we understood them, but we knew then that we really did not understand decision-making in Juba at all."

Despite their frustration, members of the Bush team were committed to the South and to the Christian constituencies who cared so much about their plight. In subsequent meetings, Salva asked President Bush for moral, political, financial, and even military support as a hedge against Khartoum. And during his final stop at 1600 Pennsylvania Avenue, just days before Bush left office in January 2009, Salva would make his biggest request yet. "I want your guarantee," he told the outgoing president, "that if they (Khartoum) cross over that line, the United States will defend us militarily."

In addition to exerting political pressure on Khartoum, the Americans had provided military training to the SPLA and "looked the other way" as Juba acquired tanks and advanced weaponry in violation of the CPA. But a public guarantee of South Sudan's security—the kind Washington avows only to NATO and a few major strategic partners? This was out of the question.

During these meetings, and the regular engagement between American diplomats and SPLM leaders, there was little time reserved for matters inside South Sudan. "To be honest, we really had no idea what was going on in the South," the White House official admits. "We didn't understand anything about South-South politics." Just as Garang had earlier stage-managed the narrative with his foreign patrons, the SPLM brass again "didn't want us looking at the South, they wanted to keep our attention elsewhere, on Khartoum."

The CPA had ended a brutal war—at least temporarily—and offered an opportunity for a new beginning in the South. Those were no mean feats in the circumstances, and on paper it was an impressive blueprint. But the dysfunction of the interim period had also illustrated that the deal had not truly delivered peace. Sudan's fundamental problem—the extreme disparity between the center and the country's multiple peripheries—remained unchanged, and the SPLM no longer sought to reform it. They wanted to opt out, and no one could blame them. And so as the end of their turbulent union neared, another North-South reckoning was in the making.

When I first arrived in Juba in 2009, an oil-funded growth spurt was in full acceleration. Foreign expatriates measured the city's evolution in roads paved, motel amenities offered, and the latest delicacy stocked (e.g. cheese), at huge markup, on the shelves of the local import shop.

On my first half dozen visits to the capital, I stayed at the aspirationally named "Oasis Camp"—a cropping of white and blue metal containers perched on the banks of the Nile River. Meals included a lot of gristly meat dishes, dried-out breaded goods, and powdered drinks mixed with bottled water. Rooms were paid for in cash, as was everything else in South Sudan, as there were few banks and no credit card machines. Oasis camp guests passed by soft-spoken Indian proprietors at the straw-roofed reception hut, down a broken sidewalk and under a rusty welcome gate, where they came upon the modest oasis itself—a small fountain shrouded by green shrubs and presided over by a life-size concrete statue of a gorilla.

Giant mango trees offered ample shade, their falling fruit gathering speed before crashing on metal roofs. A dazzling array of lizards meant one was never lonely in a rented half-container, and once stepping outside, staying upright in the sludge-like mud around the camp was always a challenge when it rained. On the occasions pumps did deliver water from the river to makeshift shower heads, it reeked, suggesting the intake was just downriver from where sewage was expelled.

As in any developing country, clean water was hard to come by. I regularly contracted the kind of funky waterborne parasites and unidentifiable amoebas which together meant an uninterrupted stretch of diarrhea for my first year in Southern Sudan. I was surely less immune than the locals, but I also enjoyed a standard of living and access to comparatively clean water and plumbing that most could only dream of.

Oasis was not unlike other camps then providing accommodations—"Mango Camp," "Bedouin," "Sahara." Some were tents, others were stacks of aluminum containers, but all were accompanied by the whirring hum of diesel generators. "Afex" was comparatively swank, one of the first to boast brick and mortar accommodations. Its "pizza night," riverside bar, and dance music were popular with expats looking for a reprieve, and a few times played host to visiting celebrity "actor-vist" George Clooney.

After becoming a highly visible member of the Save Darfur campaign, Clooney had then used his celebrity to try to draw attention to South Sudan ahead of the referendum. During one of his much-talked-about visits to Juba, his American advisers asked if I might come down to Afex and brief him on some research I'd been doing of late. The ask gave me pause, as I had reservations about the many hazards of drop-in Hollywood activism and the intimate relationship between Clooney's advisers and the SPLM. After politely declining once, I accepted a second invitation. Clooney was hoping to harness his celebrity for good, and would inevitably draw attention to South Sudan's then precarious situation, and so I tried to convince myself it was better to help shape views than to decline on principle.

After dark I joined Clooney and a handful of journalist sidekicks at a four-top bar table on the dirt banks of the river. "What's your poison?" one asked, heading toward the bar for a round of drinks. "Gin and tonic fine for me, thanks," I said, noticing the limes at the bottom of the empty glasses on the table.

I shared an informal assessment of recent violence along the North-South border, and Clooney jumped in with good questions, his intellect evident from the get-go. I offered some nuance that I hoped he'd consider. But it was late on a Saturday evening, everyone was ready to unwind, and talk of conflict dynamics soon gave way to story-telling and more drinks. Clooney talked of journalism and Hollywood and American politics and everything under the sun. Despite their varying levels of intoxication, he was also remarkably polite to the near-constant stream of tipsy aid workers who approached the table to ask for—or demand—a photo with him.

When it was my turn to buy a round, I got up and solicited Clooney's order. "Vodka-tonic," he said, "hold the tonic." When I returned he was recalling memories from his youth; first, a faux strip-tease routine Walter Cronkite once did to entertain fellow guests at a dinner party hosted by Clooney's journalist father. Then teenage years driving his aunt, famed jazz singer Rosemary Clooney, and her friends between shows at boozy lounges and velvety clubs.

When the Afex river bar closed up for the night and the music went quiet, I hitched a ride home. Exiting the compound in an SUV, we passed a row of shanties built atop of a shallow urban graveyard, then a slaughterhouse cloaked in the hot stench of rotting animal flesh. Staring emptily into the distance, I re-played the evening in my head. It had been an entertaining but bizarre night—hard to conceive of Clooney's world and this one fitting into one planet.

After Oasis Camp I graduated to the Beijing Juba Hotel. Marked by a neon-lit palm tree, the Chinese-owned property boasted an actual lobby and semi-workable televisions in every room, and so felt rather luxurious. Like other guests, I eventually grew accustomed to stepping through the floor and retrieving a heel dusted with soil—it was easy to puncture the fake wood laminate rolled directly onto the uneven ground below. Years later the compound played host to the Chinese embassy and oil workers, before being wholly bought out by Chinese enterprises and turned into a veritable "little Beijing." The hotel twice burned to the ground.

Just east and around the corner from the Beijing were the homes of Salva, Riek, and the SPLM government ministers. The big men of the SPLM occupied a long row of aging block houses, each with its own high-walled perimeter and pair of shimmering SUVs inside. Formerly occupied by officers of the Sudanese military, the houses were now among the accoutrements that came with the top government jobs—and which house a minister occupied was often a reflection of his status. In the center of town, long cream-colored walls and well-armed guards of the elite Tiger Division surrounded "J-1," an impressive new presidential office and residence built with ample petrodollars.

As in many underdeveloped economies, government jobs were most sought after. Some felt called to public service, but many aspirants were motivated by the one institution that offered a decent salary and a chance for social mobility. At the upper echelons, some were motivated by a chance, figuratively speaking, "to eat." The top jobs—cabinet, executive office, governorships—afforded luxuries of high office, jobs to dole out to loyal supporters, and huge official budgets that could be gobbled up for personal use. In a country accustomed to turbulence and changing circumstances, one would not waste a chance to get ahead during a turn at the feeding trough.

Several government ministers made semi-permanent residence at "Nimule Logistics," a motel on the north edge of town with an outdoor restaurant under a giant thatched *tukul*. Its owner had decades-old ties to the SPLA brass, and most nights one could find a handful of them at a corner table talking politics over bottles of cold beer. They weren't talking of the unity government in Khartoum, or of making unity attractive. They talked sometimes about domestic politics at home in the South. But by 2009, they talked mostly about preparing for the independence referendum, or preparing for war.

The premier spot during the interim period, however, remained the Juba Grand—the metal-container-and-concrete-courtyard mainstay where I'd met a lethargic SPLA middle man on my first visit to South Sudan. The Grand was *the* address for visiting elites and a clearing house for political ideas, deal-making, and intrigue. In addition to Juba's first-tier politicians, a stroll through the stone-paved courtyard sometimes meant exchanging *"salam aleykum"* greetings with a Darfur rebel leader, former Sudanese Prime Minister Sadiq al-Mahdi, or leading Islamist Hassan Turabi. Even President Bashir took up at the Grand on his rare overnight visits to the regional capital.

Take a right at the next roundabout and head north to find Logali House, a mainstay of Western expatriates. The three-story white hotel had a tin green roof and was buttressed by mango trees and a vacant lot where plastic bags and refuse held court. Unlike most guest accommodations, Logali was an actual house with white-linened rooms and toilets together under one roof. Accessing the property required traversing some rocky terrain and then passing narrowly between stick-fenced local homes before ascending to a clearing where a half dozen or more land cruisers were inevitably parked. Each of them was splattered with hardened mud, emblazoned with the seals of humanitarian or UN agencies, and displayed the familiar sign of an AK-47 crossed out in red—"no weapons" on board.

Logali had a recessed patio bar offering relief from the midday sun, and flowing pink bougainvillea crept over exterior walls into a small grassy courtyard filled with wooden tables and umbrellas. Its food was edible and its drinks cold. The manager was a thirty-something South African chap called Laurie, who made the rounds in khaki pants and bleached white button-down, checking on guests and advising kitchen staff. Laurie was personable, professional, and committed to his work, but his gelled hair and knowing winks gave away the party boy just beneath the surface.

Most far flung locales in the less-developed world have such a go-to place, where UN officials, aid workers, journalists, and diplomats mingle with other "expats" and wind down with a cocktail after a long and dusty day. They trade stories of doing good or escaping danger, while setting eyes on the most attractive new arrivals from Europe and America. In Juba in the late 2000s, Logali was it. Though overwhelmingly patronized by foreigners with money to spend, the occasional local joined the mix at Logali—the offspring of wealthy elites, those educated abroad who straddled two social spheres, or young entrepreneurs looking to get a piece of huge international humanitarian budgets.

The expats were, as anywhere, a mixed bag. Some were here to pitch in—making small contributions to healthcare infrastructure or clean water or the new government's payroll systems. They brought technical skills, a basic respect for their Southern Sudanese colleagues, and a healthy understanding of the limits of their reach. Others were here for adventure, career advancement, or to fulfill grandiose visions of saving poor and wretched souls. And sometimes the lines blurred.

Thursdays were barbecues and a movie screening, Fridays and Saturdays the patio lights went on and the speakers pumped pop hits from the West. On weekdays the hotel's wireless internet was more reliable than most. Its lunch tables were filled by gossiping diplomats and wire journalists tap-tapping on their laptops, racing to file their daily dispatches. At nearly $300 a crack, the guest rooms upstairs were the most expensive in town, occupied by visiting World Bank officials and well-oiled development contractors, whose daily per diems rivaled what many South Sudanese make in a year. As in other post-conflict societies, the influx of foreign cash had a hugely distorting effect on the economy.

It was at Logali that I drank my first White Bull—the local lager—under the tutelage of a Canadian friend named Dan, who did democracy and governance programming for an American NGO. The national brew "is like a holiday variety pack," Dan jested sarcastically, as the bartender popped caps off the 17oz. bottles, "every one of 'em tastes different." In truth the beer wasn't half bad, and the brewery was one of South Sudan's few private sector hopes outside the oil industry.

The sharp green and yellow labels boasted a likeness of the country's unofficial long-horned mascot and proudly announced itself the "first beer ever produced in Juba." The brewery's South African manager was an asset in promoting foreign investment, but in a symbolic blow to a dangerously one-dimensional economy, the brewery was forced to lay off its local staff and close its doors in 2016 due to the struggling economy and a crippling foreign exchange shortage.

By 2016, the laws of supply and demand had dropped the price of a night's accommodation at Logali to $100, as the number of Juba hotels continued to multiply. The new supply of hotel rooms served the growing number of foreign aid workers, diplomats, and businessmen swarming over the capital after independence. But they also catered to the huge number of South Sudanese from outside Juba, many of them state government officials who became semi-permanent residents, employing official budgets to put up in the capital for weeks and months at a time. Few wanted to pass up the comforts of the developing city or the opportunity to climb higher in the patronage scheme by remaining back home in their constituencies. The game was in Juba.

But during the interim period, as development in Juba exploded for nationals and expats alike, so too grew the gap between the capital city and the rest of Southern Sudan. The vast majority of the population lived in rural areas, and John Garang had captured their attention when he famously spoke of "bringing the towns to the people." It was a core tenet of his SPLM manifesto, which mandated a shift *away* from an "urban-based and centre-focused development paradigm." A rural and decentralized program, he explained, would pre-empt the kind of mass population movements that had crippled other capital cities, leading to mega-slums and a needless deterioration in the quality of life.

It was astute analysis, and by 2016 Juba was well on its way down the path he'd cautioned against. While "towns to the people" became a mainstay of Southern political lexicon, a short trip beyond Juba's city limits revealed how it remained little more than a catchy slogan.

Short-term international experts and visiting Western policymakers rarely ventured beyond the city limits, however, their narrowed aperture reinforcing the hyper-centralization of the government they were advising. Before long, these disparities would increasingly skew perceptions among those in the capital and become a source of resentment outside it. Juba was fast becoming an anomaly.

Two hundred miles north and east of Juba, as the crow flies, is a village called Motot. It is smack dab in the center of the Greater Upper Nile region, deep in Nuer country.

Out here the sky is a giant canvas, too large to see all at once, stretched in every direction until it wraps around the earth's edges. Multi-dimensional clouds—cirrus, cumulus, stratus—have combined forces to cover the canvas in its entirety today. Almost. The sky seems so immense in part because the land is so flat here, and there is so little on it. In Binyavanga Wainaina's satirical essay, "How to Write About Africa," the Kenyan writer lampoons the oft-caricatured depiction of Africa, one that necessarily includes naked-breasted natives, a menu of monkey-brains, and romantic notions of wildlife. "There is always a big sky," he adds, and I chuckle at this particular jab as I stare up at the clouds.

We're a long way from Juba, at least in figurative terms. Motot is only about 200 miles from the capital, a distance a Chevrolet sedan might easily cover in three hours on an American expressway. But you can't get here by motor vehicle; only by foot, or by helicopter, as there are no roads to Motot. The Sobat River, which marks the Ethiopian border to the east, is a full three days' walk. To Juba, under ideal conditions, the walk takes more than a week. Try traversing streams and swampland during the rainy season? The trek may take a month.

There are few vehicles here, except the Land Cruiser owned by "Save the Children," a humanitarian agency operating nearby, and the car sometimes dispatched by the county commissioner on local business. I hop a ride with the local staff from Save the Children. Revving his engine, the driver gathers speed and laughs nervously before plunging through a deep muddy trench, full of rainwater—it's anyone's guess how deep. In no time the sludgy goop rises almost to the level of my passenger-side window, and I can feel the powerful vehicle being pulled sideways. We've all crossed our fingers in jest, hoping not to be swallowed whole. When the rainy season stops, these trenches dry into giant swells of petrified mud, earth ripping at the undercarriage of those vehicles that manage to pass. Today we reach our destination, albeit with a flat rear tire.

The majority of South Sudanese live in rural areas like this one, in villages or smaller seasonal dwellings dotting these vast plains, some subject to the mood of the nearest river, others staking more permanent stead to farm the land. Motot is everywhere and nowhere. Salva Kiir is from here—not literally, but his own village is not unlike this one. Riek Machar is from a village, and so, too, were John Garang and most of South Sudan's biggest names. They have long since gone, but their origins are much the same as the people of Motot.

There are differences, of course, between Motot and villages elsewhere. But much is common between the lives of people here, and those in Dinka, and Shilluk, and Toposa country. Their lives are separate nonetheless, divided by space and time and formidable terrain. There are no roads between them.

As I walk through Motot, chains of smoke rise leisurely above straw-roofed huts, as mothers stoke cooking fires below. These *tukuls* are made of mud and cow dung, with conical roofs of tightly-woven brown thatch. Extended families build their tukuls in groups of three or four, and encircle them with asymmetric fences made from tree branches. Small patches of maize rise up inside the fence; chickens, cows, goats, and young children meander about.

Here the tukuls appear to be wearing skirts, as the last row of straw is left uncut and bows nearly to the ground. The homes are mostly round, and their waist-high doors demand entrants crouch to enter. Corrugated tin, tarpaulins, or other discarded synthetics sometimes supplement the natural materials, particularly in urban areas where the homes of the poorest are less permanent. "How often do you rebuild?" I ask the local staffer from Motot, who is walking with me. "Three or four years," he says, though in other places families sometimes rebuild each season, moving on account of weather patterns, access to water, or to escape inter-ethnic violence.

Sometimes life is intensely green, other times it is barren, the dusty earth and dried grasses making for a monochromatic scheme of sandy brown. Weeks of rain have washed away loose soil on the paths we walk around the village, and so the earth is packed hard, like cement. Two children pitter-patter past, their feet well accustomed. The girl and boy, each with matching shaved heads and beaded necklaces, turn back and strut by us again, masking their curiosity with chins raised proudly. There isn't any school here, and so they deploy their boundless energy wearing paths around the village together with their cattle. Hundreds of them. Thousands of them. The heavy-hooved cows plod paths of most any village, their right-of-way rarely questioned.

It is quiet today. To an outsider, time stands still; there is little cause for hurry. It is comparatively cool, the breeze and cloud cover a welcome respite from the heat, but it is going to rain again any moment. Species of acacia provide shade, as do bushwillows, soap berry, and neem trees, though on the grassy savanna beyond the village the trees are few and far between. In some regions mango trees rise high above homes and river banks, elsewhere there are banana trees, scrub bushes, and elephant grasses towering twelve feet high.

A woman carrying a hollowed-out gourd of milk on her head stops and offers us a drink. Like most women, she is wearing a *taub*—a versatile garment with brightly colored patterns, often draped across the chest and knotted at one shoulder. Two more women in scarves and flowered *taubs* follow, carrying brooms, piles of thatch, and charcoal. A young girl in pink leopard print kneels over a stone, grinding sorghum into meal. Women often do most of the work caring for children, farming the land, collecting firewood and water, cooking meals. Often girls are married young, in exchange for cattle, and Nilotic men sometimes marry multiple wives.

As anywhere, the tug-of-war between tradition and modernity is evident here; cell phone coverage expands, refugees return from abroad with urban sensibilities, and more youth are drawn to a life in Juba. Miles from any urban setting, in these furthest and most isolated reaches of the continent, one can often spot a particularly well-traveled piece of second-hand clothing, a t-shirt labeled "Kent State University," or "New York Giants Football." Women remain second-class in economic and social terms, but norms are slowly changing. Many are advancing in their communities through political activism, church networks, and increasing exposure to urban life. Traditional chiefs and customary law are vital elements of society, but with the advent of the modern state, no matter how fleeting its presence, the old order is struggling to maintain relevance.

A boy with mature features nods as he labors into his family compound, lugging a grimy yellow jerry can—ubiquitous in this part of the world—filled with water from a local stream or nearby well. His meal today will be milk and sorghum. When times are good, and where people have access to markets, meals in rural villages might also include maize, beans, dried fish, fruit, and groundnuts. When times are hard, women boil grasses, leaves, or wild greens into a dull dry paste. Or they go without.

War and the long shadow of underdevelopment are evident here and in villages across the country. And so these residents' stake in the political future and governance of this country is as important as it is for any of the big men in Juba—maybe more important. But for now, it is not something in which they have a voice, or know very much about, beyond their immediate circumstances. Most politics are local.

People know little about implementation of the CPA, or the inside politics of the North-South unity government, or plans for building institutions to govern a nation of their own. They know little about how oil revenues are being spent in their name, or the power games inside the SPLM, or the role of the Americans or the Europeans or the Chinese. What they know they learn by word of mouth from their chief, who gets it from a county commissioner, who gets it from the political chiefs in Juba.

Debates about state sovereignty are not a primary focus here, nor is the latest palace intrigue in Khartoum or Juba. National identity is not something most people wake up in the morning and think about. Independence is relevant, in that it is one potential remedy to the violence and economic neglect they have too long suffered. But it means something different here than it does to those in the center of Juba's political arena.

9

A VERY GREEDY BOY

"Shame on us, Shame on us; we failed to learn the lessons of those African liberation movements that have gone before us."

—Senior SPLM member,
detained December 2013

Something was rotten in the almost-state of South Sudan. Drunk on newly acquired power, the SPLM would go down the path of so many guerrillas-cum-governors, failing to live up to the ideals for which they ostensibly fought. Elevated by their status as custodians of the peace agreement, and milking their reputation as liberators, the ruling clique wielded power as they saw fit and erased any line between their party and the state. While most outsiders paid attention to Sudan's volatile North-South axis, the SPLM's old guard would forcibly suppress dissent at home, siphon millions from state coffers, rig national elections, and circumvent, rather than build, institutions. They had little time for democracy and cracked down on anyone who didn't appreciate it.

The party justified its firm grip on power in part through a prevailing sense of "mission not yet accomplished;" South Sudan would not be free until it got to the referendum. As the interim period approached its climax in 2011, the possibility of a return to war with Sudan was real, and there was no room for error or internal division. The great irony, however, was that the SPLM, in its heavy-handed ways, appeared to be mimicking the very regime in Khartoum that it had so long fought to escape.

The U.S. and other Western supporters, likewise focused on the country's peaceful separation, ignored the ills of a nation-in-waiting. In managing instability in Sudan, a degree of triage was necessary. Preventing a catastrophic new North-South war was the top priority. But what wasn't necessary was turning a blind eye to what was happening inside South Sudan. The two interests were not mutually exclusive.

Rather than beginning to build the kind of democracy it had articulated in its founding documents, the SPLM's top men were presiding over an increasingly concentrated, corrupt, and authoritarian system that would foster not nation-building and cohesion, but division and instability. Meanwhile, blinded by a sometimes emotional attachment to the cause, and having long been in bed with the idealized freedom-fighters, South Sudan's steadfast friends in America remained unwilling, or unable, to confront the ugly truth. Their chosen partners were failing to lay the foundations for a viable state, much less an inclusive democracy.

Gabriel Changson was no such true believer. He was among the SPLM's fiercest critics, and he readily confronted its ugly truths. A former central banker turned opposition politician, with ties to the Nuer militias that historically opposed the SPLA, Changson had long been relegated to the margins of national politics. But where others were co-opted by the increasingly well-fed party elite, Changson never surrendered his contempt for the SPLM.

I first met Changson in 2009, and we convened regularly over the next seven years to debate politics and policy. Regardless of his political stripes, it soon became evident that he was one of the country's few genuinely strategic thinkers, possessing both a national vision and ideas on how to get there. But he was almost always frustrated.

During a 2016 conversation over milky tea and dry biscuits, Changson returns to a critique I heard many times in our encounters over the years. "The CPA delivered the SPLM a monopoly of power

on the South," he begins. "The assumption was that they were liberators and the rest of us were traitors." In a familiar tone of righteous
flabbergast, he then recasts the assumption in a postwar light. "But
are you liberators if you destroy your own country?"

It is a cold June day in Nairobi, the capital of neighboring Kenya
and a kind of second home for many South Sudanese—both those
who grew up in refugee camps, and those elites who frequent the cosmopolitan regional hub for business and pleasure. The gray, overcast
afternoon is normal for this time of year, though it would surprise
Westerners who harbor visions of tropical Africa. Changson and
I share an outdoor picnic table at a local coffee joint attached to one
of Nairobi's many gargantuan shopping malls. A biting breeze comes
and goes as we eagerly await our tea, mixed in the Kenyan way with
lots of creamy milk and sugar.

An indefatigable arguer, Changson wears his mood conspicuously
on his forehead, where deep and animated grooves signal opinions
before his words do. The lines morph into caricatures of surprise and
skepticism, before softening into an inviting smile and signature slow
chuckle, "Hyeh… hyeh… hyeh." Changson sports a boxy African
safari-patterned shirt, and an ill-fitting watch dangles loosely from
his left wrist. His bald head is accented by fuzzy tufts of silver hair
on each side, and he rubs it often. He has high cheekbones and his
facial scarring—lines coupled with at least a hundred raised dots—is
common to his sub-clan of the Nuer.

Conversations in Changson's dilapidated party office were always
substantive, and always turned into sparring matches. He punctuated
debate with a succession of rhetorical questions, driving home a point
with this favorite of dramatic devices. He was a capable listener but
also virtually impossible to interrupt when he was on a roll. Years after
our first meeting, we traded spirited words over the speaker phone in
my State Department office. Upon finishing, I opened my door to find
a gaggle of colleagues assembled outside, wondering if they should be
concerned about an impending physical altercation.

Hailing from a village outside Nasir, Changson was one of many
who had roots in the *Anyanya* movements of the 1960s and 70s and

who later joined a constellation of political organizations and predominantly Nuer militias that had opposed the SPLM. While he prepared for secondary school exams in 1964, the first civil war forced school closures across the South, leaving Changson and his schoolmates few options but to join the *Anyanya* rebels.

"Then what?" I ask, prodding Changson to tell me more about his time in rebellion. But the elder shies away. "That was a long time ago," he says, his body language suggesting it was neither a proud nor a happy period. "Let us talk politics instead."

When a familiar waitress arrives, Changson teases her playfully, in a grandfatherly sort of way, before returning to his criticism of the SPLM. But as we turn to politics, one of his cell phones vibrates on the table. He picks it up without hesitation. Cell phone culture in Africa is decidedly different than in the West, and visitors to pre-independence South Sudan had to learn its own peculiar conventions. Unlike in the West, phone calls were very often answered in the middle of a meeting. Sometimes lengthy conversations would ensue, in a mixture of Arabic, English, Dinka, or other national tongue. Other times a call was answered simply to say "I'm in a meeting, I'll call you back." Any self-respecting government official carried at least three cell phones, sometimes four or five. The quantity of lines and frequency of calls received connoted a kind of social status, a currency that distinguished the politically relevant from the not.

But the real reason for carrying so many phones was technical. Before 2011, it was difficult to place a call from one service provider to another—calls simply would not connect between networks, a reflection of rudimentary infrastructure and extremely limited coverage. Thus, a government minister's business card was crowded with numbers from four or five networks—Gemtel (prefix 047), Zain (091), Viva cell (095), Sudani (012), or MTN (092). SIM cards were almost a fashion accessory. Those outside the capital city might also have a satellite telephone number (+88), which remained the only means of communication across large swaths of the country.

Also unlike in the West, where cell phone numbers of the super-elite are kept within tightly held circles, the numbers of the most influential government officials were not hard to come by. Their digits circulated among colleagues, subordinates, extended families, and hometown communities, as well as foreign businessmen, journalists, and anyone who wanted some face time. When in a pinch, asking a seasoned *boda boda* driver for the number of the deputy finance minister was worth a shot.

A peculiar call-answering protocol was one byproduct of this numerical ubiquity. I first encountered the practice late one evening during a discussion with then foreign minister Deng Alor as we slouched in flimsy plastic chairs outside the Juba Grand Hotel. One of his phalanx of phones would ring, illuminating the darkness with electronic blue, and upon identifying the correct device, Deng would squint at the screen to make out the number. If he did not recognize it, he would pick up the call, silently, and wait for the other party to identify themselves. Once the caller's identity was confirmed, he would break into a hearty greeting—"*Kefyak, Inta kwesi? Inshallah kweyas hamdullilah.*" But if the identifying caller was either unknown or unwanted, he would say nothing, terminate the call, and return the phone to the plastic tabletop among its brethren. It happened another half-dozen times that night, in exactly this manner.

It was a common practice for any high-profile figure, and a newcomer unfamiliar with this peculiar protocol could be forgiven for repeating a confused pattern with furrowed brow: place a call, hear it be answered, say, "uh, hello... *hello?*" into the silence, and then "click" as the recipient disengaged. Once I was privy to the rules of the game and had established relationships, I would call and immediately announce myself into the silence: "Hi, it's Zach from Crisis Group calling."

As Juba expanded rapidly in the pre-independence period and growing international attention focused on the emergent capital, the currency of a broad social network and the availability of cell phone numbers appeared to inversely impact government efficiency. More and more direct calls to ministers from deal-seeking entrepreneurs, international media outlets, expanding aid agencies, and growing patronage networks amounted to a huge time suck. Having long sought attention for their cause, ministers didn't suddenly adopt new approaches to time management. Meetings were more regularly interrupted, waiting rooms more crowded, and ministry staff seeking the boss's guidance were edged out.

Today, Changson has no pressing agenda, as he's been out of a job since the war's onset in late 2013. As he discusses developments in Juba with his latest caller, cell phone pressed hard to ear, I sip tea and watch Kenyan mall shoppers come and go.

⸺

Gabriel Changson began his professional career at the Central Bank of Sudan in the early 1980s, during which time he was offered a USAID scholarship to study economics at Duke University in North Carolina. He remains a proud "Blue Devil" and remembers the period fondly, one during which his wife gave birth to "an American son."

He returned to Sudan and served in various Central Bank postings before becoming politically active. Following the 1991 SPLA split, he made common cause with Riek Machar and eventually helped him launch a new opposition party in 1997. But when Riek returned to the SPLA in 2002, Changson remained outside. He maintained a small subsidiary of the political party he'd helped fashion and soon returned to Juba himself. The SPLM government appointed him to several cabinet positions between 2006 and 2013, a token opposition representative with technical skills but negligible political influence.

While many opposition figures shared Changson's views, few were as articulate about the perils of SPLM domination and the dangers of blind support from the West. Where others feared their words would come back to bite them, Changson was unafraid and his criticism unabashed. He railed against the biased nature of the CPA talks, the exclusion of anyone but the SPLM from the table, and a continuing pro-SPLM bias among Western diplomats.

With the CPA's establishment of a Southern regional government in 2005, the SPLM dominated South Sudan's political arena. It observed little separation between party and state, spent government revenue as it liked, and muzzled dissenting voices. And though the SPLM had long spouted vitriolic rhetoric against Khartoum's centralization of power, Changson saw the liberation movement simply adopting the tactics of their Northern oppressors, and using their privileged position to entrench themselves indefinitely. And he wasn't the only one to notice.

Changson represented an aggrieved minority that complained the American-backed CPA process had unduly elevated the SPLM and sowed the seeds of one-party rule. They argued that the accord's power-sharing formulas—which mandated majority SPLM control of the executive and legislative branches—gave the party unfair advantage and distorted the true nature of political demographics in the South. And because the executive arm of the new Southern government was so dominant, and the SPLM had been anointed one of two "partners" in the CPA now governing the country, its actual power was even greater than it appeared on paper.

"The NCP and the SPLM were the biggest political and military forces in the North and the South, respectively," explained one diplomat involved in the peace talks, "but they weren't alone." The two parties had dictated the peace, but "neither of them had a legitimate mandate from their people." Their power had come through the barrel of a gun. Rather than allow others into the talks, each group rightly assessed that a bilateral deal would strengthen their positions at home. The new money springing from wealth-sharing arrangements would then concretize the SPLM's control of the South, and put distance between itself and any would-be challengers. The internationally backed accord would also afford the two parties special stature in the global arena—legitimacy gained from the outside, not from within.

But Changson could do little about it. His opposition party, like all the others, was weak. Few of them had attracted substantial followings or enjoyed any name recognition outside of Juba, and limited membership meant a limited role in government. The SPLM wasn't helping, either. It used the apparatus of the state to ensure no serious challengers emerged.

Critics also argued the party monopoly was hindering institution-building, as government positions were allocated not on the basis of merit or relevant experience, but on the basis of tribe and party loyalty. The SPLM was using the government as a massive patronage pyramid to the detriment of a functioning civil service. Much-needed technocrats from outside the party were marginalized, their skills unused or lost to emigration. Others who expressed dissent were smeared as Northern collaborators, or harassed by SPLA forces. In time, the same went for journalists who penned critical columns or asked insubordinate questions.

Changson and his colleagues also resented a prevailing narrative that "the SPLM was solely responsible for 'the struggle'" and later for Southern independence. It was "a line swallowed whole by the Americans," he fumes, his words coated in chagrin. Surely the SPLM was the dominant force in realizing both, but outsiders were insulted by the lack of wider recognition. Many others had also fought for justice and equality, some long before the SPLA existed. He took it as yet another slight in an increasingly distorted history narrated by its victors. After all, he says, "While we and many other South Sudanese had advocated independence for decades, those of John Garang were busy pursuing what? A unified 'New Sudan.'" Though Garang always had the separation option in his back pocket, critics saw his SPLM co-opting the secession narrative only after he died.

In all this, the aging and disgruntled politician explains, the SPLM's foreign champions were complicit. Not only had the United States midwifed the CPA and endorsed the SPLM's exclusive participation in the talks, Washington's continuing political and financial backing was emboldening an already unaccountable SPLM and eroding hopes for multi-party democracy. Meanwhile, the SPLM vanguard continued to travel extensively in the West during the period, where its many friends welcomed visits, pulled strings on their behalf, and reminisced about the days of struggle.

One second-generation SPLM apparatchik told me he left the party after becoming "disillusioned with the U.S. relationship." He was sickened by the idea that it was "fashionable in America, you know, to have my own personal freedom fighter." Washington, he said, had been "listening to a small group of 'holy sons'" and catering to their interests. "The Americans helped to individualize this country," through preferential treatment and friendships, "at the expense of the people of South Sudan."

Between the end of the war with Khartoum in 2005 and South Sudan's independence in 2011, Washington and its Western partners—on whom the SPLM was hugely dependent—would give the movement a free pass to shape the emerging state in its own image. In more than a few of our discussions over the years, Changson delivered what would turn out to be a strikingly accurate prognosis: "The international community has been feeding a greedy boy... once that boy grows strong, he will be difficult to change. You will not be able to fight him."

The picnic table vibrates again, rattling my empty tea cup and saucer. As Changson takes another call from South Sudan, I hear the reference "Dr. Riek" several times amid his mashup of Nuer and Arabic.

Changson was a man in the middle, caught between worlds and an uncomfortable set of compromises, and it showed. He had taken up with Riek in articulating an alternative to the SPLM in the 1990s, only to be frustrated by Riek's return to the SPLM. Possessing neither his colleague's stature nor popular appeal, he was resigned to continue working with Riek to advance their shared agenda. But he was also constantly frustrated by a sense that the man was driven by narrow self-interest. It felt as though the agenda was always dispensable. My tablemate puts the cell phone down and can't help falling back into a familiar diatribe about Riek's political missteps.

Changson's relationship with SPLM governments was another uncomfortable compromise, and he was sometimes criticized for being in league with them. Like any other member of the educated elite, he coveted senior jobs and the influence that came with them. In a country with no jobs, no one would turn down a cabinet post. The ministerial appointments served his own ego and career, and paid dividends for his ailing party, his region, even his home community in

Nasir. But he was also one of the few who could de-link these paro-chial interests from the larger vision of building a nation.

Our waitress returns, and after we order another round of tea, I challenge the veteran politico. "You have such virulent criticism for the SPLM, but some people say you've worked very closely with them..." Having been down this road before, I know I'll get a rise out of him. On cue, he gives me a "you should know better" look mixed with faux contempt, as he sucks air across his teeth. In such an underdeveloped political system, Changson was conscious that he could neither wield influence nor effect change from outside govern-ment. He scoffs, however, at the notion that he was ever co-opted.

Changson is deeply principled in accounts of his own affairs and likes to back them up with evidence, so he proudly recounts his most principled stand. While he knows I'll call "bullshit" to any embroi-dering, this story has been corroborated elsewhere. In 2006 the SPLM leadership appointed him caretaker minister of finance, as they were desperate for a competent technocrat to clean up a mess made by a dubious party acolyte. By all accounts, Changson did help the Min-istry correct course, and the SPLM leadership offered to name him officially to the influential post—"on one condition." He pauses for effect. "They told me I had to convert to SPLM."

"I know, you refused," I say, pre-empting the end of the story, but he will finish it anyway. "I refused," he says, exhaling a theatrical puff of disgust.

The man in the middle also felt the frustration experienced by some Southern intellectuals who had received higher education abroad and found themselves caught between two very different worlds. They had tasted modern societies and advanced economies, which in turn nurtured a particularly poignant sense of their own country's under-development. They were frustrated by the state of their country and their people, disillusioned by the disparity between the politics of their birthplace and the modern institutions of the West. They believed they could apply their skills to help close the gap at home. And while their individual contributions were invaluable, they often felt sucked under by the ineptitude, nepotism, and waste surrounding them.

Their disappointment was born of hope and idealism about their country, but it manifested itself in different forms. Some directed their frustration at foreigners. Others, including Changson, shared disparaging judgments about backward colleagues with Westerners like me, which was always an uncomfortable experience. It seemed a misplaced search for an outlet—someone from the developed world who would understand and validate their frustrations. But I would awkwardly change the subject—an instinct really, as surely no comfort or good could come from a privileged foreigner also disparaging the locals.

On occasion, when overcome by feelings of futility, Changson would foist responsibility on the West, which he believed to be more capable. "You people," he would say, leveraging foreign diplomats to the hilt. "You must force changes" in the SPLM and in the country. "You must save us from ourselves." It was precisely the foreign dependency for which he criticized the SPLM, a plea born of frustration over the dysfunctional state of the South's institutions.

While in government and after he resigned, Changson flirted with the time-honored practice of advancing local political interests through military means. He was undoubtedly attuned to the many splinter rebellions agitating in his home state in the latter half of the interim period, and to the potential bargaining power therein. The minister was well aware of the currency of violence in his country, and he seemed to struggle with knowledge that it often seemed the only way to gain an edge or advance an agenda.

When the new war erupted in 2013, Changson joined Riek and the predominantly Nuer opposition, just as he had in the 1990s. He again became one of Riek's senior political advisers and openly advocated the overthrow of Salva's government. He surely wanted to carve out space for himself, as few had singularly pure motives. But more importantly, he saw the conflict as the opportunity to finally dislodge the SPLM that had run his country into the ground.

By 2015, familiar frustrations returned, and Changson publicly announced a break with Riek and the formation of his own splinter party. Before he did, we had several contentious telephone conversations in which I argued that despite his legitimate concerns about both Riek and the direction of the peace process, he had a better chance of advancing reforms by being at the table than by splitting the opposition. But he refused to countenance further participation. He believed Riek was again putting himself above broader Nuer interests, and he was angered that the peace deal was heading not toward political change but toward putting old SPLM wine in new bottles. He was right, and it was a principled position. But it didn't do much good.

Changson and a youthful sidekick now spend most of their days in this Nairobi cafe drinking tea, working the cellphones, keeping abreast of developments on the ground, and trying to grow his movement by luring away both political operators and local warlords. But sitting here in the recesses of this shopping mall parking lot, he's loath to admit that, for now, he's mostly irrelevant.

"See you next time, old man," I say, wrapping up our conversation with an extended handshake.

"Hyeh… hyeh… hyeh," he chuckles, then bids me farewell and relocates to a new table inside the cafe. On either side of him sit laptop-tapping Kenyan university students, visiting European safari-goers, and gabbing young professionals from Nairobi's coffee-drinking classes. They know nothing about the man in the middle.

The SPLM had a history of maintaining cohesion by relying on "force rather than persuasion," wrote one notable historian of Sudan's wars. The movement's militarized culture and hierarchical tendencies had since bled into its governance in the post-war period. Though South-erners were increasingly intent on secession, getting to the referendum and avoiding new conflict would not be easy. Until the votes were cast and independence assured, "mission not yet accomplished" remained the prevailing leitmotif in the story of South Sudan. But in time, the continuing "struggle" would clash with increasing desires for democracy at home—which was, after all, what the liberation struggle was supposed to have been about.

Given Khartoum's long and successful history of dividing South-erners, the rationalization of a heavy-handed approach could be understood, an unsavory means to the shared end. But for Changson and those outside the SPLM, it became an all-too-convenient justifi-cation for the party leadership to do whatever it wanted, regardless of its relevance to North-South politics or the goal of independence.

And yet no matter how aggravated some Southerners became—and aggravated they were—the shared desire for self-determination trumped all else. "Those of Changson" swallowed hard and filed their grievances away for later. Internal matters, they rationalized, could be addressed once the vote resolved the South's future status. "No one wants to rock the boat," Changson had told me in 2009, "until we reach the other shore."

But by 2010, the SPLM itself nearly capsized the boat. Taking the patience of its population for granted, the party usurped more power, scrapped a constitutional process, and rigged election nominations—sparking anger both inside and outside the SPLM. If party hardliners weren't careful, it seemed, their coercive style might undermine the very power and Southern unity they were so intent on preserving.

During Sudan's elections in the spring of 2010, the SPLM played conservatively on the national level, appeasing Khartoum in hopes of smoothing the way to the referendum vote Juba really cared about. But at home in the South, the party could not help itself. Feeling auda-cious and untouchable, the SPLM used the polls to reinforce its own majority position. It employed state organs to interfere in campaigns, intimidate opposition candidates, and muzzle dissent within its own ranks. Some of the SPLM's unpopular incumbents even intercepted telephone calls of opponents and manipulated communication signals to advance their campaigns.

The party's political bureau bypassed its own nomination system, ignoring local primaries and naming its preferred candidates instead. And where that wasn't enough, they rigged the vote. Allegations of fraud prompted standoffs and led to armed insurrections in three states. The SPLM then reverted to what it knew best: force. Their heavy-handed responses endangered civilians and threatened further polarization between ethnic groups and their political leaders.

Rather than preventing the kind of internal fractures that would play into the hands of enemies in Khartoum, the SPLM's greedy conduct itself seemed the greatest threat to peace, independence, and its own popularity. The party's handling of the election was an unmistakable signal of the dangerous trends it was establishing at home. But those waving red flags were ignored. Standing in a voting center alongside Salva Kiir, U.S. Congressman Donald Payne called the elections "a great day for democracy."

Nine months later, on the eve of the January 2011 referendum on self-determination, the SPLM had failed to learn the lessons of squeezing too tightly. It was the kind of dominance emblematic of the politically insecure or the politically unaccountable. Or in this case, both.

Just before the referendum vote, the SPLM called all political parties and civil society members together, attempting to patch things up. Or so it seemed. They offered those at the margins a role in shaping a constitution for the state that was to emerge, and agreed that the new South Sudan should be governed by an inclusive transitional government. But the moment referendum ballots were cast, "they went back on their word," complains an exasperated Onyoti Adigo, leader of South Sudan's decidedly small minority in parliament. The promise of political unity had evaporated, and when Onyoti and others protested, "it was, 'no thanks, we're in charge.'"

Later that month, Salva appointed what was meant to be an "inclusive" committee to revise the constitution, but it included only one non-SPLM member, Gabriel Changson, who refused to participate in the charade. Observers joked that committee proceedings amounted to two SPLM ministers simply locking themselves in a room with a crate of White Bull beer and re-writing the laws of the land as they fancied. Whether or not beer actually flowed, that is roughly what transpired, and the constitution these two party loyalists produced included an extraordinary expansion of powers for the sitting SPLM president, Salva Kiir. Rather than articulate a vision for a country now free to pursue its democratic potential, the SPLM's two hatchet men used the exercise to consolidate one-party rule and curry personal favor with the president.

Opposition parties again cried foul, but David stood no chance against Goliath. Six months later, on the eve of independence, the SPLM leadership rammed their unilateral constitution through parliament, a mostly pro-forma exercise in an institution it had never taken seriously. It didn't help that most members of parliament were lower down the SPLM pecking order than those in the cabinet. These second-tier party men enjoyed salaries and SUVs but were expected to toe the line rather than exercise any actual oversight. When they didn't, Salva and the party brass threatened to kick them to the curb.

But Onyoti, the minority leader, was intent on upholding his mandate. He held up the vote on the SPLM's constitution, citing concerns about transparency and an increasingly dangerous concentration of power. A few hours later, an army unit showed up at his office and promptly knocked his front teeth out.

Onyoti and his assistants were pummeled with fists and boots, dumped in the back of a pickup truck, and driven to an army intelligence facility where the beating resumed. It wasn't the first time. A year earlier, when Onyoti's minority party was accused of fomenting unrest, a phalanx of soldiers had arrived at his home to arrest him. The senior parliamentarian was stuffed in an overcrowded cell where, he says, he and 40 other detainees were unable to sit down and had only a bucket in which to urinate. "To get oxygen," he recalls, "we had to lie down and suck air from under the door." Asked why such behavior went unchecked, Onyoti sighs. "*Aye*, the American government did not understand the *real* SPLM."

The SPLM seemed politically tone deaf, or simply didn't care. They were disenfranchising opponents, sparking rebellions, and setting back the long-term project of democracy. What were its leaders thinking? If the new South was going to become a viable state, its leading party would have to find a better way to govern. Democracy wasn't going to materialize overnight; the process was going to be long and slow in any case, but the least the SPLM could do was not make things worse.

Dissent bubbled inside the party as well, though it remained below the surface. Changson explained that there was a shortage of trust among party cadres, and thus a structural inhibition against reform. "Any internal challenge or proposed reform," even if intended to better equip the party to govern, "would simply be reported to the boss," he said. In another of his familiar zingers, Changson would often ask rhetorically, "How can you expect them to run a democracy, when they do not even practice democracy inside their own party?"

The rot inside South Sudan was deeply worrying. But independence in 2011 would present another opportunity for a fresh start: the struggle would be over, the mission accomplished. It would take everything the party and its leading lights could muster to pull off what would be an extraordinarily difficult transition to independent government. The SPLM would need to get its own house in order, dismantle its top-down military culture, and trade coercion for something more sustainable. It would also need a new vision for the future, and a new organizing principle, if it was going to win popular trust. Failing to adjust would risk recreating the kind of hyper-centralized and unstable state from which South Sudan had finally managed to extricate itself.

~

"The SPLM was anything but democratic," I say, before detailing the record of a liberation movement that had lost its way. It's 2016, more than two years since South Sudan's collapse. I'm continuing the political autopsy, and across the table now sits the SPLM's former secretary-general, Pagan Amum. I am expecting a fierce rebuttal to my provocative opening.

"Yes, it's true," Pagan says instead, to my surprise. I didn't have to battle with him at all, he just comes right out with it. "We failed to transform."

Such an admission would never have been forthcoming before the country's unraveling, particularly from the party's chief message-man.

But since the party imploded in 2013, conversations with him and other SPLM figures reveal a willingness to acknowledge what they had long suppressed. Some are ready to own the failures, others to acknowledge them while pointing fingers elsewhere. The secretary-general shares much of Gabriel Changson's analysis, and even admits, "It is true. Those of Changson were often on the receiving end of what the SPLM was doing."

Coupling hindsight with the heart-wrenching realities of the country's undoing, I am hoping to revisit the party's failure in a new light. Pagan's surprise answer is encouraging. Piecing together this complicated and incomplete picture requires the wisdom of its own party leaders, of its most ardent critics, and of ordinary South Sudanese. I put the question to each of them: Why did the SPLM fail?

Three answers emerge: the military character of the movement, its weak links with its own population, and—most consequentially—a battle for the inheritance of the SPLM after the death of John Garang. None of these dynamics are new, but the narratives are gaining new depth as a result of time, critical distance, and the re-ordering of the country's political landscape. And until the SPLM's party dynamics helped set the country aflame in 2013, most of its foreign friends had either ignored them or were entirely in the dark.

First, John Garang's movement was highly militaristic, but it lacked political orientation. "It was never a political movement, and it never had a political architecture," huffs one disillusioned former member. Conscious of the mistakes and internal divisions that had beset earlier Southern rebellions, Garang was not about to repeat history. He resolved to maintain unity by keeping a firm—and singular—grip on the fledgling movement. After forcefully wresting control of the SPLA in its early days, Garang sidelined rival politicians, established a dominant military ethos, and dealt ruthlessly with internal dissent. "There were assassinations left and right" one former American diplomat tells me, who was deeply familiar with Garang and the movement in its contentious early days. "All of that violence, he was part of all of it."

Supporters argue that Garang's SPLM manifesto and vision were democratic, and that his forceful rule was a temporary means to a lasting end. But critics like Changson don't buy it. The language was lofty, he argues, but the icon didn't build the groundwork to support this political agenda. Garang was a visionary, and his ideas were revolutionary in the realm of Sudanese politics, but he didn't develop organized political cadres or train a class of capable administrators. Instead, he concentrated power and shaped policies in a manner to avoid internal threats. "That is why African movements fail," Changson says, "and the SPLM did the same."

Another outspoken critic later wrote that decision-making structures under Dr. John were a "glittering façade," behind which he would direct the movement "alone and unquestioned... while at the same time hoodwinking the world" into believing it was a democratic operation. The "so-called" Political Military High Command "almost never met," he says. "But somehow, Garang would announce its decisions over the radio." As power became concentrated almost entirely in his hands, Garang would become increasingly unaccountable and "surrounded by sycophants." Many began to bristle at his authoritarianism, but Garang managed to evade a reckoning; he diluted demands for reform while keeping attention on the external enemy in Khartoum.

That external enemy had presented a call to collective action. Cadres from all three regions, and from most of South Sudan's tribes, had signed up. Their collective opposition to Khartoum moderated regional and ethnic identities, and allowed those from a hodgepodge of backgrounds and ideological perspectives to combine forces: educated and illiterate, Marxists and free-market capitalists, unionists and separatists, secular atheists and devout Christians. But once the goal was achieved, the common denominator was gone, and nothing had been cultivated to take its place.

And so when it came time to govern, the party was ill-equipped. "Democracy will not just fall from heaven," the critic complains, "like we'll suddenly become democratic overnight? This is our biggest problem. We never had a democratic culture. We think that the gun is everything."

Even some of Dr. John's closest supporters now cop to his "dictatorial" ways, ascribing their party's ultimate failure, in part, to the ethos of the movement he built. "The power must come from the top," Changson explains of the SPLM's ethos, drawing a triangular structure in the air with his index fingers. "It is the culture that continues today," he says. "Salva, Riek, and the others have since graduated from the same school."

Garang did possess worthy ideas on education, administrative systems, and nation-building, but the war came first, and so did control of the tool he'd created to wage it. Despite his respect for the late guerrilla leader, the former American diplomat with inside knowledge of the movement agrees. "Garang was busy manipulating all these foreigners to put pressure on Sudan... he wasn't building up anything inside the country. He felt he could do that later." The official slows down for emphasis: "He was – not – working – on an organization... *At all.* So when he died, there was nothing left."

<hr />

The second explanation for the SPLM's failure was its lack, during the days of struggle, of a meaningful connection with its own population. It was no "people's" army, but derived legitimacy and fueled its rebellion instead through foreign support. "We were not self-reliant. We were spoiled—we had everything we needed form the start; guns, food, supporters," one founding member summarizes, "so we never had a relationship with the people." For all its Marxist rhetoric, the SPLA did little to cultivate the civilian population in furtherance of its own revolutionary cause.

Neither people, nor economic or social development, were ever at the center of the SPLA's agenda; they were secondary to military objectives and the pursuit of power. Worse yet, when the SPLA didn't get what they needed from external sources, they preyed on their fellow South Sudanese. Divisions and deep resentment were sown in the early days across Nuer, Equatorian, and other Southern communities through violent confrontations with an often predatory, and predominantly Dinka, SPLA.

Emergency food aid was delivered primarily by foreign NGOs, but rather than help to distribute it, SPLA fighters often took it for themselves. The SPLA was meanwhile receiving logistical and military support from neighboring countries, and its leading men were being feted in regional capitals. In time they enjoyed social, political, and business connections in Kenya, Uganda, Ethiopia, and further afield, as well as strong moral and political support from Washington and European capitals.

Though external support helped the SPLA achieve some military successes in the 1990s, they were not formidable enough to displace the Khartoum government. The war was unwinnable. And so they eventually needed the region and the West to deliver a peace deal in 2005. Implementation was outsourced too, explains the party critic, "Every now and then we would run to the Americans for help when things were stuck; 'please mediate, and oh by the way don't forget this is our position.'" The plight of South Sudan's people had helped earn the SPLM many supporters around the globe. But it also meant a rebel vanguard that was oriented less and less toward its people, and more and more to its friends and supporters abroad, who appeared willing to back them at any price.

Sitting in the back of a noisy hotel bar in 2016, a senior African diplomat with a long history on South Sudan laments the foundational assumptions made by regional and international backers. In between sips of cold draught beer, he articulates for me, and for himself, a belief that those assumptions made it possible for SPLM leaders "not to have any sense of accountability." The diplomat was no romanticizing "true believer," but he was from a post-colonial class that understood the injustices being done to their brothers and sisters in Southern Sudan, and had given the SPLM the benefit of the doubt. They were political peers and, in many cases, became his friends.

"They are very savvy, they were telling us exactly what we wanted to hear," he recalls. "They went to the same schools we did, they mastered the language and the narrative, and so we felt we understood each other." His words on this suffocatingly humid evening are an indictment of disappointing friends, but they are also an exercise in self-criticism—something many in the West are not yet ready to undertake. We split a pile of napkins and wipe sweat from our respective foreheads. "I think these guys... they are a diaspora elite," he continues. "No roots! No roots at all... they rode the wave of international legitimacy rather than that of their people." He takes another sip of beer and shakes his head silently, the disappointment written all over his face.

The third and most immediate cause of South Sudan's collapse was party factionalism; John's Garang's death in 2005 sparked a vicious battle for the inheritance of the SPLM. "For the next eight years, it was a fight to control Salva," says one senior official, and through him the direction of the emergent South. The war that followed is often thought of as the product of a power struggle between Salva and Riek. The latter's prominence and presidential ambitions, the devastating legacy of 1991, and a history of Dinka-Nuer violence all help to inform this narrative of a battle between two visible strongmen. But South Sudan's unmaking cannot be understood in these terms alone. An accurate rendering of the SPLM crisis, and the war it ignited, requires a wider lens.

Three camps vied for control of the decapitated movement between 2005 and 2013: "those of Garang," "those of Bahr al Ghazal," and "those of Riek." While individual positions and alliances shifted with time and circumstance, these three blocs persisted throughout the eight-year stretch, each maneuvering for influence under the banner of the SPLM.

Garang's immediate disciples—Pagan Amum, Deng Alor, Nhial Deng, and a handful of others—enjoyed the boss's personal confidence and had been entrusted to negotiate the CPA. They harbored no doubt that they, as Pagan says, were the SPLM's "true founders and legitimate heirs." Garang's men had remained wary of Salva since the 2004 "Yei incident" in which he gave voice to criticisms of Garang, and believed the movement was being hijacked by charlatans. But, more importantly, those of Garang—the party intellectuals—found Salva parochial and uneducated, and so saw him as an interim figure rather than a rightful successor to their exalted guru.

By contrast, this group was educated, cosmopolitan, and enjoyed access and personal relationships with leaders around the African continent and in the West. Though they would position themselves tactically and make inroads with Salva, their true colors were ill-concealed. Detractors resented their privileged access and presumptive air of self-importance, and derisively branded the political orphans "the Garang Boys." In time, they would be seen as power-hungry and corrupt, and skeptics scoffed at their supposedly honorable pursuit of saving the movement from vultures.

A second faction, "those of Bahr al Ghazal," included prominent politician, intellectual, and businessman Bona Malual. He and Garang were two of the most prominent sons of Southern Sudan, and they had long quarreled with one another. Malual had always believed that the younger Garang could do the fighting, but should leave the business of governing to established Southern politicians (i.e. himself). Their rift was substantive but also underpinned by an ethno-regional rivalry between their respective sections of the Dinka. A critic of Garang's management style and his politics, Malual distrusted the ascendant "Garang boys" by association. Malual had been a fixture of Sudanese national politics for decades, was well connected in Khartoum, and often critical of Garang. Opponents thus branded him an NCP collaborator, and perceived his faction—fairly or unfairly—as doing Khartoum's bidding.

When Garang died, those of Bahr al Ghazal circled the wagons around native son Salva Kiir. Stoking fears, the clique urged Salva to consolidate his personal control and secure Bahr al Ghazal's pre-eminence. They pushed Salva to sideline the Garang Boys, and he did. Some of them were removed from influential positions, others left the country for an extended hiatus abroad.

Believing their party had been "taken hostage," the Garang faction would mount a successful counter-coup in 2007. They re-asserted their position in Salva's government and engineered the dismissal of key Bahr al Ghazal surrogates. But the tide would turn yet again after independence, when these surrogates rallied to Salva's side and returned the favor.

The SPLM soap opera would play itself out over the course of the interim period and beyond, eroding internal trust and coherence. It was hard to organize for the future amid a constant tug-of-war. And that wasn't all; a third character was twisting the plot.

The third faction, "those of Riek," was predominantly Nuer. It included many of those who had followed Riek during the first devastating power struggle in 1991. In times of crisis, Riek also enjoyed the support of disenfranchised Nuer communities outside the SPLM. Their regional militias had been nominally integrated into the army at the end of the war, but had no love for, or allegiance to, any of the SPLM factions. Many didn't have any particular affinity for Riek either, or his political ambitions, but his national stature meant he was best placed to advance Nuer interests.

While Riek's No. 2 position made him a contender to succeed Garang, many in the upper echelons of the SPLM would rather die than see the old traitor prevail. Though he had picked the first party fight in 1991, Riek was sometimes an outsider in this second-generation party feud. Riek himself characterized his faction as comparatively "silent," one that offset, and sometimes even mediated between, the two feuding factions.

For all its volatility, the internal party fracas was kept mostly behind closed doors. From the outside, the SPLM may have appeared a coherent unit—its symbols, flags, and rhetoric distracting from the cancer within. But in this toxic atmosphere, governance suffered. Amid such corrosive feuding, the SPLM could hardly advance a coherent vision or program. It desperately needed to transition from a liberation army to a governing party, and to deliver on the development agenda for which Southern Sudan's people had waited so long. But the SPLM was fraying from within, consumed by its personalities and their struggle for power.

Once, during a particularly tumultuous 2008 party convention, the factionalism sucked up all the oxygen. When the meeting ended, the long-time critic of Garang and his glittering façade had had enough. He resolved to form his own party, penning a manifesto that captured just how rudderless the South Sudanese project had become:

In ten days of meetings the party never discussed a single position paper on the economy, or foreign policy or elections or anything at all. This is extreme political bankruptcy. Little wonder it failed to deliver nationally or regionally in Southern Sudan... The whole ten days were spent arguing who should or should not be removed from his party leadership position.

As the CPA era was coming to a close, and with independence on the horizon, it was time for the SPLM to mark a new chapter in its evolution. For anyone paying close attention, the writing was on the wall; without significant course correction there would be trouble in a new Republic of South Sudan.

Washington and other friendly capitals also needed to re-calibrate their relationship with the SPLM to reflect new realities, the changing political landscape, and the demand for greater democratic space both inside the party and out. This wasn't just a matter of flowery democratic aspirations, it was a fundamental question of stability.

Though foreign friends were aware of tensions inside the party and out, domestic squabbles took a back seat to the larger North-South agenda. There were bigger fish to fry—the elections, the referendum, and North-South talks, without which there would be no independent republic at all, much less discussions about its political culture. There was truth in this rationale, but there were also serious ills to be confronted if the emergent republic was ever to stand on its own two feet, and looking the other way was helping prepare it to fail.

It was time to stop treating the SPLM as friends or underdogs and start dealing with them as leaders of a sovereign state—on the basis of interests and objectives. This required a cultural shift. The SPLM needed not a chummy pal, but a true friend, someone to tell them that they didn't own the place, and it was time to get their act together. With the party dependent on its foreign patrons to help deliver the referendum and its ultimate independence prize, American leverage would never be greater.

10

DRINKING THE MILK

"Once we got to power, we forgot what we fought for and began to enrich ourselves at the expense of our people."
—Letter from President Salva Kiir, May 3, 2012

Under their beds, literally!" shouts James, exasperated. "Millions of dollars in actual cash, kept under their beds!" he says, laughing in disbelief at the near-cartoonish practice. "Ministers, officers, they'd stuff the cash into briefcases and travel with diplomatic cover to Kenya, Uganda, wherever." James (not his real name) is South Sudanese and a former official at a prominent Kenyan bank in Juba. Fake contracts, bogus companies, double-dipped invoices, and eye-popping kickback schemes; James can barely contain himself. He reels off one example of corruption and then another, and the words he's belching out are beginning to trip over one other, as he's got so much to say.

Muzzled for years by an unwritten code of silence, by 2016 he feels free to speak. By now his country has all but fallen apart, and extreme corruption was among the reasons for its collapse. "What's your guess?" I ask, "How much do you think was stolen over the past decade?" But James cuts me off before I finish, "Billions and billions," he says, shaking his head and explaining that the financial system was so out of whack it would be impossible to know for sure.

Corruption nearly devoured the state before it was born. Starting in 2005 with the signing of the CPA, petrodollars began to swell Juba's coffers, ultimately amounting to an estimated $12 billion in revenue over six years (estimates vary widely). For two decades, the SPLM had fought a guerrilla campaign from "the bush," living off the land and what was offered by—or taken from—the local population. But the peace accord's wealth-sharing provision changed everything: oil wasn't a major source of revenue for South Sudan's economy; it *was* the economy. And soon it would be a curse.

In the ensuing years, the goat herder in rural Bahr al Ghazal remained without electricity or running water, but the army chief purchased a mansion in Melbourne, Australia, that boasted a home theater, sauna, and two swimming pools. Like 70 percent of their fellow citizens, the goat herder and his wife remained illiterate, and their children had no primary school to attend. But the children of SPLM elites wore designer clothing and drove Range Rovers to premier schools in upscale London neighborhoods and leafy Nairobi suburbs.

Corruption was certainly not unfamiliar in Africa, but the circumstances seemed a particularly egregious betrayal of the SPLM's history and its stated ideals. South Sudan was fortunate to enjoy ample new revenue, and the peace deal meant the long-suffering population might finally catch a break after decades of pain and sacrifice. What could explain a collective heist of this scale, in a country so poor, neglected, and in need of development?

<hr>

American oil giant Chevron discovered oil in Sudan in 1979. In a twist of geological fate that would bind the country's two disparate halves, many of the most promising deposits were discovered underneath the boundary that divided North and South. Foreshadowing Khartoum's plans to exploit the oil, the government promptly changed the Dinka name of one new concession area to the corresponding Arabic name.

Later, it quietly introduced legislation intended to re-draw state borders and annex the valuable new oil fields to the North. When Southerners protested, the legislation was withdrawn. But the oil-and-border dispute would remain at the center of North-South tensions up to, and beyond, the partition of the country more than three decades later.

When Sudan's second civil war began in the mid-1980s, Chevron was forced to withdraw, writing off hundreds of millions in startup and exploration costs. A dark period in the development of the oil industry—and in Sudanese history—followed. The government launched a massive campaign to expel mainly Dinka and Nuer civilians from prospective oil areas. Tens of thousands were forcibly displaced and whole communities destroyed as Arab militias, and later Southern mercenaries, were enlisted to rape, pillage, and kill their way through areas pegged for extraction. New oil companies, notably a Chinese-led consortium, filled the void, built the necessary export infrastructure, and helped bring oil online in 1999. From its origin beneath Southern soil, crude oil was now flowing north through new pipelines to a refinery in Khartoum and to Sudan's port on the Red Sea. But the violence continued to intensify.

Sizable new oil proceeds helped Khartoum buy helicopter gunships, combat vehicles, and other advanced weaponry with which it could prosecute the war, continue clearing oil fields, and turn Southerners against one another. Using arms, ammunition, money, and promises of local authority, the regime's divide-and-rule strategy fueled fierce battles between independent Nuer militias, Riek Machar's breakaway SPLA, and Garang's mainstream SPLA.

Collaborating with Khartoum's military, hosting its warplanes, and turning a blind eye to the destruction of local villages, the companies developing the fields—the Chinese consortium, but also major Western firms—were later accused of complicity in war crimes and crimes against humanity. While dueling forces and war-ravaged communities were occupied, the government sucked the black gold out of the ground as fast as possible. The discovery of valuable hydrocarbons had seemed the one stroke of fortune in the Southerners' otherwise accursed history, but suddenly it was being stolen from beneath their very feet. Oil tankers were sailing out of Sudan's port at capacity and unprecedented sums were flowing back into Khartoum's treasury, but Southerners saw not a penny.

With the 2005 peace deal came a 50-50 wealth-sharing arrangement; finally, Southerners had a chance to benefit from their own precious natural resource. Nile blend crude flowed north from Unity State, the site of so much recent suffering, and Dar blend later began pumping from wells to the east, in Upper Nile State. Each flowed through pipelines that snaked across hundreds of miles of Sudanese desert before reaching Port Sudan, where it was bought by mostly Chinese oil traders for export to Asia. South Sudan then received half the proceeds. One look at the jaw-dropping number of zeroes on the incoming deposit slips and Juba's newly-appointed government ministers had to pinch themselves.

Almost overnight, the most underdeveloped place on the planet was flush with billions of petrodollars, and it could spend as it liked. Given South Sudan's place at the bottom of global development indices, would this injection of money have a pronounced impact in lifting its people out of poverty? Sadly, not so. By 2011, the Bahr al Ghazal goat herder was still resigned to traveling three days by foot to the nearest market. His family remained hungry, he had lost a child to malaria for want of cheap medication, and he had twice re-located on account of violent cattle raiding by a local warlord. Things weren't going to change overnight, but after six years there seemed almost no evidence of trickle-down effects of the boom. From zero to $12 billion and little to show for it: where had it all gone?

Like the lottery winner who struggles to manage his new-found millions and ends up worse off, poor countries that suddenly become rich can suffer a similar phenomenon. It's known as the "resource curse"—when a well-endowed nation paradoxically suffers poor economic growth and development. And there was no country more prone to the infamous scourge than South Sudan. A single new resource—oil—comprised 98 percent of its revenue. Its fat new paychecks meant GDP per capita was $1,600 in 2010, better than two-thirds of other African countries—better even than India. It wasn't even classified as a "low income country" by World Bank standards. Six years wasn't enough time to catch up after decades of neglect, to be sure. But by independence, one could point to very few tangible improvements. Outside of Juba, the place remained as impoverished as anywhere on earth.

I hopped a UN helicopter heading toward Malakal, and then another heading further north—toward the Upper Nile oil fields. It was 2010, and I was doing research for the International Crisis Group. Any decent analysis of South Sudan, I believed, required a first-hand sense of the industry that was having such colossal impact—political, financial, and otherwise—on the formation of this young state. But I also wanted to see for myself what impact oil production was having at a local level.

In addition to the 50-50 split of oil proceeds, the 2005 peace agreement had stipulated that two percent of oil revenues be earmarked for the rural communities where the oil was being extracted. This bonus, as well as other promised benefits from the oil companies, would offset the negative impacts of drilling and provide for a few islands of development. At least that was the idea.

Pakistani peacekeepers smiled and nodded shyly as I boarded their small, Soviet-made helicopter—an airframe that felt at least twice my age. With the chopper's aging doors slid open, we whizzed over tree tops at what felt like an incredibly low altitude. The soldiers jabbered among one another, in what I assumed was Urdu, but any time we made eye contact they paused and offered more shy nods. When our hovering chopper set down near Melut amid a cloud of white dust, I exhaled a sigh of relief. I smiled, clasped my hands in prayer-like thanks, and nodded once more to my diffident Pakistani friends. I still needed to get into town, so I hitched a ride with two UN military observers on their way out for a patrol. Over the dubbed tape of Britney Spears hits he proudly blasted, I asked the gregarious Samoan driver if he could drop me at the home of a local chief.

Several area chiefs had convened there, and after offering tea, they dove straight into oilfield development and relations with the petroleum companies. Relations were not good. As operations expanded in the lucrative basin, service roads, rigs, and huge pools of untreated water had swallowed up land where villages had once been. When diesel-chugging earth movers had finished plowing through thatched huts and small farming plots, the compensation and resettlement packages were not what had been promised. Complaints about groundwater contamination, which was causing a spike in reported health problems for the chiefs' people, and for their cattle, had been largely ignored. No one was answering the phone in Juba, either. The locals liked the new roads, but it was hard to find evidence of the houses, schools, or other perks oil executives had apparently promised them. I did the math in my head—a guaranteed two percent of oil revenues would have amounted to millions of dollars for this community. But there seemed scarcely a whiff of that money here.

Just before dusk I met the Melut county commissioner in his office, another converted metal shipping container. Before getting down to business, he kindly offered to let me stay the night in the aging brick house for which he was caretaker. I had been to similar houses, each lone structures of rare permanence, in other important counties. They had once accommodated visiting British colonial administrators or their local representatives and were later snatched up by Sudanese military officials.

Later, on the short drive to the house, the commissioner and I talked about Minnesota's Twin Cities, home to both of our families. Though he returned to Sudan when the war ended, he and his family had been placed in Minnesota in the 1990s as part of a refugee resettlement program that welcomed thousands of Southerners to establish new homes in American cities, from St. Paul to Omaha to Portland, Maine.

The house toilet—itself a rare find in these parts—didn't work, and so I walked down to the cracked-soil banks of the riverbed and squatted there. There was no diesel to fuel the generator, and so no electricity either, but I had a flashlight and could spend the evening hours reviewing the day's notes before getting some shut-eye. It would be a brutally hot evening, with the dead air and convection-like heat inside the house, but that was to be expected when traveling outside of Juba.

Hours later I remained awake, lying on my back, sweating and staring up into the darkness. There was a rap at the door. I put on a shirt, and opened the front entrance to find the commissioner's men silhouetted on the doorstep, Kalashnikovs in hand. I felt the muscles in my neck and arms stiffen. In broken English, their leader indicated that the commissioner had sent them to take me to "better accommodations."

"Thank you, that's generous," I said uncomfortably, "but really I am fine here." But the young man insisted, offered me no further info, and ordered his men to help load my things into their pickup. After riding quite some distance in the back of the truck, heading east I guessed, a gleaming white light appeared on the otherwise totally darkened horizon. The ride became smoother, as dirt roads changed to pavement. Soon there were street lamps. As we approached the shining mini-city, huge silver holding tanks appeared amidst a labyrinth of twisting pipes, all bathed in white light. Only then did I realize my upgraded accommodations for the night would be on the campus of Petrodar Operating Company in the Paloich oil fields.

Guards waved us through the gate, and inside stood several recently-built structures, each made from the same blue and silver materials: a hotel-like building with televisions and air-conditioned rooms for senior staff, several long rows of dormitories, a huge dining hall, and a mosque. A groggy site manager came out to greet us, having just received a phone call from the county commissioner back in Melut. Though the communities felt neglected, the bosses here were buttering the commissioner's bread, it seemed. The manager showed me inside the fluorescent-lit building and up to a second-floor unit, where I plugged in my laptop computer and cranked up the air conditioner before hitting the sack.

When I woke in the morning, dozens of oil men in black rubber boots and blue jumpsuits were already milling about the self-contained campus—Sudanese, Malaysians, Chinese, Arabs, each a cog in the machine that would lift thousands of barrels of oil from the earth's bowels that day. It was an island of sorts, this campus, a feeling reinforced by the near total absence of Southerners on site.

As I waited to hop a ride back to Melut for more interviews, I watched the scene outside the perimeter, where time seemed to move slower. Just beyond the fence were long brown grasses and a man-made ditch, half-filled with stagnant water and lined with refuse. A man in a *jalabiya*—a long, free-flowing cloak—with a rugged face and a walking stick sauntered past with a few lethargic cows. It was hard to imagine what he felt, staring back through chain links at the scene inside: the activity, the foreigners, the alien infrastructure. Was he bothered, I wondered, by the disparity of matters inside and outside the fence? Or had he years ago resigned himself to this fait accompli? It hardly seemed like the peace dividend that many communities like his had expected. If life had not improved in areas where extra resources had been specially earmarked, what then for the rest of South Sudan?

Five years after the war, the country-in-waiting remained grossly underdeveloped, beset by graft and a limited capacity to manage all the new money. In the absence of mature institutions, an extensive oil-fueled patronage network had become the South's organizing framework. Jobs and money were spread around on the basis of ethnicity and war-era credentials. Families, clans, and supporters orbited around respective patrons "from their home area"—local sons who had been atop the SPLA command and now occupied prime positions in government. Not only did they take care of themselves, but they were expected to take care of their own. This de facto system became the norm, such that one's inability to deliver largesse might garner more frowns from family, friends, and community than would stealing from the state.

Army and public sector salaries also were used to repay the debts owed to so many thousands who had sacrificed and died for the struggle. It was a welfare scheme of sorts. The huge government payroll ate up a staggering portion of the country's budget, and was drained further by a dubious list of payees. Paychecks were also regularly sent to an incalculable number of "ghosts"—idle, retired, deceased, or wholly fictitious recipients, whose salaries nonetheless made their way into someone's pockets.

Despite the money being spread around, still the handouts reached only a small portion of the population. The vast majority of average Southerners remained in dire poverty, awaiting the food, clean water, schools, clinics, and jobs that they expected would accompany the peace. While international donors provided humanitarian aid and development programming to the most needy, those at the top of the country's food chain got rich. The payments leaders gobbled up for themselves were initially condoned as "backpay" for their efforts leading two decades of struggle. But things quickly got out of hand.

Army generals and government ministers flashed the familiar accoutrements of status—Rolex watches, luxury SUVs, and expensive whiskey—but the real money was flowing out of the country unseen. Astonishing sums were being re-located to foreign bank accounts, properties, and businesses in Kenya, Uganda, and the Gulf, as well in the U.S., Canada, Europe, and Australia. In order to enjoy their foreign assets and tend to families enjoying the spoils abroad, the thieves traveled often, and in style. Although they occupied critical government positions, many soon appeared to be spending as much time outside the country as they did at home. And it was all on the government's dime.

Hundreds of millions of dollars disappeared through sometimes comically transparent schemes. Ministers appropriated official budgets for personal use and awarded inflated contracts to companies registered in the name of family members. Huge sums were paid to illegitimate companies for roads never built and services never rendered. Letters of credit authorized millions in official withdrawals from the central bank with no regard for budget appropriations. One ministry withdrew an astonishing $30 million dollars for "office equipment" in a single month, another skipped contracting altogether in a decidedly shady purchase of some four hundred Toyota SUVs. Some transactions cited dubious line items, others were shamelessly explicit in their personal nature—one letter authorized $50,000 for a cousin's medical treatment in a neighboring country.

James, the former bank executive, explained that invoices for fulfilled contracts were sometimes processed, paid, and then "cycled back into the system, again and again." One paid invoice worth nearly $2 million, he recalls, was recycled—"on the very same piece of paper" by an official inside the finance ministry, who promptly used the document to pay himself. The most notorious, and maybe most disheartening, scheme was the so-called "*dura* saga," in which an estimated $2.3 billion in government contracts were approved to purchase *dura* (sorghum), as food shortfalls were projected across Southern Sudan. Several hundred fake companies cashed in on the deal, most of which never delivered a single bag of grain.

Senior officials, and very often their spouses, children, nieces and nephews, were listed as shareholders in a wide range of holding companies, with interests in telecommunications, road construction, and mining, as well as banks, hotels, and defense contractors. One such shareholder, with a 25 percent stake in "Combined Holding Limited," was the twelve-year-old son of President Salva Kiir. The youngster's passport listed his occupation as "Son of the President." Many enjoyed tax exemptions and other sweeteners on account of the blurring of boundaries between party, state, and the military. Not only did senior officials benefit by directing government contracts to their own companies, but their shady foreign partners often greased the arrangements with kickbacks.

Because there was a limited banking system in South Sudan, and cash was hard to move, large-scale corruption also required liaisons. Willing partners were not hard to find in Nairobi, Kampala, and the Gulf. Politicians, commercial executives, bankers, lawyers, real estate agents—accomplices were needed to establish accounts that skirted rules and facilitate transfers without triggering audits. They held shares in shell companies, secured deeds for multimillion dollar properties, and ensured customs officials looked the other way. "People knew," James says of executives at his own bank, gritting his teeth. These liaisons were happy to be compensated for their services, and enjoyed sweet reciprocal arrangements when establishing their own businesses back in South Sudan.

The consequences of social and financial investment abroad would compound over time. With children being schooled abroad, assets secure elsewhere, and many afforded dual citizenship and foreign passports, there was less incentive for the ruling class to build strong institutions at home. They also had less to lose at home. When these same elites ignited South Sudan's post-independence war, the country would be ravaged, but it was not they who lost homes, livelihoods, and family members.

Corruption became so commonplace in Juba that efforts to conceal it slackened. One evening in 2010 I interviewed a government minister responsible for huge infrastructure budgets; as we spoke a young aide entered the office and quietly set a black leather suitcase at his boss's side. As the minister shared a thought, he casually opened the suitcase behind his desk, unknowingly licked his fingers, and began to thumb hundred-dollar bills behind his desk. In the reflection of glass cabinets behind him, I watched him count, fold, and stuff what must have been several thousand dollars into his pants pocket. Again without any words exchanged, the aide retrieved the suitcase and receded to the outer office, as if this was routine practice.

The pocketed bills were a comparatively small sum when compared with the hundreds of millions misappropriated, and could conceivably have been for legitimate use in a cash-driven economy, but that seemed doubtful. The ease with which the minister handled the transaction, especially in the presence of a foreigner, was indicative of the scope of the problem.

Corruption makes for complicated relationships, and wrestling with this awkward reality didn't require coming face-to-face with suitcases stuffed with illicit cash. The obvious disparities between a government official's salary and his luxury watch or high-end SUV required only basic math. And it wasn't only the wealthiest of government fat cats who cut corners.

The truth was that I, like most everyone else, had working relationships with individuals known to be corrupt. These were stones often left unturned; matters unspoken by both sides. It was both deeply uncomfortable and anything but black and white. Addressing the problem of graft on a systemic level was one thing. But a Westerner coming from a world of order and privilege to call out a Southern Sudanese whose receipts didn't add up? That was quite another. Not only might it ruin a relationship or get you thrown out of the country, but there were also questions of circumstance in an environment where right and wrong weren't always so easily distinguishable.

When it came to getting promoted in the workplace, or providing for a family in dire need, or sometimes just surviving, many South Sudanese faced different choices, starker moral compromises, or simply had to play by a different set of rules. Maybe the boss asks the mid-level bureaucrat in the finance ministry to grease an illegal transaction, or transfer illicit funds to a personal account. Does the bureaucrat refuse and risk losing a job in a country where there are so few? Does he risk the pressure that might be applied to him or even to his family? Does he report the misdeed in a place where there are no whistle-blower protections, no credible government oversight committees, no reliable courts? If the boss says "take ten percent for your trouble, too," then what? Does he raise suspicion by refusing? And how does he explain turning down the money to his uneducated and unemployed brother back in the village, whose sons and daughters have eaten only boiled grasses for weeks?

Most outsiders accepted the uncomfortable reality that in order to do business, in order to pursue what they hoped were larger aims, one sometimes had to look the other way.

⸺

In addition to corruption and problems absorbing the new oil money, another dangerous product of the oil boom was the matter of myths. Pumping some 350,000 barrels per day at independence in 2011, South Sudan was no Saudi Arabia, with its 10 million per day. It wasn't Iran (4 million) or even Nigeria (2.5 million). Juba's modest output was a mere fraction of production in these genuine petrol states, but tell that to any South Sudanese, and they will promptly correct you. Influenced by the immediate and visible flash of wealth that accompanied the boom, many Southerners believe their supply of oil is endless. In reality, production was by then already in decline.

Mabior tells me that I don't know what I'm talking about. Mabior is in his early 40s, has a secondary school education, and travels in Juba's chattering classes. Sitting, elbows on knees, in plastic chairs in the backyard of a hotel in Juba, we stumble onto the topic of oil. "I've seen it there with my own eyes," Mabior says emphatically, popping the top off a sweating bottle of water. "Bubbling up from the ground... there is so much oil underneath."

"Really?" I ask with obvious skepticism, before asking what he makes of the decidedly conservative estimates that have been put forward by geologists.

"*So* many counties, in so many counties I've seen it there, where the oil will come," he retorts. It was a claim I'd heard countless times over the years, even from the most discerning minds, and I wondered what exactly was perpetuating this blind optimism. Was it born of the country's unforgiving past, and the necessity of hope in a better future? Production was at record lows by mid-2016, but still, that seemed not to puncture the delusions of fossil fuel grandeur.

Mabior and the true believers spoke often of huge blocks of untapped land, most notably the much talked about Block B—a concession the size of New York State. French oil giant Total had rekindled its 30-year-old interest in Block B just before independence, and he was right, significant finds there were possible. But they were by no means assured, and there was good reason to be skeptical. In 2011, an industry expert from the Norwegian government—itself a longtime supporter of the SPLM—offered a sobering forecast. "Small deposits might be found near already producing fields," he explained to me between briefings to Southern government officials. "And better technology could increase recovery yields." But short of a huge, and unexpected, new discovery, he explained, South Sudan's heyday had come and gone.

Underground treasure may have been finite, but the land had much more to give. South Sudan had fertile soil, sun, and water in seemingly endless supply. Farming was the country's ticket to prosperity. "Even if you sow metal nails, they will grow here," one woman explained.

With the right investments, agriculture could be the economic engine of the future, and the answer to chronic food shortages. Watching huge sums of oil money accrue in state bank accounts, however, had a way of putting off infrastructure investments and long-term planning. And so the resource curse stymied efforts during the interim period to develop the agricultural sector or any other sustainable industry. Oil prices plummeted in 2009, and production later slowed, but even then little more than lip service was paid to an agricultural revolution. Even if the Southerners got lucky with a new oil find, it would take years to develop, leaving a short-sighted government and its economy in the lurch.

Neither did South Sudan save for a rainy day. Parliament approved a 2011 bill establishing a reserve fund that would help to absorb another price shock or otherwise stabilize the economy in the event of a crisis. But the bill languished on Salva's desk, awaiting signature, and did not become law until mid-2013. And a rainy day was coming.

In the mid-2000s, high global oil prices meant other countries were likewise experiencing an economic boom. In Russia, President Vladimir Putin was presiding over a comparatively advanced and diverse economy, but nonetheless pledged that his resurgent country would not "fall asleep under the warm blanket of petrodollars." The Russians diverted a considerable chunk of their oil profits into a reserve fund—a piggy bank that could be used to stimulate the economy when their fortunes changed. South Sudan did not. By comparison, the SPLM had not only crawled comfortably under its warm blanket of petrodollars, it had turned out the lights and taken a sleeping pill.

Efforts to combat corruption in the years before independence were mostly a charade, and those who hoped to confront it had become dispirited. But when South Sudan was dragged back into war, and its economy in a death spiral, criticism of the SPLM became more commonplace—and so too did talk of corruption. "These guys have taken us all for a ride," one young South Sudanese intellectual tells me across a small round table in a crowded cafe. My old friend—himself an SPLM member and one-time champion of the "Garang Boys"—is bitter, visibly bitter.

He now believes the ruling party's greed and disregard for the people rivals—maybe even surpasses—what Southerners experienced under Khartoum's rule. The worrying drift he's describing began long before independence, but his clear-eyed assessment appears to have been unlocked by the recent unraveling of South Sudan's fairytale story. "These missing funds, you see, they aren't just a matter of opportunity lost. You get me?" The rampant spending, disregard for the national budget, and excessive borrowing that ensued have crippled the economy and set back the development agenda. "It's even worse than you think."

Wearing a worn brown leather jacket with a high collar, he looks straight out of a 1970s television show, but in fact he wasn't born until the tail end of that decade. It's his cohort of thirty-somethings that offers the best hope for South Sudan's future—educated, fluent in progressive ideas, and tired of militarized politics. Disgusted by the opportunity wasted, for him the SPLM liberators' fall from grace has been a betrayal of monumental proportions.

"They – took – everything – for – granted," he says with a familiar staccato inflection, as he pushes up wire-framed glasses. "Flush with oil money. Babysat by the international community, they didn't think they had anything to do." He agrees that factionalism and a power struggle inside the SPLM led to the collapse, but objects to its characterization as political. "This wasn't about politics; it was about money." To call it political, he explains, would be to "legitimize what was simply a battle for the national cake."

My counterpart has left other worthy pursuits to spend time investigating corruption scandals, piecing together evidence he hopes might discredit the old guard that has run his country into the ground. Tapping a network of young and similarly disillusioned professionals, he has compiled an impressive trove; using a thumb to scroll through pictures on his smart phone, he shows me letters of credit, internal memos, bank records, transfer orders, phony contracts, and photos of illicit assets in foreign countries—a number of which have been posted on Facebook by the children of government big shots. (One shows a young woman posing in the sunroof of a BMW on a coastal highway in Australia.)

As he scrolls through the evidence he gives pause to let it sink in, and watches my face for the reactions registered. He needs the sheer obscenity of it to be acknowledged; he needs his contempt to be validated. I do. But I also can't help being concerned for his safety, as the amount of incriminating material in his pocket could surely invite the threats, beatings, and attempted assassinations that have befallen others like him. It is also hard to know if such evidence will have any impact, even if released publicly. Power has been so concentrated in the hands of a seemingly untouchable class of government elites that it is hard to imagine anyone being held accountable.

The Americans and their European partners were providing indispensable political backing, and pumping huge sums of money into Southern Sudan during the interim period. Yet it was no secret that senior officials were also stealing money out the back door. (The cash may not have been stolen directly from aid accounts, but the arrangement presented an enabling problem nonetheless.) Had the West simply turned a blind eye? Yes and no.

The focus on CPA implementation and the basic objective of preventing a renewed war remained the top priority. U.S. officials believed that, until independence, there were simply larger, more immediate concerns to tackle. Some private appeals were made to clean things up, but evidence was often anecdotal. Even when graft was undeniable, some foreign donors rationalized that they had limited power, as one told me, to "tell the Southerners what to do with their own money."

"At the end of the day, the SPLM marched to its own drummer," another diplomat reflected, dismissive of over-stated notions of Western influence. "It's a different world, and we can never understand that."

There were important truths in these explanations. But it was also true that these foreign friends had enormous leverage and chose not to use it—either in battling the SPLM's authoritarian politics, or its endemic financial corruption. The hazardously close "friendship" and continuing concerns about Khartoum had precluded firmer demands on the SPLM to tighten financial controls, particularly in the early years. Whether willfully ignored or accepted as short-term reality, corruption was effectively seen as a treatable symptom that could be dealt with later. It would hopefully come under control once institutions matured.

But left unchecked, corruption became deeply corrosive. It fostered a sense of impunity among the ruling elite and rotted the very foundations being laid to support an independent state.

⁂

"Is there some unified theory of corruption in South Sudan?" I asked, "Something to explain how and why it became so systemic?" I had confronted the issue in countless conversations over the years, but in 2016 I put this broad question to ordinary South Sudanese, to longtime observers, and to those I knew had stolen money. While no satisfying single theory emerged, their answers, taken together, help to wrap the mind around this devastating cancer.

Weak leadership was most often cited, followed by immature institutions. Indeed the kind of systems and checks and balances necessary to absorb, manage, and safeguard such huge sums of money simply didn't exist during the early interim period. The regional government had just been established. There was not yet a ministry of finance nor a Southern central bank. Most senior positions in government were filled not on the basis of credentials, but on the basis of SPLA hierarchy. A handful of fighters made an impressive transition to administrative roles, but most did not. "There were individual pockets of good governance," one senior party member explained, citing a handful of individuals with administrative experience and advanced professional degrees. "But honestly, they stood no chance in a system that lacked discipline and leadership... it was a melee."

James, the former banker, opined that some felt a sense of urgency, "They were getting old, and so felt it was time to cash in before their time was up." The rebels had lived hand-to-mouth for years, and it was naive to think they would transition overnight from a mindset of survival to one of long-term planning, even if they were ready to make the switch. Some continued to doubt the viability of the CPA, believing a return to war with Sudan was on the horizon, and so concluded it was best to eat while they could, and store up for harder times. Many international partners also shared fears that North and South might return to war, and so a "temporary" mindset, and footprint, was reflected in their sometimes halfhearted investments and development programs.

Institution-building was also hampered by the semi-autonomous character of the regional government in Juba. On one hand, South Sudan was trying to stand up the structures necessary to administer a state, but on the other, the CPA's intent to "make unity attractive" meant it was politically untenable—for Juba or donor countries—to pre-judge the outcome of the 2011 referendum. What's more, finally free of their overlords, some in the new regional government were understandably eager to stand on their own two feet; they were resistant to external help, whether from friends in the region or further afield.

These explanations shed light on what had *allowed* for extreme corruption. But I still wanted to know what *motivated* it. Was it merely human nature, such that any of us, dropped in their circumstances, would have done the same?

For a time the notion of backpay was accepted—or at least those cashing in told themselves as much: these guys had led the struggle and so deserved compensation for their sacrifices and eventual success. Their capture of the state, after so many years of subjugation and resource exploitation by Khartoum, had indeed come with a striking sense of entitlement. There was a kind of "moral licensing" at play—an idea popular in social psychology, in which a past deed of good moral behavior makes people more likely to do immoral things "without worrying about feeling or appearing immoral." The liberation struggle, waged on behalf of the people, was a deed good enough that it meant a little theft of state resources was hardly out of line. And then a lot.

The practice of buying loyalty, and with it Southern unity, is also pertinent in piecing together the corruption puzzle. The Juba Declaration of 2006—Salva's big-tent policy, in which Southern militias were brought into the SPLA, was, not surprisingly, greased with a considerable amount of cash. "There were boxes of dollars stacked in Matiep's house," one former SPLA captain told me, alluding to Nuer commander Paulino Matiep's compound. Fashioning a metaphor around the country's most revered animal, the aging antagonist had reportedly told SPLA leaders, "Our cow has delivered; let us divide and drink the milk among ourselves."

Some believe the wholesale integration of Matiep's and other enemy militias into the SPLA was the cornerstone of a larger Southern policy to use its abundant oil revenue to "buy peace." The Sudanese government had long funneled resources and armaments to Matiep and other disaffected Southern constituencies as part of a divide-and-conquer strategy. Determined not to lose the CPA and its coveted referendum, Salva's government was going to maintain unity by outspending its Northern adversary at any cost.

In addition to cash, the buy-off included positions. Just as Riek Machar was once brought back into the fold and ended up as vice president, Matiep was promptly made deputy commander-in-chief of the SPLA—the very army he'd been fighting against for years. Another Khartoum-allied militia leader was made a state governor, while others were appointed "presidential advisors"—positions which meant nothing in practice, but came with offices, SUVs, and budgets. Salva and company would spread the wealth around so as to prevent Matiep or anyone else from being tempted again by Khartoum. And spend they did, in huge amounts.

Others deny such an explicit policy. But if the collective milk chug wasn't exactly a matter of policy, events suggest the arrangement was at least understood: if an outsider like Matiep was to be fed at any expense, surely the deal also extended to the true liberators inside the SPLA. Let the milk drinking begin.

As soon as enough officials were lining their pockets, there emerged a situation analogous to the Cold War notion of mutually assured destruction. If anyone pointed the finger at someone else, he risked being outed himself. Both parties would be destroyed. One disgraced finance minister, Arthur Akwen, was fired and sent to prison in 2007 on allegations of corruption. When armed allies later broke him out of jail, the state made no attempt to put him back behind bars. He simply remained in Juba, and strangely, no action was pursued against him. "Arthur made it known... you know, in the corridors," one of his successors told me, "that should a case be brought against him, he had all the necessary documents to incriminate others... right up to the very top." And so this omertà, a mafia-like code of silence, itself opened the door for more to partake in the spoils.

Beyond the extreme cases of individual corruption was a harder question: in a society that lacks durable institutions, what is "corruption" and what is a sensible way to distribute resources? Were corruption and illicit patronage networks just the "African way"? Some Western experts see this kind of patronage not only as a central organizing principle in Africa, but one that cannot be improved upon. Peaceful states, in Africa, are a result of dividing the cake among the powerful, they argue, and hoping otherwise is simply naïve.

It is true that Westerners too often travel to developing countries dispatching ideas about liberal democratic institutions with impatience and absolutism. But this altogether defeatist argument plunges off the other end; it suggests that Africans are somehow not interested in, or capable of, more sustainable forms of self-governance. It's a cheap appeal to the simplistic: "Let's not pretend there's more possible here; this is just how it is and so we'd be wise to keep a lid on things by continuing to play the game."

The patronage model, and other ostensibly questionable means of doing business, were a reality in South Sudan, and they could be rationalized given the circumstances, at least in the short term. What's disparaging is the suggestion that the kind of social, political, and economic rules and institutions that order and advance societies elsewhere in the world just aren't possible in places like South Sudan.

※

South Sudan's high thieves were comfortable drinking the milk and felt no reason to worry. There had never been a crackdown on corruption in Juba. But on May 3, 2012, President Salva issued a letter that would change all that and send a shockwave throughout South Sudan's body politic. "An estimated $4 billion are unaccounted for or, simply put, stolen by current and former officials," read the jaw-dropping letter. Salva indicated that an account—Stolen Funds Recovery Account, No. 0810299067373—had been opened at a bank in Kenya. To the letter's secret list of 75 recipients, he wrote, "I am writing to encourage you to return these stolen funds," and he offered amnesty and confidentiality to anyone who deposited stolen cash. Those who did not comply, however, would be held accountable. Salva closed the missive to his long-time comrades with a poignant summation, "Once we got to power, we forgot what we fought for and began to enrich ourselves at the expense of our people."

By the time of Salva's 2012 letter, some high-risk decisions had already put South Sudan's economy in unexpectedly serious trouble. Resulting budget shortfalls and emergency austerity measures were undermining the state's fledging institutions, and the cash that had long lubricated the country's political system was suddenly drying up; without it the engine would grind to a halt. Rather than bailing out the ailing government, international partners had finally pressed Salva to instead take concrete steps to fight the plague that was eating the new state from the inside out. Independence had been achieved, and there could be no more excuses for crooked financial management; the time for a reckoning had come.

At first glance, Salva's so-called "letter of 75" seemed a bold move. It was exactly the kind of course correction that was needed. But while donor nations applauded the initiative, not everyone agreed. "You cannot be serious. You are issuing this letter, while you're up to your own neck in this?" James says of the reaction, "People were just laughing at him." In addition to being angry, many in Juba's political class found the letter's high-minded appeal particularly rich, as it was widely believed that Salva and those immediately around him were as crooked as anyone on the secret list. "It was never meant to produce anything meaningful, just a diversionary tactic to satisfy the donors," James asserts. "Salva had to know that it would never fly."

But the letter was, in fact, no laughing matter. Regardless of the veracity of its claims, many of the accused saw it as a political smear campaign by those now pulling the strings in Salva's inner office. Finger-pointing ensued, and speculation of who exactly was on the purported list fueled the fire. For the first time since independence, party factionalism was back, and it was out in the open. "Those of Telar," one party insider told me, referring to one of Salva's controversial new advisers. "They want to prosecute the Garang Boys, to punish the lot that was in control—and was looting—the country." Others argued the accused had not only stolen money but had done nothing to move the country forward during their reign of thievery; it was about damn time they were punished.

A poisonous buzz enveloped Juba, and it included not only well-known party factions but outsiders as well. One of them was long-time American friend and "Council" member Ted Dagne. Working quietly from inside Salva's office, Dagne had been intimately involved in the corruption investigation. His participation was a matter of considerable controversy, as it was widely believed that he had written the "letter of 75" and was behind the entire initiative. Fairly or not, some thought him interested in playing politics, or re-asserting his role in Washington-Juba relations, or caught up in a romantic ideal about righting the country he and his American colleagues had helped to create. Others alleged he was somehow out to make money for himself. In the days after the letter was circulated, Dagne was reportedly forced to flee the country for his own safety.

Cracking down on corruption was critically important, but the rollout of Salva's most high-profile anti-corruption measure seemed poorly executed. Many questioned how the $4 billion figure had been calculated and whether the president's office had obtained sufficient financial data to support its allegations. And the numbers were the easy part; the letter had sparked a political firestorm that the president and his men seemed unprepared to manage.

"Everyone was on that list!" complained one cabinet minister who received a letter. He and several other senior SPLM figures intervened with the president, arguing that he could not simply indict the whole government in this fashion. "How can I continue working, if I am discredited, I am a thief?" They told Salva he would have to dissolve the government, as the accusation meant "a cloud was hanging over all of us." Many of those who received letters were, in fact, guilty, and so they may have been trying to get Salva to bury the matter. One wonders whether they reminded Salva of the dangers of "mutually assured destruction"—if they were going to be publicly fingered for corruption, they were going to take Salva down with them.

Whatever his initial motivation, Salva backed down, and the seemingly bold crackdown petered out. No investigations were pursued, and a tiny fraction of the stolen loot was returned to the anonymous bank account in Kenya. Though it had put thieves on notice, the ill-managed probe was hardly the reckoning many South Sudanese—and their international partners—had been waiting for.

Meanwhile, those who saw the corruption probe as a way to topple political opponents would begin looking for another chance. Instead of tackling one of the country's most systemic problems, the acrimonious episode was the first signal that a dangerous political battle was on the horizon.

11

A MESSY DIVORCE

". . . the peasants alone are revolutionary, for they have nothing to lose and everything to gain . . . For him there is no compromise, no possible coming to terms; colonization and decolonization is simply a question of relative strength."
—Frantz Fanon, *The Wretched of the Earth*, 1961

I was standing in the fields, the corn fields," Pagan Amum says, "extending far into the horizon." He squints and frames the re-imagined landscape with an outstretched hand. "It was *so beautiful*. I was like in a sea, in a green sea, with a blue sky," he continues, with melodramatic effect. "But why are we not having fields like this all over the place?" Pagan could not reconcile the fields of plenty before him with the abject poverty faced by so many of his countrymen—and so he vowed to change it. "We can have this whole country with fields extending to indefinite end," he thought to himself. "It will be possible for us to be very rich."

It's the summer of 2016, and I'm sitting with Pagan, the former secretary-general of the SPLM, in a high-backed booth in a nondescript cafe in Denver, Colorado. Flat light shines through a mural of the Rocky Mountains behind him, and busboy tubs clang with coffee cups and plates. A faint soundtrack of classic rock ballads echoes about the cafe. Pagan is in exile in the United States, on terms that are not quite involuntary, but not quite voluntary either. I've come to revisit one of the most consequential episodes in Sudan's history—the tumultuous negotiations over the South's separation—with Pagan, its leading character. But before we get into the particulars, I ask him what led him to that moment, and to the enormous responsibility he assumed in the making of South Sudan.

Scooting forward and leaning into the conversation, Pagan says he had "always grown up with this sense that I have a big mission." Returning to those green fields, he explains it was in that moment that he began to understand what that mission would be. "I realized we are in a country that we do not belong to... where we are looked down upon, as if we are guests." Pagan was seventeen years old then, and from that day forward, he says, "I started to ask big questions." In time, he resolved, "my great mission was to build a nation, a country of our own."

And so begins an apocryphal tale of Pagan's childhood, in which his fate and personal transformation were bound together with that of a nation-in-waiting.

I first met Pagan in Juba in 2009. Party representatives from around the country had descended on Juba for a series of events, and Pagan was rushing from one to another to deliver remarks and shake hands with notable comrades. I followed him, stop by stop, about his busy schedule, until I was finally invited to climb into the back seat of his white and gold Toyota SUV for a meeting on the go. The "SG," as he was called by his staff, noticed my surprise at the pair of aging AK-47s lying on the floor beneath our feet. He gave a reassuring shake of the hand. "Oh, don't worry about these."

We had a lot to discuss, and as the driver sped south toward another event at a river-side hotel, Pagan suggested we begin. He was a master of spin, peddling the accolades of the indispensable party and deflecting difficult questions with ease. It would take many meetings to penetrate the polished facade of the SPLM's frontman.

Comrade Pagan had been one of John Garang's closest disciples. He was an intellectual, a Marxist-Leninist, and a capable showman—credentials that compensated for his lack of a popular political support base in his native Shilluk land, on the west bank of Upper Nile State. Pagan broke many of South Sudan's traditional molds, and his physical appearance was no exception. Short, with a round face and a rotund belly, he was something of a bowling ball. The image also fit his politics, a hardened sphere speeding toward its goal with increasing velocity and little chance of deviating from course. He was confident, brash, and had a PhD in bombast—and soon the pudgy ideologue would carry the fate of a nation in his briefcase.

In the spring of 2010, less than a year after our first meeting, teams from North and South began talks on Sudan's two possible futures—as one country or two. Appointed lead negotiator, Pagan relished the chance to finally square-off against his Northern adversaries. At ease defending his decisions to the weaker-willed Salva Kiir, Pagan assumed unparalleled power and decision-making authority in what would quickly turn into a high-stakes game of poker with Khartoum.

Years later, moderated by experience and some distance from the stormy period, the righteous agitator would mellow. Over a breakfast of two raw eggs and a handful of whole peppercorns, he'd told me his new equilibrium was thanks to his health-conscious spouse, regular meditation, and deep reflection on his preferred readings in Buddhism and Eastern philosophy. But at the time of Sudan's 2011 partition, he was more Tasmanian devil than contemplative monk. He reveled in the opportunities for brinkmanship, eager to play chicken with his Northern foes. In many ways, Pagan's career and political identity would come to be defined by his opposition to Khartoum—pursued with a zeal and certainty born of liberation ideology.

"When I was born," Pagan says, "my mother she cried out, '*This is incredible!*'" The new mother named her first born "Pagan, " he explains, which "means 'incredible' in the Shilluk language." And in recounting his path from early prophecy to prominence in the liberation of his homeland, Pagan pauses before delivering a rehearsed closer: "Since then, I have lived an *incredible* life."

Born in 1959 to educated Shilluk parents, Pagan was a child of privilege. His father served in the colonial police before succeeding his own father as a prominent chief in the Shilluk kingdom. He acquired sizable tracts of land, farmed a range of crops, and operated a series of shops in nearby Malakal, which together provided considerable wealth in comparison to the resources of most Southerners.

Pagan's grandiose accounts of his visionary youth reflected an outsize ego, and a lofty gaze, set as soon as he left home for university. Pagan got his first taste of liberation discourse at the University of Khartoum in the late 1970s, where Southern students were a tiny minority. Keen to translate their newly acquired Marxist-Leninist ideals into action, he and a group of like-minded friends enrolled in martial arts classes. "We thought we could build ourselves into invincible ninjas," he recalls, laughing.

The aspiring radicals traveled home to his father's farm, where they also tried to teach themselves to fire guns. And when they weren't preparing for revolutionary action, he explains, "we read everything we could get our hands on." On one occasion, Pagan mistook a book on yoga for a martial arts tutorial. The accidental read made an impression, and he began practicing yoga regularly, "even in the bush during the war," he claims. The introduction to yoga also sparked a wider interest in Eastern thought and meditation.

Intoxicated by Garang's vision of a "New Sudan," Pagan joined his fledgling movement in 1983. Dr. John—who oversaw all personnel deployments at home and abroad—sent him for studies in political science and party-building at the Cuban school of social sciences in Havana, where the SPLM had recently established ties to Fidel Castro's communist regime. Acting as SPLM representative to Latin America, Pagan facilitated guerrilla training for SPLA cadres and further developed his leftist ideas through exposure to Cuban revolutionaries and Nicaraguan Sandinistas.

Pagan was one of few to be offered such an opportunity. When he returned to South Sudan, he became the movement's spokesman and a member of its highest organ, the National Liberation Council. Over the next decade, the ascendant intellectual would grow closer and closer to Garang—a relationship that would define his political career, for better and worse. It would offer him and Garang's other hand-picked consiglieri a path to party prominence, but it would also provoke the ire of party foes.

~

Following Sudan's national elections in April 2010, attention turned to the next and far more consequential event on the political horizon: the referendum on Southern self-determination. The negotiating teams from North and South initiated talks on the conduct of the forth-coming vote, as well as a series of "post-referendum arrangements." Oil, security, borders, debt, currency, and citizenship would require urgent solutions, particularly if the country was to split in two. But talks quickly became politicized, and the high-stakes game of poker commenced.

Tapped to lead Juba's negotiating team, Pagan was presented with an opportunity to fulfill the grand visions of his youth. Juggling hostile opponents, domestic dissent, and international pressure, he seemed to welcome the challenge, and the spotlight. The more pressure applied, the more comfortable he seemed. If there were ten seconds left in a basketball game, with one chance for a winning shot, Pagan wanted the ball. Sometimes he succeeded, sometimes not, but Juba's audacious point man never hesitated to call his own number.

The two teams of negotiators—and the many foreign diplomats now watching—hoped talks on future arrangements would be completed before the vote took place, in January 2011. But this proved wishful thinking; North and South would remain locked in a protracted tug-of-war that lasted nearly two-and-a-half years, all the while teetering on the edge of an actual war on the ground. As negotiators shouted down proposals and caustic rhetoric hardened moods on both sides, the two armies tempted one another daily along some 1,600 miles of shared border. Near one border post of particular import, soldiers in camouflaged fatigues sat atop tanks, fiddling with their weapons and eyeing one another across fewer than 100 meters of dry scrubland. Even if the politicians managed to keep things under control at the negotiating table, one errant shot by an undisciplined soldier, or one jeep erring too close for enemy comfort, and the situation would spiral out of control.

To begin the process, Pagan affixed his first signature—led by a prominent slashing "P"—to a set of guiding principles. Idris Abdul Gadir, Khartoum's lead negotiator, signed next, and the two men thus committed their teams to peace, cooperation, and a "prosperous future" for all. They would negotiate "in good faith to promote the common interests of the people… regardless of the outcome of the referendum." This language entertained two possible outcomes—unity or separation—as the vote was still nine months away. But it was mostly for show. The South was leaving and everyone knew it.

When Southerners eventually cast their votes for independence in January 2011, the goal of post-referendum negotiations shifted to the realization of "two mutually viable states." But the magnanimous principles and pragmatic new catchphrase would soon be replaced by antagonism and zero-sum thinking. It was hardly a surprise; dividing a country in two is tricky business, after all, especially one soaked in so much blood.

Each one of the post-referendum issues on the table was thorny in its own right. Mix them all together, stir in identity politics, billions in revenue, outsized personalities, and an emotionally super-charged past, and one begins to understand just how messy the divorce would become. And given the tectonic political and economic changes separation would prompt in the North, it was fair to say that two new states were about to be born—not one.

While separation was officially a matter of states, litigated by national politicians, it was average citizens—their homes, livelihoods, safety, pocketbooks, and identities—that would be most affected by the divorce proceedings.

In dividing up their shared estate, the most coveted asset was oil. Oil was not only the source of South Sudan's potential viability as a state, it was a matter of pride and a symbol of opportunity. Petrodollars had fueled a decade-long boom in Khartoum while the South languished in extreme poverty. Not surprisingly, the black gold would quickly become the most contentious item on the agenda.

Yet it was also the item that would continue to bind the two sides together after separation. More than 75 percent of proven reserves were in the South, but the pipelines and sea port required to export the crude were in the North. If either side were to benefit from oil going forward, they would have to find a way to cooperate. This mutual dependence seemed the greatest insurance against a return to all-out war.

To make matters more complicated, Sudan's oil also happened to be concentrated in the contested borderlands between North and South—some of the most productive fields even straddled the line. But no one knew the actual coordinates of that line, and the border was in desperate need of demarcation. Since the Comprehensive Peace Agreement mandated resolution of the issue, teams from North and South had trotted the globe in search of a British colonial map that properly identified the border. They dug through dusty archives and museum basements, but it seemed the map had been lost to history.

As the two sides wrangled over contested territory, nomadic herders feared being cut off from grazing lands while families identifying as Southern worried they would be absorbed into the wrong country. Displaced elders clung to hopes of one day returning to traditional homelands from which they'd been wrongfully ousted. Because economic, cultural, and linguistic frontiers in these border regions were so fluid, a solution would require more than drawing a line on a map. It also necessitated creating the kind of "soft" border that would allow cross-boundary movement and trade, upon which millions depended, to continue.

Citizenship and nationality were also critical agenda items in a country as racially, ethnically, and religiously heterogeneous as Sudan. Decisions presented potentially life-altering consequences for the Dinka man who was born in Khartoum, married to a Northern Sudanese woman, and whose children spoke Arabic and attended school in Khartoum's suburbs. He was of Southern descent, but South Sudan was as foreign a place as any. Would he be fired from his job or denied services in Sudan when the two countries split? Would he forced to "return home" to take up citizenship in a country he'd never set foot in? Would his wife be welcomed there?

Next on the list was currency, as Juba planned to introduce its own money in the event of separation. In a predominantly cash economy, a stable rollout would be necessary to prevent a monetary crisis and public unrest. For the Azande woman who sold mangoes and groundnuts at an open-air market in Western Equatoria, the opportunity to trade in her Sudanese pounds—while they still had value—would determine whether her children were fed or not.

Divvying up the country's assets and its staggering $40 billion debt would also be a complicated affair. At night, the blue, green, and gold lights of Khartoum's impressive skyline and suspension bridges reflected off the Nile, anchored by the five-star Burj al-Fateh Hotel, its majestic facade shaped like a ship's sail. Juba's "skyline," meanwhile, consisted mostly of aluminum pre-fabs and a handful of aging single-story brick buildings. One Southerner summed up his side's opinion on the matter of assets and liabilities. "Khartoum was built using the resources of the South, and a war waged against us with our own money!" Indeed Southerners had seen little benefit from Sudan's rampant spending. "Unbelievable! Why should we leave them with all of the assets, and shoulder any of the burden?"

Finally, military men would need to hammer out a deal on security, including a demilitarized zone, a pact of mutual non-aggression, and a solution for indigenous SPLA forces remaining in Sudan. The generals would also need to settle the matter of proxy support for rebels in each other's country. Sudan was experienced in sending weapons to Southern militias to stir the pot, and on the eve of the referendum, Juba was now returning the meddlesome favor.

Beginning in mid-2010, talks alternated between Khartoum and Juba before moving to neighboring Ethiopia, a neutral site and the headquarters of the African Union (AU). Given President Salva's lack of strategic vision and his increased distance from the negotiations, Pagan assumed the mantle and proceeded as he saw fit. The indefatigable and self-confident negotiator made most decisions without consulting

Juba. When Salva was consulted, or when he traveled to participate in talks himself, Pagan occasionally over-ruled his decisions.

The bowling-ball negotiator may have been a more forceful advocate for his emergent country, but some found his self-appointed authority as dangerous as it was arrogant. "Pagan was running a parallel system!" one Southern critic told me, spouting his contempt in a high-pitched affect common to South Sudanese politics. Khartoum likewise thought Pagan too big for his britches, and several times tried to sideline him and deal instead with the more malleable Salva Kiir.

"Nonsense," Pagan says, when I ask him about the criticism. But his seamless segue to disparaging comments about Salva—"an unenlightened coward" who was "unable to take strategic decisions"—offers a good hint that Pagan had been anything but a nodding subordinate.

The negotiations began on a bilateral basis, but the parties could ask for "facilitation" if needed, from former South African President Thabo Mbeki, who had been appointed by the African Union to support the process. Some leading Africans believed Mbeki's role was critical. South Sudan was going to secede, and they thought it important that the seismic event "have an African narrative about it," one member of Mbeki's team told me. "It was important that Khartoum not feel that Africans were conspiring with the West to dismember Sudan."

After three months spinning their wheels, it was evident that the issues were too complex and too acrimonious to negotiate bilaterally. Pagan also felt his team faced a considerable disadvantage: Khartoum controlled all the important governance and economic data at a national level, including statistics on oil production, while the SPLM was flying blind. He feared that his team could not negotiate an equitable deal if they were denied access to this information, or worse, given manipulated data. And so they revisited the idea of a more active third-party mediation, which might help level the playing field.

The SPLM had some reservations about Mbeki and his mediation team, who they worried were unduly partial to Sudan and might prefer unity over separation. But Pagan also bristled at suggestions that Southerners should "buy their freedom" from Sudan. He grew concerned that outsiders—not only Mbeki, but the SPLM's friends in the West—might press them to unduly accommodate the regime under which they had so long suffered.

A handful of Southern politicians thought accommodation a prudent strategy, though they were vastly outnumbered. One party pragmatist argued the SPLM should deal amicably with Khartoum: avoid conflict, ensure independence, and initiate positive relations with the state that would—like it or not—become its most important neighbor. Culling the CPA's slogan to "make unity attractive," he argued that it was now time to "make separation attractive."

But comrade Pagan did not share this view, to put it mildly. He recalls gritting his teeth at this "take what we can be given" mentality, a dynamic he likens to that of "slave and colonial master." No, the liberation ideologue intended to approach the process as equals. Self-determination was a right for which his people owed no further debts. The conservative voices, he says, were coming from "the faction of the SPLM that had always cooperated with Khartoum," and their sentiments reflected the "psychology of the domestic slave."

Pagan's provocative characterization hangs in the air. He rolls up the sleeves on his checkered button-down shirt, plants his elbows on the table, and delves deeper into his lexicon of liberation. "Others in the SPLM, they had not internalized the rebellion… toward a revolutionary core." He separates himself and a small vanguard of like minds from the majority of party members, whose "souls," he says, "were still seized by the domination of their masters." He says he was confident that he and his more enlightened colleagues were better placed to pursue "South Sudan's true national interests… with clarity of mind."

Not surprisingly, Salva vacillated between Pagan's pugnacious camp and those few who favored appeasement. But in time Pagan appeared to prevail, whether by force or persuasion. In a September 2010 address to old friends from the Congressional Black Caucus in Washington, President Salva's remarks sounded strikingly familiar to that of his lead negotiator:

> There are rising calls that the South must make "accommodations" and "compromises," if it expects the North to accept its

independence. The terms "accommodation," "compromise" and phrases such as "buy your freedom" are troubling. These terms imply in some way that the South has not already made significant compromises and sacrifices. Anyone who knows the history of our country knows that nothing could be further from the truth.

Thabo Mbeki's team eventually assumed a more active role in mediating between the two parties, and in time invited U.S. and UN diplomats to participate as observers. Washington was the most influential foreign actor in Sudan. Its close ties to the South meant it could—in theory—lean on the SPLM when necessary. And because of its wide-ranging economic sanctions against the North, it also held the cards to Sudan's recovery and reintegration into the global economy.

But as the clock ticked down toward the referendum, progress at the negotiating table was frustratingly slow. The right to a vote on self-determination had been guaranteed on paper six years earlier, but now, with less than six months to go, the historic vote remained far from assured.

———

The best way to clear a path to the referendum—and to Khartoum's recognition of its result—was to finalize mutually acceptable arrangements on the thorny post-referendum agenda. The poll's likely outcome was sure to send shockwaves throughout political and economic systems in both North and South; putting a blueprint in place to address uncertainty and absorb shocks would mean Khartoum had less reason, and less opportunity, to deny the poll or its results. But talks were stuck—each side wanted assurances from the other, and neither wanted to move first. And so the game of chicken intensified.

Given the NCP's long record of unfulfilled promises, Pagan's team wanted concrete assurances that Khartoum would stick to the referendum and the prescribed timetable, and be the first to formally recognize an independent Republic of South Sudan. Southerners did not want to find themselves in geopolitical limbo like Kosovo, formally recognized by only half of the world after its unilateral separation from Serbia in 2008. Khartoum's swift recognition would ensure the rest of the international community followed suit. But the SPLM could do little to influence policy in Khartoum, and so relied almost exclusively on Washington and other international guarantors to hold the NCP to its CPA commitment.

The NCP, meanwhile, wanted to ensure its own stability in the wake of such a monumental event. On the eve of partition, the regime faced a cocktail of political, economic, and security risks that posed an existential threat. Rebels in Darfur continued to agitate. And SPLA-allied forces in two other Sudanese states—Southern Kordofan and Blue Nile—would soon rear their own rebellious heads if their future status was left unresolved. Regime officials also feared that the blow of partition would embolden political opponents and turn powerful domestic constituencies against them. They also worried—credibly—that Juba might double-down in supporting Sudan's other aggrieved regions once it was free to stand on its own.

Khartoum's problems were clear, but its game plan was not. Observers wondered whether the party was in a state of shock; indeed many Northerners never expected that the referendum would actually materialize, and some now appeared to be in denial. Divergent camps sent conflicting signals. Hardliners wanted to thwart the vote altogether. Others were ready to accept secession, but believed they should use any means necessary to maintain control of the Southern oil fields. A third camp of pragmatists—conscious of international pressure, a president under international criminal indictment, and the unavoidable political consequences of partition—wished only to fortify the regime's hold on power by negotiating the best possible severance package.

As time grew short, and Khartoum held its cards close to its chest, the collective blood pressure of those around the negotiating table spiked. Given the kind of brinkmanship that had long characterized Sudan's North-South politics, diplomats from the U.S., Europe, China, Africa, and the United Nations worried the two sides might wait and attempt to strike a grand bargain at the eleventh hour. With the referendum still in doubt, would Khartoum slow-roll talks and try to extort significant concessions from the SPLM—and the international community—in exchange for peace and its recognition of the poll?

It was an exceedingly dangerous moment, and the stakes couldn't have been higher. Pagan and his team dug their heels in, and so did their Northern adversaries. Only a handful of moderates, in both North and South, could extract themselves from the amped-up emotions and antagonism of the moment. Conscious of geography, economics, and historical ties, they knew the relationship between Sudan's two halves would remain the most important for years to come. But as the tenor of talks went from bad to worse, the space for pragmatic voices was squeezed, and their patriotism questioned by those spoiling for a fight.

"They didn't give a shit," one member of Mbeki's mediation team said, recalling the dangerous game being played by elites from both sides. "They didn't give a shit about the little man." The negotiators, he argued, were in a bubble of high politics, their decisions informed not by the interests of common citizens, but by outsized egos, bravado, and ideological fervor. Personal histories of war, mistreatment, and mutual resentment would prove hard to set aside, and for some of the men involved, it seemed a chance to settle old scores.

The consequences of miscalculation by either party could be catastrophic. For six years, the two sides had spent billions beefing up their armies and acquiring ever more sophisticated weapons systems, meaning a return to the battlefield would be exponentially more destructive. Neighboring states, affected by spillover effects and eager to protect regional security and economic interests, might well join the mix. It was hard not to wonder: was another continental war in the making?

<hr />

By late September 2010, temperatures were also rising outside the conference room walls. Sudanese Information Minister Kamal Obeid sent a shock wave through Southern neighborhoods in Khartoum when he announced that if the South chose secession, the estimated two million Southerners residing in the capital city, "will not enjoy citizenship rights, jobs or benefits; they will not be allowed to buy or sell in Khartoum market... we will not even give them a needle in the hospital." The Speaker of the National Assembly followed suit, warning Southerners they would soon be "second class citizens," and Southerners began to fear for their safety after Islamic councils reportedly issued fatwas against them.

At the border, each army flexed its muscles, moving in thousands of armed reinforcements. A widely-shared cartoon captured the fragility of the moment, depicting Presidents Salva and Bashir, each sneaking a toe over their shared border to provoke the other.

The increasingly bellicose rhetoric was turning heads outside Sudan too, as international attention returned to Sudan in those treacherous final months of the CPA's interim period. Washington led the charge, waging a diplomatic campaign that signaled to Khartoum, Africa, and any reluctant world powers that the referendum was an American priority, and it was not going to entertain a delay.

In New York, President Obama and world leaders convened a meeting to broadcast the urgency with which they viewed preparations for the vote and progress on post-referendum talks. Vice President Joe Biden was dispatched to the region to catalyze support, and Hillary Clinton's State Department surged diplomatic staff to Juba. "This could not be a more crucial time in the life of Sudan and also in the life of international affairs," Samantha Power, then a senior White House official, told reporters. It was critical to "show that the world is united," she said, and to "ensure that the referendum goes off on time and peacefully."

While negotiations on oil, debt and security inched forward, Khartoum used every hook possible to try to scuttle the referendum or bait Juba into making a mistake. It obstructed draft legislation governing the poll, challenged voter eligibility rules, withheld funding for the body organizing the referendum, and then challenged its work in court. In the waning months of 2010, delay seemed so plausible, and violent fallout so likely, that in my then-role at the International Crisis Group, I spent weeks preparing a report for publication titled "Managing Referendum Delay." The SPLM had the law and international public opinion on its side, but each of Khartoum's curveballs would challenge Pagan's SPLM to keep its frustrations in check. Each was intended to goad Juba into unilateral action that would damage its credibility on the world stage.

At one point, the SPLM did float a unilateral declaration of independence as an option of last resort. Such a gambit would likely have played into Khartoum's hands, delivering it a justification to forgo the referendum, and reducing South Sudan to a contested territory.

As our lunch arrives in the Denver cafe, I ask Pagan about the provocative move, and the risks. "That was me," he says, unsurprisingly. "I was the architect of that idea." He argues that it was primarily a "pressure tactic aimed at the NCP, and more importantly, the international community." By toying with such crazy ideas, Pagan says, he believed that already nervous international diplomats would redouble their efforts to ensure the referendum took place, and took place on time. It worked, to some extent, but however comfortable Pagan felt throwing the dice, such gambles were extraordinarily risky.

Now, as then, Pagan likes to project a sense of omniscience about the complicated dynamics at play. As we revisit the angles and weigh the risks, a slippery potato twice evades his fork before skidding off his plate, interrupting our conversation. "What... what is this?" he says, addressing the potato facetiously. "It is refusing to be taken to the mouth," he jokes, successfully stabbing the evasive spud before returning to geopolitics. Pagan wants to give the impression that each move was part of a masterful strategy. It was not. As lead negotiator, Pagan was as capable a representative as the SPLM had, but the politics were dangerously unpredictable, and the task far bigger than any one man—no matter how big his britches.

So jarring was the pre-referendum period, the prospect of war, and the international significance of partition, that some observers quietly contemplated whether the referendum should take place at all. And beyond the hotly contested vote, others privately pondered whether

South Sudan could really be a viable state. But by then it was too late to turn back.

⁂

After months in a hands-off posture, Mbeki finally learned what some seasoned Sudan experts had been urging all along: he needed to knock some heads together if any progress was going to be made. Though he would never drive the process in a manner many thought necessary, Mbeki's team finally assumed a more pro-active position in November and augmented his small and insulated team with international technical experts. He also invited U.S. diplomats to play a semi-formal role in the talks.

The Americans dispatched one of their most seasoned diplomats to help grease the negotiations. Princeton Lyman had been U.S. ambassador to South Africa in the early 1990s and had worked closely with Mbeki's predecessor and former boss, Nelson Mandela, during that country's historic transition. Lyman's appointment facilitated a better relationship with Mbeki's team—few others can call him "Thabo," as Lyman does—and a more active role for a small team of State Department support staff. At the same time, Mbeki and others hoped the Americans would put a package of big-ticket incentives on the table to help lubricate an otherwise stuck process. They did.

That month, John Kerry, who was then chairman of the Senate Foreign Relations Committee, made back-to-back trips to Sudan to pitch a "roadmap" on behalf of the White House. The two-page document—the product of a bitter inter-agency fight in Washington—offered to lift Sudan's designation as a state sponsor of terror, begin normalizing diplomatic relations, and ease some sanctions. It also hinted, vaguely, at the possibility of debt relief. In exchange, the so-called roadmap outlined seven conditions for Khartoum to meet, including a smooth referendum, a deal with Juba on post-referendum issues, and military de-escalation.

Though the roadmap was a seemingly lucrative package, NCP officials considered it with skepticism. Sudanese diplomats felt they had been burned in the past after Washington had reneged on similar offers, and worried about a repeat. But faced with the impending consequences of partition, the prospect of normalization with the American superpower was tempting. Though they continued to harbor doubts, they agreed to the American roadmap.

⁂

Against the odds, the January 2011 referendum was held on time. It was peaceful and credible, and millions of Southern voters affirmed their intent to secede. Khartoum quickly recognized the results. The proud sons and daughters of this nation-in-waiting inked their calendars for the 9th of July, 2011—their long-idealized Independence Day was now just six months away.

With the main event out of the way, North and South returned to the negotiating table. It was crunch time. As they dove deeper into the issues and zeroed in on the most consequential trade-offs, Pagan pursued his objectives with a religious fervor. His tactics sometimes confused and frustrated Mbeki, as well as the Americans and other international partners. The more practically-minded among them wanted solutions, and they sometimes saw his brinkmanship as hot-headed and careless, subjecting the people of South Sudan to unnecessary risk.

But Pagan was unmoved. He readily acknowledges the tension that emerged between himself and those around the talks, but, he asks rhetorically, "Who is historically responsible to achieve these goals?" Answering his own question, he says, "It is us… it is me." At the end of the day, he argues, the South Sudanese were responsible for their own fate. Everyone else—African mediators, American friends, UN observers—had limited objectives. They would move on to their next jobs, their governments would change, and they would pursue their own interests. So while their advice was well intentioned, and he would faithfully consider their proposals, only Southerners, he argued, "would have to live with the decisions" made in this moment and "live with them for generations." These were matters of long-term national interest and identity, and Pagan—the man who believed he was destined to liberate—wasn't about to compromise for the sake of expediency or someone else's short-term needs.

As we approach hour seven of our conversation in Denver, I press Pagan on the risks. It's no surprise that Pagan—talker, egotist, and political animal—could go on seemingly indefinitely. "This single-mindedness was necessary" to achieve independence, he maintains. As usual, his argument is wrapped in existential terms.

Pagan's argument is intellectually sound; defending the long-term national interest he has articulated surely demands steely resolve in the face of outside pressure or calls for expediency. But it also seems easy to get caught up in such a grandiose justification, to risk going one step too far. As he continues his defense, I can't help but think of the gaping chasm between those dealing in brinkmanship and those ordinary citizens—the goat herder, the fruit seller, the dislocated elder—whose lives hung in the balance.

Earlier Pagan spoke in Eastern philosophical terms about the importance of being realistic and accepting human limitations. "The ideal is something to strive for," he had said, "but something that can never be reached." As we spar over the handling of North-South talks, I wonder whether he'd considered this maxim back then, during the negotiations.

The case for principled single-mindedness would have been harder to defend had the gamble gone wrong in 2011—if talks had collapsed, the referendum had been sabotaged, and the parties had returned to war. None of this came to pass. But before long, Pagan's rationale would again be tested, and this time it would be harder to reconcile given the extraordinary sacrifices forced upon ordinary Southerners.

12

INCEPTION

"We have made Italy; now we must make Italians."
—Massimo D'Azeglio, Italian nationalist,
upon the unification of Italy, 1861

Before the sun rose on January 9, 2011, the people of Southern Sudan were waiting in line. In towns and rural outposts across the South, tens of thousands stood ready to cast their votes for separation, and they could not have been happier to wait. In Juba, seemingly endless lines snaked back and forth outside polling stations, row after row, before circling around the block. Many voters were dressed in their Sunday best. They flashed toothy smiles and proudly posed for photos with their laminated blue and white voter cards. Some had carried cinder blocks to sit on for the hours-long wait, others stood without feeling tired. Women carried infants on their backs, and the elderly inched forward in line, aided by the steadying arms of younger compatriots.

Nearly four million people had registered to vote in the historic referendum. Six inches wide and seven inches long, the white and blue paper ballots awaiting them offered a simple choice. In one box the word *"Unity"* accompanied an image of two hands clasped together. Below it, in a second box marked *"Secession"* was an image of a single, open, and free hand. "You dip this finger in purple ink," one yellow-vested poll worker explained proudly, "and then," he paused for a beat, gesturing toward the ballot with a wry smile, "choose wisely."

Though each man and woman would mark just one ballot, they were casting their votes for their forefathers, for countless loved ones lost to the struggle, and for their children, who they hoped would be the greatest beneficiaries of this unforgettable day. Whether standing in line in Eastern Equatoria, or Northern Bahr al Ghazal, or in the center of Juba, on this day each of them was South Sudanese.

In the months leading up to the poll, the government-in-waiting had bankrolled a campaign to educate, register, and turn out voters, and its position on the matter was unambiguous. "Vote for Dignity" and "Vote for Development" read billboards and posters blanketing the country—each of them depicting the favored open hand of secession. That hand, some explained, was waving goodbye to Sudan, and to decades of suffering. At a central roundabout in Juba, a towering countdown clock—its red letters displaying "39 days, 6 hours, 44 minutes"—fueled the excitement.

Trucks and cargo planes delivered boxes of ballots to the furthest reaches of the country, radio messages offered information and updates, and officials traveled county by county to train poll workers and issue them official yellow vests. The U.S. government and the United Nations together spearheaded an incredible effort, in political, logistical, and resource terms, to ensure the vote would take place as planned. President Jimmy Carter and former UN Secretary-General Kofi Annan were among those on hand to monitor the vote. George Clooney paid another visit during the campaign, snapping photos with locals and posing with the open hand of secession. They were but a few of the many dignitaries who had shown their faces in Juba in recent months, each appearance lending visibility, and a sense of inevitability, to an exercise that had for so long been in doubt.

Southerners living all across Sudan were free to vote. So too were the many refugees who had fled the war and remained in neighboring countries, in the U.S., UK, Canada, and Australia. At the handful of polling stations in Khartoum, voter turnout was comparably limited, as North-South hostility and widespread opposition to secession had made for a tense atmosphere. Nonetheless, there were Southerners in the North who would not shy from making their voices heard.

Seven hundred miles to the South, a crowd buzzed at John Garang mausoleum in Juba, where there was no such cause for restraint. There, in the most visible of the nearly 3,000 nation-wide polling stations, yellow-vested poll workers prepared a ballot for the country's most famous voter. A wail of police sirens was audible in the distance, and the collective excitement swelled as they drew near. A phalanx of speeding black SUVs suddenly arrived in a cloud of dust, each adorned with a pair of whipping SPLM flags. Stern-faced bodyguards in tight-fitting business suits leaned out the doors of the vehicles. As the convoy came to a halt, the guards dismounted and huddled around a rear door. A familiar cowboy hat emerged: President Salva ascended the steps of the tented platform as referendum officials, dignitaries, journalists, and ordinary Southerners pushed close to catch a glimpse. John Kerry and George Clooney were among the onlookers, as was Clooney's principal sidekick, "Council" member John Prendergast. After stamping his fingerprint, the president looked up and flashed his ballot and a smile to the boisterous crowd. Photographers snapped shots of his purple-inked index finger, and the cheers spiked as he dropped his ballot through the slot of a clear plastic box cinched with yellow zip-ties. It was a simple act, but one for which Salva had taken up arms four decades earlier. One could only wonder what his former commander, interred in the tomb below, would have felt on this day.

When all the ballot boxes had been emptied, and the millions of fingerprints tallied, a whopping 99 percent of Southerners who had voted for secession. Though the outcome was no surprise, the announcement felt miraculous nonetheless. Celebrations erupted in the streets of Juba and elsewhere across the South, as breathless Southerners rejoiced, marched to the beat of drums, and praised God. "I am so happy!" one sweaty young man in a boxy dress shirt exulted. "Imagine having schools, no fear, no war... Imagine feeling like any other people in their own country."

Messages of support and congratulations poured in from around the world. President Obama called the exercise an "inspiration to the world," and Secretary of State Hillary Clinton lauded the "compelling statement" made by the people of Southern Sudan. But most importantly, Sudanese President Omar al-Bashir appeared on national television and announced that he would "accept and welcome these results because they represent the will of the Southern people." It was official. Africa's largest country would be split in two, and it was set to happen peacefully.

Six months later, invitations would be issued for South Sudan's emotional coming-out party. And it was a sight to see. On July 9, 2011, I woke early, thinking I might beat some of the crowds to Freedom Square. But by the time I arrived and claimed a spot on the grandstand, a sea of jubilant Southern Sudanese stretched across the square, seemingly without end. Many waved miniature flags of red, black, green, blue, and yellow—what was yesterday the flag of the SPLM would today fly for an independent republic.

"We have waited 56 years for this day," Salva later exclaimed from atop the raised platform to the throng of new citizens below. "It is a dream that has come true!" The crowd roared at an ear-splitting pitch, again and again. People climbed trees, stood on the roofs of buses, and sat on each other's shoulders to get a glimpse of the president taking the oath of office and then, with two hands, triumphantly hoisting a copy of the new constitution in the air. The crowd roared again, and the military band struck up the recently unveiled national anthem. Those familiar with the lyrics joined in its uplifting final crescendo: "*Ohhhhh* God... Bless South Sudan!"

Pagan Amum, the master of ceremonies, basked in the spotlight, rallying the crowd in a mix of Arabic and English, "*Mabrouk Jenub* Sudan! South Sudan *Oyyyy-aaayyh*!" The flag of the world's 193rd country was raised to join the long row of other nations' banners flying over the square. It was no coincidence that America's stars and stripes waved from the flagpole immediately next to it.

Juba was the happiest place on earth. On my way to the event that morning, I'd heard cars honking endlessly and women ululating at an ear-splitting pitch as celebrants made their way through the city's pulsing streets to enter the square. Many had been celebrating since the stroke of midnight. In addition to its freshly painted roads and new landscaping, the city was blanketed by signs celebrating independence, thanking John Garang, and paying tribute to martyrs. Each was signed by an eager celebrant—the Chamber of Commerce, the Nuer Youth Union, an Equatorian church congregation. Private businesses did the same, from oil companies to White Bull beer, whose giant billboard depicted three men raising bottles in "A Toast to a New Nation."

With blue and red lights flashing and sirens wailing, roaring motorcycle escorts accompanied convoy after convoy of VIPs to the grandstand, each ferrying a head of state or prominent delegation from Africa, Europe, the Gulf, and Asia. Among them was Sudanese President Omar al-Bashir—the man who, for many Southerners, embodied a generation of hate, destruction, and death. Dressed in a white robe and matching white turban, Bashir stepped out of the back of a white SUV and was met with a mix of surprise, cheers, and boos. For many the moment was bittersweet—painful to see him there, in the heart of their joyous celebration, yet vindicating to have him bear witness to their assertion of sovereignty and self-worth.

"We shall honor our oath in being supportive of the South's independence," Bashir announced to the crowd in familiar Arabic, removing all doubts and paving the way for global recognition. From the White House, President Obama issued a declaration honoring the world's newest state. "After the darkness of war, the light of a new dawn is possible," it read. "A proud flag flies over Juba and the map of the world has been redrawn."

Riek Machar's unmistakable voice was next to ring from the speakers. "Modest, courageous, and noble," he proclaimed, introducing his boss and political nemesis with surprising enthusiasm. History, he told the crowd, "would attribute the outstanding achievement of independence" to Salva Kiir. His voice rose in volume and energy as he described Salva, a "brave fighter and leader" who had success-fully navigated the most troubled of waters and so "earned his place among the world's greatest heroes!"

It was hard not to raise an eyebrow at Riek's conspicuously gushing praise, even amid the elevated oratory of the day. Whether a genuine reflection of hatchets buried or political prudence, it was notable. Of a man whose abilities he did not respect, Riek exclaimed to the crowds that he had been honored and privileged to have every day experienced his cowboy-hatted leader's "unwavering courage and clarity of purpose."

Salva returned to the bright green podium emblazoned with the seal of the Republic. In humble and benevolent tones, the normally under-whelming president rose to the occasion. His confidence-inspiring remarks seemed to hit all the right notes: humility, gratitude, selfless-ness, and forgiveness. He spoke of economic development, the delivery of services, accountability, self-reliance, and reconciliation. Conscious that a state had been born, but a nation was still in the making, the president appealed to the many communities that stood before him, "We may be Zande, Kakwa, Nuer, Toposa, Dinka, Lotuko, Anyuak, Bari and Shilluk, but remember, remember you are South Sudanese first." Though it piqued no particular interest on a day of such unre-mitting joy, Salva told his fellow countrymen, "They say we will slip into civil war as soon as our flag is hoisted... that we are incapable of resolving our problems through dialogue... that we are quick to revert to violence. It is incumbent upon us to prove them all wrong!"

Popular expectations—already high—were buoyed by the excite-ment of independence and the lofty rhetoric of promise. After decades of struggle, there was no more foreign enemy to combat, no more sacrifices to be made, and no more swallowing of legitimate griev-ances for the sake of a greater good. The slate was clean, and it was time to reap the rewards.

—

Among the Southern Sudanese celebrating in Khartoum that day was Ayen, a Dinka woman originally from Kwajok, near the birthplace of

Salva Kiir. In her neighborhood, a low-income suburb of Khartoum, she and her fellow Southern Sudanese rejoiced. They could hardly believe what they'd done. Though Ayen, like most Southerners on her street, had spent her entire adult life in Khartoum, she too had cast a vote for secession. Just six months earlier, she had arrived at the polling station feeling nervous and excited, having never before voted in an election. Now she'd helped birth a nation. It was a simple act, and an extraordinary one. Like millions of others displaced by war, she decided that day to return from Sudan to the land of her birth, enthralled by the prospect of a new beginning.

Ayen and I sit outside on plastic chairs, in an empty dirt lot on the western outskirts of Juba. As we talk, she sucks air across her teeth. It's 2016—five years have passed since those initial heady days of independence, and Ayen is reflecting now on a life shaped by two migrations. She wears a maroon dress trimmed in cream and green, covered with an elegant black *taub* knotted at the right shoulder. Her facial features are sharp and strong, and her braided hair is pulled back in a ponytail, displaying double-studded earrings and a beaded white necklace. She communicates as much with her arms, eyebrows, and tilts of the head as she does through her rapid-fire Arabic.

Ayen carries herself with the kind of assured posture born of experience. But she was not always this way. In 1998, she explains to me, Sudan's civil war had become too much for her family to endure. Arab tribes from the border region north of Kwajok had been mobilized, armed, and sent south to prosecute a scorched-earth campaign in communities like her own. During one raid in Ayen's village, militia men raped women deliberately in front of their helpless fathers—an act, with racial overtones, meant to intimidate and demoralize. Growing nervous and angry, her father sent Ayen, then 23, and her six siblings to seek refuge in the relative calm of Khartoum. He stayed behind to join the SPLA.

Ayen settled in one of Khartoum's low-income suburbs, where she washed clothes, brewed *marissa*, a traditional sorghum-based beer, and attended Catholic church. She married a fellow Southerner, had four children, and made friends with both Arabs and Southerners, as well as people from Nuba, Darfur, and elsewhere across the country's diverse periphery. But for nearly thirteen years, she never had the chance to return to Southern Sudan. Estranged from her family and her village, she had lost a sense of who she was and where she belonged.

In 2011, Ayen got her chance to go home. When news of South Sudan's referendum result was announced, she joined hundreds of others in Khartoum dancing and carrying celebratory banners in an impromptu parade through neighborhoods home to fellow Southerners. Weeks later, she and her husband finalized plans, she explains, to "bring their children home, to see their own country." Like so many of her neighbors, they would "return" to a country they'd never set foot in.

By the end of 2012, almost two million refugees like Ayen had returned to South Sudan, and they would continue streaming home until the onset of war in 2013. A first wave returned just prior to the 2011 referendum, encouraged by Southern leaders to "come home and vote." They came from Kenya, Uganda, Ethiopia, Congo, and beyond, but most came from Sudan. Many in this initial wave undertook the journey themselves, but ill-informed about costs and transport options, they endured arduous journeys and often got stuck along the way. The "returnees" found little government support upon arrival, and the sudden influx of huge numbers of people put undue strain on local populations and markets.

Ayen was part of a second wave that returned just after the referendum in 2011. She and many others left Khartoum under real (and perceived) pressure. Life in the city had suddenly been made difficult. Not granted citizenship rights as initially envisioned in North-South talks, many were forced to register as aliens. They were dismissed from jobs and subjected to increased school and hospital fees. Religious tension spiked, as did intimidating rhetoric. The impending partition had stirred raw emotions in the North and brought racial, cultural, and class differences to the fore. As Ayen went about her normal business, she says she felt like an "other," constantly wondering what was behind the eyes of Northerners she passed on the streets.

"Suddenly, they were treated like foreigners," explained one Southern aid worker who helped facilitate returns. This time, the International Organization for Migration and a government partner provided assistance—flying, bussing, and barging returnees like Ayen to the South. Though haphazard and rushed, the operation was impressive nonetheless.

On the morning of her departure from Khartoum, Ayen tells me through a translator, "my best friend Chendi, from Nuba, she came to deliver a package of food she had prepared, and extra clothing for the children." Chendi tried to be positive, but she quickly succumbed to tears. "*Ooooooh,*" Ayen hoots at a soprano's pitch, recalling the poignant moment with pursed lips and a bittersweet expression. The two women embraced with the unspoken knowledge that they would likely never see each other again.

In addition to her own four children, Ayen would bring three from her husband's first wife, who had passed away. "My husband and I sold our plot and nearly everything inside" to finance the journey, she says. They boarded one of the hundreds of ramshackle buses ferrying returnees south, each topped with mountains of chairs, foam mattresses, cookware, suitcases, baskets, and a rainbow of overstuffed plastic bags. Re-creating the scene with her strong hands, Ayen motions in the air, stacking each item on an imaginary bus. With yellow jerry cans of water bobbing on ropes out the bus windows, Ayen's delegation of nine bounced south across inhospitable terrain toward the border town of Renk.

There the family switched modes of transport, joining thousands of other hopefuls aboard a group of barges—three large, flat, makeshift river ferries tied together for the two-week upstream journey to Juba. It would be long and onerous, but they had one another, she explains, and there was a certain camaraderie about their shared experience. Each morning at sunrise, a pastor led their group in prayer, Ayen says, now making the sign of the cross. She then prepared tea for the children and washed their clothes at the riverbank before setting off on the day's ten-hour trip. They were given a modest allocation of foodstuffs—sorghum, lentils, salt, and other items—supplemented on the few occasions they docked within walking distance of a market.

I recall the period, telling Ayen that I watched some of those barges arrive in Juba, each of them extraordinarily cramped. "How much space did your family have?" I ask. Ayen extends two index fingers and draws the size of their allocated space in the rusty soil around where we are sitting—it seems barely enough for her group of nine to sit down. The family slept on the barge and queued in line for hours to use one of eight latrines. Disease flourished, and the days caring for a child suffering from diarrhea were harried, as Ayen pleaded with those waiting in long lines to allow her first entry. She sucks air across her teeth again, and shakes her head. Halfway through the trip, bars of soap were distributed after three fellow travelers died of illnesses contracted en route.

On each leg of the trip, Ayen and Chendi spoke by phone, except when cell coverage was inadequate. Chendi lived vicariously through Ayen's static-interrupted descriptions, and she regularly asked about each of the children. Amid all the uncertainty, these conversations meant a great deal to Ayen. Her account of the journey is replete with small acts of humanity, and she spends considerable time talking about them: guidance from a pastor on a particularly difficult evening, food shared with a fellow traveler, encouragement from a grieving friend back home. The acts seem magnified—in my mind, and in hers—amid the unimaginably difficult conditions.

Ayen's whole life was here, condensed into a few square yards on a crowded boat—halfway between a past she'd left behind and a future upriver she could not yet imagine.

—∞—

Standing atop a milk crate at Freedom Square on the 9th of July, 2011, the White House's representative, Susan Rice, signaled America's continuing commitment to the project it had helped get off the ground two decades earlier:

> My government will stand with you as you build up the institutions that enshrine your liberty. We will stand with you as you write a constitution for all South Sudanese. We will stand by you as you forge the conditions for lasting peace,

prosperity, and justice. And we will work with you as you shoulder the obligations of a full and responsible member of the international community.

But the lofty rhetoric of commitment would not be matched in practice. Though Washington continued to funnel huge amounts of aid to South Sudan, it would not sustain the outsize political engagement it had during years of peace negotiations or the run-up to independence. Satisfied with a job well done, many of South Sudan's champions brushed the metaphorical dust from their hands and moved on; they believed the leaders they had backed would not only flourish in their own state, but be forever indebted to America for the freedom it had helped deliver at long last.

But they appeared to have misunderstood independence as the finish, rather than the beginning, of the South Sudanese project. Not only was the world's newest state also its least developed, it was beset by poisonous social dynamics, and its transition to democracy had gotten off on the wrong foot—concerns few outsiders appreciated or wanted to acknowledge.

When the euphoria of independence began to subside, the challenge of building a country came into starker relief. "Our country, as it stands today, is a four-legged animal," South Sudanese intellectual Jok Madut Jok remarked, "but the legs are broken." Each of the legs of a functioning nation, he explained—government service delivery, a disciplined military, a vibrant civil society, and political unity—were "crooked"; the young animal was in serious trouble. "If we do not fix these legs, the future is going to be very, very difficult." Jok's was a striking metaphor: one could envision a young wildebeest birthed on the vast East African plains during the rush of migration season, when the herd could afford it only a few minutes to learn to walk, or it would be left behind.

South Sudan was poor, landlocked, and had no formal economy to speak of. Private investment was scant, and the lack of production had created a crippling dependence on imports. Nine out of ten people lived on less than a dollar per day. Development indicators—poverty, education, health, clean water—seemed to reach new lows on global indices. With no services, no roads, and no electricity, few outside the capital had any meaningful experience of the state. What few services were available were usually provided not by the government, but by international aid groups.

Juba already had its hands full establishing institutions of governance in 2005, but with sovereignty in 2011 came an additional menu of responsibilities, from central banking and monetary policy to customs enforcement and foreign policy. There were plenty of practical matters too; American diplomats helped out by putting together a "how to become a country" binder, with tabs ranging from postal codes to UN membership to registering a country code for telephone numbers. (Whereas phone numbers in the U.S. begin with the number one, Southerners chose "211"—a nod to the year of their independence.)

Establishing a bureaucracy and functioning civil service was essential if the new state was to implement policy and drive the basic functions of government. But human capital was scarce. A handful of educated professionals was hardly enough to run a country. In the halls of government, former SPLA generals were far more numerous than experienced civil servants. Southerners returning from administrative jobs in Khartoum would be a huge asset, but they were sometimes sidelined by those whose participation in the liberation struggle had translated into a sense of entitlement. Meanwhile, a disproportionate focus on the capital, often reinforced by international partners, meant the disparity between Juba and the rest of the country—where most people lived—continued to grow. And the rural majority wasn't happy about it.

Just as the state-making got underway, several new rebellions emerged. Each was led by a disaffected strongman, attempting to settle old scores with the government or re-negotiate their position in the new state. Each response effort sucked up attention and precious resources, displaced civilians, and undermined development. And each put strain on an already unstable national army, where ethnic and wartime divisions lingered just below the surface.

Outside the army, the average Southerner was too accustomed to a life of conflict and deprivation. He had not yet had an opportunity to reconcile the wrongs done to his neighbor, nor had either of them seen any tangible dividends of independence. And so each continued to vest his family's well-being in a local strongman, a member of his tribe who spoke to his grievances and promised security, while using him, in turn, to amass personal power.

The everyman's empty pockets and hungry children, when juxtaposed with visions of a corrupt elite, often underwrote ethnic prejudices. Real or not, this experience fueled perceptions of a Dinka-dominated central government, and reinforced an already widely held notion that marginalized communities could prosper only when one of their sons occupied the presidential throne.

For all the talk of state-building, Jok Madut was among the few who wrote and spoke widely about the danger of neglecting an equally important challenge: nation-building. South Sudan was a country in name only, an internationally-recognized veneer that represented little more than a defined territory. Roads and schools and services would form the skeleton of a state, but this body politic would also require flesh and blood. Nation-building was about the people themselves, Jok preached, it was about fostering in them a sense of loyalty and belonging. And this was no fluffy aspiration; national identity was exactly the kind of connective tissue without which this project would come apart.

"People's first entity of affiliation, and respect, and loyalty is the tribe," Jok lamented, "not the nation." Apart from their shared struggle against Sudan, precious little defined Southerners as members of this new unit. The label "Southerner" itself derived meaning only in its contrast to the North. "We have never had a chance to ask ourselves: what are the threads that connect all of us?" Jok said to a youthful audience in Juba one year after independence, "What is the glue that binds us together?" A new narrative would be required if any member of this new club was to think of themselves not first as Dinka or Nuer or Bari but instead as "South Sudanese." It wouldn't be easy; nations do not simply happen; they are intentional projects forged through conscious effort.

In its formative days, America, too, had overcome an external foe. It cultivated a set of symbols, themes, and ideas that together became a national identity. Though the stains of American slavery and racism could not be ignored, the national project had captured a majority of the citizenry from its earliest generations, and endured. From the Boston Tea Party and the legends of the American Revolution, to the ideals of Lincoln affirmed through the Civil War years, there was a narrative of shared history. Notions of freedom and exceptionalism had been staked out by the founding fathers and sustained for generations. From John Winthrop's vision of the Massachusetts Bay Colony to President Ronald Reagan's reprise generations later, America believed itself to be a "shining city upon a hill." From the "American Dream" to the Statue of Liberty, from the Star-Spangled Banner to rock-and-roll, and from hamburgers to apple pie—the state had been underwritten by stories and symbols that helped to shape a national ethos.

Jok and a handful of South Sudan's other big minds saw that they would need to do the same. Beyond the shared history of victimhood and struggle, their own founders would have to champion institutions, language, art, memorials, colors, an anthem—"things that every South Sudanese can look and point to," Jok says, "and say 'this represents all of us.'" It could not be done without harnessing the country's many cultures, languages, songs, religions, and customs, and somehow turning diversity into a strength.

The old Sudan, from which the Southern Sudanese had finally extricated themselves, offered a useful lesson. Not only had the NCP regime's attempt to force a nation-wide Arab and Islamic identity denied the country's diversity; it was also the basis on which Southerners were excluded from political power, socio-economic advancement, and any sense of belonging. These grievances were what had ultimately torn Sudan in half. But now that South Sudan stood on its own two feet, ethnic divisions were being exploited, dissent suppressed, and jobs and resources doled out to members of one's own tribe. Had the South's ascendant leaders learned that lesson, some wondered, or were they simply repeating the mistake?

The challenges were sobering, to say the least, and yet it seemed important for outsiders to keep things in perspective. How much gets accomplished in a single four-year term for an American president, or one session of Congress? The regional government in Juba had only existed for six years, in an environment full of constraints, and its task—creating a nation-state from scratch—was no walk in the park.

There were bright spots. Cell phone technology was rapidly closing a communication gap, foreign investors were testing the waters beyond the petroleum sector, and nascent progress was visible in terms of roads and basic infrastructure. Sound legislation had been debated and passed, if not yet implemented. Though musically underwhelming, a government-sponsored competition had yielded a national anthem, "South Sudan Oyee!"

Despite the modest gains, it was also clear by 2011 that the regional government hadn't always put its best foot forward during its six-year dress rehearsal. The SPLM had prioritized instruments of central authority while underperforming when it came to serving the average citizen. Many Southerners criticized their government's failures, but others had so little experience of the state that they had simply abandoned expectations altogether. If the new government was going to win them back, it would have to demonstrate progress on the two issues that most impacted their everyday lives: security and the economy.

For all its hard luck, South Sudan was blessed with oil revenue, at least in the near term. Though developing other sectors would be critical, oil revenue could jump start an economic engine that could propel the country into the future. But the SPLM would have to do a far better job managing its revenue than they'd done to date. Weighed down by defense and public sector salaries, the national budget was in need of an overhaul. Budget execution required attention, too: one year the finance ministry—itself responsible for fiscal management—exceeded its own budget by an astonishing 1900 percent. Capable financial administrators would need to be recruited if Juba was to corral spending and make sound investments. A clearer tax and regulatory framework was also required if Juba was to woo responsible foreign investment.

The state-making endeavor would need a blueprint, and so the cabinet adopted an ambitious 411-page plan intended to "drive the country's development" into the future. And while framing the enormous agenda was a worthwhile undertaking, there was something undeniably alien about the plan's scope, assumptions, and Western technocratic speak. The process that created the document was ultimately more geared to satisfy Western donors than it was an organic exercise. The finished product was a blueprint for a modern liberal democracy, composed mostly by foreign development professionals, too few of whom had ever set foot outside of Juba.

Meanwhile, the state-building efforts weren't taking place in a vacuum. Continuing political tension with Sudan—now a wholly separate country—was preventing a fresh start, not least in economic terms. Amid the ongoing litigation over oil, debt, security, and other divorce matters, Khartoum sought to squeeze its departing spouse by implementing a trade blockade. Huge swathes of Bahr al Ghazal and Upper Nile were normally supplied with goods from across the country's northern border, as these Southern states were better connected to Sudan than they were to Juba. But when the normally steady stream of trucks and traders was halted at border crossings, markets in Southern states emptied. Prices spiked, more people went hungry, and the flames of domestic unrest were fanned. Shortly thereafter, when Pagan Amum's negotiating team and their Northern adversaries failed to agree on a plan to convert to a new currency, the haphazard introduction of new and competing currencies further shook economic confidence.

Despite South Sudan's uphill battle, hopes remained high that the anticipated boost in oil revenues after independence would liberate the new country and help make up for time lost.

PART II
THE UNMAKING

13

THE NUCLEAR OPTION

"If you think you are the smartest guy in the room, someone is going to check mate you."

—African mediator

To say South Sudan was oil dependent is like saying the Arctic is sometimes chilly in the winter. On the eve of independence, petroleum constituted a whopping 98 percent of revenue. It was the very wellspring of the emerging state's viability, and many hoped it meant an end to decades of neglect.

In the world's most underdeveloped plot of land, there was little formal economy to speak of, almost no infrastructure, and a largely unskilled labor force. People were hungry, insecure, and in dire need of basic services. After separation, the oil would belong to the Southerners, but they would still need Khartoum's infrastructure and Red Sea access to get it to market. Without steady revenue from oil, the new country's economy would swiftly collapse.

In the North, the oil boom that began in 1999 had stabilized Sudan's ailing economy and catalyzed a decade of growth. Despite American sanctions, billions of petrodollars had energized commerce in the capital, pumped the army full of steroids, and sparked new building, infrastructure, and foreign investment. It also fueled a vast patronage pyramid that helped the regime remain in power. But like its neighbor to the south, Khartoum failed to sufficiently diversify its economy. By 2011, with the South's departure imminent, everything was about to change overnight. The loss of some 60 percent of Sudan's total revenue (and more than 90 percent of exports) could destabilize the country and deal a fatal blow to its ruling party.

Oil was a matter of survival for both North and South. Despite all the blood, sweat, and tears spent during months of negotiation on other post-referendum arrangements, the fate of talks would ultimately hinge on this matter of most strategic import.

Mediators urged the two teams to pursue "win-win" oil arrangements that would ensure continued production during a rocky transition and maximize value for both states. During early talks, one proposal was floated for a 50-50 "wealth-sharing" deal—North and South would *share* Southern oil revenue for a fixed period after independence. U.S. Envoy Princeton Lyman appealed to Southern negotiators to consider the plan. Juba had a huge task ahead of it, he argued, and could not afford to waste any attention on a hostile neighbor—better to compensate Khartoum and get on with their own business. It was a pragmatic play.

In the years immediately before and after independence, Pagan Amum and I discussed the topic of oil countless times—from extraction technology, to contract negotiations with the Chinese, to transport and processing fees. When we meet for a second day of discussions in Denver, in 2016, I'm eager to revisit it, as the politics of oil—and the decisions Pagan helped to engineer—have since shaped his country more than either of us could have imagined at the time.

I drive us to an unremarkable suburban hotel, and we grab jackets, as the temperature has dipped considerably. On the way in, I catch myself striding ahead and slow to wait for him. Pagan sometimes walks in a relaxed, slow manner. It may be the Zen maestro within, but I can't help thinking it is the learned gait of a man keenly aware of power and political optics. Presidents, dignitaries, leaders—these are the kind of great men who need not rush; for them the show will wait.

We park ourselves on stools at a high-table in the lobby, and I open by asking about Ambassador Lyman. Pagan breaks into a wistful smile. "He is so good, so genuine," he says, recounting the American's diplomatic arts fondly, and the many months Lyman spent pushing Pagan's team toward compromise. "He sneaks, he *sneaks* into your soul and then tries to fight you from within." Pagan breaks into a hearty chuckle. "It is so hard to turn him down." But Pagan did turn Lyman down when it came to wealth sharing with Khartoum—that was a bridge too far.

"This is not the business of sovereign states," he says. Any arrangement not based on "clear Southern ownership of its own resources," he believed, would set a bad precedent and perpetuate a sense of inequality. "The U.S. would *never* do such a thing; you would just say, 'are you crazy? We are sovereign here.'" Pagan pauses, satisfied that he's about to land a point, and I can feel another rhetorical question coming. "So why should we?"

The two negotiating parties spent months squabbling over fees—how much South would pay North to use its pipelines, processing centers, and export terminal. Desperate to compensate for the hole partition was about to blow in its economy, Khartoum opened by proposing hugely inflated fees. Formula after formula was proposed, debated, and shouted down—at one stage it was suggested that Juba pay a lump sum to Khartoum as a kind of national alimony.

"But whatever the proposal," Ambassador Lyman explained when I asked him in 2016, "Pagan devised offsets that would effectively yield no net payment" from Juba to Khartoum. Lyman laughed out loud, recalling Pagan's doggedness with a mixture of frustration and admiration. "He was *a very... tough... negotiator*," he said, "always extracting the most he could get." But the American again appealed to Pagan's team. "Look, guys, it's not whether it's *just*, or *right*," he had told them, "it is simply the price for peace."

Pagan countered with a proposal to pay reasonable pipeline fees while also "offering assistance" to Sudan, provided Khartoum acknowledged the South's undisputed ownership of the oil, and agreed to other concessions. For a country still coming to terms with giving away a third of its territory, and 60 percent of its revenue, the notion of a handout from its junior brother came as a slap in the face to Sudanese negotiators.

But Pagan balked at the idea that his team should be unduly deferential. "Because they have an ego that we are supposed to respect? Don't *we* have an ego?" Where others sought compromise and face-saving, Pagan stood on principle. "You cannot tell me that I must *share*, or that I must mind my language," Pagan continues, "just because we are an emerging underdog?"

Pagan's was not an unreasonable position, and one could appreciate the strength of character and desire to be treated as equal. Nonetheless, his approach antagonized those around the negotiating table, and there's no doubt he reveled at the chance to deliver a blow to Khartoum's collective ego.

Pagan shifts in his seat, and after a long pause, he says of his posture throughout the talks, "I was firm, but engaging." When I suggest that others might replace "firm" with "pain in the ass," he spouts a laugh of acknowledgment, but insists he was always guided by national interests, never stubborn for the sake of stubbornness.

With no deal in sight, each side looked elsewhere for more leverage. As the dominant commercial player in the oil sector, China suddenly found itself caught in the middle. Beijing's state-owned oil giant operated the oil fields and purchased and refined almost all of the crude from both countries. It still owned majority stakes in the country's pipelines, refinery, and export terminals—all built by Chinese companies. Each side subjected Chinese representatives to intense pressure, prompting considerable anxiety in Beijing. Many assumed that Chinese officials would weigh in more assertively, but perceptions of Beijing's influence and its readiness to employ it were unrealistic. It wanted desperately to remain on the sidelines, and to maintain balanced relations with both North and South.

China wasn't the only lever the parties tried. Juba also made showy consideration of bids to build an alternative oil pipeline—one that would free it from its dependency on the North. If Juba appeared to have another export lifeline, the thinking went, Khartoum might compromise on fees rather than get cut out of the equation altogether. One pipeline plan connected Juba to a proposed new port on the Kenyan coast, another snaked through Ethiopia to an established port in coastal Djibouti. But Khartoum was not fooled. Technical obstacles aside, South Sudan's proven reserves were not enough to justify building a new pipeline. A new pipeline would take years to complete and could well cost more than all the oil that might ever flow through it.

The months-long saga reached a dangerous climax in January 2012 after Khartoum took a turn trying to strong-arm a deal. And a provocative attempt it was. Pagan and Southern negotiators woke up one morning to urgent telephone calls informing them that a series of the South's oil shipments had been confiscated at Port Sudan. Khartoum had loaded Southern oil onto its own tankers and was effectively holding hundreds of millions of Juba's revenue hostage. When journalists swarmed Khartoum's petroleum minister for comment, he confirmed that Juba's oil exports "would be halted at port until a settlement is reached." Later he added that the shipments had been taken "in lieu of" fees allegedly owed by South Sudan for previous exports.

Pagan was livid. Southern oil sector spokesmen disputed the claim and fingered the "blatant theft" as an attempt by Khartoum to force their hand. The SPLM refused to continue discussions and publicly threatened to shut down the entire oil sector—a move which would bring both economies to a screeching halt. Of all the threats leveled to date, none was more consequential than this. The so-called "'nuclear option" had been the subject of occasional murmurs, but few believed the Southerners would go so far.

But days later, Juba made good on its word. After an emergency cabinet meeting, government spokesperson Barnaba Marial emerged to make a stunning announcement. "The council of ministers decided today," he told assembled reporters, that in light of the oil being "looted" by Khartoum, the petroleum ministry had been instructed to begin "a complete shutdown of oil production."

Those scribbling in their notebooks outside could hardly believe it. The men gathered inside the cabinet room had just hit the big red button. Juba would see Khartoum's extortionist provocation and raise it one better—South Sudan would forgo its own national revenue entirely in order to deprive Khartoum.

"*What the fuck*?" That was the response of one American official close to the process, when I asked her to characterize Washington's collective reaction to the shutdown. South Sudan's biggest patron was caught totally off guard by the decision, and was none too pleased. American diplomats had heard the threats before, but never believed the SPLM would go through with it. "People in DC were irate," the official said. "These guys are meanwhile asking us for help, they're asking us for everything from humanitarian aid to weapons systems, and now they do this?" She shook her head in disbelief. "They strangle their own economy and we're going to have to feed their people again?"

Oil company managers placed frantic calls to the ministry, distressed about the potentially irreversible damage a shutdown would cause to infrastructure. Diplomats likewise flooded the phone lines to try to walk the SPLM back from the brink. But Pagan announced that Juba would not be pushed around, telling reporters the shutdown was a "matter of national pride." He would rather "leave the oil in the ground, than lose it to Sudan... that is even worse." The SPLM issued a list of demands for the North to meet before they would turn the oil spigots on again. They framed the decision as an assertion of sovereignty and an act of defiance against their former overlords. And at the time, their principled stand was met by cheers and nationalistic pride in parliament and across South Sudan.

But the opportunity cost was staggering. Southerners had waited for a generation to see the development gains long promised to them. And while oil talks continued in Addis Ababa, some people back home in rural communities were still forced to subsist on grass and leaves; others died of preventable disease. When it came to bailing them out—food and clean water, education and health care, agriculture and economic growth—the amount of wealth in the ground offered huge potential. Even the country's comparatively modest oil reserves presented far greater value than whatever aid the Americans could reasonably provide. But now they were leveraging it—all of it—and for what?

To most of South Sudan's friends, the move by Juba's negotiators suggested a shocking disregard for their own people. "Yeah, that warm fuzzy feeling about South Sudan and independence and all that?" the American official continued. "It promptly took a nose dive." Re-living the frustration of the moment, the official recounted a meeting with the SPLM's chief negotiator shortly after the shutdown was announced. "He talked and talked endlessly about their decision, as Pagan does, but it's clear he doesn't have a serious plan. They didn't. They had no plan!"

Ambassador Lyman's team had been busy forging compromise solutions and pressing the SPLM to be reasonable, all while managing an increasingly skittish Washington from afar. But the broader historical relationship with the United States—in which the SPLM had long been coddled and its interests protected—was undermining their efforts. SPLM leaders weren't listening to their American colleagues as they once had, but they continued to make decisions with the belief that Washington would never let them collapse.

"Yes, they thought we would save them," said the American diplomat. "Yeah, what do you call that? Yes, a moral hazard."

Officials in Juba announced that the shutdown would take less than a week to complete. Racing to try and reverse the decision, Mbeki and regional leaders convened an emergency heads-of-state summit in Addis Ababa. Chinese officials also finally stepped forward, pleading with both sides to reach a compromise. More diplomatic heavyweights intervened directly with Pagan, but there was no deviating the bowling ball from its course. When Presidents Salva and Bashir arrived in Addis, Mbeki circulated a compromise proposal to defuse the standoff and steer talks back toward a mutually beneficial arrangement.

In a meeting that Pagan did not attend, Salva told Mbeki and his fellow heads of state that he was ready to sign the proposed compromise. They announced a breakthrough and planned a ceremony for later that evening in the Sheraton Hotel's grand ballroom. Moments before the event was to begin, as Salva stood just outside the ballroom, he got wind that his chief negotiator—still in his hotel room—was not on board.

Pagan was summoned to the anteroom and told his boss, "Mr. President, I will not sign an agreement that I have not been a party to negotiating." He outlined his concerns, and indicated that if the president supported the agreement, he should sign it himself, adding not so subtly, "If you sign this agreement, you will be received with stones when you return to Juba."

Dumbfounding the crowd already assembled inside, Salva then entered the ballroom and promptly reneged. It wasn't the first time the president would reverse himself at Pagan's insistence, or the last. Both Mbeki and the NCP were furious. The move hurt Juba's credibility as an honest broker and disappointed Salva's regional peers who already held him in low esteem. Salva blamed the latest reversal on "my people," but everyone in Addis zeroed in on just one person.

"He torpedoed it," one frustrated mediator explained of Pagan, as suspicion grew that the South's frontman was angling for more than just a fair deal. "At that moment, everyone was convinced... this guy is out for regime change in Khartoum."

Aides reported that Sudan's President Bashir later chided Salva. "What do you mean 'your people?'" he asked angrily. "We know it is this American boy Pagan. It is he and the Americans."

Now resting his elbows on the table, Pagan smiles, relishing his influence and maverick reputation. "They believed I was implementing a U.S. conspiracy to dismember Sudan... actually, they even believed that I was CIA." Pagan explains that such perceptions helped him during the talks, as anyone acting with such nerve must surely be backed by a powerful benefactor. Whether Pagan's adversaries believed such a fanciful ruse—and it is likely a stretch—paranoid perceptions were not uncommon given the SPLM's established ties to Washington.

Bashir again pressed Salva to replace Juba's brash pointman, calling him a "warlord who has no interest in peace" and no sense of belonging to the land or its people. Another Sudanese official echoed the president's disdain, blasting Pagan's "notorious hostility towards the North and the Arabs."

Pagan's contempt for the NCP regime was real, but it also played well at home. Even amid the three-dimensional chess match he was playing with Khartoum's negotiators, Pagan had his eye on the presidency. "He was playing domestic politics all the time," Ambassador Lyman recalled, "at each phase calculating, 'is this deal or that deal going to hurt or help me back home?'"

As the face of the South's referendum vote, and its defiant warrior at the negotiating table, Pagan saw his stock rising. After all, he believed himself the legitimate heir of the grand project started by his mentor, John Garang. For him, neither the weak-willed Salva nor the traitorous Riek was fit to carry the torch.

※

The Southerners were determined to be treated as equals, and understandably so. But following independence, their robust assertion of sovereignty meant they would risk over-playing their hand. Their decision to shut down the oil sector was about ending Khartoum's illegal confiscations and about securing a fair deal on exports. But it was also being leveraged against a much larger goal—toppling the NCP government.

Some in the SPLM saw an opportunity; not only could the South win its independence, it could do one better by unseating the regime that had ruined Sudan for more than two decades. With the body blow dealt to Khartoum's economy, they believed the NCP was on the verge of collapse. All it needed was a firm push. But their analysis was clouded by emotion and the chest-thumping pride of the moment, and the voices of caution inside the party were again extinguished. The NCP was surely facing its greatest challenge yet, but it had weathered economic storms before. Every few years prognosticators surmised that unsustainable economic forces would finally spell the end of Bashir's regime, but the NCP had a reputation for proving them wrong. "Guys, you keep saying this," Lyman told Pagan and his SPLM counterparts, "but they're still here."

In addition to misjudging their financial position, the SPLM bravado colored military assessments as well. "Grossly naive" was how one insider described Juba's cabinet meetings during the decisive period. "It was: 'just surge funds to the SPLA and we'll be at the gates of Khartoum in no time.'" Buoyed by their newfound sense of strength, South Sudan would indeed test the military option in April 2012. After a series of hostile engagements and finger-pointing between Northern and Southern armies, the SPLA charged north and captured the symbolic Heglig oil fields just outside the disputed territory of Abyei. It was a provocative and stunning military victory, one that was celebrated in Juba and briefly validated the chest-thumpers.

"Nobody saw it coming," another American official told me, "and it freaked everyone out." The incident prompted a short but dangerous series of border battles, and the SPLA was forced to withdraw after an unexpected, and unequivocal, rebuke from the Americans and the wider international community. "I call on South Sudan to immediately withdraw its forces," said the UN Secretary-General from New York. "This is an infringement on the sovereignty of Sudan and a clearly illegal act."

The provocation had nearly ignited a wider war, just months after the two sides had narrowly avoided one. It further polarized relations between the two countries, and temporarily bolstered—rather than dislodged—the embattled NCP regime. Neither side was innocent, but the event was a public image disaster for the "good guys" in the South, and even earned them a threat of UN Security Council sanctions.

The sheen was starting to come off the underdogs in South Sudan. The SPLM was unaccustomed to this degree of international opprobrium, and could no longer play the victim. Taken together, the continued support to proxies in Sudan, the assault on Heglig, and the oil shutdown seemed to confirm the notion that Juba, now free to stand on its own two feet, was bent on ousting the regime in Khartoum.

The oil shutdown was arguably the biggest strategic decision in the young country's short history, and by most accounts, it had been engineered by Pagan and very few others. With oil talks frozen, Juba was locked into the most dangerous and costly game of chicken yet. As hostilities along the border subsided, an economic war of attrition ensued, each side hoping it could outlast the other. But despite hopes for Khartoum's capitulation, it was Juba that would be forced to flinch first.

The SPLM government had announced that it had sufficient reserves in the bank to hold out, but those funds would dry up in remarkably short order, leaving the newly sovereign state in dire financial straits. The oil would stay in the ground, untapped, and so too would the promises of development and government services.

Despite the obvious trouble it was now in, the SPLM defended its decision, peddling a familiar talking point: "Our people have suffered for generations, they are prepared to suffer a little longer." But it wasn't government elites or negotiators who would do the suffering, of course. Though the shutdown decision had initially enjoyed populist acclaim, Southerners would soon begin to feel the pain. Inflation soared. Commodities became scarce, and the World Bank warned of economic disaster. The government slashed budgets, cut allowances, and scrambled to secure advances from predatory lenders. And then things went from bad to worse.

States governors, who normally received funds from Juba for state business, soon found their mailboxes empty. Day laborers went to buy dinner for their families, but found their earnings bought only half as much as they had the week before. Long lines formed at petrol stations, and frustrated drivers shouted at one another. The price of a bag of *dura* doubled, and then it tripled. Popular support for the audacious shutdown decision began to evaporate. The SPLM had been riding the wave that had come with independence and its defiance of Khartoum, but its political reserves would not last forever.

As the economy deteriorated and Juba held its own financial lifeline hostage underground, SPLM ministers went on a roadshow looking for loans. Piqued by their rash decision, Western donors refused to throw more money at them, calling the shutdown a "self-inflicted wound." And so the SPLM gang went hopping around Europe, the Gulf, and Asia looking for anyone who would listen.

First stop, Beijing, where they hoped their oil partners would come through with the kind of eye-popping loan that had characterized its investments elsewhere in Africa. The SPLM licked its lips over the kind of "no strings attached" package that might finance infrastructure projects and build an alternative oil pipeline to East Africa. But China's state banks were more conservative these days, and because Beijing had been so uncomfortably caught in the tug-of-war between North and South, it wasn't keen to make any big moves. Stability was China's top priority; its leaders preferred that Juba strike a deal with Khartoum and end the standoff, which would be best for both parties and protect Chinese investments in the two countries.

But this wasn't the answer the Southern delegation had gone looking for. Betraying their increasing desperation, government officials made a foolhardy attempt to force China's hand. After Salva took tea with the Chinese premier on an official visit to Beijing's Great Hall of the People, Information Minister Barnaba Marial made a surprise announcement that China had granted South Sudan an $8 billion financing package. But Chinese officials were mum on the matter, and no such deal ever materialized. One top diplomat from Beijing later confided with a puzzled chuckle, "I was in every one of those meetings, and there was no such loan discussed."

Offering up future oil sales at a discount, the SPLM leadership did manage to cobble together smaller loans from other sources: oil companies, banks in the Gulf, and most worryingly—shady private lenders. Given their desperate position, the sharks had smelled blood, and the SPLM ministers had agreed to predatory terms that would put their young country in the red for years to come. Rather than climbing out of the hole in which their young country was starting, they appeared to have hopped in with shovels and begun digging. It was hardly the prosperous start so many had envisioned.

***

Frustrated with Juba's misplaced braggadocio, disastrous new domestic security problems, and an economic death spiral, Secretary of State Hillary Clinton flew to Juba in August 2012 to deliver some stern advice. Enough was enough, she told President Salva. The oil shutoff was destroying their new country, and in the war of attrition with Sudan, they were going to lose. A failed state would be devastating for

South Sudan's weary people, but it would also reflect poorly on the Americans—their state-making project gone belly up.

"A percentage of something is better than a percentage of nothing," Clinton said at a joint press conference in Juba, reiterating the sentiments she'd delivered to Salva. "You've made your point" about "*your* rights to *your* resources." Now, she told them, it was time to deal. Clinton's visit came at a point of maximum international pressure, coinciding with a deadline from the UN Security Council and the looming threat of international sanctions if the two sides did not come to an agreement.

The two sides finalized an oil deal in the ensuing days, and a comprehensive set of arrangements—security, borders, debt, banking, trade, citizenship, and a temporary fix for Abyei—was inked six weeks later. After more than two years of battlefield brinkmanship and bitter divorce proceedings, economic survival and continued inter-dependence had trumped all else.

The "September 2012 Agreement" by no means settled everything between the two nations; implementation was slow and some cans were kicked down the road. But after more than a year off-line, oil would begin flowing again in the spring of 2013, an emergency infusion of essential nutrients into two economies on life support.

Pagan worked with Northern negotiators to conclude each element of the agreement, but also registered his opposition publicly. "It is true… the negotiating team, including myself personally as a chief negotiator were subjected to extreme pressure from the Americans, British, the Norwegians," he complained in a press conference, ensuring his defiant nationalism was on record. "They were forcing us to give away the resources of South Sudan."

Whether a matter of conviction or political posturing, Pagan maintains that the shutdown was the right choice, and that the SPLM should have held out longer, leveraging more against oil. "History has proven this was a bad deal," he says to me, four years after the fact. I shoot him a decidedly skeptical frown in return, and pepper him with counterpoints. But Pagan maintains that the oil shutdown "achieved its desired effect" and that Sudanese negotiators immediately started scaling back their demands.

"Really?" I ask. "Many people think you did not get a better deal in the end—in fact some argue it was worse." He laughs incredulously at the suggestion, and offers further rebuttals.

But Pagan is in the minority. Many observers, and some of his fellow countrymen, have a less glowing assessment of his handling of the oil talks. They see less virtue in Pagan's motivations and cite the damage to the economy, reputational costs, and opportunities lost as a result of the shutdown. "It was a disastrous idea, just dumb," Ambassador Lyman told me in 2016 without reserve. "The stupidest thing they could have done." South Sudan's once flush economy was put under such duress that Juba, many believed, had been forced to negotiate from a position of weakness. It did not get a better deal in the end, and the political and economic consequences of its self-inflicted wound would prove deep and lasting.

"I really like Pagan, he has a vision, and there is an innocence underneath it all," one member of the Mbeki-led mediation team said of Pagan's posture during the negotiations. "But this guy didn't understand what it takes to run a country... he was self-deluded about his own intelligence, thinking he was the smartest guy on the block after Garang. And if you think you are smart, well... someone is going to check mate you."

Most consequentially, critics—both South Sudanese and foreign—also draw a causal line from the oil shutdown to South Sudan's civil war two years later, in 2013. Turning off the wells meant turning off the profits, and that, they argue, broke the patronage system that had lubricated the country's powertrain for years. The emptying of the national coffers exacerbated the personal, political, and ethnic divisions that led to total breakdown. It is too simplistic to suggest the patronage shortfall was the cause of South Sudan's fratricidal war, but it surely was a contributing factor.

Less than a year after the agreements were signed, as focus shifted to the home front, Pagan would openly criticize President Salva and signal his intent to mount a challenge for SPLM party chairman and for the presidency. But he would not get his chance. Pagan was detained by the president's forces in December 2013, accused as a co-conspirator in the alleged plot to overthrow the government.

Now, sitting in Denver, more than 8,000 miles away from South Sudan's political arena, Pagan insists he has no plans or interest to return. "No, not until President Salva is gone. It is useless." But what I hear is a man who has not yet identified an opportunity. Against the advice of many, Pagan had already engineered one return to Juba, in 2015, seemingly bent on re-claiming his party position and mounting another challenge amid the chaos and disunity. But undermined by Salva's new power circle and with his life again threatened, he relented and boarded a plane for the United States.

After two full days debating the events at the height of his political influence, Pagan, wearing khaki pants and a maroon Oxford button-down, stands on the lawn of his modest split-level home in an unremarkable Denver suburb and waves goodbye. Trees sway in the summer breeze, and a single blue car turns leisurely down the adjacent street.

In one way he seems content with the change of pace, making up for time lost with three school-age children, eating healthy, and "reflecting on the meaning of his personal journey," from whence it began, in the green fields of Upper Nile. But the political animal abhors his own irrelevance, and I can't imagine him enjoying all this pleasant normalcy for long.

In fact, just two months after our discussion, Pagan would return to his familiar place in the headlines, announcing a new campaign he was launching from Denver, "South Sudan Reborn."

14

WALDORF ASTORIA

"The saddest thing about betrayal is that it never comes from your enemies."

—Anonymous

I n August 2011 I hopped a series of UN flights to Bentiu, the capital of Unity State, roughly 300 miles northwest of Juba. In addition to sharing volatile borderlands with neighboring Sudan, Unity then faced a cocktail of internal challenges arguably unparalleled in South Sudan. Feeding on compounding economic, social, and political grievances, local rebellions had been wreaking havoc for months. Insecurity of this kind could, like an ailing economy, undermine popular confidence in the barely-baptized new Republic. But struggling to assert its authority, the new government appeared to be making things worse.

Throughout the tumultuous period between 2010 and 2012, all eyes had been fixed on North-South talks, with the aims of averting a new war and ensuring Southern independence. Little attention was reserved for the domestic situation in the new country, though its health and trajectory would be shaped by decisions in these critical years as much as at any other time. South Sudan's foreign champions sought not to draw too much attention to worrisome domestic political and security trends at a moment of existential consequence. But the turbulent episodes of this period—including internal rebellions and violence between feuding tribes—were exposing a dangerously fragile new state.

After touching down in a single-engine Cessna at Bentiu's rust-red dirt airstrip, I set up at a local guest house, comprising half a dozen weathered metal containers, a two-stall wooden outhouse, a plastic water tank propped atop a wooden fence, and a small communal tent. I spent sticky nights sleeping on an aluminum bed frame criss-crossed with plastic-coated wires of yellow and green. Each morning I filled up a small wash basin, peeled off the night's sweat-drenched clothes, and washed while wearing boots to manage the mud. Most evenings I ate "chips," the potatoes sliced and fried in a cauldron of hot oil sitting in the long grasses outside the main tent. Ducking into the tent, I cracked the spine on a new notebook and started making calls to local contacts, hoping to get a handle on the many pressures causing instability in this tempestuous border state.

What they reported was worse than I expected. After rebels defected from the SPLA and recruited young men from aggrieved communities, the government sent trucks of SPLA reinforcements rumbling into the area, intending to put down the rebellion. Bloody battles had ensued, killing scores on both sides, sending thousands of civilians fleeing into the inhospitable hinterlands, and flattening whole settlements. The still-militarized government was intolerant, inexperienced, and predisposed to violence. Just a few hours on the ground and the hypothesis was confirmed: Juba was its own worst enemy.

"No question about it! No *question*, security was our biggest problem," recalled one former county commissioner, repeating himself and shaking his head at the scale of the challenge. Not only were fracas like the one in Unity endangering civilians and undermining national authority, the armed forces themselves were in need of an overhaul. Transforming a fractious guerrilla army into a set of professional security institutions that could protect and defend was no small order. In the meantime, the bloated army was more often a source of instability than the antidote.

Security woes aside, the economic shocks of Khartoum's trade blockade were immediately evident, even before I'd left the tent at the guest house. The orange Fanta soda I'd eagerly slurped was the temperature of warm tea, as the fuel-deprived generator and the refrigerator it powered sat idle. Meanwhile the women frying up a batch of chips had just returned from the local market empty-handed. In a fiery mix of English, Nuer, and frustrated gesticulations, I heard them complaining of another spike in the cost of basic staples—grain, sugar, cooking oil, even clean water.

Just beyond Bentiu's increasingly barren market, I would later find a makeshift camp full of Southern returnees—people like Ayen, the hopeful mother whose family had journeyed south by bus and barge—their piles of furniture and belongings splayed about as if a hurricane had just barreled through town. Nearly 85,000 of them had already arrived here from Sudan. Some had been harassed and extorted by Arab militias along the way, and many were now marooned here without land or means for further transport. Insecurity was gripping the city, markets were emptying, and more and more people were showing up.

Unity state was also among the many places where the unreconciled legacies of Sudan's 20-year war were driving not only contemporary politics, but the new insurrection. The rebellions were a reminder of President Salva's 2006 big-tent policy, through which Nuer commander Paulino Matiep and tens of thousands of armed militia men—a great many of them from here—had been absorbed into the SPLA. Though their integration was intended to preserve unity, the new arrivals were marginalized and denied upward mobility.

Among the disgruntled was Peter Gadet, the most notorious of the new rebel commanders now demanding change in Unity. It was no coincidence he and several other commanders were from nearby Mayom County, the home of Matiep. Long an adversary of the SPLA, Mayom remained one of the country's most ostracized and disaffected communities. Peter Gadet's new militia was one of seven groups that declared opposition to the Southern government in 2010 and fought throughout 2011. As Sudan's partition approached, such strongmen saw an opportunity to redefine their place in the new order.

Some were motivated by personal gain, others saw rebellion as the only means through which grievances would be heard. Citing governance failures, rampant corruption, and corrosive tribalism in the army and government, "those of" Peter Gadet had issued a scathing declaration on the eve of independence. Among other things, it had blasted the SPLM for "intimidation" and a "politics of exclusion."

Southerners had for years suppressed their grievances in service of the greater good, choosing, as opposition minister Changson had explained, "not to rock the boat." As a result, a fragile unity had been more or less preserved since the CPA. But now, as I moved about town, and then visited outlying villages, I heard more and more examples that suggested it was cracking.

During one firefight in Gadet's Mayom County, locals described how an SPLA division had set fire to seven villages perceived to be sympathetic to the rebels, destroying more than 7,000 *tukuls*. When terrorized civilians trickled back to find the charred remains of their homes, what was not destroyed had been looted by the army. It was difficult to distinguish between the two forces clashing here; Gadet's "rebels" weren't a haphazard band of warrior delinquents, they were organized units, clad in SPLA uniforms, marching under the command of officers, and deploying weapons as formidable as any the actual army was wielding. Eager to bolster their credibility, rebel supporters showed me videos of their foot soldiers, draped in ribbons of ammunition, chanting war songs, and rallying to the battle cries of their impassioned leader. South Sudan had just achieved independence, and yet Unity State felt like a war zone.

Hoping to get a sense of the SPLA's counter-insurgency strategy, I hopped a ride on a *boda boda* to the nearby headquarters of the SPLA's 4th division, where morale was low after weeks of fratricidal convulsion. Once there, I found a gaggle of officers reclining under a drooping shade tree, machine guns resting across their knees. After explaining the reason for my visit, the low man on the totem rose, in lethargic fashion, and escorted me inside.

The office of the 4th division commander was hot, dank, and heavily curtained. The portly man behind the desk wore dark green fatigues and a formidable scowl. His English was as limited as my Nuer, but I could tell by his expression that he was deeply suspicious of my interest in Bentiu's security nightmare.

After considerable vetting with the help of a young army translator, and pledges that I was not a CIA agent, the commander barked an angry order at the private. He saluted the boss and then hurried out of the room. Unsure if I was about to be detained or expelled, the young man returned moments later with two spoons and a plate covered in a mound of smooth pale brown. As the commander handed me a spoon, his frown gave way to a wide smile and an invitational nod to the plate. And so my new friend and I talked at length over a plate of peanut butter. He was eager to understand what was happening in Juba, and I wanted to understand what was happening here.

Given ongoing tensions between Khartoum and Juba, Sudanese armed forces were massing at the border less than 40 miles away. The changing of the seasons was also due to bring an annual migration of armed cattle herders south from Sudan. The rebellions, meanwhile, had fractured the the commander's division and turned much of the local population against his soldiers. And not without controversy, the commander was taking orders not from SPLA headquarters but from the local governor, Taban Deng, who was reviled by a majority of Bentiu's residents. I asked the commander about each concern, but between mouthfuls of peanut butter, he could not help but turn the discussion instead to the high politics of Juba. After all, Unity state was home to Riek Machar, and thus an important piece in the unspoken chess match now well underway between Salva and Riek. Their maneuvers for political and military control of the state were complicating matters in a town already confronting too many dangers.

I spent several more days talking to residents, politicians, and local chiefs in Bentiu and the surrounding counties, after which I packed up to head back to Juba. I settled up at the guest house and fought my way through increasingly ferocious winds back to the small dirt airstrip. Turning my back on the driving wind and shielding my eyes from the hail of dirt, it seemed I was the only passenger intending to catch the twice-weekly air service shuttle. In most state capitals, there are no airport terminals, no tickets, no airfield staff, no set flight times. Humanitarian NGOs receive scratchy radio signals when an aircraft is en route; standbys like me keep an ear to the sky, waiting to hear for an approach. Prior to setting down, caravan pilots often buzz the airstrip to clear it of cattle, wild animals, and wandering children.

As I awaited my air taxi, it seemed a nasty seasonal dust storm known as a *haboob* was in the making, threatening my commute. I heard the single-engine Cessna approach, and shielding my eyes with a defensive elbow, I looked up to see its faint outline circling above the dust cloud. Trying to land, it circled once, twice, three times before the dull buzz of the propeller faded into the distance, signaling surrender. I dropped my head in disappointment and voiced a few choice expletives. The next flight out was four days later.

I spent the next morning walking the dirt paths on the outskirts of town, where the rains had transformed ditches and low-lying areas into a network of meandering canals. Splashing and jousting playfully, two children bathed in a pool sequestered by tufts of long, almost fluorescent green grasses. They tired into an affectionate embrace, catching their breath. A gaggle of young women in colorful *taubs*, each of them tall, with hair braided in tight rows, sat on stools bent over piles of sudsy clothing. They spoke at the kind of high-speed tempo that only young women are capable of, and laughed hysterically as they washed. At least four decades their elder, a woman passed by silently with a giant bundle of branches balancing on her head, sweat pouring down her face.

Farther down the path, two passing acquaintances set down bags of laundry to exchange friendly slaps on the shoulder. They turned to offer deferential nods to an old man passing by on a rickety bicycle, who reciprocated with a mostly toothless smile. Three young boys sat sideways atop a two-wheeled wooden donkey-cart, they and their cargo bouncing in rhythm as their creaking axle stumbled over hardened swells of earth. Returning from a nearby tributary, a boy in dirty blue shorts and blue shirt stopped and proudly lifted a string to display the fish he'd just outwitted.

Despite the array of pressures being exerted on Bentiu, there remained a kind of intermittent normalcy to the place. It was something not uncommon to unstable parts of the country, where if you have no choice but to get on with it, well, then you simply get on with it. The normalcy of that quiet morning would soon be interrupted, however, by another bout of fighting, each episode making it harder to distinguish between the normal and the aberrant.

A series of retaliatory attacks ensued that week, after which retreating rebels planted land mines on each of the roads running into Bentiu. Arguably the most indiscriminate of weapons, it was, of course, civilians who suffered the consequences. The next two days saw innocents traveling by foot or by bus maimed or killed on three of the four primary access roads, leaving only the westward route toward the UN base where I had re-located to await my return flight. Early the next morning I stood at the gate, looking out beyond the swaying grasses at the rust-colored dirt road, and recalling the gruesome images I'd been shown—a stunned and bloodied bus passenger contemplating a leg blown to pieces. I envisioned teenage soldiers digging up the earth at the apex of the arched road and planting the deadly devices under the cover of night. We could not risk traveling to town and making it four-for-four.

Sometimes the rebellions were met with force, yielding more violence and deepening popular resentment of an already mistrusted government. When that failed, Juba doubled-down on a buyout policy which effectively rewarded rebellion. Born during the fractious civil war, and continued through the interim period, the pattern was well-established: dissatisfied commander instigates violence, weak central government buys back his loyalty. The armed entrepreneur might score a promotion in rank, a suitcase of cash, salaries for his fighters, or increased control over his local community. The buyout program purchased a temporary peace, but it also gave others incentive to follow suit. And they did. The political leadership in Juba knew the practice was unsustainable, but it was a hard policy to break. Domestic unrest could ill be afforded at such a fragile moment.

And so the Unity State rebel Peter Gadet would eventually be re-integrated into the army, again, his latest in a long career of defections and returns. "This guy is a professional," one cadet told me of Gadet's history of flip-flops, "Six, seven times?... We have lost count." Gadet's buyback in 2011 was undoubtedly greased with cash, a new command, and other perks, but the reforms he ostensibly demanded for his home state would never materialize, and the Unity state rebellions continued without him.

Two years later, when the army collapsed, Gadet would defect to join Riek Machar. He would again demand justice and reforms, while at the same time leading some of the civil war's most brutal attacks on civilians.

<hr />

As South Sudan struggled to find its footing in the wake of independence, its relationship with its most important bilateral partner was about to change, in a way that Washington had not foreseen.

America had long ago chosen sides in Sudan, and its reflexive opposition to the government in Khartoum meant it continued to suppress criticism of Juba even after independence. South Sudan was not yet out of the woods, and advertising the underdog's domestic failures, the thinking went, would indirectly benefit Khartoum. North-South negotiations remained unfinished, and until matters of partition were resolved and the South free to stand on its own, a return to war was not out of the question.

There was truth in this rationale, as Juba would be starting off in a hole if they didn't manage to negotiate equitable deals. But there was another reason to mute criticism; shining a light on the South's missteps—weak governance, security failures, corruption—might also reflect poorly on Washington, its state-making project not yet coming up roses. But continuing to defer a much-needed re-calibration with Juba was perpetuating an unhelpful dynamic.

While I was on the ground in Bentiu, Salva Kiir was en route to New York City, where an uncomfortable meeting would serve as a harbinger of a fundamental shift between the United States and South Sudan. Though the public face of the relationship remained intact, the episode would begin to expose the cold reality of how badly Western actors had misjudged their role, influence, and perceived relationships in South Sudan, and the dangers of emotional attachment in foreign policy.

President Salva arrived in Midtown East in September 2011 for his first meeting of the UN General Assembly. The year's annual gathering of global leaders would be a coming out party for the world's newest state. Salva's visit would also include the first official meeting with President Obama as a fellow head of state, and both sides deemed it critically important. During President Bush's second term, Salva had been received numerous times in the Oval Office, and he resented the fact that he had not yet met Barack Obama. Now was his chance to make an impression.

The agenda for the bilateral meeting included mostly congratulatory sentiments and ideas on continued partnership, but Obama's talking points included one more substantive concern. It, too, pertained to the complex security environment in Unity state. Salva's government had been covertly supplying weapons through Unity and across its northern border—now an international boundary—to their rebel brothers in Sudan.

Cut off and weakened by the secession of South Sudan, these former comrades-in-arms were left to continue the fight against Khartoum. They had been members of the SPLM since the beginning; their communities had been on the front lines of the civil war, suffering some of its greatest devastation. The sacrifices they made ultimately allowed for the South to be free. But the CPA had ultimately yielded nothing for them. And so few in the South were comfortable simply cutting off their weapons supply or denying rearguard support. SPLM leaders in Juba, still deeply suspicious of Khartoum, also believed they would be better off with friends controlling the territory between Sudan and the South's oil fields.

Already feeling buoyed by their newly attained independence and presumed position of strength, some believed that their old enemies in Khartoum—now reeling from oil revenue losses—might finally be ripe for toppling. The ultimate cherry atop the independence sundae would be for Sudan's remaining rebels to finish off the regime. After all, what could be better than a friendly new government in this most important neighboring capital? It was audacious thinking.

Juba's gun-running to former SPLM battalions was a serious problem for Khartoum; technically speaking, the South Sudanese were now meddling in the affairs of a sovereign neighbor. It not only threatened to undermine the delicate post-referendum negotiations over oil, borders, citizenship, currency, and debt, but also risked inviting new conflict. Some in the South seemed cavalier about it, but the Americans assessed the risk seriously. Few in Washington wanted to cut off these longtime SPLM fighters either, but as one U.S. diplomat remarked at the time, "That battle will have to be fought another day. There is too much at stake."

The continued stream of weapons was the worst kept secret in the region. But previous attempts by American diplomats to get the South Sudanese to rein in this activity were dismissed or denied. They decided to enlist POTUS, and should it be necessary, they armed him with satellite imagery that, according to one official present, "left no doubts."

As the sun dipped behind the skyscrapers on Manhattan's west side, Salva and his entourage arrived at the famed Waldorf Astoria Hotel for the meet. Built in 1931, the glamorous art deco monument to high society has played host to kings and queens, gangsters and powerbrokers, and generations of A-list celebrities, from Marilyn Monroe to Muhammad Ali. New York's premier hotel address also becomes the seat of the American Presidency for a few days every September, when the White House and State Department take over the historic property for diplomatic engagements around the UN General Assembly. In a reception room on one of the Waldorf's upper floors, Obama was joined by then Secretary of State Hillary Clinton, UN Ambassador Susan Rice, Assistant Secretary of State Johnnie Carson, and Special Envoy Princeton Lyman.

"Don't lie to the president," one official recalled, paraphrasing the appeal U.S. diplomats had reiterated just moments before the meeting.

"We implored them—'don't lie to the president.'" In advance of the important bilateral, American diplomats had twice met with South Sudanese foreign minister Nhial Deng and officials from Salva's office to prepare this critical first engagement. They found the new country's diplomats decidedly arrogant; their brazen remarks and a "who needs you guys?" tone worried their U.S. counterparts. The Americans spelled out the intelligence briefings Obama had received about the weapons, and tried to offer a way for Salva to save face. "We even suggested he could offer a 'non-denial denial'"—Salva would indicate that he would look into the matter, and thus begin a conversation about solutions. But they pleaded with Salva's men that he not lie to the naturally skeptical Obama, who would not take kindly to the obvious deceits attempted thus far.

After a brief photo spray with the White House press corps, the two presidents and their delegations settled into ornate wooden chairs around a beige oval table, flanked by respective flags of their two young countries. The meeting proceeded as planned, smooth and friendly. Obama saved the cross-border weapons shipments for last. Explaining that the intelligence reports were clear, he told Salva that as a sovereign state, the new government couldn't be meddling in the affairs of another country. All eyes fixed on the man in the cowboy hat. After a pregnant pause, Salva looked across the table. "Mr. President, if your satellites are telling you we are sending weapons across the border, you had better check on your satellites."

The Americans were stunned. "We nearly fell off our chairs!" Ambassador Lyman recounted years later with as much shock as on the night it happened. Piqued, Obama promptly ended the meeting, and aides say, he had little time for Salva Kiir from that point forward. According to Lyman, Susan Rice later found Salva in a Waldorf suite and "ripped into" him, castigating him for the inexplicable affront, one which surely embarrassed her, South Sudan's top advocate inside the administration. From then on, Lyman explained, "it was difficult to enlist Obama's help" with Salva Kiir, and when he did place calls from the Oval Office, the exchanges between the two men were unmistakably "chilly."

Though relations would remain close with most of Washington's champions—all of whose involvement long predated Obama—a rift with an American president was unfamiliar territory. Salva had become a huge fan of George W. Bush, but was now on the outs with the man who had underwritten South Sudan's independence and invested huge capital in seeing him succeed.

Weeks after the jarring exchange, Salva appeared to backpedal. In an awkwardly contorted letter to the White House, Salva suggested "new information" had come to light regarding the issue. It was a half-hearted apology. Denis McDonough, Obama's closest advisor and eventual Chief of Staff, traveled to Juba together with Lyman, assuming Salva's government was seeking to patch things up. But when they arrived, Salva suggested he had no knowledge of the letter sent in his name, and again denied the weapons shipments. A reportedly "furious" McDonough returned to Washington, again feeling hoodwinked by a seemingly ungrateful ally.

The cooling feelings were mutual, it seemed. Though it didn't register widely in either Washington or Juba, some believe the rocky round of communication was the first indication of a major shift in an otherwise long and warm relationship. For years, the Southerners had depended on America to protect them from Khartoum. They had depended on them to safeguard their right to self-determination and the sanctity of the referendum poll itself. But with independence now in hand, the ascendant leaders in Juba no longer needed a benefactor in the same way. They were on a post-independence high, and they weren't about to be taking orders from equals. The gap would gradually widen in the period to come, and with it began a slow decline in American influence.

Washington would continue to go to bat for South Sudan, as neither Rice nor the vocal American constituencies would allow the relationship to spoil. But the favors were more begrudging for some inside the administration, as the taste of independence had soured. In time, the shift would ultimately surprise many of Juba's American backers who believed, naively, that the liberation fighters would be forever indebted to their unwavering "friends."

But the relationship had always been asymmetric; Washington was sympathetic to the Southern cause, while Juba was pursuing a strategic interest. Important bonds were forged, but this fundamental asymmetry was lost on the true believers. Citing a lesson learned during decades representing Washington abroad, Princeton Lyman opined, "Warm relations are essential to diplomacy and foreign relations, but they should *never* be mistaken for 'friendship.' Friends are willing to do something for your sake," he explained, "not simply for their own."

Lyman agrees the die of U.S.-SPLM relations had been cast long before, but believes the U.S. policy establishment "should have seen," when the Southern rebels achieved independence, "that these guys were not what we all hoped they'd be." Obama himself did not have a long history with South Sudan; he was not part of the club that had for decades been so close to the SPLM. "We couldn't keep lionizing them," Lyman reflected, "and the first guy to see that was Obama."

A UN helicopter circled its designated landing site near a village in a remote region in southeastern Jonglei state. From inside, its VIP passenger could see chains of smoke rising on the horizon. Peering below, he also caught a stunning glimpse of what everyone had been talking about. Alarm had spread in recent days after UN patrols snapped startling aerial photos of some 8,000 young men marching across Jonglei's vast marshlands. They were Nuer youth from across northern Jonglei, they were armed to the teeth, and their destination was no secret: Pibor county, home of the ethnic Murle people.

South Sudan's leaders had just toasted their independence on the world stage in New York City, but back home, Jonglei state—South Sudan's largest—was coming apart at the seams. As in Unity state, the government and its armed forces had been struggling to contain armed rebellions. But here, each of them drew upon and exacerbated an even larger concern: tribal violence. Over the summer of 2011, an escalating cycle of attacks between ethnic Nuer and Murle communities had left hundreds of civilians dead and radicalized young men on both sides. Spewing hate speech and threatening to "wipe out" the minority ethnic group, the angry wave of Nuer avengers had now arrived in Pibor, ready to make good on their word.

The UN chopper came to a halt, and off stepped a man in a short-sleeved checkered shirt, sunglasses, and a brown felt hat. He carried a walking stick in his dominant left hand. Vice President Riek Machar might easily have been mistaken for someone else, if not for his entourage and the signature gap between his two front teeth. He was received by local SPLA officers, whose units stood no chance of deterring the heavily armed attackers, and neither did the vastly outnumbered UN peacekeepers. And so Riek Machar, the country's most formidable Nuer "big man," had flown in to intercept the mob. Or so he hoped.

Vast, underdeveloped, and home to an England-size swamp, Jonglei was one of mother nature's more formidable opponents during the rainy season. Its flooded marshland and muddy black soils were the kind where 4x4 vehicles were sucked down and then swallowed whole. Enigmatic and often impenetrable, its legendary landscape was part of its personality, inseparable from the lives of its pastoralist people and the challenge of projecting state authority in a land history had left behind. "You have the Wild West in your country," one local administrator told me, attempting to offer some context, "well, this is the Wild East."

I first visited Jonglei in 2009, two years before independence, as cycles of inter-communal violence reached a worrying peak. Such feuds were not uncommon, as the centrality of cattle to all aspects of Nilotic life made them a trigger for confrontation between communities. But that year the cycle of cattle raiding was different. A stunning number of people had been slain in a series of attacks and counterattacks, and the violence had become dangerously politicized.

Raids between local Nuer, Murle, and Dinka tribes were larger, more coordinated, and increasingly targeted at civilians—including women and children. These weren't young men with sticks and spears stealing cattle to replenish stocks or earn respect in their villages, as had been done for centuries. These were armed militias, in military fatigues, draped with rounds of ammunition, and communicating tactics by satellite phone. Some of the calls incoming on those expensive phones, I'd learned, were coming from national politicians, who appeared to be stirring the pot.

Unable to contain the situation, Juba put out to the world that old enemies in Khartoum were instigating the violence. The claim lacked evidence and complicated local dynamics, but it convinced many foreign observers who had long ago chosen sides. The real sources of the problem were rooted at home, and together revealed much about the country's largest state: political and economic marginalization, elite manipulation of ethnic tensions, a history of violence, the absence of roads and communications infrastructure, land disputes, a lack of justice mechanisms, a breakdown of traditional authority, and the huge numbers of weapons in the hands of ordinary civilians. These weren't people bent on senseless barbarity; they had real grievances, and their responses, while shocking in scale, were not necessarily irrational. Lack of trust in government and neighbor alike meant communities felt the need to guarantee their own security.

Jonglei's violence was a window into a society too accustomed to war. Young men in Akobo County sometimes didn't have shoes or schoolbooks, but they had AKM and G3 assault rifles and rocket-propelled grenades. Their counterparts in Pibor were regularly short of food and clean water, but they had 60-millimeter mortars, anti-personnel mines, and RPM machine guns. When disputes arose, the mostly hapless police were too far away to engage. When they did, they were outmanned and outgunned. Under pressure to take action, the government usually responded in familiar and reflexive fashion, with force.

Among the catalysts for Jonglei's cycle of violence was an earlier, and ruthless, campaign of forcible disarmament undertaken by the SPLA in two Nuer communities. That operation had netted some 3,000 weapons, but weeks of firefighting between the SPLA and community protection groups left 1,200 civilians and 400 soldiers dead. The Nuer felt singled out by a government they didn't trust, and were then attacked by cattle raiders from Dinka and Murle communities.

And so they rearmed to exact revenge. It was the kind of story that repeated itself over and over in the years before and after independence, each time infused with more vitriol, more weapons, and more casualties.

By late 2011, when Riek Machar was dispatched to intervene, Jonglei's violence had again spiraled out of control, this time fueled by genocidal language and another brutal state response. Church-led conflict resolution efforts and interventions by UN peacekeepers occasionally helped deter or delay the violence, but could not halt it. The narratives were more polarized than ever, and each community identified as the aggrieved party: the government was not only failing to protect them against rival tribes, each complained, it was singling them out more broadly. "No education, no health, no water, no roads, and no positions in government!" one frustrated leader of the Murle community told me, throwing up his hands. "How would you react?"

As Riek Machar arrived to address the wave of fellow Nuer who had marched on Pibor county, the battle cries grew louder. "*Boh Char Juc e Naath!*" shouted one amped-up ring leader in rhythmic tones, his arms and fingers outstretched to the crowd ("The Lou Nuer defeat people!"). Waving rifles above their heads, thousands of his brethren responded in chorus, echoing his cries from past battle glory. Tall, lanky figures in a range of military fatigues streamed in from every direction, joining in song and amassing a crowd of jaw-dropping proportions. Riek stood on a stool and delivered a deep-throated appeal in his native Nuer tongue, urging them not to be goaded into a fight. Men of Riek's stature, especially those in senior government positions, usually have huge sway over their ethnic communities. But this time, the crowd ignored the big man.

Social scientists like Germany's Max Weber had long identified a "monopoly on violence" as the single most defining characteristic of the modern state, a concept refined in the twentieth century but rooted as far back as Thomas Hobbes' landmark treatise, *Leviathan*, in 1651. South Sudan's government enjoyed no such monopoly. They were hardly the only modern state to lack this key ingredient, but this particular rebuke was as stunning as it was portentous: the Nuer youth had told the new republic's vice president, and its army, to simply get out of the way.

"They didn't want to hear it," one county commissioner from the Nuer heartland told me. "Riek was part and parcel of the SPLM that had been focused on Juba, focused on divvying up oil revenues… these leaders that had all ignored people at the grassroots." The ruling elite in Juba had been occupied with the huge task of partition. Capacity was stretched thin, but they had also turned a deaf ear to grievances while over-estimating their political capital at home.

"Now Riek shows up, months into the crisis, with all these cameras," the commissioner continued, his voice gathering pace. "They believed he was here just to win political points." They resented the fact that his eleventh-hour intervention "made them look like the bad guys." After Riek made numerous appeals, and his helicopter departed, their march across Pibor resumed. A vicious series of attacks followed, with body count estimates as high as 1,000—enough to make it the single deadliest episode of tribal violence since the 1991 Bor Massacre. Believing the SPLA to be either indifferent to the assault, or actively involved, bands of Murle youth soon set out for Nuer villages. The cycle continued.

As the deadly tit-for-tat escalated throughout 2012, the SPLA again intervened, hoping to end the violence by removing weapons from the hands of these warrior civilians, by whatever means necessary. This time they zeroed in on Murle land, and the reports that began trickling out were harrowing. Murle civilians were raped, tortured, and killed. Investigations found children had been strangled, burned with wax, and their heads submerged under water in simulated drownings.

Curiously, the SPLA units assigned to lead the campaign were predominantly Nuer, seemingly given carte blanche to avenge prior Murle attacks against their relatives. Rather than breaking the cycles of deadly violence, the national army was being employed to exact ethnic revenge. Foreign diplomats began scrutinizing the government's approach, but Juba was not much interested in criticism. They responded by preventing United Nations peacekeepers from accessing the area, ordering international human rights monitors to leave the country, and eventually shooting down a UN helicopter in the skies over Pibor—a war crime under international law.

Like those in Unity State's Mayom County, the Murle were hated for the alliance their leaders had made with Khartoum during Sudan's long civil war. And the long-stigmatized minority group had provoked new ire in 2010 for sympathizing with another local rebel, David Yau Yau. Angered over perceived election rigging, Yau Yau had rebelled against the government, and, as per the government's long-standing buyout policy, he was brought back to the fold with an attractive package: military rank, house, car, and cash. But the SPLA's 2012 atrocities in Murle villages re-ignited the rebellion and drove thousands of angry youth into Yau Yau's corner. After they bloodied the SPLA's nose on several occasions, President Salva ordered a full-scale counter-insurgency campaign. It was the spring of 2013, and yet again, the Republic was at war with a constituency of its own people.

Erasing the line between combatant and civilian, the revised SPLA operation seemed designed to terrorize the population, or wipe it out altogether. "They cordoned off the area, and then slaughtered civilians," the dismayed Nuer commissioner from Jonglei admitted to me. The SPLA had funneled weapons, ammunition, and other support to youth militias from his own Nuer community, effectively creating a joint campaign against the much-maligned Murle. Foreign diplomats in Juba sent urgent reports home to their capitals, fearing a campaign of state-sponsored ethnic cleansing was now underway.

Thousands were dead, hundreds of thousands displaced, and there was talk of genocide. During the Sudanese civil war, more Southerners died fighting one another than fighting Arabs from Sudan. Now it was happening again. One had to wonder whether that war had really ended eight years ago, or had only been temporarily paused. It was hard to know whether these were the birth pangs of a nation struggling to find its footing, or a red flag foretelling a much larger breakdown to come.

The SPLA's war in Jonglei finally sounded alarm bells in Washington in the spring of 2013. Until that point, "it wasn't really on our radar," one U.S. official told me in 2017. Preventing a new North-South war and finalizing the September 2012 agreement on post-referendum issues had sucked up all the attention. The hard reality was that Jonglei—where large-scale violence had become the norm—received less attention than it might have under other circumstances.

"We knew bad stuff was happening," the same official reported, but there was no shortage of rationalizations. "To be honest," she continued, the increasingly common episodes had, for some, reflected a crass sentiment that "this is Africa, this is just the way it is." Others lumped domestic insecurity in the category of continuing tension with Sudan, given new evidence that Khartoum was arming some of the militias.

Despite other pressing concerns, U.S. officials admit Washington was slow to recognize the nature and scale of the problem in Jonglei. "There wasn't really an understanding of the larger politics at play," said another official, "or the state's role in targeting its own citizens." SPLM liaisons had been "spinning a story" about domestic challenges, he told me. "These guys we were working with every day, they had put a good face on it."

When Washington did come to understand the scale of the crisis, many of the SPLM's long-time friends were slow to accept inconvenient truths, says former US Envoy Princeton Lyman. Until then, advocates and members of Congress "were quick to attribute almost any criticism of South Sudan as engaging in the fallacy of moral equivalency." Nothing South Sudan could do would ever match the evils perpetrated by Sudan, the thinking went, and losing sight of that amounted to "betraying the [American] friendship with the South."

Guided by their visceral contempt for Khartoum, supporters continued to believe any criticism of the South would indirectly benefit the Sudanese. But willful ignorance was also at play; having so long sided with the good guys, some were not ready to accept that the freedom fighters were now mimicking the behavior of their northern oppressors.

By mid-2013, the government's troubling counter-insurgency campaign was matched by an increasingly authoritarian drift in the political arena, and a disturbing picture began to emerge. "That's when we knew this was bigger," the U.S. official said. "That's when we knew South Sudan was really headed in the wrong direction."

15

ROCKING THE BOAT

"War is the continuation of politics by other means."
— Carl von Clausewitz, *On War*, 1832

JUBA, MARCH 2013–DECEMBER 2013

I, General Salva Kiir Mayardit, do hereby issue this republican decree," the radio announcer began, reciting the president's words. It was a familiar start to an executive order, dictates which often concerned matters of benign administration. Those lending one ear to scratchy radio broadcasts in mechanics' garages, church rectories, and market stalls might normally tune out at this stage. Not today. It was Tuesday, July 23, 2013, and the man on the radio was about to deliver a bombshell.

Decree No. 49, the radio announcer continued, was "for the relief of Dr. Riek Machar as Vice President of the Republic." Those half-listening turned their heads in surprise and reached for the volume knobs on their radios. Before the stunning announcement could sink in, the announcer began reciting another decree. Salva and his new circle of advisers had prepared not one but four sweeping orders to be issued that day. Decrees 50 and 51 relieved "All National Ministers of the Government," and their deputies. The final order, the announcer explained, came under Salva's signature as SPLM Chairman: "Suspension and Formation of the Committee to Investigate Secretary General, Comrade Pagan Amum." In one fell swoop, the 55 most powerful government officials in South Sudan had been sacked.

The president's office was peppered with questions, and his lieutenants attempted to downplay the action as a normal cabinet "reshuffle." But as they spoke, army units were fanning out across the city to preempt any reactions. There was no camouflaging the enormity of the day's political massacre.

Months of internal discord had preceded the day's provocative announcements, as a fight for control of the SPLM was in high gear. In response to agitation from party challengers, Salva had played defense by going on offense: he canceled meetings of the SPLM's highest organs, dismissed state governors and army generals, and suspended high-profile ministers on account of perceived disloyalty. He used government funds and positions to shore up support inside a divided party and tighten his hold on state governments. Opponents had cried foul at what appeared to be an increasingly authoritarian drift in the world's newest democracy.

As news of the vice president's firing circulated, angry supporters gathered at his house, eager to take up arms against their president-turned-tyrant. Enough was enough, they argued. Friends and observers watching from afar held their breath, worried that South Sudan—having just celebrated its second anniversary—was about to explode.

From his seventh-floor office at the State Department in Washington's Foggy Bottom neighborhood, Secretary of State John Kerry phoned Salva to appeal for restraint. Six blocks east at the White House, national security officials dialed Riek with the same message. Hours later, as tension in the capital city mounted, Secretary Kerry issued what would be a portentous statement: "The world is watching to see if South Sudan pursues the path of peace and prosperity, or the tragic path of violence and conflict that has characterized much of its past."

TOP: The Nile River and its tributaries during the rainy season, Jonglei State. (*Zach Vertin*) CENTER: Two young boys carry jerry cans of water from a nearby stream, Western Equatoria State. (*Zach Vertin*) BOTTOM: Young boys watch a herd of long-horned cattle pass by their village; *tukuls* in the background, 2012. (*John Wollwerth/shutterstock.com*)

ABOVE: Vice President-turned-rebel leader Riek Machar on a satellite phone from his impromptu headquarters in the bush, Jonglei state. February 2014. (*REUTERS/Goran Tomasevic*) BELOW: Riek Machar exits a cabinet meeting in Juba with members of his entourage. (*Alfred Gonzales Farran*)

ABOVE: Salva Kiir, then chairman of the SPLM and First Vice President of a united Sudan, meets with U.S. President George W. Bush in the Oval Office, 2007. (*Public Domain/White House/Eric Draper*) BELOW: President Salva Kiir. (*Tim McKulka*)

TOP: A rusting military tank in its final resting place, a remnant of Sudan's civil war. Juba, 2009. (*Zach Vertin*) CENTER: Women await an international food distribution amid famine conditions in 2016, Pibor. (*UN*) BOTTOM: An all-terrain vehicle is towed out of a muddy pit in Western Equatoria state, 2014. South Sudan's limited road network becomes nearly impassable during the rainy season. (*UN*)

TOP: A popular 2005 cartoon captures Salva Kiir's tall (and unexpected) task—filling the shoes of SPLM chairman, Dr. John Garang. (*GADO cartoons*) CENTER LEFT: After a day of grazing, a young Dinka man proudly poses with one of his herd, 2009. (*Zach Vertin*) CENTER RIGHT: The late Dr. John Garang depicted on South Sudan's inaugural currency, which was issued upon independence in 2011. (*Zach Vertin*) BOTTOM LEFT: A girl uses a stone to grind sorghum into flour, Jonglei state, 2016. (*Zach Vertin*) BOTTOM RIGHT: Men greeting each other in the traditional way.

TOP: Rebel soldiers patrol and protect Nuer civilians as they make their way through flooded areas to a makeshift camp for the displaced. Unity State, 2014. (*AP Photo/ Matthew Abbott*) CENTER: An SPLA soldier stands at attention, 2011. (*REUTERS/ Goran Tomasevic*) BOTTOM: An ASPLA commando draped in ammunition belts, Upper Nile State, 2014. (*punghi/shutterstock.com*)

ABOVE: A Nuer woman, Upper Nile state, 2010. (*Zach Vertin*) BELOW: Three Dinka boys in a cattle camp. As night falls, they cover themselves with ash to deter mosquitoes, 2009. (*Zach Vertin*)

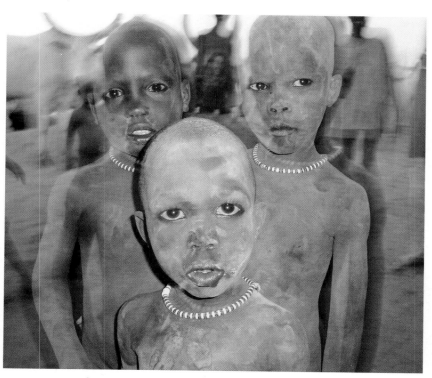

ABOVE: Salva Kiir (in cowboy hat) waves to crowds of fellow voters after casting his ballot in the long-awaited referendum on self-determination, Juba, 2011. (*Tim McKulka*) BELOW: Former U.S. President Jimmy Carter and former UN Secretary-General Kofi Annan—each of whom played significant roles in efforts to bring peace to Sudan—speak to reporters during the referendum, Juba, 2011. (*Tim McKulka*)

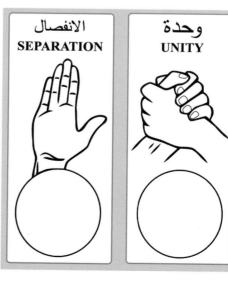

TOP: Celebrity activist George Clooney meets with senior Southern Sudanese officials ahead of the self-determination referendum and poses with the preferred vote—the hand of separation. (*Larco Lomayat*) CENTER: Eager referendum voters wait in line on the first day of voting in January 2011, proudly displaying their registration cards. (*Zach Vertin*) BOTTOM: The official ballot used in the 2011 Referendum on Self-Determination. (*Public Domain*)

ABOVE: A young man at Independence Day celebrations, July 9, 2011. (*Steve Evans*) BELOW: The cheers reach an ear-splitting crescendo at the moment of South Sudan's independence; the Sudanese flag is lowered (left) and the new South Sudanese flag raised (right), Freedom Square, Juba, 2011. (*Zach Vertin*)

ABOVE: The crowds at Freedom Square in Juba, Independence Day, 2011. (*REUTERS/ Thomas Mukoya*) BELOW: U.S. Ambassador to the United Nations Susan Rice greets Vice President Riek Machar on Independence Day in Juba, 2011. (*USAID/Jen Warren/Flickr*)

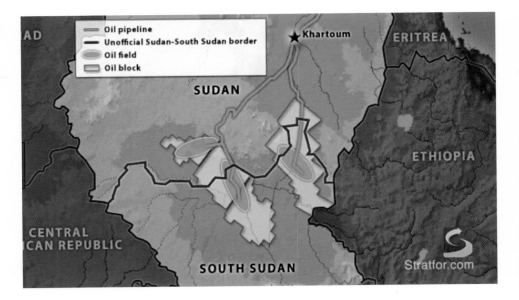

ABOVE: The oil fields in Sudan and South Sudan on the eve of separation, and the pipelines that transported all of the oil to Port Sudan (in the North) for export. (*Courtesy of Stratfor Worldview, a geopolitical intelligence firm*) BELOW: A boy hangs out of a bus full of "returnees" and their personal belongings, one of hundreds of thousands who "returned home" to South Sudan before and after the 2011 referendum. (*Heida Kolsoe, 2011*)

TOP: SPLM Secretary-General and lead negotiator for Southern Sudan, Pagan Amum. (*Chatham House*) CENTER: A cartoon published during the contentious North-South talks over separation, when both sides amassed troops and provoked each other along their shared border. (*Khalid Albaih*) BOTTOM: Surrounded by their belongings, a woman and her child—both "returnees"—in their makeshift home after returning from Khartoum to South Sudan, 2011. (*Tim McKulka*)

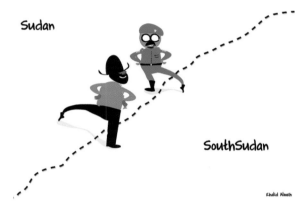

Sudan

SouthSudan

Khalid Albaih

TOP: Salva Kiir addresses the nation wearing military fatigues one day after fighting erupts in Juba. He alleges that Riek Machar has attempted a *coup d'état*. December 16, 2013. (*REUTERS*)
CENTER: SPLA soldiers stand guard outside a government office in Juba. (*Tim McKulka*)
BOTTOM: Flooding and awful conditions in an overcrowded camp for displaced persons in Juba, 2014. Some 200,000 civilians sought refuge from the civil war at these impromptu protection camps. (*UN*)

ABOVE: Youth from the so-called "White Army" mobilize for battle, Upper Nile State, 2014. (*REUTERS/Goran Tomasevic*) BELOW: The aftermath of vicious fighting between government and opposition forces in Malakal, Upper Nile State. (*Albert Gonzalez Farran*)

TOP LEFT: Representatives of the SPLM "former detainees" Kosti Manibe (left) and Deng Alor (right) at peace talks in Addis Ababa, 2015. (*Acquired by Author*) TOP RIGHT: The Government's lead negotiator Nhial Deng (right) and deputy Michael Makwei (left). (*Acquired by Author*) CENTER LEFT: Salva Kiir greets Secretary of State John Kerry in Juba ahead of a tense meeting on the peace process, May 2014. (*State Department/Public Domain*) CENTER RIGHT: The Opposition, or SPLM-IO, lead negotiator, Taban Deng. (*Acquired by Author*) BOTTOM: President Obama delivers an address at the African Union headquarters, one day after hosting a summit of regional leaders on South Sudan. He references the stalled peace talks and a deadline set for the warring factions to secure a peace deal. (*White House.Gov*)

Salva's July 2013 bombshell pushed the SPLM's internal power struggle into the public arena for the first time. But those who were paying close attention knew the party crisis had been brewing for nearly a year. It began on the heels of a nation-wide tour in the summer of 2012, when senior party figures traveled the country to celebrate independence with Southern communities, to give thanks, and to take credit. The tour was meant to be a kind of victory lap, but what party leaders heard instead was frustration and discontent. Ordinary citizens were fed up; a year had passed and too little had changed. Generations of sacrifice were supposed to be over, they argued. Where were the dividends of independence?

The disappointing roadshow spiked internal party debate, and Riek sensed an opportunity to strike. He could use popular discontent to finally launch his bid for the presidency.

By then elite party factions had already begun to quietly size one another up, as minds wandered from the enormous challenge of nation-building to the seductive allure of the presidential throne. After all, the country's first national elections—scheduled for 2015—were on the horizon. Finally unencumbered by Khartoum, the polls would present an opportunity to succeed Salva, the accidental president, and party stalwarts believed a change at the top was long overdue. Riek and other would-be challengers lamented the party's loss of vision and direction, though they, too, were responsible for the rot. They sought change, but it was power they coveted most. And now was their chance.

Just weeks after Independence Day in 2011, Salva had first told foreign confidants of his uneasiness about internal party dissent, citing three would-be contenders for his seat: Riek Machar, Pagan Amum, and Mama Rebecca, the widow of John Garang. He found the increasing defiance seeping into party meetings uncomfortable, particularly when coming from these bolder and more cunning personalities. By early 2013, it appeared Salva had had enough of politics; he confided to former AU mediator Thabo Mbeki that he was ready to step down at the end of his term. Though it was not an official announcement, late night gatherings among party aristocrats were instantly abuzz with the news that the big man would not contest in 2015. The challengers licked their lips: Salva's seat was theirs for the taking.

Two months later, in March 2013, party organs convened to review the SPLM's constitution, party rules, and voting procedures. While a seemingly mundane exercise, control of the party—and by extension, control of the republic—was vested in these documents. A battle quickly erupted, forcing the question of party leadership to the floor. It seemed Salva, the sitting president, had changed his mind. Intent on keeping challengers at bay, he moved to outlaw secret balloting, and signaled that he wanted sole authority to convene party meetings and appoint members of its powerful central committee.

Opponents were furious. Not only had Salva reversed his decision not to run, he was now strong-arming party mechanisms to fortify his position. The acrimonious sessions ended in a stalemate, but before they did, Riek Machar and Pagan Amum declared their intention to challenge him for the SPLM chairmanship, and thus for the presidential nomination. Riek, Pagan, and other aspirants had for years pledged party unity and loyalty to Salva, but the time for keeping up appearances had suddenly expired. A power struggle was now underway. Months of tense politicking ensued, yielding less and less time for any of the country's leaders to deliver on the promises they had long ago made to their citizens.

The days when a lid had been kept on internal party quarrels were over. This was the movement's first open political challenge, and it was unfamiliar territory for a hierarchal military organization and for its politically deficient leader. Salva and those around him responded the only way they knew how; they purged threats, neutralized opposition, and harnessed the instruments of state to maintain ever greater control. Ironically, the party intelligentsia now opposing Salva had themselves helped to erase the line between the SPLM and the state in recent years. Now they were being bullied by the greedy boy they'd helped create.

Encouraged by those newly appointed to positions of power, Salva would begin to strike a drum, and the beats that resounded through South Sudan's political circles would gather pace and volume over the course of 2013.

Deeply concerned by the acrimony, party middlemen began shuttling frantically between the SPLM's competing camps, hoping to broker a compromise. But just a few short weeks later, Salva would strike the drum again. Having already dismissed a prominent governor and upwards of a hundred army generals, Salva and his men moved up the food chain. As vice president, Riek had often proven a more capable administrator than his boss, and the wily operator had recently begun using popular national initiatives for political advancement. But before he could fly any further, Salva clipped his wings. In April 2013, Republican Order No. 3 stripped the vice president of his constitutional powers. Party operatives had been struggling to forge some kind of reconciliation, but neither side was in the mood, and the unexpected order signaled their failure.

Conscious of the gathering storm, and doubtful that they could resolve the leadership dispute on their own, a senior party man named Deng Alor boarded a plane to Washington.

⁂

Deng Alor is a striking figure. Standing six foot eight inches tall, he is a gentle giant, and his slender frame glides with the grace of a giraffe. With a personality and hushed tones to match, he might be aptly branded "the big smooth." Deng is comfortable in suits and smart ties, though his flashy watch also complements short-sleeve shirts—very large ones—in dark blues, grays, and African prints.

Unlike some of his SPLM colleagues, the two-time foreign minister and senior party man neither needs nor is predisposed to dominate a conversation. At rest, Deng can be still, quiet, and measured. With eyes sometimes open only a slit, it's easy to think he's succumbed to a narcoleptic interlude. He speaks in a smooth, milky timbre, infusing more volume and rhythm when a topic animates him. I have seen Deng frustrated on rare occasions, but I have never seen him angry.

When greeting a foreign delegation, Deng endears himself by shaking hands, making eye contact, and showing interest in the lowly note-taker as well as the big-shot with the fancy title. He is polished, but not detached; his warmth is natural, not practiced.

Deng has a remarkable memory for recounting dialogue, and regales foreigners with stories of political intrigue. Re-enacting scenes from lavish dinners at Qaddafi's palaces and backroom horse-trading on state visits to China, he is a captivating story-teller, both apocryphal and otherwise. He also loves to laugh. After dropping a subtle gag into the end of story, sly and knowing eye contact follows; he pauses to let it sink in, and then punctuates the silence with a crack of boisterous laughter. Joking with Deng is a physical experience; he laughs from the shoulders and his punch lines are accompanied by back-slaps and high-fives.

The lanky diplomat can be persuasive, and he knows it. Sidling up to a counterpart, understanding his interests and motivations, and speaking his language, Deng was always well-suited to the art of foreign affairs. Throughout the years of struggle, he became particularly skilled in connecting with those from the United States and Europe, understanding the value of these relationships for his cause, and for himself.

Deng is an effective emissary, bordering on manipulative, but he takes care not to cross a line. His efforts to advance an interest are never rooted in malevolence. When seasoned observers call him on his tactics, Deng concedes with laughter—acknowledging the game rather than losing someone's confidence. He is decidedly likable, a fact which can both endear him to foreigners and blind them to larger and more inconvenient truths.

Like many South Sudanese of his class, Deng is a man between worlds. Born "around 1951" in a disputed border territory called Abyei, his homeland has long been a tempestuous microcosm of the larger struggle between Sudan's North and South—wracked by divisive battles over race, culture, boundaries, resources, and nationality. Deng's years, and his identity, have thus been divided between North and South, as well as between Ethiopia, America, and the political capitals of Africa. He belongs to each of them, and also to none of them.

Roughly the size of Connecticut, Abyei (*AH-be-yay*) is small and generally unremarkable. But, like Kashmir or Gaza, its history as an epicenter of territorial conflict could fill volumes. Settled by Deng's Ngok Dinka tribe, the area is also traversed by Misseriya Arab herders from Sudan, whose centuries-old routes to dry-season water sources in the South are an existential matter. Abyei gained national significance when oil was found there in 1979, a discovery which renewed a fight over whether it should be part of North or South. But after multiple promises of a right to decide their own future went unfulfilled, the Ngok Dinka people remain in a kind of stateless purgatory. Like Deng, they are at once part of both worlds—and part of neither.

When Deng was a teenager, a spat erupted between his Ngok Dinka and the neighboring Misseriya. Deng's mother, sister, and niece were among the many residents corralled and taken to a local police station, allegedly for their own safety. They were being held in a traditional thatched hut, when a mob of Misseriya militiamen set it on fire, burning his mother and relatives alive. "It... that experience—it shaped my outlook on the whole thing," Deng says, referring to Sudan's complicated political experiment, the marginalization of black Africans, and a history of violence.

Deng attended primary and secondary school in Sudan, in Muglad and Wad Medani respectively, before moving on to college and student political activism at the University of Cairo in neighboring Egypt. He made friends with Arabs from Sudan's privileged riverine tribes, more than a few of whom rose to join Khartoum's premier political class. Orphaned by the age of fourteen, the bright teenager spent holidays and school breaks at their homes, developing lasting ties to their families and embracing Sudanese Arab social mores. Years later, after decades of violence and political acrimony between North and South, he paid school fees and helped to secure jobs for the children of one boyhood friend, a Northerner active in the reviled National Congress Party (NCP) government.

Another prominent Sudanese politician, Ahmed Haroun, was indicted in 2007 on war crimes charges by the International Criminal Court. Haroun was an architect of the Darfur war, and before that he mobilized ruthless militias who targeted and displaced Southern civilians—including in Deng's home—during the 1990s. He was then governor of the Sudanese state that claimed and twice invaded Abyei, once burning Deng's home town to the ground. But Deng bought him shoes anyway. Haroun was born with a foot ailment that required specialized shoes—which, due to his international indictment, he could not travel abroad to purchase. After trips to Europe as a government minister, Deng several times returned with a pair of special shoes for Haroun—his peer, neighbor, and foe.

Deng's relationships reflect a unique capacity among Northern and Southern Sudanese to compartmentalize, separating gracious social interaction from often hostile political affairs and divergent world views. "This is Sudanese culture, which is something very strange," Deng says, "something unique, to be studied... the psychology of the Sudanese." Before rounds of the no-holds-barred negotiations over separation in 2010–2011, opposing teams from Khartoum and Juba would first engage in the warm and extended social greetings that are a mainstay of Sudanese social life. Conversing in Arabic, exchanging repeated well wishes and asking about one another's families, the rivals laughed and embraced while Western diplomats looked on, befuddled.

In the early 1980s, upon hearing of the secret rebellion taking shape in South, Deng returned home from university and joined the fledgling SPLA. Deng—code name "FIRE"—grew close to John Garang and eventually ascended to the highest ranks of the SPLM pecking order. He served the movement in Addis Ababa, and when peace came he rose to influential positions in government—first tours as cabinet and foreign minister in the unity government in Khartoum, followed by two stints as foreign minister in Juba.

Deng is a widely recognized figure in both Sudans, and has for years traded on his seniority and reputation among both national and international elites. In a nation where hundreds of thousands bear this most common name, Deng is first among Dengs. When one refers simply to "Deng," no one is in doubt about whom they are speaking.

"I consider myself a Pan-Africanist and a very liberal person," Deng says, a worldview he says is the result of extensive travel, his foreign wife, and early readings in world history and the American civil rights movement. John Garang introduced him to civil rights-era America and its diversity, concepts he says were at the core of Garang's political philosophy; "We can build another United States here in Sudan," he had told them. "The whole New Sudan thing," Deng explains, "was born of his experience in America." And so Deng, too, was turned on to an America he had not yet visited, but one that would soon become his second home.

With a Washington rolodex that would impress any aspiring lobbyist, Deng was long the standard-bearer of the American-South Sudanese friendship. He hosted Susan Rice on her first trip to SPLA-liberated areas in the early 1990s, when she was accompanied by several members of the so-called "Council" of American supporters. "She came with JP—John Prendergast, and Ted (Dagne)." Chuckling, he recalls Rice "dancing with Dinka ladies" and "jumping over bulls" they had sacrificed in honor of her visit. "We became very close after that," he says of Rice, "she became a *very* big supporter of the SPLA."

In addition to befriending legions of humanitarians and activists over the ensuing decades, Deng has worked with three American presidents, their national security advisers, secretaries of state, and all seven American special envoys, not to mention Frank Wolf and the SPLM's bi-partisan champions in Congress. His extensive travels make for a similar record of engagement across Europe and Africa. It is a record not lost on political opponents, who see Deng and the other "Garang boys" as drawing their legitimacy not from domestic constituencies but from their ties to the American foreign policy establishment.

Deng is married to a charming Ethiopian woman named Mesrak, with whom he has three sons. Mesrak and their boys acquired refugee status in 2001 and re-located to Sacramento, California. Sporting fashionable gear and casual demeanor, their sons are unmistakably Californian. Each was educated in a local Catholic school and later pursued degrees at West Coast universities.

As is the case for many SPLM elites, rumors of corruption have followed Deng for years. In the years before independence, many took notice of his re-decorated home and office in Juba, his expensive shoes, and his fleet of SUVs, accoutrements enjoyed across the top tier of Juba's ruling class. But given the collective milk chugging, no one was particularly interested in digging into such allegations. The Americans, too, harbored doubts about the personal checkbooks of the SPLM vanguard, but this was an allied region struggling to escape Islamist tyranny. And in case you forgot, Deng is just so darn likable.

The big smooth enjoyed personal and professional relationships that spanned tribe, religion, nationality, ideology, and profession. His credibility was due in part to personality, and partly to his position of privilege. He moved as easily in Islamic and Arabic-speaking circles in the North as he did in pan-Africanist confabs across East and Southern Africa. He took tea with Arab despots in the Middle East, macchiatos with diplomats in Europe, and soda with evangelical Christians in America. And like few others, he bridged ethnic and regional divides across the SPLM, and enjoyed rapport with both its intellectuals and its military men.

Like many Southern Sudanese elites, Deng's is a life divided, best understood in dichotomy: North and South, Arab and African; local and national, African and American. Deng is a guerrilla and a cabinet minister, a member of Abyei's village elders and a class of international jet-setting elite.

———

The official reason for Deng's April 2013 visit to Washington was a series of meetings about South Sudan's ailing economy, and he was accompanied by finance minister, SPLM veteran, and political ally Kosti Manibe. But Deng had another more pressing message to convey to his friends in America.

Following scheduled consultations at the State Department and White House, Deng privately pulled aside senior American counterparts to express alarm. Salva was showing increasingly authoritarian tendencies, he complained, and the schism inside the SPLM was becoming dangerous. He wanted the Americans to get involved. After all, past disputes had required external mediation, and the SPLM was accustomed to looking abroad to solve its problems at home. Congressmen in Washington had attempted to mediate between Garang and Riek in 1993, and other influential friends had acted as intermediaries on subsequent occasions.

Deng was a Garang loyalist, and together with Pagan Amum, would become known as one of the principal "Garang Boys" after their mentor's death. As such, he was reviled by the opposing faction now coalescing around Salva—the one group with whom there was friction. Like few other partisans, Deng had made inroads with those of Riek as well as those of Salva, a fellow Dinka with whom he shared personal, familial, and cultural ties. When it came to personal rapport, he was as close to a bridge as the SPLM had.

Deng had the best interests of his young country at heart in reaching out to the Americans. But given his established ties to Washington's foreign policy intelligentsia, "those of Deng" also believed they would be well-served by American engagement. They might even be able to translate their Western connections into a needed boost in the party horse race. Deng's opponents back home made the same calculation. They viewed his trip with paranoia, as it was already widely believed that Deng Alor and Pagan Amum were Washington's golden boys, and they worried he might engineer secret support in de-throning Salva.

When Deng returned from the United States, another republican order was coming down the pike, and this one had his name on it. Gayle Smith, a senior White House official and ally of Susan Rice, came to Juba in response to Deng's plea. She hoped to promote intra-party dialogue, but for some her visit only confirmed their paranoia about Deng's cozy relations with Uncle Sam.

Issued on June 18, 2013, Order No. 12 suspended Deng Alor and Kosti Manibe from their cabinet positions, and lifted their prosecutorial immunity in connection with corruption allegations. Another drum beat reverberated, this one louder than the last. Corruption was widespread in the upper echelons of the SPLM, but the singling out of these two seemed a conspicuous indication of an intensifying political row. "A simple case of character assassination; nothing more," said one senior party insider of Deng and Kosti's suspension, "Salva is out to undermine his rivals." Deng ceased communication with the president, the bridge across the ever-widening chasm now burned.

Factionalism was back. Though it was Salva's signature at the bottom of each republican order, it was hard to imagine this president masterminding such a sweeping crackdown. Under fire from both Riek and the Garang Boys, the lonely president had found refuge in a handful of surrogates who had backed him in the past: those of Bahr al Ghazal.

The pendulum of party power had swung again, it seemed, the Bahr al Ghazal faction re-capturing the ear of the president and the powers of his office. The self-proclaimed "rightful heirs" of the SPLM—Deng, Pagan, and other mainstream party barons—blamed one member of the Bar al Ghazal clique: Telar Deng. The shadowy figure working behind the scenes from inside the palace had become the subject of intense scrutiny. "The devil" some called him, "Lucifer himself" another said. Telar was evoking the most diabolical of adjectives. He had a sinister grin and seemed almost to relish the role of dark knight. He even fashioned embossed black business cards with gold lettering, which seemed the perfect prop for this saga's new villain.

Telar had been at Salva's side when things got dicey with John Garang in 2004. And so, in one of the party coups and counter-coups over the subsequent decade, the Garang Boys had engineered Telar's excommunication from the party. "It was Deng and Pagan who had given Salva the knife to kill him," the same party insider explained, in political metaphor. "But they left the knife on the table" and Telar was now in position "to turn the knife on them."

The palace intrigue seemed almost Shakespearean, entertaining if it weren't for the cold reality that South Sudan's people were getting tired of it, and they would ultimately suffer the consequences when the drama finally destroyed the party.

After being ousted from the SPLM in 2009, Telar had joined the NCP, Sudan's national party and the sworn enemy of the SPLM.

Whether their belief was founded or not, the Garang Boys and many others in the SPLM seized on this fact, branding him a stooge of Khartoum. "This card-carrying member of the NCP," they argued to South Sudanese and foreign diplomats in 2013, was "infiltrating" the office of the president and corrupting the new state on behalf of old enemies.

Given Khartoum's penchant for such nefarious plots, the allegation was plausible. And the enemy-branding was a tool SPLM leaders had employed in the past with great success. Anything that implicated Sudan's brutal regime had currency in South Sudan; it was a kind of scarlet letter. Telar did maintain worrisome connections to NCP powerbrokers, and Salva was then looking to improve relations with Khartoum, as he could not juggle a political war on two fronts. And so where the SPLM challengers saw smoke, they declared fire.

"What is happening now is a crisis in the ruling party," one civil society activist commented at the time, a crisis that he warned was being "transferred" to the state. "It is not the state itself that is sick. The sickness is in the party."

In the early morning hours of July 9, 2013, Salva Kiir put on a gray suit, bright red tie, cowboy hat, and a lapel pin of his young country's flag. In his left front jacket pocket he slid a pair of thin-framed reading glasses, and an aide delivered a black portfolio emblazoned in gold with the seal of the republic. Inside were remarks his speechwriters had prepared for his address that day at Freedom Square, on the occasion of the Republic's second birthday.

The speaking platform at Freedom Square had once again been draped in colorful national banners, flower bouquets adorned railings, and the steps were carpeted in ceremonial red. The SPLA marching band was already warming up. While celebrants had begun packing the grounds at dawn, waving flags just as they had two years earlier, the country's tenuous state of affairs was hard to ignore. The tensions in the SPLM's top echelon were unfolding against a backdrop of increasing popular frustration. Expectations remained unfulfilled. Economic austerity measures continued to pinch. Chatter about high-level corruption was widespread.

Conscious of his colleagues' attempts to hang popular discontent around his neck, Salva addressed those standing in the crowd below. "I went to the bush not (for) myself," he told them, nor for his SPLM comrades or his cabinet ministers. He had waged a lifetime of guerrilla war for the *people*, telling them, "My dear citizens, I have not forgotten you." Hanging on the grandstand above was a banner announcing the day's theme, *Toward Effective Nation Building and Prosperity for All.* "I am aware that many of you cannot afford a meal every day," Salva continued, "that you struggle to pay rent, feed your family, pay school fees for your kids, and pay medical treatment."

Like the speech American presidents rise to deliver before a full Congress once every January, this was effectively Salva's State of the Union address. In a familiar and flat monotone, the president outlined his administration's accomplishments, detailed budget priorities for the coming year, and pledged solutions to the everyday concerns of his electorate—clean water, jobs, education, infrastructure, and security. It was more read-and-recite than soaring oratory, and Salva interrupted himself regularly to pull out a white handkerchief and wipe the sweat from his face. Despite the characteristically underwhelming delivery, Salva's speechwriters had hit the right notes.

The president then left the podium and stood at attention, flanked by saluting generals, as a military parade processed before him: marching infantry units, green camouflage jeeps mounted with heavy guns, hulking flatbed trucks loaded with surface-to-air missiles, and eighteen wheelers topped with battle tanks, their long guns rising at low angle. But close observers were not distracted by the speech nor the day's pageantry; they were focused instead on the subtle hints that betrayed the political acrimony now just below the surface. Unlike the joyous celebration in 2011, today there was no rousing speech from Riek Machar, nor even a mention of him. Today there were no rousing call-and-responses from emcee Pagan Amum, as he was conspicuously absent. Though Salva did not use the occasion to beat the drum, nor even make reference to the open feud then gripping the political establishment, his subtle hint of a "major shift in my government" lent credence to the rumors then swirling about the capital city.

But before the president could act, Riek Machar threw down the gauntlet. Within days of the second anniversary celebration, Riek publicly indicted Salva on six counts of failure: corruption, tribalism, insecurity, a struggling economy, poor foreign relations, and the SPLM's loss of direction. The time for pretenses was over. "To avoid authoritarianism and dictatorship, it is better to change," Riek told journalists, "I have been serving under Salva Kiir... I think it is time for a change now."

Years later when I asked Riek to reflect on his pushing the party fight into the public sphere, he argued, "We were an independent state. We [could] discuss matters of governance freely." He was right, but given the fragility of the state and its institutions, I pushed him further. "Sure, but did you and the others sufficiently consider the risks of taking matters outside the party..." He cut me off, "We did. We did discuss it. There was no tolerance in the party," he says, alluding to Salva's suppression of internal dialogue. "There was no other way."

The six charges Riek leveled were incontrovertible, but it was also hard to dissociate the move from the man. Riek could no longer wait to scratch his presidential itch. The gap-toothed descendant of the prophet had kept his ambition bridled for eight years. He could contain it no longer, especially now that Salva—pledging to remain in power—seemed to have acquired the same disease that had afflicted so many African presidents-for-life.

Riek lobbied party cadres to support his candidacy, citing his superior education and believing himself best positioned to mobilize a coalition of ethnic minorities that could challenge "Dinka hegemony" in the new South Sudan. His Nuer power base would not be enough; he needed to win over other party power brokers, and that would not be easy. While many of them were ready to move on Salva, they were not about to sign up with Riek. When it came to his assuming the mantle, "over my dead body" had been the maxim of the party's mainstream elite since the 1991 split.

Deng, Pagan, and the new anti-Salva coalition would separate tactics from strategy: ride Riek through an internal battle against Salva, they plotted, but then push him aside before he could capture the presidency. They would not disrespect the late Dr. John by handing the SPLM chairmanship to its most notorious traitor.

Within days of Riek's public challenge, the Republican Orders dismissing him and the cabinet were read over the radio. Riek, Pagan, Deng Alor and the rest of the SPLM establishment had been sent to the guillotine.

News of their ouster spread rapidly throughout Juba and then further afield. Cell phones buzzed, diners gossiped in local canteens, and *boda boda* drivers sought to break the news to one another: "Have you heard?" In relatively short order, several hundred army supporters and senior SPLM figures showed up at Riek's home, eager to take matters into their own hands. But Riek talked them down. Any retaliatory action, he argued, would play into the president's hands.

"Please remain calm," Riek then said in a message to supporters later that evening, "be assured that our aspiration to lead this country to prosperity and stability won't be intimidated by anything. We've chosen to handle everything politically and this is how we're going to continue."

In Washington, Obama administration officials were shocked when they awoke to find "President sacks VP and Cabinet" flashing across their Blackberry phones. They scrambled to arrange high-level calls from the White House and State Department, hoping to reach both Salva and Riek and plead for restraint. U.S. officials had been aware of the quickening drumbeat, but neither embassy nor intelligence reporting had foretold of such a drastic event. "We didn't see it coming," one told me, "didn't really know what it meant, and had not much beyond phone calls and prayers to throw at it."

The following morning, the freshly unemployed vice president called a press conference in the courtyard of his home to reiterate his message of restraint. Dressed in a long white *jalabiya*, sandals, and rectangular sunglasses, a relaxed Machar greeted those present warmly and shook hands before casually taking a seat behind a folding table draped in a pale pink cloth. "I want the nation to be calm," he said, speaking in a quiet and measured tone to a spray of journalists and television cameras assembled before him. "I want no violence to happen."

Though legions of his supporters were spoiling for a fight, and the political motivation behind the surprise dismissals not in doubt, Riek insisted that it was within the president's constitutional mandate to dismiss a cabinet and remove him as vice president. Rejecting the calls to arms, Riek maintained that political change must come through democratic processes, and he urged the army to maintain its neutrality.

Like many inside and outside South Sudan, the U.S. officials were equally surprised by Riek's measured appeal for calm. He had taken the high road. And for the time being, it gave him the moral high ground. It was a rare moment of statesmanship amid the menacing drumbeat.

Riek and the ousted members of cabinet—some of whom commanded considerable support within the military ranks—had chosen not to contest the provocative decision by force. But the avenues for political resolution were closing fast. In the weeks and months that followed, Salva continued to flex institutional muscle and stack his government with supporters, while Deng and the newly unemployed challengers focused on leveraging their weight inside the SPLM.

By September, each faction was counting its votes within the SPLM's powerful central committee, where nineteen votes could decide the fate of the party. Riek and the Garang Boys believed they might outnumber the president. Salva's men came up with the same numbers—he would come up short, and so Salva repeatedly prevented the powerful group from convening.

Why would the challengers not simply leave the SPLM, and form their own political party? It was a question that Riek and others had been asked many times before, and the response was always the same: "trademark." The only four letters that mattered in South Sudan were

"SPLM;" for many, they were synonymous with liberation, and they represented the only national organization of any kind. To surrender them was to surrender any chance of electoral victory. What's more, the SPLM controlled all of the country's resources, without which it would be impossible to mount a serious challenge.

Deng Alor was among those most attached to the party, and he privately characterized the view of those opposing Salva. "Government dissolution is one thing. But the party is a red line." If Salva went any further, Deng explained, if he tried to dominate the party in the way he was now dominating the state, "Then there will be violence... no question."

⁓

On a relatively quiet morning in mid-November, Salva's motorcade arrived at the newly designated party headquarters for an opening ceremony. "SPLM House," as it was christened, was a square yellow structure with a Spanish-tile roof, situated inside matching yellow walls just off a main thoroughfare in the center of Juba.

To the crowd of loyalists assembled for the ceremony, Salva asked rhetorically, "Do you think that today the [party] structures still have the legitimacy to continue functioning?" No, he answered his own question, citing their dysfunction and expired mandates. Salva would remain chairman, he announced, but the party's highest councils would be dissolved until a new convention was held. The red line had been crossed.

Three weeks later, on December 6, Riek, Pagan, Deng, and the challengers responded. Descending upon the same yellow-walled compound, they convened a press conference that would change the course of their young country's history.

It was a sunny afternoon on the grounds of SPLM House, where a crowd of party members, journalists, and onlookers buzzed with anticipation as one shiny SUV after another delivered the party heavyweights. The political tension in Juba was palpable, and as Salva's detractors arrived, it was hard not to think something provocative was afoot. Riek Machar stepped out of his vehicle in pinstripe black suit, white shirt, and red tie, and flashed his unmistakable smile. Today he would join forces with Pagan Amum, who was greeting the crowds milling about the white tents on the grounds. Deng Alor sauntered forward toward the main tent to round out the influential triumvirate.

The men seemed to walk with a knowing bravado, as the day's event was to be a liberation in itself. They would tell the world of the "true state of affairs in the SPLM," and how comrade Salva was driving the "beloved Republic into chaos and disorder." Pagan rose first and stood before a bouquet of assembled media microphones. Looking out over the guests, the natural-born performer opened the event in characteristically over-the-top fashion. "*Ohhh Motherland,*" he began his prayer, singing in the rhythmic tones of Martin Luther King, Jr., "we rise raising flags with the guiding star, sing-ing songggs of *free*-dom." He introduced the dozen party bosses who flanked him left and right, and behind them stood rows of whispering supporters and aides, each eager to be close to the action.

Riek, as ranking member, then read a prepared statement on behalf of the group. "We, the SPLM leaders," he announced, beads of sweat trickling down his forehead and left cheek, called the press conference in order to "enlighten our people on the internal crisis that has engulfed the SPLM and paralyzed the government." He bared all: party factionalism, dysfunction, Salva's usurpation of decision-making power, and the corrupting influence of the Bahr al Ghazal lobby.

On behalf of the group, he indicted Salva and the vultures around him for attempting to dissolve party structures, and for betraying South Sudan by collaborating with the enemy in Khartoum. Spectators' eyes widened and journalists scribbled furiously in their notebooks, as each statement was more damning than the last. Looking down through the tinted lenses of his wire-framed glasses, Riek continued, "Salva Kiir has surrendered the SPLM power to opportunists and foreign agents," and was "plunging the party, and the country, into the abyss."

The challengers had brought their own mallet, and each took a turn banging the drum. In addition to political manhandling, they hinted that Salva had also been assembling a personal army "in the guise of presidential guards." For months, concern had spread in party circles about the recruitment of several thousand youths—exclusively from Bahr al Ghazal—to the president's personal compound in nearby Luri. The army chief of staff, himself a Nuer, had angrily complained that their recruitment and command was happening outside official structures, but his protestations were ignored.

Soon it was Deng Alor's turn to air grievances, and he spoke for 25 minutes. For those who knew him well, the mild-mannered veteran's voice and body language carried an uncommon note of contempt. "Yesterday we were very good boys, who struggled for this country, brought independence, and raised the flag here," he said, caricaturing the position in which he and his lot now found themselves. "Today, we are bad boys," he continued sarcastically, eliciting a laugh from the crowd. The division inside the party was not new, Deng said, and Khartoum had now "planted people in the government, and they were implementing the agenda" of the enemy. The big smooth raised a finger and shook it in frustration at his friend and colleague Salva: "His mission is to destroy the SPLM, to destroy all of us."

It was true; over the course of 2013 Salva had drifted toward the despotic. He had abused state power and breached party rules to undermine agitating rivals and weaken the party. But it was hard not to take a wider view. Those posturing in front of the media today were styling themselves as democrats, and exhibiting an air of self-righteousness. But the rot in the SPLM had begun well before 2013. Factionalism, corruption, militarization, the estrangement from the common man, and the detour from democratic principles—these bacteria had been eating away at the party and at state institutions for years, all while the men speaking today occupied positions of leadership. Were they not also responsible for the nation's rotten state of affairs?

The press conference was a scathing rebuke of the president, the kind of public quarrel never before seen in the SPLM or South Sudan. The challengers may have been right, but they were also playing with fire.

Salva tapped James Wani Igga, a comparatively non-threatening Equatorian, to replace Riek as vice president. The new VP was decidedly short, and had a taste for shiny double-breasted suits and flashy accessories (think glittering yellow tie atop bright red shirt). Wani was a senior party figure who had been around the block, and had seen the SPLM at its best and its worst.

On the evening of December 11, just after dark, Wani got in his SUV alongside aides and bodyguards and headed toward home. He looked worried. He had just left a rather unsettling meeting of security chiefs at the president's office, and he needed to get a message to Riek's camp. Wani would himself become highly partisan once the crisis erupted, toeing the government's line with vigor. But prior to it, his actions suggested a larger concern for the country. Wani had been through leadership battles in the past, and knew very well how dangerous they could be. He summoned an aide, Lam, to deliver a message.

Lam was a kind and physically awkward young man who had previously worked for Riek, and was one of just a few Nuer who remained on staff in the office of the vice president. Wani knew that Lam, who had grown up under Riek's wing, would be a discreet and reliable messenger. The president had just concluded a "what to do about Riek" meeting, he confided, where there was talk of eliminating the threat. Lam dutifully relayed the news, which corroborated rumors of arrest or assassination that had already made their way to Riek. But when his bodyguards pressed him to leave town for his own safety, Riek declined. Lam worried that his longtime benefactor seemed to be discounting the ominous warning.

Meanwhile, party bosses continued to grapple over which SPLM organ should be convened, when, and under what rules. But the bureaucratic jiu-jistu belied an underlying reality: a reckoning was coming. As the drum beat grew faster and faster, cooler heads attempted once more to shuttle between the SPLM's dangerously polarized camps. They reached across divides to blood relatives and old colleagues, quietly urging them to refrain from any moves that might push the party—and the country—over the edge.

Three days later, on Saturday, December 14, scores of party officials from Juba and across the country migrated to Nyakuron Cultural Center. They had received invitations from the president for a meeting of the SPLM's National Liberation Council (NLC)—a group that had not convened in years. While outnumbered in smaller party organs, Salva determined that he could use his position and resources to ensure support in this larger body.

En route to the event, participants noticed a beefed-up security presence around the city. When they arrived at Nyakuron, they found heavily armed soldiers guarding the entryways, and a palpably charged atmosphere inside. They filed into rows of high-backed chairs draped in green and red, the stadium seating arranged in a semi-circle around a central stage. Riek Machar was present, but several other notable figures were conspicuously absent—Deng Alor was out of the country, and Pagan Amum had been barred by security forces from leaving his house. The American ambassador and other foreign diplomats had been invited to the party convention as observers, but they too stayed away, citing growing tension and associated security risks.

When the crowd settled into their seats, several South Sudanese church leaders took to the stage to open the NLC meeting with a prayer. But they also took the opportunity to confront the elephant in the room, appealing to all those present to exercise restraint, even suggesting the meeting be postponed. Despite widespread respect for the churches, and the critical peace-brokering roles their leaders had played at tense moments in the past, their pleas for a cooling-off period fell on deaf ears.

The military band's horn section then blared an off-key tune as Salva took to the podium. The president had just returned from South Africa where he had attended the funeral of president and world-renowned peacemaker Nelson Mandela. Salva dedicated the first part of his speech to the revered leader, "a great inspiration for all the oppressed peoples across the African continent... including the people of South Sudan." He asked attendees to stand for a moment of silence, and reflect on a man whose dignity, restraint, and forgiveness had inspired the world. But it was hard to reconcile Salva's ensuing remarks with the legacy of Mandela. Though the party chairman spoke of unity and democratic ideals, his most notable stanzas were divisive ones, their implication not lost on anyone present. "Some comrades abandoned the struggle, others even joined the enemy," he said, beginning a series of thinly veiled warnings to Riek Machar and other party challengers. They had humiliated Salva in their press conference just a week earlier, and today was his opportunity to remind them who was in charge.

As he made a disparaging reference to the 1991 split in the SPLM, the traitor to whom he was referring sat slouched in an armchair in the front row. Riek stared back at the president skeptically, head resting in hand. Though 24 years had passed, the reference to Riek's 1991 split and its painful ethnic divisions remained evocative.

Salva then turned his elliptical criticisms to Deng, Pagan, and the rest of the deposed cabinet ministers now opposing him. "They took their positions for granted, they got spoiled by the luxuries of office and forgot that we are servants of the people." To those now challenging his decisions, "I must warn," he continued, "that this behavior is tantamount to indiscipline which will take us back to the days of the 1991 split. We all know where the split took us... I am not prepared to allow this to happen again."

Near the end of Salva's remarks, a woman in the crowd broke into a song in the Dinka language, and the president joined her, chuckling. "Anguen thou wen kuan janub!" It was an old war song from Bahr al Ghazal, sung by the SPLA's wolf battalion during the days of liberation, which proclaimed it better to fight and die than to be humiliated.

"It wasn't a party meeting," one frustrated participant later reported, "it was a war rally." It was a bitter irony that the increasingly divisive party confab was unfolding at Nyakuron Hall—the nation's only cultural center. Built in the 1970s during the South's first short period of self-rule, it was meant to be a place to celebrate the South's many cultures, and a symbol of national cohesion.

While Riek and other opponents sat idly like spectators, the president's men engineered resolutions to the disputes over party procedures, thus affirming his control of the SPLM. "There was nothing procedural about it," another participant remarked of the process skewed in Salva's favor, "Everything in that meeting was coerced." Salva's opponents cried foul, and boycotted the second day of the meeting.

The drumbeat had lost all cadence as its speeding beats ran together. The banging was overwhelming the senses; nothing else could be felt, heard, touched, or tasted save the banging of the war drum.

Political institutions are designed to provide a buffer against violent conflict. And while such institutions nominally existed in the young country, they were anything but mature. In *On War*, a triad of volumes published in 1832, Prussian general and military theorist Carl von Clausewitz famously wrote that "War is the continuation of politics by other means." Indeed after a year of tumult in South Sudan, politics appeared to have run its course.

In the early evening hours of Sunday, December 15, shortly after the second and final day of the NLC meeting was concluded, a fight broke out between Salva and Riek's men at the presidential guard headquarters in Juba. The membrane stretched across the head of the drum, beaten one too many times, was finally giving way.

16

WAR

*"Even if it is a god who killed our people, we can go
and fight with the god. We don't mind."*
—White Army fighter

JUBA / BOR, DECEMBER, 2013

Dusk gave way to darkness on the evening of December 15
at the headquarters of the presidential guard at Giyada, in
central Juba. An order passed through the ranks; Dinka
members of the guard were to disarm their Nuer counterparts. But
the unusual move did not go as planned. Suspicious Nuer elements
resisted, and the barracks were soon a cacophony of shouting and
small arms fire. A close-quarters battle left scores of soldiers on both
sides dead.

When the metallic rat-a-tats of gunfire abated temporarily, people
in the surrounding neighborhoods breathed a sigh of relief, assuming
it would be an isolated incident. They were wrong.

The fight burst through Giyada's gates and spilled into residential neighborhoods, one faction pursuing another, the battle lines
confused by men in common uniform. Military facilities and arms

depots elsewhere in Juba were soon sites of mayhem, as word spread and army units fractured on ethnic lines. Crack-crack-crack-crack, the rattling sequences of automatic rifles overlapped one another. Then chest-pulsing thuds and explosions as heavier weapons were deployed. Before long, stunned civilians watched battle tanks rumble down the capital's streets, and then turn off-road, crushing *tukuls* and whoever was inside.

As the chaos closed in, Nyakueth, a Nuer woman of small stature, huddled with her four children inside their mud-and-thatch hut. She could hear it, feel it—soldiers exchanging fire, explosions shaking the ground below her feet, and screams of voices she thought she recognized.

Nyakueth's husband was an SPLA soldier, and they lived with their four children in New Site—a predominantly Nuer neighborhood of military families just across the road from army headquarters at Bilpam, on the north edge of the city. But her husband was away on training exercises, and she was alone caring for their children, the youngest a new infant. Her mind raced. She had no idea what was happening outside, and wondered if she should—or could—make a move.

Suddenly a hail of bullets tore through thatch and corrugated tin, then another. It sounded like the house next door. The gunfight was now on top of them. Nyakueth pushed her children to the ground, covering them as best she could with her slender frame. "If I die," she thought to herself, "it is up to god."

As Nyakueth cowered in her hut, and the fighting pushed into its second full hour, Deng Alor, Pagan Amum, and other SPLM figures were frantically making phone calls, trying desperately to put a lid on the situation they had, however indirectly, helped to create. With their bridges to Salva burned, they called the American and British ambassadors, the UN's chief representative, and anyone else they could reach. Only immediate and unambiguous public signals from Salva and Riek could prevent a full-scale urban war, they warned. Worse yet, "No matter who controls Juba," one of them told the American ambassador, "no one can control ethnic violence if it spreads to rural areas."

Spasms of fighting continued throughout the night of the 15th, and the battle resumed as the sun came up on Monday the 16th. Dinka units of the presidential guard flushed most of the Nuer fighting forces out of the city, and then began scouring the town looking for remaining soldiers. Some, they believed, had shed their uniforms and blended back into their communities. But as the president's guards and other security organs fanned out across Nuer neighborhoods, the line between soldier and civilian was all but erased.

At nine o'clock that morning, Nyakueth's phone rang. It was her brother, Pot, who worked as a local staff member for the UN. "Come to the base right away," he told her. She hadn't heard much gunfire in the last couple hours. Possessing little understanding of what had happened overnight, or the larger forces at play, she asked Pot whether that was still necessary. "Come *now*," her brother repeated, his plea now unmistakably insistent, and this time he shared the details.

In the last hour, hundreds, maybe thousands of men, women and children had swarmed the gates of the UN camp. Some were crying, shouting, or in shock, others had arrived severely beaten, bloodied, even unconscious. Several had been carried to the base with gunshot wounds, many of whom were not soldiers. Pot explained that the masses now accumulating there had fled from New Site and Manga Ten and other Nuer neighborhoods, and they were reporting horrifying scenes.

Soldiers were breaking into homes, questioning male inhabitants in the Dinka language. "*Yin col nga?*—what is your name?" they asked. Those who failed such language tests were dragged out and beaten; others were shot or had their throats slit as their children watched. Nuer families were terrorized and their homes looted. Some reported having seen dozens of Nuer men, tied together, being led away. Others, attempting to flee, were shot in the back. This was no longer a battle between rival army factions. It seemed the Nuer were being hunted.

Elsewhere in Juba, most Southern Sudanese, as well as international diplomats and aid workers, remained hunkered inside. Tidbits of information and rumors circulated by cell phone and two-way radio, but it was hard to get a handle on what was happening outside.

Whatever it was, the stories being pieced together suggested civilians were in grave danger.

The UN peacekeeping mission was headquartered in Juba, split between two bases on opposite ends of town. While its blue-helmed soldiers were not expected to insert themselves between warring combatants, protecting innocent civilians was a core element of their mandate. It is a task easier said than done, and the mission's peacekeepers—fairly or not—had a reputation for inaction. Though the two bases were guarded by blue helmets, the majority of peacekeepers were deployed outside the capital, leaving the UN bases vulnerable in such extraordinary circumstances. Despite these handicaps, UN representatives made one momentous decision that day—to open their gates. By the afternoon of December 16, more than 10,000 people had rushed through its gates seeking refuge—most of them Nuer. Twenty-four hours later, the number surged past 16,000.

Pot's frightening accounts spurred Nyakueth into action. Bending to exit through the waist-high door of her hut and then slowly standing erect, she emerged cautiously to find a startling scene. There was evidence of destruction everywhere, and hundreds of her neighbors were either gone or then fleeing the neighborhood. Her heart suddenly pumped with a new sense of urgency. She tied her youngest child in a *taub* on her back, grabbed the others by the hand, and raced to join the thousands heading to the UN base at Tomping. Security cameras mounted atop the walls of the U.S. Embassy compound delivered a video feed to a group of wide-eyed American aid officials watching inside. "More and more, first a trickle and then a steady stream," explained one, "people just *flooding.*"

Nyakueth arrived safely at the UN base and attempted to calm her children. But there, amid the swelling throngs of new arrivals, she found no food, no water, and no place to rest. The UN had opened its gates to provide safe haven, but was in no way prepared to accommodate the incredible numbers that had unexpectedly shown up on its doorstep. As more bodies crowded into an ever-shrinking space, sanitary conditions became abysmal. People drank filthy water and defecated in the open, and aid agencies raced to build latrines and fight dehydration and diarrhea. The sick and elderly struggled to get care, and many children were separated from their parents. At the camp's perimeter, reports of shootings, rape, and abduction fueled anxiety, and rumors of SPLA infiltrators inside the camp followed.

"It was *so* terrible a day," Nyakueth remembers, shaking her head. Her pained grimace conveys as much weight as all of the details she's just recounted. It is now the summer of 2016, and I have come to one of the UN's protection camps on the western outskirts of Juba, where tens of thousands like Nyakueth remain.

Nyakueth's palms are glued together as if in prayer, and her soft eyes stare out the open window over her right shoulder as she recounts the events of that awful night. Her hair is braided in three tight rows, and dry cracked toenails peek out from under a red-and-pink-flowered *taub*. Her cheeks are sunken and her face offers few expressions; around her mouth are a series of evenly-spaced raised dots, the *gaar* of many Nuer women. Though more than two years have passed, she appears to carry the events of that fateful night with her—in her chest, in her throat, in her semi-vacant stare.

Nyakueth is originally from Bentiu, and she re-located to Juba in 2008 when her husband was assigned to a post at army headquarters. On account of its location and demographics, New Site was one of a handful of neighborhoods where Dinka and Nuer soldiers squared off that night and into the next morning, as the army split in two. Unlike a great many of her neighbors, Nyakueth and her children survived those first fateful hours. Today, she remains inside this makeshift and overcrowded tent city—tired of this synthetic existence but too afraid to venture beyond the camp's gates.

Nyakueth says she was able to speak to her husband by phone upon arriving at the camp, to confirm that she and the children were all right, if uncomfortable and scared. She recounted to him the night's events. Though he was far outside Juba, he was well aware of the unraveling underway, she explains, as his own unit had already divided on ethnic lines. He told Nyakueth that he had defected from the army. He would not come home to her and the children but was instead en route to Nuer lands in Jonglei state on foot. It was the last time she would ever speak to him.

<hr/>

Shortly after 1:00pm that day, December 16, Salva Kiir entered a crowded press room at the presidential compound. Cameras flashed, murmuring journalists took their seats, and the national television station went live. "The purpose of this press statement is to inform you all of the events that unfolded last night," the president began, but it was hard to soak up these first words given the shocking image at the podium. Surrounded by his cabinet, and bathed in white TV lights, Salva was dressed not in his normal Western business suit, but in full military fatigues. He wore the familiar camouflage print of the elite Tiger battalion, a matching hat, and red-and-gold insignia like those he wore during the days of struggle. It was an unprecedented spectacle, and a reminder of how blurred the lines between army, party, and state remained. General Salva Kiir was sending a message.

The commander-in-chief then leveled a shocking accusation: Riek Machar had attempted a *coup d'état*. The "prophet of doom," as Salva called him, had failed to overthrow the government, and he and his co-conspirators would be brought to justice. Turning to the details of the previous evening, Salva explained that upon closing the tense NLC meeting at Nyakuron Center, an unidentified gunman had fired shots in the air. The government believed—or rather, promoted a narrative—that these shots were a signal to renegade forces to launch a planned attack on the Giyada guard headquarters and other SPLA posts.

"I would like to inform you all, my dear citizens, that your government is in full control of the security situation in Juba," Salva asserted, seeking to project authority and snuff out any would-be defectors. Government forces had driven the criminal attackers out of town, he said, and were still in hot pursuit.

"Rest assured that the government is doing all it can to make sure that citizens are secured and safe," he continued, making no reference to the Nuer civilians then being hunted. In fact, few of those taking notes or watching on television were even aware of the atrocities that had already been committed, a campaign that would continue over the next 48 hours.

"I will not allow or tolerate the incidents of 1991 to repeat themselves," the president warned. It was the second provocative reference to the painful split that had sown a generation of hatred between Salva's Dinka and Riek's Nuer, and for many, it was a call to war. The president had drawn a dangerous line in the sand, and whether intended or not, that line was an ethnic one.

Salva announced that Juba's citizens would be under curfew from 6pm to 6am, and then closed his prepared remarks. "Long live SPLM/SPLA, long live the unity of our people, long live the Republic of South Sudan." The irony of his parting words was that party, national unity, and the very survival of the republic were all now in question.

In the catastrophic days that followed, government spokesmen peddled the story of a *coup d'état* at home and abroad. But there was just one problem: it did not seem to add up. No attempt to capture or kill the president himself, nor his security chiefs? No evidence of advance planning, nor confessions by thwarted coup plotters? And the man allegedly behind the putsch, Riek Machar, was reportedly at home in his pajamas at the time it was launched?

It is hard to say what Salva actually believed about the events of December 15 and 16. Was he convinced that a coup had in fact been attempted? That one was in the making? Or was it, as the evidence suggested, simply a convenient cover story—a ruse designed to allow him to crack down on political opponents and finally eliminate his presumptive nemesis?

The man in the red T-shirt sitting across from me extends his left arm straight in front of him. He raises an index finger. As he talks, he reaches out with the other arm, and pulls the index finger back, before flicking it forward in release. It's a familiar mimic for the discharge of a rifle, and one David returns to often as he tells of the events witnessed on the morning of the December 16.

Government soldiers had been conducting house-to-house searches, David explains, looking for Nuer soldiers. But whether ordered from on high, or the result of liberties taken in the heat of the moment, the search squads also began targeting ordinary civilians—men, women, and children—simply because they were Nuer.

Those leading the campaign in David's neighborhood were Dinka members of the presidential guard, but they appeared to have swelled in number. The rumored Dinka recruits—those who had been trained at the president's farm at Luri, just 50 miles away—were now apparently in Juba. And their alleged new moniker, "*Dot ke beny*," Dinka for "rescue the president," left no doubt as to their intentions. They were to eliminate any and all threats.

Senior security sector officials would later testify to investigators that the president's off-the-books militia had not simply been called in as back-up, but had been in Juba before the crisis began. A week earlier, the sources alleged, the Luri recruits had been sent on a "clean-up" duty around Juba. But collecting litter, they explained, had been a pretext for the new force to conduct reconnaissance and map Nuer areas for later targeting.

David is 44 years old, with a lean frame and shoulders that cave forward. As he speaks, the words seem to come out of the left side of his mouth. Like Nyakueth, he remains inside a UN protection camp. David bows forward toward me, elbows on knees, and describes soldiers busting into *tukuls*, ordering inhabitants outside, and assaulting them. At first the camouflaged men angrily questioned those inside, and demanded money. But soon they were beating his neighbors with the butts of their guns, ordering them to lay face-down on the ground, and kicking screaming victims with black gum boots before—David discharges his index-finger rifle again—shooting them in the back. It was surreal, all happening right there in the middle of the dirt path that ran through his neighborhood, in broad daylight.

"Everyone began fleeing to the bush outside of town." As David, too, ran in search of safer territory, he and several others were intercepted by a group of soldiers and ordered to lie down. He thought of the scene he had just witnessed, but had no choice but to comply. He slowly lowered himself to the ground, and lay with cheek pressed against the gravel road. His muscles contracted. He flinched as shots were fired into the bodies next to him. But when the assailants moved on, David found himself somehow spared.

He picked himself up and ran as fast as he could. As he made his way west, he spotted the gaggle of soldiers again, now shouting at a feeble old man and forcing him to sit atop a pile of bloodied corpses. He despaired at the scene, wishing he could intervene, but he could not dare to tempt fate again.

David ran until he found an empty house, where he climbed through an open window and waited, in silence, for several hours. Suddenly the silence was broken, "Checking, checking, they are checking," a voice said, startling him. "You will be killed now. Come out, come out!" David says, mimicking the hushed urgency of the voice. It belonged to an Equatorian man who lived nearby, and the stranger ushered David into his own home.

"They gave me a cap," David explains, and told him, "'you sit here, together with the old mama.'" The cap helped to conceal the raised *gaar* on his forehead, and his impromptu hosts nestled him up next to the elderly woman sitting against a back wall. David would pose as her elderly male counterpart. Members of minority Equatorian tribes were of little interest to the men roaming in search of Nuer like David. After security units completed their search of the area and moved on, the Equatorian family then helped arrange David's safe passage to the UN base.

"Why do you think the Equatorian man helped you?" I ask David. What I don't have to vocalize is the shared understanding that the good Samaritan, by taking in a marked man, had put himself and his family in extraordinary danger. David had no time to think about it then, and suggests he doesn't know now either; he says only that the family was conscious that he was not a combatant, but an innocent fellow citizen who, like them, wanted no part of this dispute. Because David remains inside the UN protection camp, he hasn't seen the man since, and did not get a name. But he wants to make very clear that he intends to find him one day and express his gratitude. "I know the place... I know the man."

As David finishes his story, I look behind him at rows and rows of white tents and plastic-roofed huts, and know that this story is anything but unique. This camp is filled with survivors whose stories are as grim as his. As with Nyakueth, I've arranged to speak with David and others here with the guidance of a professional organization doing trauma counseling in camps like this one. Such interviews require sensitivity to a survivor's experience, environment, and sense of control, as well as to potential triggers that might re-traumatize. There are ethical questions to consider, too, in asking about one's experience of violence, and multiple reasons why these survivors choose to tell their stories. Many here are eager to talk, and to be heard.

Michael, another middle-aged Nuer man, describes the afternoon that he and his cousin were rounded up with a dozen other men and driven in a heavy-duty truck to Gudele prison. After handing over their money and ID cards, Michael and his cousin were told to remove their shoes and pile them atop the others already there. "The stack of shoes was as tall as me," he says, raising a horizontal hand to show its height. His cousin began to sob. SPLA soldiers locked the two men inside a large room, its floor covered by rotting corpses, many lying where they had met their frantic end the night before. The floor was stained with the fluid of decomposing remains, making for an overwhelming stench. Michael finishes his story, and goes quiet. "*Full* of dead bodies," he says again moments later. When I ask how many he shakes a finger; "I cannot, I cannot," he repeats twice, "there were too many to count."

Gatluak, who runs a small shop in another Nuer neighborhood, had locked up for the day and returned home to tend to his chronically ill sister. Like so many others, he was forced to flee on the 16th, and he had no choice but to leave his sister behind. After a night in hiding, and in anguish, he made the hugely risky decision to return to her. "If I let her die alone there, my life will be cursed," Gatluak told himself.

Patrolling soldiers soon found him there, preparing food for his sister, and demanded he come outside. The "baby-faced one" pointed the barrel of his Kalashnikov "right into my face," he explains. "You look up at the sun now," he said, "it is the last time you will see it." Tense long seconds passed, and Gatluak winced as another of the soldiers pushed the gun barrel into the air, telling his partner to let the man care for his sister, adding, "We can return for him later."

⸻

By December 18, Nyakueth was desperate to feed her children. She shuddered at the danger beyond the fence of the UN camp, but resolved it was the only way. "If you don't go," she told herself, "your children are going to die, same as these people that are already dead." Just make it through this day, she thought, and then thank God that you won't have to go out again. When the noise of gunfire slowed, she and four other women made a run for it, intending to scour the nearby Manga Ten neighborhood for anything they could find.

Outside the fence she found a war zone. She was careful to keep her distance, but spotted soldiers in army, national security, and police uniforms moving about in the distance, some on foot, other patrolling in army trucks and looted cars. En route to Manga Ten she passed five lifeless bodies lined up side-by-side at the edge of the road, each with visible gunshot wounds. A hundred hurried paces later, another three bodies. Then another, lying contorted and lifeless in the deserted Manga Ten market. Elsewhere, government soldiers had begun collecting bodies and dumping them in unmarked mass graves—their superiors hoping to conceal the scale and brutality of the murderous events.

Nyakueth and the others found the market already looted, the shelves in its rusting tin shacks mostly empty. So they broke up and began searching house to house, hoping to find grain, beans, powdered milk—anything with calories they could ferry back to their children. As Nyakueth exited one house empty-handed and turned left toward the next, a camouflage-painted Toyota pickup truck— green, tan, and black—roared up in front of her. Five soldiers hopped out, guns cocked. Shouting at the women, one of the men picked

Nyakueth up and put her in the bed of the pickup, and then the others. Bumping along the uneven road, the soldiers drove their captives to another area, and ordered them to get out.

"We had no power to resist," she says, resigned. "I believed they were going to kill me."

Nyakueth and the other women were directed at gunpoint inside a *tukul*, one by one ducking their heads as they entered. Inside was a badly burned body. Nyakueth has little to share about that moment, except to say the deceased was so burned that it conveyed almost nothing in the way of identity—not even a gender. It was anyone. It was no one. Seemingly hopped up on adrenaline, the soldiers began debating among themselves in Arabic, before one of them aggressively announced the result of their deliberations. Nyakueth and the other women had a choice: eat the charred corpse at their feet or be raped.

As the soldiers raised their voices, shaking their assault rifles and demanding an answer to the ultimatum, another man entered the *tukul*. Nyakueth doesn't know how or why this man arrived, but she brightens up and straightens in her chair as she recalls his fortuitous arrival. She recognized him, a Dinka officer called Deng, who was an acquaintance of her husband. Deng recognized Nyakueth, too, and the superior officer insisted forcefully that his fellow soldiers desist and return to their patrols.

As they sped away, Nyakueth and the others hurried back to the UN base empty-handed. "I never went out again."

<hr />

At the U.S. embassy, staff members fielded a flood of calls from local contacts. It had been difficult to piece together what had been happening over the last 48 hours, but reports were now doubling and tripling up from different sources. Soldiers had set up checkpoints, pulling passengers out onto the street, and executing any of them with a Nuer name or facial scarring. Nuer neighborhoods were being cleansed of their residents, and the reports detailed both extreme brutality and a clear intent to intimidate. Heavy-duty trucks full of bodies were heading toward the outskirts of town, their payloads to be dumped at unmarked sites.

When the violence abated, one of the first assessments by international observers found some Nuer neighborhoods "totally depopulated." They were barred by government forces from visiting some neighborhoods, where soldiers had yet to "clean" the area of evidence. In others, they found homes ransacked, the ground littered with spent bullet cartridges, and evidence of sudden flight, including "prepared meals left untouched in homes." One man—feet and hands bound, with a gunshot wound to the chest—appeared to be put on display at an entrance to a Nuer neighborhood.

Months later, formal investigations by the UN and the African Union corroborated testimony of the worst reports: some Nuer civilians were tied up and burned alive inside their homes; others were forced to drink the blood of murdered family members. Women of all ages were gang raped, left unconscious and bleeding. Some were tortured for days in secret locations, others simply disappeared. No one knows how many were killed in those first three days, nor where all the deceased are buried.

You can't help but try to imagine it: the scenes of violence, the individual acts. Looking out over a rust-colored dirt road in a still-emptied neighborhood, now two years on, I think of all the stories I've heard about what happened here. It's hard to imagine them. Or maybe it isn't; maybe it just seems hard, or wrong, to try to match an ephemeral image with the gravity of an act of extreme violence. The imagining itself seems somehow unjust, and the inherent curiosity shameful. But ignoring the reality of what happened, curating it into a faceless or less gruesome form seems even worse.

Beyond the deeply painful nature of the atrocities was the question of responsibility. Had there been an order from on high to deliberately target Nuer—from Salva or other senior politicians or military men? Evidence of a "systematic" policy to commit such egregious crimes has been a central question in massacres and genocides from Nazi Germany in the 1940s, to Cambodia under the Khmer Rouge in the 1970s, to the slaughter of Tutsis in Rwanda in 1994. A "systematic" campaign is the threshold by which "crimes against humanity" are determined under international law.

In 1963, political theorist Hannah Arendt sparked lasting controversy during her famous reporting of the trial of Nazi war criminal Alfred Eichmann when she introduced the notion of the "banality of evil." Eichmann, she argued, was neither an ideologue nor motivated by a particular hatred for the Jews he helped to exterminate. He was not extraordinary but rather an unthinking cog in a machine, following orders as they were handed down in a system that had normalized the unthinkable.

Half a century later, in South Sudan, the same difficult question applied: Were those individual Dinka soldiers (and later their Nuer counterparts) committing such conscience-shocking acts motivated by a deep-seated sense of ethnic hate? Or were they following an order, doing as they were told, and thus accountability rested with their bosses?

Such orders are rarely written down, and ultimate authority can be difficult to pin down. However, the African Union's 2014 investigation resolved that the crimes in Juba were indeed committed in a "widespread or systematic nature," and carried out "in furtherance of a state policy." The United Nations came to the same conclusions, and both investigations inferred advance planning and coordination. The evidence was established, though personal accountability for these crimes would be for a future court to determine. What was not in question was the heinous nature of the acts committed, and the power they had in fueling widespread feelings of fear and thirst for revenge.

"I myself, I don't want Salva to be president," explains Ker (*KAIR*), a twenty-something member of the "White Army," from his lavender plastic chair. The bright afternoon sun injects a diagonal beam into an otherwise dark *tukul* in Waat, a comparatively sizable village deep in the Nuer heartland. Just five miles from where we sit is the legendary mound of the most famous Nuer prophet of the nineteenth century, the hallowed ground where he performed ceremonial rites, dispensed advice, and sang songs that allegedly foretold of South Sudan's violent reckoning.

The light cuts a harsh silhouette of Ker's angular frame, and before us on a matching lavender plastic table are empty pots which until recently contained a generous meal of rice, gristly chunks of goat, and mush of stewed wild greens. With the fighting nominally over, I have come back to South Sudan to speak with those like Ker who were directly involved.

"Most of us, we used to say, Salva can be our president," Ker says, looking me in the eye. "But we didn't know he could do these things." He shakes his head in disgust. "We cannot suffer what he has done to us." But Ker is talking not only of the massacres that caused so much pain and anger among members of his tribe. "We the Nuer, we have been marginalized." To get a job, an education, healthcare, or to realize any sense of security, Ker explains, you cannot get it here in Nuer country. "We don't have roads, facilities, hospitals, education, what, what, what—everything must be got from [the capital]."

In addition to his native Nuer and Arabic, Ker speaks more fluent English than his peers, though with some familiar quirks; he uniformly exchanges the letter "p" for "f," thus recounting his "exference" in the war, and why so many of his Lou Nuer community remain deeply "unhaffy." In rhythmic tones that rise and fall for emphasis, Ker is confident in offering his thoughts on politics, tribalism, and the war itself, all while maintaining direct eye contact—even in telling of some of the murderous attacks against Dinka civilians in which he participated. Outside, two roosters crow with impressive volume, occasionally strutting into the doorway to listen in on Ker's version of events.

Ker was pursuing his studies in Jonglei's state capital, Bor, when the fighting began. In the early morning hours of December 16 and throughout the following day, his cell phone rang incessantly. Ker's wife, then residing in Juba with their two children, spoke at a quickened pace as she recounted the chaos then enveloping the capital. Other friends and relatives called to detail the scouring of Nuer neighborhoods and the deaths of mutual friends. As he triangulated information, Ker felt anger welling up in his body. "I cannot even describe it," he says, his voice slowing and the muscles in his arms constricting as he revisits the painful night.

A sense of helplessness mounted as he exchanged news and reactions by cell phone with peers in Bor and across Nuer areas further north. "What do we do, what do we do?" He imitates the exasperation he felt, slapping open palms on his thighs and bowing his head.

Ker and his fellow students watched on television as the president took to the podium in his military fatigues, summoning the ghosts of the past. "I will not allow incidents of 1991 to happen..." Ker trails off after quoting Salva's words almost verbatim. Visibly frustrated, he explains how the legacy of 1991, the Bor massacre, and the turbulent years that followed still resonate in Bor, even for those who were then just young children. "We always used to hear from locals, 'You Nuer are here in Bor, but you forgot what you did to us in 1991.'" Ker shakes his head, his tone now frustrated, "This is 2000-and-something, not 1991. Why are we talking about this?"

By the evening of the 17th, Ker explains how a rumor materialized in Bor that "all the Nuer in Juba have been killed, and the rest have scattered to camps and the bush." Without electricity at home, most citizens power-up their phone batteries at charging stations set up at local markets. But after two days of fighting, those civilians hunkering down in Juba were not able to charge their phones, which would have required movement outside of their homes. And so the preponderance of dead phones exacerbated fears outside the capital—Ker and many others thought it meant that "all the Nuer were dead," a realization he says helped catalyze reprisal attacks against the Dinka in Bor.

On December 17, a government spokesperson in Juba notified the public that ten senior political figures had been arrested "in connection with the foiled coup attempt." Among the detained were "Garang Boys" Deng Alor and Pagan Amum, and anyone else that had participated in the press conference at SPLM House on December 6.

All of the detainees were party heavyweights, and most had been recently fired from their posts. But when it came to ethnicity they were a heterogeneous bunch—Bor and Bahr al Ghazal Dinkas, Lou and Jikany Nuers, Shilluks, and Equatorians. Their tribal diversity underscored the political, rather than ethnic, origins of the crisis. With the government's *coup* narrative already in doubt, it was hard to see anything other than political motivations behind their arrest. Many feared the high-profile group might be assassinated, as there were plenty of opponents now in positions of influence who would be happy to see them eliminated.

Several other wanted men remained at-large, most notably the alleged mastermind himself, Riek Machar. For government and SPLA hardliners, the country's most infamous traitor had long been the object of both personal animus and ethnic hatred. They had opposed Riek's return to the SPLA in 2003, and were not about to tolerate another cushy accommodation. It was a visceral hate, and they wanted him dead. They wanted his people dead, too—loyal soldiers, bodyguards, family members, and known affiliates.

On the morning of the 17th, senior military men amassed a sizable force to storm Riek's house. Draped in ammunition belts, perched atop tanks, and manning machine-gun-mounted technicals, SPLA commandos surrounded the home. There was no more time for talk, no more time for politics, no more time for compromise.

Two T-72 army tanks smashed through the compound's walls and fired high explosive shells into the brick house. Dozens of commandos bull-rushed the compound, exchanging fire with those inside. Some of Riek's guards were killed in the shootout, but when the dust settled, Riek was nowhere to be found.

No one had been able to reach him by phone, either. Party allies, the UN chief, the American ambassador, and anyone else dialing Riek or his associates had found their mobile phones shut off. Riek was well aware of the phone-tracking capacity his young government had acquired, an instrument undoubtedly now trained on public enemy No. 1.

Rumors began swirling as to Riek's hiding place, one of which was soon passing across lips all over town: "Riek has been given refuge at the U.S. embassy." Frustrated government officials questioned the Americans, but Riek was not on their compound. Nor was he at the UN camp. The truth was, at the time his house was destroyed, the deposed vice president was holed up in a *tukul* several miles to the north and west, his location known only to the trusted bodyguards who had ferried him there in an unmarked car under the cover of darkness.

Hours after his house was destroyed, Riek and his entourage decided they could not afford to stay any longer. They escaped from Juba and headed north, where they forced their way onto a hired barge and crossed the Nile at Mongalla. Waiting in the long grasses on the other side were the forces of General Peter Gadet, commander of the SPLA's 8th Division and the first senior Nuer officer to defect.

Gadet had already killed his deputy—a Dinka—and taken control of military facilities south of Bor. One soldier present told me Gadet had unexpectedly pulled a pistol from his holster and, before anyone could react, walked right up to his deputy and shot him at point blank range. Gadet's forces then seized control of Bor, where they would link up with Ker and thousands of Nuer youth bent on revenge.

Two days later, on December 19th, Riek spoke publicly for the first time. Railing against Salva, he denied the alleged *coup d'état*, calling it a fabrication intended solely to destroy political opponents. But then he went a step further. "We want him to leave, that's it." Citing Salva's campaign of murder and ethnic incitement, Riek announced that he had called on the national army to "remove Salva Kiir from the leadership of the country."

The genie was out of the bottle, and there was no going back. What had begun as a reaction had just officially become a rebellion. Two years after achieving its independence, South Sudan was at war with itself.

Ker tied a red band around his forehead and a scrap of white cloth around his left elbow. So too did hundreds of his Nuer brethren. The fight, they learned, was coming to Bor. These foot soldiers—the so-called "White Army"—then overpowered local security forces and began exacting revenge against the town's majority Dinka community.

Ker explains that the White Army is an informal community protection mechanism that was created generations ago, "by our grand grandfathers, to defend families and cattle." The stories and traditions of the White Army have since been passed down, he says, and when you become a man at age 15, you receive a gun and are obliged to uphold its sacred duty. For Ker and men of his age, battlefield toughness is a matter of identity. "If you are fighting on the frontline, and you do not shoot someone, you are not a man."

Historically, the need for self-protection has been felt particularly strongly by Ker's section of the Nuer; the "Lou" from this remote region enjoy less access to water than their neighbors, though their cows and livelihoods are no less dependent. But the White Army took on an entirely new dimension during Sudan's civil war in the 1990s. Mobilized by Riek Machar following the 1991 split, they became a more distinct fighting entity and assumed an active role in the South's internal conflict. Ker's uncles and cousins were given guns and joined Riek's breakaway forces on the brutal rampage that would later become known as the "Bor Massacre."

In the days after Nuer civilians were massacred in Juba, that awful event repeated itself in Bor—this time in reverse. Nuer assailants went house-to-house, shooting men, women, children, and the elderly. Soldiers and skinny young men in red headbands looted markets, burned homes to the ground, and taunted local civilians. Thousands of Dinkas fled to the UN base in Bor. Tens of thousands more fled across the river. Some were shot in the back as they fled to the riverbank. Others drowned, swept away by powerful currents after they jumped out of boats to take cover from incoming fire.

Dozens of decaying bodies soon lay in the streets of Bor, scores more were seen floating down river. When it was all over, survivors would bury hundreds of family members and neighbors in mass graves. As the town emptied, soldiers and White Army members made off not only with captured weapons, but stolen goods, money, and cattle. The attacks were reminiscent of the infamous massacre some 22 years earlier, and for those unfamiliar with the political machinations at the heart of the crisis, they helped cement an ethnic narrative of the violence in the war's first days.

"Why should civilians in Bor be the target of the same awful violence visited on the Nuer in Juba?", I ask. Ker anticipates the question and interrupts me: "They should be killed." I ask him to explain his logic, and he vacillates between pangs of frustration at the wrongs done to his community, and cool explanations of a code of revenge shared by many South Sudanese. "We live together [with the Dinka], we share many things together, and *in a minute*—they turn to kill our people? Our mothers, our brothers, our children—with no reason?" He explains that he has an obligation to ensure justice is done. "If my mother is killed by you, I cannot leave your mother in life. Never." Ker suggests the retribution is born of a moral imperative, and there are no exceptions. "Even if it is a god who killed our people, we can go and fight with the god."

During their second occupation of Bor, Nuer fighters murdered fourteen elderly women who were hiding inside St. Andrew's Episcopal Church. Some reports suggested the women were subjected to sexual violence. When I present Ker with the facts reported about this tragic event, he responds reflexively, "Not true." Ker asserts his Christian bona fides, and suggests such an act would be out of bounds: "Even if you burn all the *tukuls* in town, you cannot burn a church." I share some of the details corroborated by witnesses and investigators, but Ker interrupts again, "Not true."

Ker does not shy away from the fact that many Dinka civilians were killed. But in confronting this gruesome and indefensible episode, the rightness and purity of the vengeful act seem thrown into question. Ker denies several more of the worst incidents that occurred during these periods of lawlessness, as if to block out that which clouds the clear justifications he's made for avenging the dead. He changes the subject.

The egregious killings of innocent Nuer in Juba had initiated a cycle of violence. But in the ensuing days, weeks, and months, the rapidly spreading war and unspeakable crimes committed would leave victims on all sides—Dinka, Nuer, and innocents from many other ethnic communities. No group was spared. And no group had clean hands.

"All of us are not happy about what happened," Ker says, reflecting on the whole period and the state of his country. "We are all sad. Even Salva, if you get him alone." But just moments later in the same conversation, Ker returns again to the reprisal killings with a note that hangs solemnly in the air. "We did our part," he says. It seems he is trying to convince himself as much as convince me. I ask him to clarify, and he repeats, "We did our part. Revenge."

After Juba and Bor, the war metastasized. Six of eight army divisions split on ethnic lines. Tens of thousands of mostly Nuer soldiers defected. Battles raged in towns and military outposts across the country. The violence multiplied at an unprecedented speed, and with it came a singularly ethnic narrative of conflict.

Because the Nuer comprised as much as 65 percent of the still fractious SPLA ranks, the impromptu opposition may have constituted the larger of the two armies now squaring off across much of South Sudan. And they weren't alone. Tens of thousands of White Army fighters like Ker had mobilized to join them, chanting the songs of war. Dinka communities, likewise subjected to violence and now fearing the "other," were also being called to action by their president. Not only did each side feel a duty to avenge what had been done, but the fight was increasingly being framed as an existential one. It was a zero-sum game of tribal hate, they were told. Kill or be killed.

A power-hungry and dominant class of elites had been unable to resolve their differences by political means, and so the population would fight a war on their behalf. By appealing to their tribal bases, Salva and Riek were most responsible for turning a political conflict into an ethnic one. But the widespread reporting of an ethnic war also helped to solidify that transition and re-frame the violence.

Over the next two weeks, the three state capitals of Greater Upper Nile were each up for grabs. In Bentiu, heavy fighting enveloped the capital after Major General James Koang defected with his 4th division forces, drove the sitting governor out of town, and announced control on December 21. Three days later, on December 24, Malakal—the capital of the country's primary oil-producing state—fell to defecting rebels of the SPLA's 7th division and their White Army comrades. Meanwhile, Peter Gadet's forces withdrew from Bor, only to re-take it a week later and further their campaign of revenge.

Each town traded hands as many as a dozen times, each counterattack yielding more devastation. Everywhere one looked were the signs of violent ruin: smoldering skeletons of torched market stalls, charred foundations of homes, and eerily emptied neighborhoods, save the bloated corpses strewn about the streets. Little remained amid the ash—metal bed frames, pots and pans, shreds of blackened clothing—the remnants of the lives, and the normality that was here until, suddenly, it wasn't.

The scenes were the same everywhere: skies filled with smoke, burned-out vehicles tipped on their sides, and rag-tag bands of soldiers and youths ferrying away booty. Food, fuel, chairs, mattresses, clothing, tools, motorbikes, cattle—they disappeared with anything that could be carried, carted, or driven away. A kind of hellscape remained, where every bit of life and hope had been sucked out. No voices, no commerce, no color, no nothing. All that remained was lawlessness and fear and the haunting smell of death.

As in Juba, terrified survivors overwhelmed UN bases in all three state capitals. UN officials grew anxious as fighting raged just beyond camp gates. For anyone wanting to destroy members of an opposing tribe, the bases were now highly concentrated ethnic enclaves, and the thousands inside were sitting ducks. Even with peacekeepers manning fences and razor-wired embankments, their defenses would not withstand a full-on assault. And though they provided a modicum of safety from the terrors beyond the wire, inside, there was little food, water, or privacy. There was only mud, sewage, anger and uncertainty.

At the presidential palace in Juba, Salva and his trusted generals made war plans. They were intent on crushing Riek and his new rebellion. Salva the politician had always been out of his depth, but Salva the general was at home poring over a map of the battlefield. His country was being torn apart on his watch, and his legacy as a unifier was quickly being erased from the history books. But operationally, he was now in familiar territory.

Riek meanwhile mobilized from his new headquarters at Gadiang, deep in Nuer country. It seemed history was repeating itself. The aging politician and presidential aspirant could hardly have imagined returning to fight another bush war, another war against an authoritarian Dinka he wanted to replace. But here he was, working the satellite phones and two-way radios from a plastic chair, under a tree, in a makeshift rebel camp. And he had little time to indulge in déjà vu. Not only was he busy cobbling Nuer militias into a coherent opposition force, he needed to procure weapons, ammunition, and supplies—and he was dialing abroad in search of sponsors.

As the fight spread to more and more locations, military alliances evolved, defections continued, and foreign actors were enticed into the fight. The flow of precious crude oil from the Unity State fields was stopped altogether, handicapping an already ailing economy. Hoping to stem the rebellious tide, Salva reinstated retired military allies and courted Nuer generals who remained on the fence, hoping to pre-empt them and their supporters from joining the rapidly growing rebellion. Riek cultivated the same Nuer heavyweights and the influential Nuer prophet, who commanded thousands of White Army youth. But he also looked beyond Nuer territory, appealing to South Sudan's other aggrieved tribes in hopes of turning his ethnic resistance into a national one.

As each side jostled for advantage, communities were co-opted or forced into the fight—the Shilluk in Upper Nile, the Bul Nuer in Unity, the Murle in Jonglei. Many Equatorian groups were caught in the middle of a war they wanted nothing to do with. Some aligned with the rebels and quietly assumed strategic positions around Juba, others kept on side with the government, wondering whether they might leverage their loyalty toward greater local autonomy. Still others, tired of yet another fight, wanted only to remain on the sidelines.

In just two weeks of fighting, some 200,000 citizens had been driven from their homes. Two weeks more, and the number was half a million. Seemingly endless chains of people trekked across vast distances to escape the violence, their destination uncertain. Tens of thousands crossed into neighboring countries, including huge numbers back into Sudan. Like Ayen, the "returnee" mother of six who had come from Khartoum, many of those now fleeing back to Sudan had only just "come home" to the independent Republic in the South. To go back to Sudan of all places, where Southerners had long been treated as second-class citizens, was a poignant symbol of the promise lost.

Despite the highly visible men in the middle, this wasn't simply a fight between Salva and Riek, or between feuding SPLM factions. In time it would transcend the Dinka-Nuer axis, too. The metastasizing war would fuel local grievances, exacerbate latent conflicts, destroy the economy, and leave millions at risk of starvation. It would shred an already delicate social fabric and return Southerners to a mindset of survival that, after five decades of war, they thought had finally been left behind. South Sudan had come undone.

17

ALARM

"South Sudan stands at the precipice. Recent fighting threatens to plunge South Sudan back into the dark days of its past... Too much blood has been spilled and too many lives have been lost to allow South Sudan's moment of hope and opportunity to slip from its grasp"
—President Barack Obama, December 19, 2013

WASHINGTON / JUBA / BOR, DECEMBER 2013

Under the lights at Rockefeller Center's Studio 3B in New York, NBC nightly news anchor Brian Williams appeared for the evening news. "Tonight there is a new crisis spot for the world," he announced to millions of primetime television viewers on December 23, "and that means [for] the U.S. as well... Southern Sudan is in the grip of non-stop violence, and there's growing fear there of an all-out war."

During the first week of the crisis, few on the outside had any sense of what was happening in South Sudan. But by Christmas, CNN, NBC, the BBC, Al Jazeera and news outlets around the world were broadcasting chilling images of carnage from the world's newest state.

Battle tanks roared through the capital, waves of civilians swelled UN camps, and mutilated bodies lay in the streets—all this, in a place where the last international news story had been that of a nation's triumphant birth.

Shocked by the sudden onset of violence, the international community scrambled to stop it. For many, the specter of Rwanda still loomed large, when the world sat by as a 1994 genocide of haunting proportions unfolded in slow motion. Here, in another off-the-beaten-path locale just 400 miles north of Rwanda, it seemed another was in the making. Even for those who sensed South Sudan's boiling undercurrents, the pace of its unraveling was hard to comprehend. "We knew there were tensions," announced the UN's chief diplomat on the ground, "but the speed, the gravity, and the scale... I think nobody could have expected."

U.S. Ambassador Samantha Power joined an emergency session of the UN Security Council in New York, its members expressing outrage and voting to send another 5,000 peacekeepers to South Sudan. "Let me be absolutely clear. The world is watching all sides in South Sudan," said the UN's Secretary-General. "Stop the violence... Save your proud and newly independent country. There is no time to lose."

Diplomats from Africa and the West boarded planes bound for Juba, hoping to stave off a humanitarian disaster. Appeals for restraint came from leaders around the world, and Salva's office was flooded with phone calls from African presidents, from Susan Rice and John Kerry in Washington, and from Prime Minister David Cameron in London. Former presidents Jimmy Carter and George Bush would also be patched through Juba's spotty telephone networks in the ensuing weeks, in hopes that gravitas and personal relationships with Salva might make the difference. Even the Pope weighed in.

"We pray for social harmony in South Sudan," Pope Francis announced from high above the Christmas Day masses gathered at St. Peter's Square in the Vatican, "where current tensions have already caused too many victims." The Holy Father had already reached out to the warring factions and dispatched an emissary to Juba, deeply concerned by the threat to "peaceful coexistence in that young state."

Meanwhile, an exodus of biblical proportions had begun. Civilians were escaping Juba by foot, bus, or any means possible. Foreign nationals were being evacuated by air, and those Southerners with means or connections likewise flocked to the airport, desperate to get a seat aboard anything with wings.

The high-definition television screen divided in two, then into three, four, and five boxes. As in many such crisis situations, U.S. National Security Adviser Susan Rice would appear in one box, then Secretary of State Kerry in another, then Defense Secretary Chuck Hagel and other members of the Obama National Security Council, as the White House situation room connected video feeds for an emergency "principals committee" meeting. The government's highest-level decision-making body had been convened in response to the crisis, and their evolving assessments were being briefed to President Obama.

Washington was focused on the rapidly deteriorating situation and diplomatic options to help slow the violence. But its first concern was the safety of U.S. government personnel and other American citizens on the ground. It was December 2013, and memories of the attack a year earlier on the American embassy in Benghazi, Libya—during which the Ambassador and three other U.S. personnel were killed—were still fresh. Beyond those tragic losses, the incident had been heavily scrutinized and used as a divisive political wedge in Washington, and the White House wasn't about to let it happen again. Threat assessments and contingencies for embassy evacuation were reviewed and updated around the clock.

The U.S. Embassy in Juba had already suspended normal operations and evacuated nearly 700 Americans and other foreign nationals. Several American C-130 military aircraft had arrived at Juba airport to ferry away the evacuees: first U.S. personnel, then close foreign allies, then anyone who could get their name on a list. Military aircraft from the UK, Germany, and East African neighbors followed suit. As those departing queued to board, Juba's national security agents lurked on the tarmac, determined to intercept any Nuer attempting to escape. In the coming weeks these agents would monitor all flight manifests, sometimes stopping taxiing aircraft and dragging Nuer politicians and businessmen off departing flights.

North of the capital, meanwhile, several dozen American aid workers remained trapped in Bor, as government and allied forces bombed nearby rebel positions. On December 21, U.S. Special Forces were ordered to mount a rescue operation. Three U.S. military V-22 Osprey helicopters lifted off from an American air base in Djibouti, en route from the tiny East African country to South Sudan. Air Force Major Ryan Mittelstet piloted "Rooster 73," the lead Osprey. In the rear cabin of his aircraft, and the two others tailing him, Navy SEALs checked their gear and readied to extract the stranded Americans.

South Sudan presented nowhere near the threat U.S. forces faced in war zones like Iraq or Afghanistan, nor had Americans ever been targets in the country that owed Washington its independence. But the fighting underway in Bor made for a less benign environment than special forces teams had been told. As Major Mittelstet led the Ospreys in a final turn toward the airstrip in Bor, their hulking dual-rotor choppers drew the attention of Peter Gadet's rebel forces on the ground.

Ker was on the ground, too, and was stunned when he looked up to see the foreign-looking aircraft approaching. "Some kind of airplanes, very fast, *very* fast!" he says, explaining that the unidentified helicopters had arrived in Bor just after a series of attacks by the SPLA's own helicopters. A communications breakdown meant Gadet's forces were unaware of the planned rescue mission, and so assumed the approaching Ospreys—now pulsating just overhead—were hostile.

"Taking fire!" Mittelstet shouted into the radio seconds later, "Go around! Go around!" More than 100 rounds of AK-47 and .50 caliber rifle fire riddled the Ospreys' fuselage, and smoke spewed from the rear of Rooster 73. Inside Mittelstet's aircraft, the cabin was awash in blood, the barrage of unexpected fire wounding four SEALS. The Ospreys aborted the mission and veered south, racing toward Uganda without their intended cargo.

The failed operation weighed heavily in Washington, where officials would also have to contemplate whether to keep the embassy in Juba open or pull up stakes and leave town. For those familiar with the situation, the threat to the embassy seemed low, but conservative hedging was a reality in the post-Benghazi attack period.

A decision to close the embassy potentially carried far greater implications than ensuring the safety of those inside. Leaving would mean no tough diplomatic engagement with the government or the rebels, and no bearing witness to whatever happened next. And if the U.S.—as South Sudan's most important foreign partner—lowered its flag and withdrew, most other nations would follow.

Some of Obama's top officials had been involved in a similar decision two decades earlier in Rwanda. During the first days of the 1994 genocide, American diplomats were evacuated and the embassy in Kigali closed. There is no certainty that remaining would have altered the course of history, nonetheless it was hard to dissociate from what happened next. Over the ensuing 100 days, three-quarters of a million Rwandans were brutally slaughtered in one of the worst bloodbaths in modern history.

After round-the-clock deliberations, Obama's National Security team decided to draw down the number of personnel at the embassy, but keep the post open. Only the Ambassador and a skeleton staff would remain, and emergency security squads would be flown in to protect them. The flag would continue flying, and South Sudan's most important partner would remain, its remaining diplomats pressing Salva to change course before his country collapsed.

While constant diplomatic interventions and efforts to slow the fighting sometimes felt futile, the counter-factual was hard to imagine. "The absence of eyes on the ground?" one European official asked rhetorically at the time, hinting at the possibility that the violence could multiply dramatically. "These guys, both sides, would be totally unrestrained."

At the time the Ospreys took fire, U.S. Special Envoy Donald Booth and I were en route to South Sudan. Hours earlier, we had left a series of crisis meetings at the State Department in Washington's Foggy Bottom district, packed our bags for a three-day trip, and re-convened at Dulles International Airport. As we boarded the overnight flight, we talked strategy on how to push Salva and Riek to the negotiating table.

Given the United States' role in creating South Sudan, its continuing political and financial support, and the grave risks now confronting the country's war-weary people, Washington believed—and so too did many others—that it had to step up and try to contain the situation. Booth was the sixth "U.S. Special Envoy to Sudan and South Sudan" to be appointed by an American president, a position that existed precisely for this kind of high-level engagement. Such special envoys occupy a unique role in American diplomacy, assigned to a limited number of portfolios deemed foreign policy priorities.

Booth had recently wrapped up a thirty-six-year foreign service career with ambassadorships in Liberia, Zambia, and Ethiopia. He had a reserved demeanor, listened before talking, and valued substance over flash. From his most recent perch in neighboring Ethiopia (2010–13), he had become well acquainted with Sudan's messy politics and the South's tumultuous birth. At the time he accepted the Sudans post, some had wondered whether a special envoy role was any longer necessary, given North and South had inked a blueprint on post-separation arrangements. Neither they, nor Booth, could have known how quickly South Sudan would be thrust back into the spotlight, and how quickly the role would once again be characterized by high-stress, round-the-clock crisis diplomacy.

Despite all that had transpired, there was still a chance to prevent South Sudan's hostile factions from plunging their people into a violent abyss. But doing so would require repeated interventions from anyone with relationships, leverage, or creative ideas.

We stopped first in Ethiopia to consult with concerned regional governments and lay plans for ceasefire talks. Diplomats from the African Union and neighboring countries had already paid an emergency visit to Juba, but reported that their intervention with Salva "had had little impact." Stopping the bloodshed and preventing collapse were interests shared by all of South Sudan's foreign partners, but the potential spillover impacts—destabilization, refugee flows, economic collapse—presented acute risks for neighboring Ethiopia, Kenya, Uganda, and Sudan.

After receiving word that South Sudan's national airport had been re-opened after several days of closure, we boarded an Ethiopian Airlines flight for Juba. Ascending the fold-out steps and ducking inside the familiar Bombardier Dash-8 aircraft, Booth and I found just one poor soul on a normally crowded plane fit for 70 passengers. Forty-five minutes into the journey, as twin-engine turboprops droned a mind-numbing drone, I made a mental map of the flight path, and grew concerned. A direct route from Addis to Juba would mean descending over rebel-held territory south of Bor, the epicenter of the battle for South Sudan.

Communication on the ground was very poor, the situation was fast-evolving, and ongoing rumors about airspace restrictions created uncertainty. The Osprey incident 48 hours earlier was also a sharp reminder that it was not uncommon for unidentified aircraft to be fired upon. I walked to the back of the plane and found a flight attendant. "Do you have a map of our flight plan?" I asked. She shrugged, called the captain in the cockpit over the cabin phone, and then—to my surprise—handed me the receiver.

I repeated my flight path query to the captain. After beginning to describe the route to me, he then realized why I'd asked and interrupted himself. "Oh don't worry, everything's fine," he said, the onboard phone crackling, "I heard they signed a peace agreement." Not so, I told him. We wouldn't be on this flight if that were true, and his aircraft would likely be sold out as it was on most days. "Oh... Ok, I see," he said, with some pause, and then hung up.

As we began our descent into Juba, I thought of the corkscrew landings pilots often make in hostile zones. I also noticed our lone fellow passenger peering out the window anxiously. Fortunately, no rebels mistook us for enemy aircraft.

I did, however, notice something unusual during our final approach. The normally teeming neighborhoods below were empty. There was not a soul on the streets, no movement at all amid the hundreds of homes dotting rows of streets below. It was *totally* empty.

We touched down and Ambassador Susan Page greeted us on the tarmac, surrounded by her security detail. We climbed into embassy SUVs and sped directly to the presidential residence.

Special Envoy Booth pressed Salva to get a handle on the violence before it tore his country to shreds. Announce readiness to negotiate a ceasefire, go on television to calm rising ethnic tensions, and release the eleven high-profile politicians he had jailed, Booth urged him. The longer you wait, he told the president, the more civilians will die "in a senseless conflict they want no part of."

"You are putting me under duress," Salva responded. "It is like when someone is tortured for information. You wouldn't want that done to you." Booth rebutted that he, and President Obama, wanted only to prevent an all-out civil war. To do that, South Sudan's leader needed to act.

We also used the meeting to question whether the hardliners surrounding Salva were giving him good advice, though this last message was difficult to convey. The hardliners in question had invited themselves to the meeting and occupied the black leather couch next to Salva. They intervened on occasion, stiffening the president's posture. They also made known their resentment of our unwillingness to accept the coup plot story they'd helped to fabricate. After an extended and sometimes contentious exchange, the president agreed to consider our entreaties. "I am ready to work with you," he said. But he quickly pivoted to spew contempt for Riek. The prophet of doom, he argued, was in no position to negotiate a ceasefire. "He cannot control the Nuer forces now fighting across the country."

After reiterating our messages to other influential government officials, we flew back out—this time to Nairobi to consult with Kenyan leaders. While transiting Jomo Kenyatta International Airport in Nairobi, Booth received a call from Secretary John Kerry. "Go back," the secretary told him. Kerry had just stepped out of another emergency meeting in Washington, where senior officials were debating our latest assessment from Juba as well as new intelligence reporting. With each passing hour, the severity of recent events was becoming clearer, as was the growing specter of full-scale war. Kerry would call Salva again in the coming hours, but in the meantime we were to return to Juba as soon as possible to keep the pressure on.

Booth and I would return to the United States nine weeks later.

Shortly after we'd left Juba, the government closed the airport to commercial flights. The State Department contracted a small twin-prop eight-seater to fly us back in. Over the next week, we met Salva three more times, each meeting buttressed by calls from Secretary Kerry. We pressed for a ceasefire, peace talks, and assurance that increasingly desperate civilians could get access to emergency humanitarian aid. Salva complained of our regularly coming to "torture" him, "morning, noon, and night... and then in telephone calls." He recounted one contentious call, when Kerry had wrapped up the conversation with a farewell wish that Salva could get some sleep despite the awful situation. But a frustrated and testy Salva interrupted him. "I will not sleep well," the president barked, "I know you will call to fight me again in the morning!"

In addition to warning that the U.S. and others would consider sanctions against Salva, Riek, and anyone directing the violence, we relayed Washington's message that the United States was re-assessing its relationship with South Sudan. Booth told Salva and his advisers that President Obama would not continue working with a government that was waging a senseless war against its own people, and we signaled our intent to draw down the embassy to a minimum presence. It was a security precaution first and foremost, but in political terms, it would also be a visible vote of no confidence from Juba's oldest friend. Salva's government was desperate to demonstrate its legitimacy, and Washington's diplomatic posture would inevitably influence decisions in other foreign capitals and at the UN Security Council.

The gravity of the situation demanded stern messages, but we also believed that President Salva—insecure, under threat, and always looking for refuge—might respond to offers of support and reassurance. And so we also expressed our readiness to help the embattled leader forge a peaceful solution. We spent hours brainstorming ways out of the crisis. "If you are able to exercise leadership, rise above the fray, and halt the violence, you will have Washington's firm support, and that of the region," Booth told him, over and over and over. Riek would have no grounds to continue. But the prevaricating president was in over his head, and he would not—or could not—grab the lifeline that friendly nations were together trying to throw him.

Salva repeated that he was "ready" for a ceasefire and open to talks "in principle," but he was short on action. Sometimes he was deliberately slow-playing, seeking to put down the rebellion in the one way he knew how. But the president also understood that things had gotten out of control, and part of him wanted nothing more than to rewind the mess he'd created and try this all over again a different way. His legacy as a unifier, as the leader who carried South Sudan across the historic threshold to independence, was quickly evaporating. But our repeated appeals to this legacy, to his Christian values, and to his paternal sense of responsibility—all of which he cared about—fell flat. He was stuck, suddenly under immense pressure from all sides, and seemed incapable of leading his government out of the war in which it now found itself.

In this decisive moment, Salva's vacillation proved devastating, as the stronger men around him appealed to his worst instincts. As the government came under ever more pressure, and as its *coup d'état* allegations were almost universally dismissed, its leader and cabinet of hardliners turned inward. Those men around Salva with the most to lose would hang on tighter and tighter as the situation deteriorated, their siege mentality and paranoia infecting the impressionable president.

In another difficult phone call days later, Secretary Kerry hounded Salva to release the eleven political detainees and finalize a ceasefire—acts which could prevent further deterioration. If he failed to show some leadership now, the secretary argued, "it's going to be very difficult for people but to conclude that you've made a choice… the wrong choice." Salva interrupted and snapped back, "No. It's a decision you have already taken; *you* have chosen to support the military coup!"

In a speech to parliament days later, the president called for restraint and dialogue while expressing sadness at the "despicable atrocities" committed. But then he switched direction, blaming the "power thirsty" coup plotters for destroying the country. Just as he did during our private meetings, the president seemed genuinely wounded by the challenge mounted against him by his own SPLM colleagues. But he appeared to have made a leap from recognizing their political challenge to fearing an attempt to overthrow him by military force—a leap for which his government offered no hard evidence.

Salva changed tack yet again in the ensuing days, this time delivering conciliatory remarks in a Christmas Day sermon at St. Theresa's Catholic Church. "Anyone that is going out to kill people, or to loot… in the name of supporting me, [know] that you are destroying me," he told the congregation and those watching on television. He called for healing, unity, and a return to order. But meanwhile the military campaigns continued. Tens of thousands of frightened civilians spent their Christmas holiday hiding in UN camps or in the bush.

The schizophrenic incoherence of Salva's government was painful to watch, and only further exposed the bankruptcy of the narrative they were peddling. It was like watching a tug-of-war, Salva pulled between good angels and bad ones. Switching tactics and mixing messages, he again appeared to be influenced by whoever was drafting his speeches, and whoever was last in his ear. And the bad angels were winning. The government continued its military offensives, refused to release the eleven political detainees, and refused to talk peace.

Resentment swelled inside the president's camp, and it was re-directed at anyone—home or abroad—who questioned the government's narrative, its authority, or its heavy-handed solutions. Anyone not with them must be against them, they surmised, and they played defense by going on offense. And so the international community that had helped deliver Juba its freedom was now also the object of mistrust and suspicion. UN chief Hilde Johnson, U.S. Ambassador Page, and other prominent figures had their cell phones, movements, and meetings monitored. The UN peacekeeping mission itself was deemed a hostile entity; government hardliners organized anti-UN demonstrations, advanced baseless claims that UN officials were aiding Riek's opposition forces, and tried to force their way into UN refuge camps they alleged were doubling as rebel safe havens.

The West was aiming "to take over their newly sovereign country," Salva's bad angels claimed, while privately telling him that the all-powerful Americans wanted him out. At the end of one of our meetings with the president, Interior Minister Aleu Aleu, a Bahr al Ghazal Dinka and leading warmonger, chimed in with a comment that characterized the hardliners' view not only of the Americans, but of anyone giving Salva alternative advice. "You know, Booth is a Nuer name," he said, its provocative suggestion not lost on anyone present.

The reality, however, was that the U.S., the region, and other partners were putting equal pressure on Riek Machar. Secretary Kerry and White House officials had all the while been fighting a similar telephone battle with Riek, who was directing anti-government forces from deep in the bush. He, too, was told that he would be held accountable for the awful retributions Nuer soldiers were carrying out against Dinka civilians. He, too, was told that he had no choice but to sit down and talk. But a consistently combative Riek interrupted at every turn, complaining of government offensives and Salva's butchery.

Riek was gambling. The veteran rebel wanted to sustain military pressure on the government while demanding preconditions for negotiations, each time frustrating the army of international diplomats dialing his satellite telephones. "The guy was over-playing his hand," one foreign diplomat huffed, recalling the unflinching belligerence that was grating on those calling to broker peace. "He damn near pushed the international community into the government's corner," recalled another. In fact, on a few occasions Riek very nearly invited frustrated neighboring countries to mount a military campaign against him.

Riek's principal demand was the release of the eleven detainees—a pre-condition for his participation in peace talks. He needed help. No matter how tactical their alliance, he knew these allies from the December 6 press conference at SPLM House—Pagan, Deng, and the others—could help him counter Salva at the negotiating table.

We first visited the eleven high-profile detainees on December 23 after Salva succumbed to Secretary Kerry's relentless appeals. The group was sequestered in a government house inside a walled compound in central Juba. Normally a suit-and-tie crowd, they were scruffy, clad in dirty t-shirts, track pants, and sandals. But they were generally well cared for, if exceedingly bored. While they had smuggled in the occasional cell phone through a sympathetic guard, they otherwise lacked contact with anyone outside. They sat on plastic chairs under a towering shade tree, passing the hours speculating about developments outside.

As we approached the compound, it was impossible to ignore the incredible amount of firepower guarding the perimeter, a nod to the influence of the men inside and the concern they registered in Salva's inner circle. As our white SUVs entered the gates, the men rose from their chairs anxiously, unaware of the identity of their visitors. When car doors opened and they spotted familiar faces, their shoulders relaxed and they breathed sighs of relief. They knew well that a visit from foreigners—the Americans no less—was as good a warranty as any against their being assassinated.

The detainees' historical animosity toward Riek was as strong as any in the SPLM, but they had forged a marriage of convenience with him in challenging the president and his newly implanted advisors. Those of Salva worried that, if released, these men could tip the scales against the government.

The detained were almost all former ranking SPLA commanders who later assumed cabinet posts, state governorships, or leading party positions. They were educated, cosmopolitan, and well-connected in foreign capitals. Many of them had been close to Garang and were ranking central committee members. A few had strong state power bases; others were revered military officers who still commanded broad loyalty among the army ranks. Some were fabulously wealthy, having cashed in on their positions of influence. If released, they would surely join the voices of dissent. Worse yet, the president's men worried they might join the fight, engineering more defections and turning the tide on the battlefield. Of greatest concern was presidential aspirant Pagan Amum, whose visceral contempt for them was no secret. We visited the group several times, hoping to facilitate their release, but also hoping they might be able to bridge the growing chasm between two polarized ethnic camps.

"You too bear responsibility for the crisis," we told them pointedly. The reality was that their hands were not clean. No, they had not taken up arms, nor attempted a coup. And they had been treated unfairly during Salva's authoritarian campaign over the last six months. But the origins of the crisis required a wider lens. These were among the most influential figures in the new nation; they were at the center of the party's power struggle, and they knew the threat it posed to stability. One could argue—and we did on several visits—that this bunch shared as much responsibility for the country's unraveling as Salva, Riek, or anyone else.

Conscious of weak institutions, poverty, a militarized population, and a delicate social balance, these and other SPLM leaders had a responsibility to the citizens of South Sudan. Instead, the party elite had together gotten high on power, disregarded the values of their cause, and lost touch with the people they claimed to represent. Their shared responsibility for the crisis had begun not during the tumult of 2013, but in 2005 when the SPLM assumed control of the new Southern government. Eventually, detained former minister John Luk admitted in front of the group, "shame on us; shame on us for failing to learn the lessons of those African liberation movements that have gone before us."

The focus on the eleven was a double-edged sword, and I worried about how much attention it had sucked up in the first weeks of the crisis. If anything happened to these high-profile figures, the crisis—which was not yet a civil war—could intensify. But the perception that the eleven, many with lasting ties to Washington, were inherently a U.S. priority served in the minds of the president and those around him to fuel paranoia. "Because they are so dear to you," an exasperated Salva had told Kerry, "you can take them with you."

After sustained pressure from Southern Sudanese, other Africans, the Europeans, and us, Salva entertained the notion of their release. But he wanted to neutralize or retain leverage over them somehow, and his adviser, Telar Deng, cooked up various schemes to this end. The lengths Salva and Riek went to in order to control these detainees indicated their degree of concern, and the precariousness of the battle for South Sudan.

We continued shuttling between Juba and regional capitals, working with influential leaders to force Salva and Riek to the negotiating table. Neither side wanted to give an inch, nor were they interested in talking—they wanted to have it out on the battlefield. The first two weeks of the crisis had seen one massacre after another; thousands were already dead, and many had lost friends or a family member. Emotions ran hot.

On December 27, the presidents of East Africa convened for an emergency summit. Recalling the "hope for freedom, justice, and prosperity" expressed by the South Sudanese people on their joyous independence day, the leaders decried the "bankrupt and opportunistic ideology" of ethnic sectarianism, and demanded the fighting stop—and ceasefire talks begin—within 96 hours.

As the deadline approached, diplomats from Ethiopia, Kenya, Uganda, Europe, the United States, the African Union, and the UN together pressed Salva and Riek. And on December 31, the two men capitulated. They agreed to send teams to peace talks in neighboring Addis Ababa. The conflict in South Sudan was by no means ripe for a negotiated settlement, as the conflict was fast and fluid, each side intent on crushing the other. But the human costs of the conflict demanded a response. An immediate end to hostilities was the only way to spare the millions of civilians now in grave danger.

On New Year's Eve 2013, the very day Salva and Riek had reluctantly consented to peace talks, the battle for the ultimate prize—Juba—intensified. These men had decades of experience fighting and negotiating, and they knew enough to try to maximize their control of territory before sitting down to talk. Better yet, Riek hoped, he would simply capture Juba and topple Salva's government.

Ker moved south of Bor to participate in the most pivotal battle of the war, and he was not alone. General Peter Gadet's 8th division forces would lead the assault, now flanked by thousands of White Army fighters. Reports indicated that as many as 25,000 Nuer men had amassed at Riek's de facto headquarters in Gadiang in recent days. They had been organized by Nuer commanders, community leaders and, most notably, the Nuer prophet. His blessings were a divine sanction believed to protect them from harm. "Waat, Yuai, Piri, Lankien, Akobo," Ker rattles off the hubs of the Nuer nation, "We came. We are one."

Tall and lanky, the White Army volunteers were similar in stature but otherwise a rag-tag bunch. They wore shorts, t-shirts, a mish-mash of camouflage fatigues, basketball jerseys, bandanas, flip-flop sandals, and red headbands. Despite resembling nothing like an "army," and lacking supplies as basic as water, they were often very well armed. Marching alongside the defected army divisions now fighting for Riek, the hybrid force's southward push would come within 35 miles of the capital city.

Rumbling north out of Juba, meanwhile, a column of army tanks, camouflage pickup trucks, artillery units, and other heavy weapons had been dispatched to intercept the advancing rebels. Two more infantry battalions headed north by boat, reinforced by young Dinka recruits from Bahr al Ghazal who were mobilized and given uniforms, but in reality were no more skilled or disciplined than those coming south to meet them.

Though the war was metastasizing across the country, for ten days all eyes fixed on this single stretch of rust-colored road north of the capital city. This was no street fight, no tactical advance on a rural zone of influence. The heavyweight battle for South Sudan was on, and it would be won or lost on this axis.

Back and forth the warring factions pushed, attack and counter, as each side sustained heavy casualties. Just as the rebels dreamed of capturing Juba, they were met with some unusually formidable resistance. Overhead, Ker and his cohort saw giant camouflage-painted machines bearing down on them. They looked like hornets, he thought, and the sound was deafening. "*Gunship*? Never in my life had I seen a helicopter gunship," Ker recalls with eyes widened. As weaponized Ugandan attack helicopters whooshed overhead and bombs fell from the sky, the impromptu rebellion soon realized it was fighting more than Salva's government forces.

Across the border in neighboring Uganda, President Yoweri Museveni had been watching the situation with interest and concern. Ten days earlier, on December 20, Salva had invited Museveni's army—the Ugandan Peoples' Defense Forces (UPDF)—into South Sudan to save his government. Unconfirmed reports later indicated that Ugandan troops had in fact been inside the country several days *before* the crisis, on account of Salva's concerns about rising tension.

Whatever the case, it wouldn't have taken much to enlist the regional strongman. Having sent his forces into wars in Sudan, Rwanda and the Democratic Republic of Congo during the 1990s, Museveni was no stranger to foreign interventions. The self-styled "Bismarck of Africa" made no bones about dictating outcomes in neighboring countries. And what's more, he despised Riek Machar. Upon Salva's invitation, Ugandan fighter jets had entered South Sudanese air space and were seen screaming north to bomb rebel positions around Bor, as well as the huge columns of White Army reinforcements. Ugandan Mi-24 helicopter gunships followed, and were soon leading the SPLA's northward push to recapture territory.

On December 30, Museveni paid a visit to Juba, an appearance that would inflame anti-government sentiment and ultimately mobilize more Nuer youth fighters. Shaking hands with Salva, Museveni announced that if Riek did not agree to an immediate ceasefire, "we shall have to go for him, all of us... defeat him." Regional leaders understood that Riek's rebels had legitimate reason to be outraged. But they had also made clear to Riek that they were not going to stand by and watch him topple the capital. Museveni had gone one further, and the optics of his visit erased any doubts about his country's neutrality. Uganda had chosen sides in South Sudan.

Rebel forces would be stopped short of the capital. But beyond defending Juba, other governments in the region chafed at Museveni's aggressive intervention. They shared our concern that his pledge to defend Juba would embolden Salva's government, inflate its confidence in a military solution, and deter it from negotiating an end to the conflict.

Ker, like most every Nuer fighter, believes their forces would have captured Juba if not for Uganda's intervention. But they also wondered whether the ethnic targeting in Juba had in fact been part of a broader campaign of extermination now spreading to the Nuer heartland. And Uganda's lighting-fast intervention on behalf of the government was under-writing those fears. "It happened so fast," one Nuer fighter reported, "Ugandan airplanes and bombs... it seemed to us that this had been a coordinated attack on the Nuer, something planned in advance." Uganda's entry was not part of a deliberate or pre-meditated campaign of ethnic cleansing. But in war, perceptions are paramount, and the damage was done.

The first two weeks of the conflict were fluid, chaotic, and the prospect of an expanding regional war was becoming ever more real. But beyond the immediate impacts of violence, and beyond the focus on its most decisive battle, the war was inducing a deeper regression to regional and local identity, and not only among the army rank-and-file. One Southern Sudanese intellectual later offered testimony that helped to understand the slide to wider war:

> While the conflict that has engulfed the country today is essentially a struggle for power between the politico-military elites at the center, these leaders are only able to draw everyone into their senseless war because the country's citizens have long been so deprived of basic necessities and so pitted against one another along ethnic lines that so many ordinary people came to think that their survival rests with giving support, military and otherwise, to their ethnic leaders.

The shared experience of independence had been a formative first step in the long-term development of a national consciousness. But in the space of just two weeks in December 2013, the euphoria of those first national memories was all but erased.

PART III

PICKING UP
THE PIECES

18

TIPPING POINT

"The great question which, in all ages, has disturbed mankind, and brought on them the greatest part of their mischiefs . . . has been, not whether be power in the world, nor whence it came, but who should have it."
—John Locke, *The First Treatise of Government,* 1689

ADDIS ABABA, ETHIOPIA, JANUARY 2014

On January 2, 2014, two delegations representing the warring factions arrived at the Sheraton Hotel in Addis Ababa, under pressure to negotiate a ceasefire. Few could have foreseen that this would be the first of many days, then weeks, then months at the capital city's premier address. The Sheraton is the most luxurious edifice in the capital—maybe in all of Ethiopia. Its gleaming balconies, magisterial flags, lush gardens, and symphony-synchronized fountains stand in stark contrast to the poverty just beyond its walls, where the dirty browns and grays of slum dwellings blur into the muddy soil they rest on.

Prominent hotels have been a unique part of post-colonial history across much of Africa; as author Michela Wrong wrote, they are often "microcosms of their countries' tumultuous histories." Built in the late 1960s and early 1970s, they are stage sets for real-life dramas about politics, revolution, money, violence, and power. They represent continuity through volatile periods of change, and have developed familiar personalities. Repositories of legends and myths, they infuse new dramas with palpable reminders of the past.

Most countries in the region have one—the Panafric in Nairobi, the Mille Collines in Kigali, the Hilton Addis Ababa. At the old Apollo in Kampala, the ghost of Idi Amin, flanked by female companions, still strides confidently around the azure-hued oval pool. The hotels are dated by their furniture and décor and waft with signature scents—the odors and aromas that have saturated over time and can't be bleached away. Full-service accommodations evoke a bygone era, while the more ambitious excesses—fountains, music venues, mini-golf courses—today stand weathered and unused. Lobbies teem with government ministers, journalists, intelligence operatives, and naive tourists. Stirring drinks and eyeing one another across low-lot lounges are shady businessmen, retired army generals, and scantily clad hookers.

To begin talks, Special Envoy Booth and I also put up at the Sheraton, which recently supplanted the Hilton (dedicated in 1969 by Emperor Haile Selassie) as Ethiopia's go-to political theater. It was among the first in a new generation of premier hotels, and had already staged a number of dramas, including South Sudan's most formative productions. Addis's premier classes enjoyed international cuisine, cocktails, and live music there, its choice restaurants and bars charging triple that of most establishments in town. The hotel's opulent and sterile interior stood in even greater contrast to the scorched earth and smoking villages back in South Sudan. Its macchiatos and cream puff pastries were not on offer at the overcrowded protection camps in Bentiu, Bor, and Malakal.

Peace talks would later re-locate to the Radisson Blu, another upscale venue that competes for business among African dignitaries, foreign diplomats, and continent-hopping entrepreneurs. (Not surprisingly, it is widely assumed that Ethiopian intelligence services have thoroughly bugged both properties.)

The Sheraton and the Radisson Blu each played host to North-South talks over Sudan's separation in 2011, and both are frequented by South Sudan's traveling elite. And so the newly arrived delegates were already familiar with the hotels, their staffs, even their restaurant menus—a strange reminder of just how much of the country's short history had been defined not by governing, but by conflict and negotiation. What was troubling was not the hotels themselves or the fact that talks were held there, as politics is an elite business everywhere. It was instead the ease with which many of the country's warring elite settled into a comfortable routine, collected per diem allowances, and waxed adversarial, while their country burned.

The peace process which began that January would last more than two years. Though the Sheraton and the Radisson were primary locales, eleven rounds of talks took place at five venues in three Ethiopian cities. Regional countries would run the peace process, supported by a phalanx of diplomats from Africa and the West. Special Envoy Booth and I would spend weeks in Ethiopia supporting the talks, then shuttle back and forth to Juba, other regional capitals, and Washington between rounds of negotiations. The leading regional organization convened seven head-of-state summits, and the United States hosted two more. The African Union and the UN Security Council committed resources and political capital, while the U.S. and other international donors poured billions into emergency humanitarian relief.

The stakes were high. The process offered an opportunity to correct course, a path to salvage South Sudan's promise and avoid the new country's disintegration. It was an emotional rollercoaster; spectacular highs and spirit-puncturing lows, intense days and dynamic progress followed by months of mundane technicality and delay. Bold actions breathed life into the talks, only for the oxygen to be sucked out by antagonism and obfuscation. A divided region, a weak mediation, and tricky dynamics between Africa and the West would complicate a deck already stacked against success.

But the story of the peace process would ultimately belong to the South Sudanese themselves, and to the contrast between its voices and its voiceless. It was mostly a story about power. Big men and big egos meeting in conference rooms and hotel lobbies deciding not only who had power and how it should be wielded, but how long the suffering would continue. Despite sustained efforts to include more seats at the table—for elders, women, opposition parties, youth representatives, and faith leaders—the two warring parties would dominate the talks throughout. And too often, the story would be characterized by these leaders' seeming indifference to the plight of the people they claimed to represent.

—

Given the ramifications of a new war on their border, South Sudan's immediate neighbors wanted to be directly involved in the mediation effort. After all, each had been intimately involved in Sudan's civil war, the peace talks that ended it in 2005, and in supporting the South's realization of independence. Now, they would be most vulnerable to potential spillover from the war.

In the closing days of 2013, diplomats had moved swiftly to put the Intergovernmental Authority on Development, or IGAD, in charge of peace talks, as it was critical that the international community rallied around a single mediation effort. IGAD is a regional organization whose member-states—which include Ethiopia, Uganda, Kenya, and Sudan—cooperate on a range of shared interests, including matters of peace and security.

Ethiopia, as chair of IGAD, tapped Seyoum Mesfin, a legendary Ethiopian politician and diplomat, to be chief mediator. Deeply acquainted with regional politics, Seyoum had served as his country's foreign minister for 20 years. He was not only a member of the ruling party's central committee, but a founding member of its Tigrayan core—the minority northern constituency which has dominated Ethiopia's government since their coalition of rebel forces toppled the Cold War-era military junta.

Seyoum was then serving as Ethiopia's ambassador to China. The Beijing post was one of his government's most important, given shared notions of "revolutionary democracy" and an expanding economic partnership. Among Seyoum's principal tasks was securing billion-dollar "mega infrastructure" projects to continue driving his country's modernization—the signs of which were already evident in the rapidly transforming capital.

But Seyoum was also eager to come home. He wanted to re-engage in the regional politics he found so important, and also to be closer to the action as Ethiopian national elections approached, his own political ambitions not yet quenched. But politics in East Africa were not what they used to be, and in time the peace process and regional divisions would drive Seyoum to his wits' end.

Seyoum had been foreign minister during Sudan's civil war and throughout the CPA process, and was deeply acquainted with the pivotal role the United States had played, particularly in its latter stages. With this in mind, Seyoum met with Special Envoy Booth and me before the peace talks began. In a quiet fourth-floor lounge at the Sheraton, he made clear that his accepting the role of IGAD mediator would be contingent upon "a strong partnership with, and backing from, Washington." We agreed to help in any way we could.

Seyoum is bald on top, and the short hair remaining on the sides of his head is graying, as is his mustache. His resting face can be intense, but it belies the beaming smile underneath. He is a likable elder, quick to joke and quicker to laugh. Seyoum is old school, raised in the disciplined ranks of a Marxist-Leninist rebellion and the highly centralized ruling party he and his comrades fashioned upon seizing power. He expected loyalty, and had a reputation for professionalism. He was skilled in the diplomatic art of flattery, and espoused an ego-free readiness to adopt good ideas from trusted advisers. The veteran diplomat would commit himself to the thankless process admirably. But critically, despite his credentials at home and abroad, it was soon apparent that Seyoum also had less mediation expertise than many had assumed.

Given its historical role as host to the process that yielded Sudan's 2005 CPA, Kenya's government had likewise hoped to host the new peace talks. When they materialized instead in Ethiopia, Nairobi chafed. The relationship between these two "frenemy" neighbors—sometimes cooperative, sometimes not—was defined by latent tension. Their competition and thinly veiled antagonism, together with regional power dynamics, would later paralyze the mediation and nearly undermine the peace process.

Not wanting to be left out, the Kenyans ensured Lazarus Sumbeiywo (*Soom-BAY-woh*) would also be part of the IGAD negotiating team. An ex-army general with close ties to former Kenyan President Daniel Arap Moi, Sumbeiywo had been the lead mediator during Sudan's CPA talks. More than a decade later, the general still traded on this most significant career role, and on a self-styled "no nonsense, I'm not a diplomat" persona. Because of the support Washington had provided behind the scenes during the CPA mediation, Sumbeiywo was also a familiar and welcome face for Africa veterans now directing policy in the Obama administration.

In early December, before the conflict erupted, I had stopped in Nairobi to pay a visit to Sumbeiywo. Taking tea on a sunny afternoon at one of Nairobi's ubiquitous Java House coffee-chain spots, I asked if he would consider informally mediating between SPLM factions if internal divisions were not soon resolved on their own. Sumbeiywo was not abreast of the day-to-day situation, and so asked for my analysis; we discussed the rot within the party, its lack of a program, and the specifics of the power struggle that was filling the void. In principle, he said, he was open to mediating and we agreed to stay in touch in the coming weeks. But the awful events that would shake Juba shortly thereafter would demand far more than a quiet intervention by a familiar face.

Sumbeiywo would have his chance to contribute, appointed as deputy to Seyoum. What was not clear then, and would later surprise and dismay seasoned observers, was just how much the man had changed in the intervening decade.

⚬⚬⚬

"If you can't get a handle on it in the first two weeks," opined one seasoned African diplomat on the urgency of talks in any new conflict, "it will last for months or years... there is usually no middle ground." With this tipping point in mind, the first order of business was an immediate ceasefire. As delegations were called for initial consultations in a first-floor Sheraton conference room, fighting continued in Bentiu, Malakal, and Bor, as did the highly concentrated battle on the Juba-Bor axis, each side probing the other's defenses.

If the advancing Nuer militias broke through, a gruesome battle for the city would surely follow, possibly with more devastating civilian costs than any to date. Riek privately made assurances that he had no intention of going all the way to Juba, but few believed he would pull back the reins if the opportunity presented itself. Foreign governments watched closely, inundating the two sides with high-level calls and pressure while preparing to evacuate their diplomats should the fight draw too close for comfort. A ceasefire was a matter of urgency, but would not likely be agreed to or sustained without the release of the political detainees and some kind of political settlement. Even then, one wondered whether the spreading violence could be contained by those now sitting in Addis, or whether it had taken on a life of its own.

The government's delegation arrived in Addis Ababa peddling its narrative of events, even circulating glossy red pamphlets entitled, *"The Truth about the Aborted Coup."* But no one was buying. This collective rebuttal was essential, as a peace process skewed in the government's favor would neither win sufficient trust nor produce lasting solutions.

The first days were intensive. Mediators consulted each delegation privately, then convened the parties together, then broke and repeated the cycle. During these breaks, U.S., UN, and European diplomats would sit with each side in hotel corridors and anterooms, applying pressure and trying to narrow the gaps. The cycle would continue into the early hours of the morning, usually ending with a debrief between the mediators and diplomatic partners in Special Envoy Booth's cramped hotel suite. We would then begin telephone and video conferences with Washington and our embassy in Juba, which were monitoring the situation around the clock, completing evacuations, assessing options, and updating President Obama.

The sense of urgency was palpable as the fate of South Sudan's capital city hung in the balance.

—⁂—

Nhial Deng headed the government's delegation to the peace talks. He was a first-tier SPLM figure and the most experienced negotiator available, a fact of which his close-cropped gray hair reminded younger opponents. Aloof, elitist, and erudite, the always well-tailored senior minister struck some as more British aristocrat than Bahr al Ghazal Dinka. One could imagine him—fast talking, legalistic, eager to deconstruct a foe's argument—comfortable at any negotiating table.

Because Nhial's historical loyalties and sensibilities aligned more closely with those of the eleven SPLM detainees, his decision to stick with the government—let alone become its public face—came as a surprise. One confidant told me Nhial had privately confided his divided sympathies: "disappointed" in Salva but also angry with the SPLM challengers for taking their complaints public instead of "keeping matters inside the party, where they belonged."

It was a plausible peek inside Nhial's brain, though I never saw him betray even a whiff of uncertainty in public. Once a presidential prospect and possessing ideal regional and familial pedigrees for the job, I wondered whether he sought to revive his princely standing and await a succession nod. In any case, Nhial's mixed feelings were surely softened by his $2,000 daily stipend, a government payout that outraged citizens and would ultimately net him hundreds of thousands of dollars on top of his government salary.

Nhial was flanked by a dozen ministers and senior officials, many of whom had been promoted or assumed new authority following Salva's 2013 purge of top-tier SPLM opponents. The information minister and world-class belligerent Michael Makwei acted as deputy. The bespectacled Bor Dinka was among a handful of legally trained party intellectuals, and his fierce loyalty to the president in recent months meant his stock too had risen. Argumentative, manipulative, and able, the finger-wagging Makwei seemed to value above all the sound of his own belittling commentary. He relished his elevated importance, and wasn't about to give it up—often making up government policy as he went along, even when it contradicted the views of his president.

Riek's rebel delegation was a junior varsity squad by comparison. Its only first-tier SPLM figure was lead negotiator Taban Deng. Experience and talent dropped off precipitously from there, as the opposition's established political types were fewer, and some of them remained directing troops in the bush. After being retrieved from the battleground by an Ethiopian army helicopter and delivered to Addis, Taban went straight to a local market to upgrade his muddy military fatigues for a suit and dress shoes. As much as any guerrilla-cum-government official, Taban was a singular embodiment of all South Sudan's contradictions: its hopes and its cynicism, its overlapping ethnic and regional identities, its economic asymmetries, its short and long memory, its rebellions, reunions, and hatchets buried.

Taban was born in Unity state to a Nuer mother and a father from an Arab tribe in Northern Sudan. He was raised by the family of his cousin, Angelina, who just so happened to be the first wife of Riek Machar. What unfolded thereafter was pure soap opera.

Before independence, Salva installed Taban as governor of Unity State, in part to constrain Riek Machar's influence in his home state. But seen as an SPLM elitist and a stooge of a Dinka-dominated government, Taban was despised by the state's electorate. Seeking to capitalize on his unpopularity, Angelina challenged her cousin, Taban, in a heated and deeply divisive race for the governor's seat in 2010. The election was flawed, but when Angelina cried foul, her allegations of fraud were dismissed and the SPLM brass declared Taban the winner.

Salva and Taban were always unlikely bedfellows, though, and it was only a matter of time before their alliance would collapse. The president removed Taban from his gubernatorial post in 2013 as the SPLM began to fray. Throwing his lot in with Riek, Taban the opportunist would ultimately complete his 180-degree about-face by linking up with Riek's rebellion in its very first days. Despite the animus among them, Riek, Angelina, and Taban would set aside their disputes and sit together in Addis Ababa as a powerful triumvirate atop the mostly-Nuer rebellion. "Only in Sudan," seasoned observers would say.

Taban would become both a pivotal and divisive figure throughout the war. One of the rebellion's principal architects, financiers, and operational commanders, he was also reviled by many of its rank-and-file members. But he had thick skin, was pragmatic, and always kept his eyes on the political horizon. He seemed most interested in securing access to levers of power in Juba. Howsoever and with whomever he might do that seemed a secondary concern.

Taban was flexible, had relationships with brokers in all camps, and proved to be a moderating force on Riek. He established a constructive working partnership with Nhial, his government counterpart, while fortifying ties with old enemies in Khartoum. But this jack-of-all-trades didn't stop there, and I wondered why Taban occasionally ducked out of negotiating sessions, retreated out of earshot to take phone calls, or sometimes disappeared altogether for days. Taban, we learned, was also the rebels' principal broker for surreptitious arms and ammunition procurement, and allegedly arranged financial and materiel support for the rebels from allies in the Gulf and further afield. These relationships, the story went, had been cultivated during his time as governor of oil-rich Unity State, where it was widely believed he had lined his own pockets as thoroughly as anyone in the country.

I had spent considerable time in Unity in 2011 writing a report on the instability that made Taban's state a dangerous tinderbox. Taban was not only a perceived sell-out, but a ruthless autocrat, and his draconian rule featured prominently in my publication. After a copy landed on Taban's desk, I was persona non grata in Unity, and later learned that Taban had appealed to the presidency to have me thrown out of the country. Two years later, as the peace talks commenced, I was apprehensive about our first meeting with him, in my new capacity as a U.S. diplomat. But to my surprise, Taban bounded through the door and greeted me warmly, offering familiar greetings in his native Nuer language and a firm embrace. Only in Sudan.

During nineteen days of non-stop negotiations, fighting continued to spread, as key towns were captured and re-captured, and more and more South Sudanese were drawn into the fight. Ayen was pinned down in her neighborhood in Juba, Nyakueth in the makeshift UN camp. Each worried most about feeding her family. Nyakueth's husband, meanwhile, had joined those of Ker, the White Army fighter who'd exacted revenge in Bor. And those of Ker had joined with young men from Simon's village. Tens of thousands waging a war of retaliation in towns and villages where families just like their own struggled to survive.

Between seemingly endless days of negotiations at the Sheraton, mediators and Western diplomats shuttled to regional capitals, as well as to Salva's house in Juba and Riek's base deep in rebel-held territory. Stop the bleeding, they told the parties, and rein in the ethnic propaganda before it was too late.

On the evening of January 23, Seyoum invited a gaggle of journalists, exhausted diplomats, and negotiators into a Sheraton conference room. Nhial and Taban took their seats at a head table between the mediators. The old comrades-turned-rivals each put on reading glasses, picked up a pen, and flipped to their respective signature pages. Cameras flashed as they signed their names to a ceasefire agreement and an accompanying pact releasing the eleven detainees.

"Excellencies, Ladies and Gentlemen," Seyoum began, reading in a hoarse voice from prepared remarks. "The signing of the agreements mark an important milestone." But he asked all to be mindful of the work ahead to achieve a lasting peace. "We have only achieved a successful beginning toward that end. But the Chinese say the journey of a thousand miles begins with one step."

Seyoum was visibly fatigued but buoyed by the breakthrough. "We recognize that South Sudan is still a young and nascent state," he continued, "still in the process of state-building, which cannot be achieved overnight." But the hard-won ceasefire, he argued, was a turning point, one that could preserve their sacred project. It was a moment of genuine jubilation, a high point for anyone involved in the combative talks and exhaustive shuttle diplomacy.

From the White House, President Obama welcomed the "critical first step toward building a lasting peace." Echoing our desire to move swiftly to the next agenda item, he urged the parties to immediately "start an inclusive political dialogue to resolve the underlying causes of the conflict."

The situation remained incredibly fluid; chaos and reactivity reigned, positions had not yet hardened, and I thought of the old African diplomat's remarks about curtailing a conflict before it reached a tipping point. The ceasefire was a first step, necessary but not sufficient. Many believed it might at least bring the boil down to a temperature where the Southern Sudanese could engage in constructive political talks.

We were wrong. While the ceasefire may have prevented wider conflagration, fighting quickly resumed. It seemed the proverbial tipping point had been passed.

19

BUSINESS AS USUAL

"For the fire consumes all but the arsonist."
—Wole Soyinka

ADDIS ABABA / JUBA / KAMPALA, JANUARY-APRIL 2014

Despite its limitations, the ceasefire signed on January 23 nominally provided a basis on which to begin talks on the underlying causes of the conflict, rather than just its immediate symptoms. The crisis had exposed a hard reality: South Sudan wasn't a failed state, it had failed before it had ever really become a state.

Many South Sudanese at home and abroad clamored for more than just a division of the cake between Salva and Riek. They wanted justice for what had been done. They wanted accountability, and better government. They wanted to sleep at night not fearing for their children or their homes or their cattle. They wanted schools and healthcare and a chance to put food on the table. They wanted to see their national revenue spent on a road to their village. They were tired of watching from the outside as a small group of self-entitled big men simply shared the spoils among themselves, dictated the direction of their country, and abused anyone who objected.

We shared their belief that "phase two" of the talks could be an entry point for more transformational changes, ideally through an *inclusive* political negotiation. In a memo to Seyoum and Sumbeiywo, I conveyed our sense of the way forward:

> The SPLM factions at the core of the conflict cannot simply return to the status quo of 14 December; a quick-fix elite accommodation will simply set the stage for a repeat of the country's recent unraveling. The next phase of negotiations must be structured so as to address immediate political and military concerns while investing a much broader swathe of South Sudanese in a process.

Unless the peace talks included more than the warring parties and their power-hungry leaders, its solutions would fail to win popular support or bring a lasting peace. But this would be no easy task. The memo proposed activities that Seyoum and Sumbeiywo could undertake inside South Sudan to foster broader participation.

A tour of the country, including town halls and roundtable consultations with communities, churches, and civic groups might invest people in the process and create more seats at the negotiating table. It would allow the mediators to demonstrate that this was not a foreign process but one by, and for, Southerners. Dedicated radio programming could provide regular updates from Addis Ababa, and networks could be established to funnel public opinion back to the negotiating table. Talking directly to ordinary Southerners might also give the mediators a justification to introduce the kind of reforms that their embattled government would otherwise resist.

We also offered to fund a technical secretariat to support the mediators. Seyoum could handpick advisers in process design, law, strategic communications, governance, security, and finance to help run the peace process and inform its solutions.

Special Envoy Booth and I developed a close working relationship with the mediation team in the early months; we provided ideas and support behind the scenes—usually in the late night hours in Seyoum's hotel suite—and the mediators used what they saw fit. We were conscious of offering such ideas, but never forcing them. Our shared interest in peace allowed for a natural "supporting cast" arrangement, and Seyoum's small and under-resourced team appreciated the division of labor.

While they drew on many of our inputs, Seyoum and Sumbeiywo chose not to go on a tour of Southern Sudanese communities, nor to staff up a secretariat with technical experts. They simply didn't think it was necessary. They were old school, born of different cultural and political experiences, and skeptical of ceding any control. Their own governments were powerful and highly centralized institutions, and they were used to dealing with the kind of political strongmen they saw when they looked in the mirror. But they were also operating on a very short leash, as the region's heads of state had given them limited space to operate. Seyoum also had to navigate difficult waters inside his own government, where powerful political and military officials took an interest in the peace talks, their outcome, and the implications for Ethiopia's standing in the region.

Their "no thank you" to these offers turned out to be the first in a series of poor decisions that would handicap the mediation and limit its chances to broker a lasting peace. There was no one way to run a peace process, but such decisions would come to reflect larger philosophical differences and ultimately a different idea of success.

"African states and the West share a common interest in ending conflicts," Booth later reflected in a speech, citing the kind of collaboration that had been instrumental in ending wars elsewhere on the continent. But, he explained, "balancing sometimes different approaches and different priorities presents constant challenges— which, if not carefully managed, can complicate peace processes or compromise outcomes."

Booth was alluding to the many such examples encountered during the process: should talks include many voices, or only the warring parties? Should the mediators propose reforms and suggest compromises, or simply facilitate a conversation? Should the talks be secretive or open to the Southern Sudanese public? And finally, what role should outsiders have in fashioning solutions or implementing them? The questions appeared to some as mundane matters of process, but in fact they concerned the very remaking of South Sudan—what exactly would be made of the world's newest and most troubled state, and who would do the re-making?

⸺⸺

"Now that's one promise broken, Mr. Minister," an unusually candid television news presenter said to the official spokesperson sitting opposite him. The government had pledged a peaceful South Sudan, the young journalist probed, so why were thousands now being forced to flee a new war? Michael Makwei, the government's leading spin doctor and its No. 2 negotiator, had been using the interview on state television to project a sense of normalcy. But now he was frowning. Before he could reply, the interviewer pushed further. "Be it you the government or the rebel group, are you not losing your credibility in the eyes of the people?"

Makwei breathed deep, gathering oxygen for one of his characteristically acerbic attacks. Launching in to a critique of Riek's attempt to overthrow a "government elected by the people," Makwei's voice gathered speed. The people "know very well that the problem is not with their government, but the problem is with these people who are power-hungry."

The government had begun to deliver on its promises, he had explained, "but before we could finalize anything, we were interrupted by this unfortunate situation." It was the kind of "business as usual" narrative Makwei and the government's salesmen promoted ad nauseam during the first months of 2014. The narrative went like this: Salva's government was stable, constitutionally legitimate, and in control; under its principled leadership, the work of providing for the people would continue, just as soon as this pesky and senseless rebellion was subdued. But it was a fiction. Tens of thousands of citizens had already fled their new country, the army had collapsed, major towns were ablaze, and nearly half the population believed their government was out to exterminate them.

Government ministers were dispatched on spin-junkets to world capitals and to UN embassies in New York, tasked to project legitimacy and the business as usual narrative, just as they were doing in Addis Ababa. They dismissed the underlying concerns of opponents and painted them simply as bloodthirsty coup-plotters—a characterization which would justify a military campaign against them. But the reality was that Salva's government was neither stable nor in control of the security situation. It had already lost a slice of legitimacy with its authoritarian drift before the conflict, then another with the atrocities perpetrated in its earliest days. Its remaining legitimacy would continue to diminish as months of war and suffering dragged on while government officials pretended otherwise.

Minimizing the crisis may have temporarily shored up support among some domestic audiences, and successfully clouded reality for some outside the country. But the propaganda infuriated citizens who sought real change. It also set the government on a collision course with the mediators, with Washington, and with other foreign capitals. Each of them was backing a peace process intended to prevent what was really at stake: total disintegration.

At the talks, Nhial and his team of government negotiators obfuscated at every turn, objected to every proposal, and sometimes simply refused to engage. They saw no need for political dialogue or for involving any other citizens in the process. "We need only to negotiate a limited ceasefire, and only with the armed opposition," they said to anyone who asked. Any political concerns could be considered later, back in Juba. It was an ironic posture from a government of recently-retired SPLA rebels, who during their own war against Khartoum would never have agreed to a ceasefire, laid down their weapons, or gone to Khartoum without a negotiated political solution in hand.

Riek's opposition team also frustrated mediators with caustic rhetoric and absolutist positions—"We won't discuss any solution until Salva steps down," his men would insert into almost every conversation. Equating belligerence with stature, Riek's team would sometimes be intentionally difficult—refusing to show up, holding out over minor issues, or overreacting in the media—just so they would be treated on equal terms with the government. It felt like a race to the bottom. But it was the rebels, and other non-governmental groups, who sought change nonetheless. The hard line belonged to Salva's government, and it quickly earned the ire of most every diplomat working the halls of the Sheraton.

Fast-paced, round-the-clock negotiations had helped secure a temporary ceasefire in less than three weeks—a remarkable pace in comparison to many wars. But talks were losing this edge. Competing narratives meant each party had a different idea as to the origins of the conflict, and thus to its solution. And so the quality and pace of results in Addis Ababa was fast diminishing. Delegations and mediators alike settled into a more established routine, to the chagrin of those who suffered and whose well-being depended on more urgent results.

Tens of thousands meanwhile toiled in squalid protection camps, including Simon, the student from Manga Ten, and Nyakueth, the young mother from New Site. Before long, millions would face famine conditions. But the negotiating parties in Addis were not about to interrupt a meal or exert themselves on a Sunday.

"So, you're telling me the only way to get my government's attention is to pick up a gun?" The young woman from a Juba-based civil society organization was furious. She and other participants had been invited to the peace talks by the mediators, but when they arrived at the Radisson Blu Hotel, they found themselves having to lobby for a seat at the table. When they tried to appeal to government negotiators, some of them flat out refused to speak to them. "This is a right," she fumed. "We shouldn't have to ask permission. This country doesn't belong to you or any particular individuals."

We pushed hard for a "multi-stakeholder" format for the talks, and worked hand-in-hand with Seyoum and other Southern Sudanese to ensure a place at the table not just for Salva and Riek's warring factions, but for political parties, the eleven detainees, civil society groups, women's organizations, churches, and elders. But the government refused. For weeks, an increasingly frustrated Seyoum attempted to secure agreement simply on the structure and rules for the talks, while Nhial and his team fought hard to curtail the scope and the list of participants.

Seyoum finally announced the official opening session of the multi-stakeholder process, and a large seven-sided table was erected to accommodate all participants. But when a South Sudanese priest began the opening prayers, one side of the heptagon remained conspicuously empty. Next to each of its vacant chairs were name plates that read "Government of South Sudan." Seyoum seethed, his normal poker face surrendering to visible anger.

To break the deadlock, IGAD's chairman—Ethiopian Prime Minister Hailemariam Desalegn—convened an emergency summit of the body's heads of state, who issued a resolution affirming an inclusive and multi-stakeholder dialogue. Salva's government announced a boycott and refused to return to Addis Ababa, nearly collapsing a peace process that was yet to begin in earnest. Nhial Deng met with chairman Hailemariam to explain the government's demand that "neither the group of detainees, nor any others, participate in the talks." The IGAD heads of state, who were dedicating an incredible amount of time and political capital to the mess the South Sudanese had created in their backyard, were livid.

"They are testing you," we told Seyoum and Hailemariam. "If the mediators bow to these attempts to strong-arm the process, or reject inclusivity, it will all be over." A precedent would be set that would undermine any chance for real political change. Hailemariam flexed his muscle. "IGAD is not going to be taken for a ride," he told Salva. "I expect your delegation will return to Addis on time." If Salva allowed the talks to fail, while his country descended into total chaos, Hailemariam told him, "no one could comprehend such a decision."

Salva's team returned, tails between their legs. But before long, they and their rebel counterparts would grind the process to a halt with more frustrating tactics, more delays, more bickering over petty detail. The IGAD heads of state would meet regularly to try to break the stalemate, and though they said all the right things publicly, they failed to hold the parties accountable or to empower the men they'd asked to mediate. As soon as the big dogs flew back to their respective capitals, their empty threats were ignored, and dysfunction again reigned supreme.

Both parties were to blame, but Nhial, Makwei, and the rest of Team Belligerent had made undermining dialogue their *raison d'être*. Until something changed, government hardliners would continue to dictate events, and the real negotiation would continue on the battlefield.

Riek's junior varsity squad in Addis Ababa was outmatched. He needed more political muscle, and so he bet big on the eleven detainees. A prospective union with these influential party men might give his new resistance movement a national profile, rather than simply a Nuer one. Just as he had combined forces with them in the days before the crisis, Riek hoped they could help him bring down the president, and assumed their time in jail had only fueled their antipathy toward Salva. And so he had made their release one of his primary demands, hoping they would then join his team.

The only problem with this scenario was that while Riek was negotiating their release, they hadn't actually asked for his help. During their time in detention, as the war turned ugly, the detainees realized they would be better off remaining neutral. Not only could they serve as a potential bridge between the warring factions, they also thought it politically prudent to let the two sides sully one another while keeping their own hands clean. When the detainees finally walked free and announced they would join the talks as an "independent third bloc," Riek bristled. He had helped secure their release and expected the favor to be returned. Relations between the potential allies quickly soured.

"We feel we have a contribution to give," Deng Alor told a room full of journalists upon arriving in Addis. "We hope we will help our people," he said, who had suffered too much on account of a war that was "completely senseless. It has no justification." After weeks of politically motivated incarceration, he also used the opportunity to set the record straight. "People talk about a military coup, there was no coup. It was just a fake coup. It was a fabrication to get rid of political opponents... and that's why we are here."

The mediators, Seyoum and Sumbeiywo, were well acquainted with the eleven and likewise believed they would help shake up the stagnant talks. Not only were Pagan, Deng, and the others familiar faces, they were experienced negotiators, ethnically diverse, and had ties to all parties to the conflict. When they arrived, we pressed the eleven hard: play a constructive role, advocate a multi-stakeholder process, and avoid being perceived as in it only for yourselves.

Both the government and opposition courted the eleven, but when they refused to join either team, Nhial and Taban conspired to marginalize them. The two lead negotiators held an inconspicuous late-night meeting in a Sheraton hotel suite, and agreed: If the eleven weren't going to aid either side, better to banish them altogether and divide the spoils among themselves.

The arrival of the former detainees presented an opportunity to pry open the process—not just for them but for other voices as well. But our own sustained diplomatic efforts to support wider participation prompted suspicions of renewed Western favoritism for the eleven. Many had long resented the cachet Garang and his boys had in the West, their links to Congressmen and powerful foreign policy types. And the eleven didn't help themselves, immediately appealing to old allies in the U.S. and Europe for resources and support—even asking Western friends to bankroll their personal expenses and a British lobbying firm to work on their behalf.

Long-time SPLM critic Gabriel Changson, who had joined Riek's team as a negotiator, derided foreign diplomats for "believing the Mandela of South Sudan will come from this group." Government hardliners also used the detainees' arrival to advance their conspiracy theories about a foreign regime change agenda—each time distancing Salva from the outside world and from a negotiated solution.

In truth, Washington's affinity for the eleven had expired—at least inside the government, where they were increasingly seen as a disappointment. Not only had they contributed to the country's collapse, but they failed to play a constructive role once they arrived in Addis.

"We are very excited you are here," one hopeful European diplomat had told them upon their arrival in Addis. "We believe you have an opportunity to make a critical contribution." But he too would be dismayed by the group's response. Some of the eleven were believed to have stolen money or otherwise profited from their senior government positions, and they were receiving a daily allowance during their participation in the peace process. But rather than tend to the urgent task of salvaging their country, "the very first issue they wanted to discuss was getting someone to pay for their laundry bills!" the diplomat fulminated, shaking his head. "It was appalling." In time, those who had high hopes for the group found them lazy and unimaginative. As space for the former detainees shrank, a number of them disengaged or simply left town.

In the early months of 2014, while Seyoum, his international supporters, and Southern constituencies pushed for an inclusive process, a competing peace initiative materialized that undermined those efforts. The ill-conceived "Arusha process," named for the Tanzanian city in which it was convened, sought to negotiate peace in the country by reconciling the SPLM's competing factions. Its creation reflected the lack of consensus about both the nature of the conflict and its ideal remedy, as well as emerging frustrations with the peace talks in Addis Ababa. But Arusha's singular focus on the party brass seemed to endorse, rather than diffuse, the elitism at the heart of South Sudan's crisis.

Spearheaded by dominant political parties from Tanzania and South Africa, and facilitated by consultants for hire, Arusha added another thread to an already tangled web of regional politics. Despite forceful and repeated warnings from many corners on the dangers of two competing peace processes, the Arusha organizers proceeded, as naive as they were eager to make a name for themselves. Dysfunction multiplied.

This was a worst case scenario for the new country; an elite stitch-up between the very actors who had just managed to tear it apart. Putting the band back together again would simply re-establish the status quo. Not only did it ignore the corruption, mismanagement, and poor performance that had characterized their leadership thus far, but it risked setting the country up for a repeat breakdown.

In theory, a truly complementary process that prompted serious soul-searching inside the SPLM, reflected on mistakes made, and devised a path to a more democratic ethos could be valuable. But one shouldn't invite old dogs and expect new tricks. Arusha's elite group of invitees had little interest in genuine party reform; most sought only to reclaim control of the goose that laid the golden eggs. While the IGAD mediators and their backers were fighting for an inclusive process and the kind of reforms that might diffuse power and strengthen institutions, Arusha was conspicuously aristocratic in its pursuits, and its organizers' knowledge of South Sudanese politics seemed dangerously superficial.

Arusha broke the cardinal rule of peacemaking by offering an opportunity to "forum shop." If one party did not like where things were going in one forum (IGAD), they could simply take their chances at another (Arusha). Moreover, they could play one forum against the other, in an attempt to undermine both. And that is exactly what they did.

Seasoned observers could see that all three SPLM groups—Salva's, Riek's, and the eleven—were motivated by narrow self-interest. Upset that its tales of a coup had been dismissed, Salva's government was increasingly wary that the IGAD process would force it to concede some degree of power, and they bristled at being put on an equal footing with Riek's opposition. And so "following a request by SPLM Chairman, President Salva Kiir," the Tanzanians established the alternative process, though Salva did not advertise his hope that it would sabotage the talks in Addis Ababa.

Riek Machar, meanwhile, had run the numbers. He knew that a largely Nuer vote would never net him the presidency. He needed the SPLM trademark, as its candidate retained a virtual lock on electoral victory. (Riek had even named the impromptu rebellion the "SPLM-In-Opposition," to the chagrin of many of its members.) Reclaiming his position as deputy party chairman offered the best odds at succession, and Arusha was his re-entry stamp to the party. His nomination as the party's next candidate was far from assured, but the No. 2 perch would give him control of party hierarchy and state resources—a formidable bulwark against would-be challengers. But it was a personal agenda; his own rebel forces, which blamed the SPLM top brass for the war, were openly hostile to Arusha. His participation strained already tenuous relations with his own commanders, and exposed the premium he put on his own ambitions.

The third SPLM group, the eleven former detainees, had been effectively sidelined from the IGAD process by mid-2014. Eager to find an alternative route back to power, they believed Arusha would be their ticket. Their prior cabinet appointments reflected not popular legitimacy but their membership in an aristocratic club increasingly detached from South Sudanese society. Re-asserting themselves within a strong SPLM would put them back in the driver's seat.

But those facilitating Arusha appeared to miss—or ignore—the ulterior motives of all three SPLM factions. Their competing process frustrated not only the IGAD mediators, but many South Sudanese who weren't keen on serving the state up again to the SPLM on a silver platter. "A bunch of spoiled brats," one young woman said of Arusha's participants, who she believed to be most responsible for South Sudan's undoing. "*Everything* is always focused on them. As if *we* have nothing to offer?"

Prominent SPLM figures more often defended Arusha not by arguing the merits of a one-party state or genuine party renewal. They warned instead of worst-case scenarios: "Only the SPLM," one argued, "could be the vehicle through which to prevent ethnic politics and violence." But such warnings appeared to deny the reality on the ground, where ethnic violence had just fractured the country, not in spite of the SPLM, but because of it.

"Isn't it time to hang it up?" I asked long-time party members during informal late-night discussions at the Radisson. "Maybe it's time the SPLM is relegated to a museum?" The movement could be rightfully honored for its place in history, I suggested, but it would also necessarily remain there—in history. New political parties could be formed, and given ongoing fights over an outdated trademark, no new political party would be authorized to use the four letters "SPLM."

The movement had been the driving force behind South Sudan's long struggle for independence, but it was now an empty shell. "Doesn't South Sudan need to look to its future, instead of the past?" But for those whose identity had been forged through liberation, it was hard to let go.

In the end the Arusha charade would melt away, when each group failed to use the process to advance its own narrow interests. Many would hang on to the "SPLM" letters, but its leading men would not come together again under a common banner.

While peace talks in both Ethiopia and Tanzania foundered, the war was tearing South Sudan to pieces. Having effectively ripped up the ceasefire agreement, each side launched new assaults. Government troops rampaged through Leer, the birthplace of Riek Machar, and after flattening whole neighborhoods, they chased thousands of people into the bush. One of those who fled was Diang, an elegant woman with close-cropped salt-and-pepper hair, who I met at a UN protection camp.

Diang is grandmother to nine children. The home in which she lived had been reduced to ash. After running for several miles, she recalls, she and the children waded into flooded swamplands to take cover. She hid there day and night, clutching the youngest child to her body, as soldiers searched the area. Several times, she and the child submerged up to their necks to avoid detection. It was neither the first nor the last time she fled the fighting in Leer.

Heavy fighting resumed in all three states of Greater Upper Nile and spread to other regions, stirring up local grievances and adding more and more layers to the conflict. Targeting civilians became the norm, and by April 2014, the abhorrent nature of the crimes sounded renewed international alarm about the risk of an outright genocide. When rebel forces re-captured Bentiu that month, Nuer commanders took to the radio waves, telling Dinka civilians they would be hunted, and calling on their supporters to rape Dinka women.

Some townspeople left their homes to take refuge at religious sites, where they assumed they might be safer. But rebel forces spent the next two days searching hospitals, churches, and mosques, separating out the Dinka and other perceived enemies and executing them. At one mosque in Bentiu, rebel soldiers opened the doors and unleashed a hail of bullets into the crowd huddled inside. Some 250 bodies were moved out of town in the middle of the night and dumped in a drainage ditch. Yellow tractors later ferried away the remaining dead, their buckets overflowing with limbs of the deceased.

"We are horrified," announced White House Press Secretary Jay Carney upon receipt of the news in Washington. Expressing the Obama administration's outrage at such an "abomination," his statement noted, "Images and accounts of the attacks shock the conscience." On the floor of the House of Representatives, Congressman Frank Wolf took to the podium while an aide displayed an enlarged photograph from Bentiu on an easel next to him. In it, a pile of nameless, faceless corpses lay rotting in the sun, their bellies bloated, their legs and arms twisted at awkward angles. *"President Obama!"* he called out twice, separated by a dramatic pause. *"Vice President Biden!"* he called out again, as if the two men were present in the chamber. "This is happening on your watch!"

Railing against failure and inaction in a country "America helped birth," Wolf went from zero to outrage in no time. "South Sudan is headed the way of Rwanda," he warned, rousing the haunting shame that still resonated in Washington. "Will we see the content of the reports only after it is too late?" he asked rhetorically, his voice spiking in volume. "When enterprising filmmakers and authors dredge up the documents and wonder why no one mustered the will to act?"

The Congressman who had spent so many years rallying others to the cause of South Sudan was now frantically trying to salvage it.

"I stand before you as concerned as I have ever been about the state of affairs in South Sudan and the potential for the recent violence to spiral into genocide."

Back in South Sudan, Riek's rebels were pushing dangerously close to the oil fields of Upper Nile. Having failed to capture Juba, they trained their sights on the next best bounty. Seizing the fields could cut off all revenue to Juba and hasten its collapse.

As the space for moderate-minded Southerners shrank, it became clear that the government's military campaign was not being directed by the SPLA Chief of Staff, a Nuer who had remained neutral. Dinka generals were calling the shots, most notably Paul Malong, a ruthless strongman from Salva's homeland who entertained no notions of neutrality. By the end of April, Malong was announced as the new chief of the army, or what remained of it—a predominantly Dinka force drawing new recruits from his native Bahr al Ghazal.

As state resources and attention were directed almost entirely to the war effort, the business of governing ceased almost entirely. Plummeting oil production meant an economy in shambles. With each battle, each town destroyed, and each father, sister, and cousin lost to violence, South Sudan plunged further into the abyss. The prospects for salvaging the republic were disappearing fast.

Belligerence was expected from the warring parties, but not from those supposedly brokering the peace. Yet just months into the process, it was clear that the countries of the immediate region were themselves complicating the already difficult task of making peace, both on the battlefield and at the negotiating table in Addis Ababa. It was a dizzying mix of competing interests and egos, all playing out on a South Sudanese canvas, its own suffering people sometimes getting lost in the mix.

Uganda's army was doubling down in supporting government offensives, provoking strong reactions from a long-time adversary in Sudan, which did not fancy UPDF fighter jets approaching its southern border. Ethiopia was infuriated by Uganda's engagement, while weapons and ammunition continued to flow into the country from Kenya and Sudan. Regional rivalries meant Egypt and Eritrea were also paying close attention and suspected of partisan involvement. Meanwhile the rest of the continent, and the world, shuddered at the thought of a regional war.

Competing national interests were also poisoning the peace talks. Kenya remained bitter over losing the talks to Ethiopia, and its president tried on several occasions to secretly convene the factions and broker a deal on Kenyan soil. Nairobi's governing class was also known for prioritizing financial gain over any coherent foreign policy, and so private business interests also shaded Kenyan engagement. Its financial barons owned businesses in Juba, but had also helped hide mountains of stolen Southern Sudanese cash in Nairobi. Every time the international community threatened economic sanctions against Juba, Kenyan diplomats paid public lip service while privately campaigning to subvert them. After all, if investigators began digging into the illicit financial holdings of South Sudanese officials, they would unearth not only stolen assets in Kenya, but the complicity of Nairobi's political and financial elite.

Sudan meanwhile relished the chance to meddle in Southern affairs again. Its leaders made public shows of support to the government while privately feeding enough ammunition to the rebels to keep them afloat. They kept a foot in both camps, should they need to play one against another in service of their own interests. Ethiopia was the most credible actor in the process, guided most by a desire for regional stability in an already dangerous neighborhood. But frustrated by its impotence in uniting the region or delivering a peace deal, it became a prisoner of its own perceived prestige as chair of IGAD. Seyoum and the normally even-mannered Hailemariam resented Kenya's antics and were apoplectic behind closed doors about the adventurism of Ugandan President Yoweri Museveni and his army. For months, every private conversation we had with them included venting about Museveni, and it was hard to blame them.

Having unabashedly chosen sides in the civil war, Uganda's role was second to none. Its military intervention on behalf of Salva's government and unilateral decisions were a constant strain on the peace process, an x-factor that made an already complicated knot that much harder to untie. In addition to undermining IGAD's neutrality as a mediator, the tension between an uncooperative President Museveni and what he saw as his "junior brothers" in Ethiopia and Kenya prevented regional consensus at moments when it was needed most.

The January ceasefire agreement had called for the "withdrawal of allied forces invited by either side"—a clear reference to Uganda's army. But they hadn't budged. In late-night salons on flame-lit hotel patios, observers speculated about Museveni's motivations. "He's protecting his economic interests in South Sudan," one argued. "No, he despises Riek, and he will do anything to prevent him from power," rebutted another. Still others wondered aloud whether Museveni was pushing a security buffer northward in furtherance of his outdated campaign to prevent Arab-Islamic expansion into the "real Africa."

Uganda's own stated rationale—that its army prevented Juba's collapse and with it another round of ethnic butchery—held some truth. But it was hardly the whole story. The UPDF's presence had also exacerbated tensions, fueled Nuer resentment, and given the government an inflated sense of its own inviolability. Salva's dependence on the Ugandan military for his own survival was in fact an unmistakable sign of his government's vulnerability, but it appeared not to phase Juba's fast-talking ministers, who kept on peddling "business as usual." Many believed Museveni's security guarantee was delaying meaningful negotiations and prolonging the war. He was the only actor with credible leverage; only he could puncture this fantasy and force Salva to compromise. But Museveni chose not to play his card, frustrating IGAD members, international partners, and anti-government forces.

In the first weeks of the crisis, a rumor had circulated that Washington had solicited the UPDF intervention—even supplied it with materiel support—and was secretly backing Uganda's assault on the rebels. For one 48-hour period it was on the lips of every machiatto-sipping diplomat and South Sudanese delegate in the Sheraton lobby. Washington's long-standing regional security relationship with

Kampala lent credence to the theory. But where there is smoke, there isn't always fire. Not only was it untrue, but senior U.S. officials repeatedly engaged Museveni and his security advisers, urging them to rein in their army. Securing the airport and preventing collapse in Juba was one thing, choosing sides and raining cluster bombs over rebel-held territory was quite another.

Washington could have cleared up this rumor, and possibly altered the dynamics of the war by taking a more forceful stance with Uganda. But given cooperation in other regional hotspots, and lingering concerns about Juba's vulnerability, American officials demurred from a public spat with Museveni. What signals were sent publicly were met with unflinching rebuke. In one February statement issued by the State Department, we warned of "the serious consequences which could result from any regionalization of this conflict," and reiterated the need for a "withdrawal of foreign forces." It was a thinly veiled reference, and Ugandan army spokesman Paddy Ankunda immediately fired back on Twitter, "What if violence rolls back into Bor, Juba after UPDF withdraw, will the U.S. be there to help?"

Special Envoy Booth and I shuttled to Uganda to try our luck in private—engage Museveni on his views of the evolving situation and encourage his army's withdrawal. We arrived at his Kampala estate on a pleasant afternoon, the thick green grass and well-kept gardens illuminated by a bright golden sun. Attended by like-minded diplomats from the UK and Norway, the meeting would encapsulate the famously eccentric president and his unhelpful posture toward the war in South Sudan.

When summoned we crossed the lawn toward an outdoor gazebo to greet the 70-year-old president, an enigmatic figure about whom everyone had a bizarre story. Museveni—or "M7" as he's informally called by Westerners—wore a vest, camouflage military pants, boots, and a signature round safari hat, its drawstring dangling beneath his chin. He politely declined to shake our hands, citing concerns about germs, and instead turned to ascend the Gazebo's throne. There he presided not so subtly from a raised platform a foot above us, leaving no doubts as to the inequality of the men now gathered in his garden court.

M7 was sometimes rambling and incoherent, other times highly incisive and self-aware. Today was no exception. Deflecting opening questions about the conflict, he transitioned swiftly into one of his legendary monologues, meandering from Marcel Proust to Winston Churchill to the demerits of 20th-century European colonialism. My mind wandered. I assessed his bulky torso, contemplating the popular rumor that the former rebel—who helped topple two Ugandan presidents before him—wears a bulletproof vest at all times.

A seemingly interminable amount of time passed, until, suddenly content with his wide-ranging sermon, M7 turned to South Sudan. The other diplomats in the gazebo, whose eyes had glazed over, shook themselves out of their semi-catatonic states. "They have no interest in the people, no program," the president said of the SPLM leadership, "they have only aspirations for high office." It was a hollow party, he said dismissively, registering his disappointment that none of the current crop had measured up to his old ally John Garang. "There is only, 'I want to be president.' Being president is not a political program."

M7 also made no secret of his particular distaste for Riek Machar. Citing the 1991 split, he said "the old mistake-maker" was not to be trusted. Riek, he said with a tone of derision, was an opportunist who had "betrayed the cause of the black people in South Sudan and went to work for Khartoum."

When M7 finally gave the floor back to our group, Booth and his fellow envoys peppered the president with questions about the war, Salva's posture, and the negative consequences of Ugandan's involvement. But the president feigned ignorance, saying he "had not been following" the situation closely. His knowledgeable and connected advisers aside, this notion was hard to believe. Prior to the crisis, M7 had personally engaged with key SPLM players, several times flying them to his farm to brief him on the latest developments inside the party. And when the war began, he had made a controversial military investment that carried considerable political and economic implications. Above all, his desire to maintain supremacy in regional security affairs was axiomatic.

Pressed again on the negative impacts of the UPDF presence, he refused to engage. "My job is a simple one: don't allow Juba to be taken by anyone with guns." When encouraged to consider a phased withdrawal, he said that Ugandan forces would withdraw as soon as Salva asked.

We turned to politics, urging M7 to engage Salva on a negotiated solution. In a response that underscored the charade-like nature of the meeting, Museveni asserted that he was "always reluctant to get involved in the politics of another country." As the remark hung in the air, I glanced across at my fellow diplomats, wondering just how many of them might fall off their chairs. Not only had Museveni directly intervened to save Salva's government, his belt-notches in the 1990s alone included grooming Paul Kagame and backing his Tutsi rebellion's capture of Rwanda, helping plot the invasions that toppled two Congolese presidents, and fighting directly on behalf of John Garang's SPLA in Sudan. His army had also deployed around the region to plunder timber, coltan, diamonds, and other valuable resources. All this made his principled nod to non-interventionism seem particularly rich.

More than a few similar meetings with M7 followed—with Africans, Americans, Europeans, and UN officials singing from the same song sheet. But it would take almost two years and mounting international scrutiny before the old man would alter his position.

On April 3, 2014, President Obama signed Executive Order 13664 establishing a sanctions regime to target South Sudanese belligerents. Washington had hoped to impose wider multilateral sanctions, so as to achieve maximum impact, together with the regional countries where South Sudanese elites traveled and hid their money. But while regional diplomats paid lip service to punitive threats, they remained reluctant to pull the trigger.

After months of lobbying, Washington decided to deliver what substantive and symbolic punch it could on its own. Obama's order authorized travel bans and asset freezes for anyone disrupting peace talks, committing atrocities, or interfering with life-saving humanitarian aid. "The United States will not stand by as those entrusted to lead South Sudan put their own interests above those of their people," the White House announcement read. South Sudanese citizens "expected their leaders to be statesmen, not strongmen."

Meanwhile, Special Envoy Booth and I prepared the ground for an early May visit from Secretary of State John Kerry. The secretary had worked the phones for months, but while Salva's team continued to refuse negotiations, South Sudan burned. It was time for Kerry to deliver tough love in person. The goal? Convince Salva to negotiate a political transition—a new government and major reforms that could rescue the country and restore some semblance of national legitimacy.

Special Envoy Booth and I flew to Juba to meet Salva. While much had transpired over the four months since we first pressed him to talk peace, I felt a distinct sense of déjà vu. Again Salva was skilled in discussing the military situation, and again his lack of a political vision was painfully evident. When it came to the peace talks, he spoke as if they were somehow happening independent of Juba and his own leadership. It was as if he was not even party to the process, but that his government would await its decisions and react accordingly. "President as passive recipient of politics," I wrote in my notes, "rather than the country's principal political actor."

Secretary Kerry's 757 passenger plane touched down in Ethiopia days later, the first stop on a four-nation African tour. Before continuing to Juba, Kerry had come to consult regional leaders, now well aware that regional consensus was an essential ingredient of any fix for South Sudan. "If they aren't part of the solution," Booth had explained, "they will be part of the problem." In a rendezvous the next morning with IGAD, AU, and UN leaders, Kerry asked how the group could together set South Sudan's parties on a path to "transition," and signaled his intent to secure Salva's direct participation in talks. He also worked with the group to endorse a plan to send additional peacekeepers and secured their commitment to impose sanctions if immediate progress was not made.

On the following afternoon, May 2, the secretary's delegation strode across the airport tarmac and climbed into the belly of a hulking grey beast. The secretary's 757 would not fly the next leg of the trip to Juba, but was swapped out for a C-17 U.S. military transport aircraft, one equipped with the kind of advanced counter-measures that can neutralize an attack. Normally employed to carry troops and heavy-duty cargo, the airframe's four giant turbines and bulging fuselage make for an imposing presence. In customary navy blue suit, Kerry made the rounds inside the windowless cavern, shaking hands with flight crew and staffers before ascending stairs to a VIP seat in the cockpit. As is the never-ending business of a secretary, he sandwiched preparations for Juba between a briefing book on the latest from Libya and a phone call to German Chancellor Angela Merkel on the unfolding European debt crisis.

Ninety minutes later the flying behemoth set down in Juba. While it was Kerry's first visit to the independent republic, it was not his first to South Sudan. Three years prior, a salmon-tied Senator Kerry had milled in a crowded tent at John Garang Memorial park, chatting with George Clooney and posing for photos with exuberant South Sudanese elections workers. After watching Salva Kiir cast his vote in the South's 2011 referendum, he had marked the momentous day by gifting Salva a new black cowboy hat—building on the tradition George W. Bush had started. Now Kerry was back, and it was hard to believe just how much the relationship had changed. Kerry was flying in on a military plane to deliver a very different message, and this time there would be no gifts exchanged.

After a round of handshakes with a South Sudanese welcome party, a convoy of armored white Land Cruisers whisked our delegation away—first stop the president's office. Normally bustling with cars, mini-buses, *boda bodas*, boys selling phone credit, herds of cattle, and other unseemly travelers, the streets were empty, cordoned off more thoroughly than I'd ever seen. It was incredibly efficient, but also an uncomfortable optic, the bolt of gleaming SUVs registering no self-doubt about the American right-of-way.

Jogging up red-carpeted stairs at the president's stately office, Kerry entered a fluorescent-bright conference room and took his seat across from Salva, each chief flanked by two rows of advisers. Forced pleasantries betrayed an unmistakable tension. The once unwavering bilateral relationship was now on the rocks, and everyone knew the forthcoming exchange was going to be uncomfortable. Salva began by awkwardly reciting prepared remarks, their content reflecting the voice of the hardliners now occupying the high-backed black chairs to his right and left. Air conditioning units wafted icy cold air and hummed so loud they nearly drowned out the president's muted tones.

Secretary Kerry waited patiently for him to finish, but then got right down to business. "I come as a friend," he began, but then pivoted and pressed hard, arguing that an end to fighting must be accompanied by an inclusive political transition. Leaning in across the table, Kerry explained that the United States would support his presidency and the constitutional order, but only if Salva exercised leadership, and fast. Once again appealing to Salva's legacy as a unifier, Kerry argued that he had to "seize the moment" to save his country from disaster.

When Salva attempted to counter with half measures, Kerry interrupted him. A re-birth of South Sudan required bolder action, he argued. A ceasefire was not enough, he needed to send a visible signal of the government's commitment to change. The reluctant president then nodded his head and mumbled in agreement. He would travel to Ethiopia, and per Kerry's request, meet Machar and attempt to jump-start the stalled peace process.

As the meeting broke up, the two men made their way down a balconied corridor. Kerry—conscious of those minding the reluctant president—spoke to Salva privately as they walked alone. Kerry invited the president to make a joint announcement of his commitments. Salva awkwardly demurred, and suggested Kerry could do it for him. And he did.

"I just completed an in-depth, very frank, and thorough discussion with President Kiir," Kerry began, standing against a deep blue backdrop and a seal of the American embassy. "I told President Kiir that the choices that both he and the [rebels] face are *stark* and *clear*, and that the unspeakable human costs that we have seen over the course of the last months... are unacceptable to the global community." The room full of journalists scribbled as Kerry then announced Salva's commitment to negotiate a political transition, as well as his readiness to participate directly in the next round of talks in Addis Ababa. "Before the promise of South Sudan's future is soaked in more blood," he continued, the two sides must take steps to end the violence, lest they "completely destroy what they are fighting to inherit."

The trip had accomplished as much as could be hoped for. The South Sudan government could no longer deny serious and substantive political talks, and the table was set for a breakthrough.

20

FROM THE BUSH
TO THE PALACE

"If you want peace, then you give us what we want!"
—South Sudanese negotiator

JUBA / NASIR / ADDIS ABABA /
WASHINGTON, MAY 2014-JUNE 2015

uilt in 1955 by Emperor Haile Selassie, Ethiopia's Jubilee Palace was an opulent tribute to its monarch's 25th year on the throne. Selassie was no stranger to ceremony or excess, and his splendid palace and symmetrical gardens have an undeniably imperial air. Up the steps onto one of three grand colonnaded porticoes, one encounters red carpets and velvet-draped doors framing not only a physical threshold, but a portal to another time. Few edifices feel as stuck in history as this one, its stylized grandeur as remarkable as it is incongruous to the modern Ethiopia bustling beyond its walls.

Inside, ornate furniture, wall-mounted chandeliers, and 30-foot ceilings make for a stately foyer. Gold-trimmed wood paneling rises high above two-tone parquet wood floors, the design and materials evoking a distinct 1960s aura. In the grand ballroom, giant tapestries grace the walls, and the throne room houses the audacious Emperor's coronation robes and jeweled crown.

Modestly nicknamed the "Lion of Judah," the Emperor also had a taste for cats. Symbolic stone lions adorn the palace porticoes and guard its gates, while smaller golden versions adorn the imperial thrones inside. Selassie also kept actual lions and cheetahs on the compound. A famed photograph depicts the late leader in military regalia and feathered hat, minding his tamed beasts on the palace steps. Another shows him flanked by two regal-looking cheetahs, guardians of imperial hubris. These very cats, now stuffed versions of their former selves, are on display inside the palace today, the most striking relics of a bygone era. Stuffed lions hold court at the center of several palace rooms, while cheetahs, antelope, and other preserved pets perch on marble-top tables and antique sideboards.

The furniture is original, and feels it. Frayed royal carpeting has come loose from the stairs, and browning water stains blemish an aging ceiling. The lack of upkeep has incubated the time-capsule ambience. Squinting hard, you can almost catch a glimpse of the emperor arriving in his Rolls-Royce, escorting through the foyer a magisterial delegation of African nobility, the Queen of England, or American presidential aspirant Bobby Kennedy—just some of the dignitaries who came to pay homage. Neither the Soviet-aligned military Derg nor the Marxist-Leninist peasant rebellions that succeeded Selassie did much to revive the palace, a reminder of both the Emperor's excesses and the turbulent periods that followed.

On May 9, 2014, after five months directing rebel forces from makeshift camps in the Nuer heartland, Riek Machar was airlifted from the bush to Selassie's imperial address for a tête-à-tête with his nemesis, Salva Kiir. Succumbing to the relentless appeals of Secretary of State Kerry and many others, Riek and Salva were set to convene for the first time under the aegis of Prime Minister Hailemariam, in what would prove the highest-profile attempt yet to end the war.

Sharing more than a thousand miles with its neighbors to the west, Ethiopia was no stranger to the turbulent history of Sudan and South

Sudan. Nor was it a bystander. Forty years earlier, Selassie himself had convened the Sudanese government and Southern *Anyanya* rebels at this very palace in a bid to end the country's first civil war. The 1972 Addis Ababa Agreement yielded political and security compromises not unlike those now being arbitrated between Juba and the newest of Southern rebellions. It had also given the South its first taste of self-government, a precedent upon which separatists would build towards independence. Now, the Ethiopian-led mediation had called South Sudan's parties back to Jubilee Palace in hopes of catalyzing serious peace talks and giving independence a second chance.

Choosing such a prestigious venue was no accident. It was intended to create a sense of occasion, to appeal to one's sense of history; moments of great leadership are exercised in venues of matching grandeur. Peace brokers hope such gravitas will introduce elements of pressure and accountability. But like the palatial Sheraton across the street, this actual palace also presented a jarring juxtaposition to the dire situation of millions of South Sudanese. Many opined on the optics—the men responsible for this senseless crisis convening in luxury as the death toll mounted and more civilians were forced across borders in search of food and refuge. They were right: it seemed everyone but the conflict's protagonists felt a sense of urgency.

***

Few had seen Riek Machar since the war began. When he arrived, the contradictions of the South Sudanese experiment were captured in his appearance: a finely tailored London suit complemented by the unruly beard of a rebel commander. It was his first time out of the country since the conflict had erupted. Showing up was in his interest, but he was also concerned about being able to cross back into his country.

Days earlier government troops had launched a multi-pronged attack on rebel-held territories, including the Sobat river town of Nasir, deep in Nuer territory. Nasir was not only the location of Riek's latest bush camp, it carried symbolic weight. Two decades earlier, it had been the site of Riek's headquarters after the infamous 1991 split.

Just 36 hours prior, Salva had told John Kerry he would cease all military offensives. The attacks ahead of the May 9 summit could not be dressed up as anything but gross violations of the ceasefire. But Juba may have deemed it worth the gamble, as capturing strategic locations on the eve of talks was a way to strengthen one's hand at the negotiating table. Salva ran the risk of being slapped with U.S. sanctions, but he was so engulfed by pressures at home that he hadn't the luxury to worry about international censure. Short of sending combat troops to intervene, the limits of foreign pressure were becoming increasingly clear.

Washington was concerned that hitting Salva or Riek with sanctions might complicate matters, and so responded by penalizing two senior commanders, one on each side of the conflict. The sanctions barred each man from traveling to the United States, and gave the U.S. Treasury Department a green light to freeze any assets within its reach. But the primary intent was political—a stamp from Uncle Sam that made clear the offenders were on the wrong side of history, and had earned the ire of a global superpower. Though the announcement turned heads in Juba, the commanders were not high enough up the chain to prompt a change in behavior. Moreover, most South Sudanese traveled and held assets primarily in the region, which American sanctions could not touch. Until there was enough appetite—both in Washington and in regional capitals—to target the leaders themselves, Salva and company would continue to call their bluff.

When government forces closed in on Nasir, Riek had retreated east, crossing the border into Ethiopia. There he had been scooped up by an Ethiopian army helicopter and ferried to Addis Ababa, just as his lead negotiator had been. Though the rebels were now decidedly weaker than they'd been in the first days of resistance, they were far from defeat.

As Salva's plane entered Ethiopian airspace, Booth and I worked with Seyoum and Hailemariam to shape an agenda, discuss tactics, and gather final inputs from the parties. Late into the evening, we then tapped out elements of a draft agreement on a laptop computer, its blue screen glowing in an otherwise darkened grand lobby at the

Sheraton. When the sun rose, Hailemariam summoned each leader several times, spending hours hashing out differences, channeling their respective anger, and imploring them to do the right thing. The aim was to get the two men to concretize new ceasefire terms, lock in Secretary Kerry's commitment to an inclusive transitional government, and empower their teams to negotiate the specifics.

It was a make-or-break moment, and the sense of urgency and consequence grew with each passing hour. Continued intransigence from both parties was threatening to collapse the talks; starting over again from scratch would not be easy, and would enable months of unrestrained war to rage in the interim. Southern Sudanese negotiators and diplomats paced the halls, each fielding anxious calls for updates from Juba and their respective foreign capitals. Then, in the late afternoon, Prime Minister Hailemariam's office sent word to the diplomatic corps: "Please come to Jubilee Palace."

A procession of cars made their way to the palace gates, though much remained to be negotiated, the deal still far from assured. Salva and Riek had yet to meet face to face as had been hoped, casting doubt on the evening's prospects. The mediators instead shuttled between the two camps, which now occupied opposing wings of the Palace. As the sun set and the temperature dipped, cool air and the steady chirp of crickets flowed through the foyer's open doors. Diplomats and journalists milled about in a familiar game of "hurry-up-and-wait." They passed the hours trading gossip and placing bets on the night's outcome. Each time Seyoum and Sumbeiywo crossed the foyer en route to the opposing wing of the palace, the onlookers watched for clues in their body language and murmured their speculations.

Around 8pm, the sides were close to a deal, but Riek was holding out over some final items. Seyoum asked us to take one more turn leaning on his delegation. An arduous exchange ensued as we fine-tuned lines of text in the draft agreement—a word here, a phrase there. Booth asked me to read a proposed fix to the last contentious passage, and Riek's team held their collective breath as they waited for their boss to commit. "Zach... if you say it like that," Riek said, pausing, and then exhaling, "then it is fine."

Booth agreed to recommend the edits to the mediation, but warned Riek against turning this into a protracted negotiation. We reminded him that he was losing ground on the battlefield, and fast. This agreement would be a major step toward ending the war and bringing other South Sudanese voices to the table, most of whom shared the rebels' demands for reforms. It would commit Salva to critical reforms, a constitutional review, and a mechanism to account for crimes committed. "You should agree to this deal," Booth told them. "You won't see anything better."

Returning to the foyer, I lay down flat on the parquet floor, propped on elbows, to type the revisions on a laptop computer. Seyoum's team printed final copies of the deal and hurried them back to the parties. As he waited, Seyoum and his staff paced anxiously, filling the tense minutes with the kind of distracted small talk indicative of taut nerves. Around 11:00pm, the throng of exhausted diplomats, negotiating teams, and guests were invited into the main hall for a signing ceremony. The deal wasn't yet done, but it seemed Hailemariam wanted to stage an atmosphere of inevitability. He was not about to let the warring factions leave the building without signing a deal.

One more heartburn-inducing round of back-and-forth on the text ensued, this time over seemingly picayune tradeoffs. Maybe the two men were buying a few last minutes of consideration, contemplating the pros and cons of signing the deal altogether or reneging and finding an escape route out of the back of the palace. But 20 minutes later, a dozen suited Ethiopian protocol men suddenly appeared, escorting Riek and then Salva into the packed hall. The rows of murmuring diplomatic guests were now flanked by a phalanx of television cameras, snapping photographers, and notebook-wielding journalists.

As the midnight hour approached, all eyes fixed on the two protagonists. Camera bulbs flashed as two South Sudanese religious leaders stretched out their hands and convened the men in prayer, which they recited while avoiding eye contact. Retreating to a long table and gilded chairs on each side of Hailemariam, the two men then inked their signatures—Salva with right hand and Riek with left. Without a smile or a handshake, they stood and awkwardly exchanged copies of the

"May 9th agreement." The crowd applauded and exhaled a collective sigh of relief, but the tension was palpable. The two men were finally in the same room, but they had not even looked each other in the eye.

Each man was then invited to address the audience. "I had no reason to return South Sudan to war," Riek told the crowd, his hands gripping each side of the podium. Finally afforded a public platform, Riek was not going to pass up the opportunity to dismiss the allegations against him once and for all. Despite a room crowded with reporters, diplomats, and political big men, you could hear a pin drop. "There has been no coup attempt in South Sudan," he said into a lone microphone, his delivery dripping with characteristic intensity. "I hope President Salva has come to the same conclusion."

Having set the record straight, he turned to the matter at hand. "By me signing today... I am sending a signal that this conflict must be ended peacefully. I hope the other side will also be serious."

Reacting to his opponent, Salva took to the podium but scrapped the prepared remarks placed there for him. "I don't want to talk about whether there was a coup or no coup." But he couldn't help himself, adding: "A gun does not fire itself alone." Seeking to exceed the magnanimity of his enemy, now seated just a few meters to his right, Salva touted his own peacemaking credentials and pledged that he, his party, and his army would make good on their commitment. "This bleeding will stop. Nobody will again open fire on another person." But the line that most remembered was his last. "I'm the president of South Sudan, and I must always remain in that position... the leader of that country."

A handshake might have sent a powerful signal to their respective supporters, but even this minimal gesture would not materialize. Their body language instead betrayed a raw and mutual contempt. But the deal was done.

Back at the hotel, after midnight in an emptying lobby lounge, negotiators and diplomats embraced one another in a rare moment of jubilation. The sensation was one of release; the contemplation of possibility—of hope—drew hardened cynics out of their corners.

The grind of the process had been emotionally exhausting—the delays, the waiting, the late nights arguing, the pointed rhetoric, the losing of larger significance in the minutiae. Days and nights of painstaking work would build an elemental footing, block-by-block, only for someone to knock it down with an eleventh-hour demand. The variables were innumerable, even before mixing in the styles, egos, and agendas of several dozen negotiators.

Moments of flexibility from the lead negotiators, Taban and Nhial, were reeled in by deep-seated grudges; flashes of magnanimity were consumed by mistrust and zero-sum thinking. Sometimes Seyoum summoned the factions to talks and sometimes not; the hours grind on, souls tethered to conference rooms around the clock. The highs and lows wore on individuals and on relationships. Inertia was an increasingly powerful force, routine a blunting instrument. Each party, and each individual, developed a narrative of what had happened, how they had been wronged, how those wrongs must be redressed. The longer the talks went on, the more the narratives diverged.

But the reflexive cynicism of the daily grind was suspended in those wee hours of May 10, replaced by an ephemeral sensation of breakthrough. A handful of Southern negotiators tried awkwardly not to betray it, but they were contemplating the possible. Some of them had demonstrated little faith in dialogue over recent months; during the day they went through the motions of a peace process, only to exercise more familiar muscles at night: plotting delay tactics, procuring ammunition, and soliciting battlefield defectors back home.

But for a moment on this night, a few of them became unmoored. They spoke of larger goals for their new nation, and contemplated more principled versions of themselves. They were aging men, having second thoughts about the path they were now so far down. Was this violence, and the sustained acrimony of Radisson Hotel battle, worth it? Or might compromise be a more gratifying path? When the men in the hotel lobby escaped the adversarial tug-of-war, the constant antagonism, they thought of their communities back home.

They wondered about how they would be judged, and what they had made of their newfound freedom. Was this what the years of liberation struggle had been meant to achieve... or were they capable of something more?

The air was briefly lighter, guards were let down. Stories and backslaps and chuckles are now permitted. Nhial was caught smiling. Taban hugged indiscriminately. A bridge existed, however fleetingly, between opponents whose experience of the moment is shared. The partisans had been replaced by a room full of South Sudanese.

Though a breakthrough moment, May 9 had not been pretty. Temporary releases aside, the tenor and body language of the late night ceremony foreshadowed a long road ahead. Emotions were still running high. Fighting would slow, but neither side was exhausted militarily. The war wasn't about to end in one fell swoop, and the May 9 Agreement—like the ceasefire before it—would not end the fighting.

But the night would alter the trajectory of the peace talks. It would bring more South Sudanese into the process and affirm the goal of a negotiated political transition. This was not simply a matter of silencing the guns, after all. It was an opportunity to start over, to lay a stronger foundation for the making of South Sudan.

Days later, a small group of Western diplomats was strategizing with Seyoum when a cell phone rang. He interrupted our meeting to answer the call. I watched him receive the news, a deflated expression followed by drooping shoulders. The first ceasefire violation had been reported. The parties were pointing fingers with the ink on the May 9 Agreement barely dry. It was an all-too-familiar pattern, the high of the palace breakthrough followed by a discouraging low. Seyoum, his government, and fellow IGAD officials were furious. After all the time, energy, and political capital they'd invested, the warring parties' disregard for their own commitments came as a painful blow. "I remember his face getting very, very red," said one of Seyoum's advisers. "He felt personally betrayed."

Telephones soon rang off the hook in Washington and other Western capitals. Ethiopian officials demanded resources and political support for a regional military intervention. Neighboring governments had several times threatened to send their armies across the border, but they had been unable to produce the troops or money to make it happen. Over time, the empty bluster had further weakened IGAD credibility. But frustration was mounting, and with their pride and reputation in question, the Ethiopians wanted to respond with a show of force. There was a genuine desire to stop the bloodshed, but as chair of IGAD and de facto owners of the peace process, the Ethiopians were also concerned about being perceived as weak.

If Salva and Riek's legions weren't going to get serious about peace, the thinking went, maybe they needed the kind of forceful encouragement they couldn't ignore. If a few bloody noses would send a message, so be it. UN troops were not about to insert themselves between South Sudan's warring factions, nor were they mandated to do so, but regional troops would have no such reservations. It was a risky proposition.

Those clamoring for more muscle had a second rationale: the intervention of a capable and neutral force would also provide reason for Uganda's partisan troops to finally exit the battlefield.

Back home in South Sudan, the war was beginning to soak in deep. Opportunistic army commanders were reducing the country into ever more isolated, and militarized, ethnic blocs. Salva and Riek each sought to improve their lot by buying up these free agents. Local warlords who demonstrated value—in capturing territory, delivering weapons, or swaying communities—were courted with offers of money, positions, and local authority. And the auction extended well beyond the Dinka-Nuer fault line. Armed entrepreneurs from smaller marginalized communities (the Shilluk and Murle), or those still sitting on the fence (the Equatorians), were particularly sought after.

Warlords wanted a piece of the power game, as well as control over local community interests. And the aims of Salva and Riek's opposing coalitions were simple: swell their ranks, tip the balance on the battlefield, and purchase loyalty before the other side could do so. Troublesome commanders had bargaining power; just as they'd been bought off after the North-South war, and again during the interim period, the rules of the game still applied. In fact, the market was now especially good for warlords, as Salva and Riek were both bidding at the loyalty auction.

But with each purchase, Salva and Riek were ceding power to local strongmen and undermining the nation-state each man was fighting so hard to capture. When the war was over, would either man be able to project authority from a faraway capital? Would either enjoy any legitimacy? What did this Balkanization mean for the creation of a national identity? These were crucial questions, but ones neither side seemed inclined to consider—this was a battle for survival.

As the fire sale intensified, the entrepreneurial-minded drove up the price. Johnson Olony was one such enterprising commander. A former rebel from the Shilluk community, Olony is a towering physical presence who once proclaimed to a public rally that he had a "Ph.D. in war-fighting." Olony began the war on the side of the government, having accepted a buyout from Salva just six months before the war began. His loyalty and battlefield successes in strategic Shilluk land prompted the SPLA to deliver him more weaponry and ammunition to battle the rebels. But when the government's commitment to his Shilluk community proved insincere, Olony simply turned on it. He captured Malakal and charged north in a dramatic assault on the government's only remaining oil fields.

Tantalized by Olony's strategic wins and considerable weaponry, Riek pounced. Following a deal that preserved Olony's local interests, netted him and his colleagues senior positions in the movement, and was surely sweetened with cash, the commander announced his new allegiance. He would henceforth fight the government with the very weapons they had just supplied to him. Though Olony's about-face was arguably most influential in altering South Sudan's chess board, the dynamics played out in other ethnic enclaves as well, where one-time rebels—and opposition politicians—were bought back by the government.

The regression was likely to be felt long after South Sudan's conflict ended. The very concept of a "nation" inside this hollowed-out state rested on building ties across ethnic and regional boundaries, however the state was organized. Just as they were beginning to fade, these boundaries again became more pronounced, as communities and individuals retreated, physically and psychologically, to the safety of their tribes.

This retreat was most evident in rural and tribally homogenous regions, but it didn't stop there. Even Simon, the young Nuer man whose urban youth and education had helped him see beyond tribalism, was not immune. While I was riding with him through rush hour traffic in Juba one afternoon in 2016, a *boda boda* driver cut in front of our vehicle heedlessly while shifting lanes. It was a comparatively minor offense in Juba's rowdy game of traffic, but from the back of the van I heard Simon mumble under his breath, "Pssh, these Dinka... *just animals.*"

Despite the setbacks following the May 9 Agreement, Seyoum jump-started political talks three weeks later, in early June. Though some of the warring elites wanted simply to re-capture the state, other South Sudanese voiced a hunger for real reforms. And so we worked with them and Seyoum's staff to develop five tracks for discussion: transitional governance, security, economic and financial management, justice and reconciliation, and constitution-making.

We developed questions for the parties to debate in each area, flew in international experts to facilitate discussions, and convened a two-day symposium that allowed participants to explore a range of post-conflict arrangements employed elsewhere in the world. Suddenly, participants took off their partisan hats and began debating ideas. The meeting halls were abuzz with unfamiliar energy, as opponents who'd barely spoken to each other in months were now talking creatively about models that might be adapted in rebuilding their own state. It was a remarkable respite from the months of cynical antagonism.

But the spirit vanished as quickly as it had arrived. Talking in the abstract was one thing, but actually giving up ground for the greater good? Hours after the symposium ended, Nhial's and Taban's teams were back to talking raw power—how to get it, how to hang on to it, and how to wield it. They did everything to dilute the process, make life difficult for the mediation, and limit anyone else from participating in the power games.

Gabriel Changson, the principled critic of the SPLM, had once spoken with conviction about the dangers of excluding stakeholders from peace talks. The CPA, he'd long argued, had been a narrow process that ultimately helped bring about South Sudan's current war, precisely because important voices, including his own, had been excluded. But now, as a representative on Riek's negotiating team, he too was trying to shut the doors on all other stakeholders.

I confronted my old sparring partner about his seeming hypocrisy, which led to more than one spirited late night debate with voices raised, fingers pointed, and walk-outs staged. Changson said that he wanted to prevent the SPLM from re-asserting its dominant position, which he saw as a recipe for national disaster. He believed a bargain between Salva's government and the rebels (again, many of whom despised the SPLM) was the only way to preserve that chance. He was willing to exclude all others—just as he had once been excluded—to achieve that end. His logic seemed twisted, and underscored the still rudderless nature of the peace process and its likely tack back toward a division of spoils among South Sudan's strongmen.

While we joined the voices pushing a reform agenda, time and again talks would return to the matter of Salva and Riek. Proposals for governance arrangements that did not include the two men had fallen on deaf ears; the game was all about how they would share power. A dozen options were debated—one included two vice presidents, another a prime minister, and a third outlined a time-bound succession in which Salva would eventually hand the reins to Riek. Twice the IGAD heads of state convened to try to broker an arrangement, but their failed attempts were followed by disillusionment and delay.

At the outset of the peace process, there had been a great sense of ambition. Friends in the region and around the world believed South Sudan's hard-won independence was worth fighting for; these early growing pains could not be allowed to drag a war-weary people back into conflict, nor ruin the decades of global support for their righteous cause. But in time, these sentiments would be soured by the parties' bellicose rhetoric, their seeming detachment from their people's intense suffering, and their inability to put the nation ahead of themselves.

"If you want peace," one hot-tempered negotiator told a collection of mediators and peace process supporters at the tail end of a protracted round of talks, "then you give us what we want!" Those across the table sat silent, stunned at the seeming inversion of roles. All too often it seemed the outsiders wanted peace more than the South Sudanese delegates themselves. "Only in Sudan," frustrated diplomats would mumble. This was surely cause for cynicism, but in fact it was not unique to this corner of the world. One wondered what experiences, what circumstances, what calculations could bring this negotiator to a point of such seeming indifference.

I sat down to draft an informal note on the state of the talks, heading it: "Parties Not Serious About Peace; Process Risks Foundering." It was the first in a series of missives arguing that the IGAD process could not succeed, at least in its current form. The pressure, the sustained diplomacy, the sanctions, the summits, and the agreements negotiated had failed to create an inclusive process or nudge the parties down a path of negotiated settlement.

Juba, meanwhile, was a pressure cooker. A disastrous economic outlook was prompting murmurs about an actual *coup d'état*—this time from inside Salva's government. After fighting had destroyed important oil fields and forced others offline, oil production had been cut by half. Meanwhile, global oil prices began declining in June

2014, and would soon be in free-fall. By the end of the year, the price of oil had dropped by 50 percent—from more than $110 per barrel to roughly $55. A year later, it had plummeted below $40. Despite Juba's emptying pockets, the terms of its separation agreement with Sudan meant it still had to pay Khartoum $24 in fees for every barrel pumped from beneath its soil.

For a country wholly dependent on oil, collapse was now a very real prospect. The government had re-directed a majority of its budget to the war effort, slashing health, education, and humanitarian budgets and withholding paychecks from federal employees. Rather than provide its people with services, it was buying ammunition with which to fight them.

Salva's government was meanwhile mortgaging the country's future at breakneck speed. Focused only on its immediate survival, it sold contracts for future oil sales at deep discounts, agreed to predatory loans from shady foreign financiers, and racked up hundreds of millions of dollars in debt. With citizens long accustomed to fending for themselves, the government could theoretically hold out longer than more developed states, but the piper would have to be paid.

As macroeconomic stability teetered, those close to the president would get what they could while they could. Returning to old tricks, they manipulated the exchange rate, tendered themselves dubious contracts and letters of credit, and pocketed kickbacks on weapons purchases. The damage to institutional development aside, the life was being sucked out of an economy already in critical condition.

"*No one* knows the indebtedness of this country," Aggrey Tisa Sabuni tells me, when I ask just how deep a hole has been dug. The stout and demonstrative Equatorian crosses his right leg over left knee, presses his palms down into the brown sofa, and leans back in a posture reflective of his frustration. "There's something like $16 billion in arrears, I mean—that's the order of magnitude, I don't know the exact figure."

377

"This is the off-books debt, not reflected in the budget?" I ask. "Not reflected in the budget," he parrots back, implying the hole is deeper than anyone thinks.

Aggrey was appointed Juba's minister of finance in August 2013, shortly after the agreement with Khartoum brought oil revenues back online. Hailing from the town of Kajo Keji, Aggrey, a trained economist, is a committed bureaucrat with sound financial management principles. Over the course of his short and turbulent tenure, he would come under intense pressure from powerful interests who opposed the standardized controls and belt-tightening he had in mind.

"I did a lot of soul searching," he says, before getting to work trying to corral outrageous spending practices, ballooning debt, and a new wave of war-related corruption. He knew it would be an uphill battle.

It's the summer of 2016, and I've come to visit Aggrey in Juba to discuss the efforts that got him fired after just seventeen months on the job. On my drive to his office, the evidence of a massive fuel shortage is everywhere: idle generators, long lines at petrol stations, an argument at one empty pump that turned to fisticuffs. We pass Juba hospital, where patients lie in wait of life-saving care as there is no electricity to fuel its generators. My driver pulls over when he spots a boy selling a used water bottle filled with petrol. It is a quantity that once went for 9 South Sudanese pounds. "How much?" he asks the young black marketeer. "Two hundred forty pounds."

It's dark inside Aggrey's office, and a flat screen television plays the news on a constant loop in the background. It's tuned to Al Jazeera English, and blaring so loud I can barely hear him. The office sits in a vacant sand lot across the road from the president's office. Aggrey has been demoted to the post of "presidential advisor"—a lofty title that often means little in practice. He is still making important contributions where he can, but such presidential advisor appointments have historically been doled out as patronage positions, their appointees' advice rarely solicited by the powers that be.

He's frustrated, he says, by the "*wrrrongness*"—he rolls the 'r' hard—"of the leadership, the assembly, even civil society in managing the affairs of a sovereign country, the economy, foreign policy." Aggrey wears a dark suit, starched white shirt, striped tie, and lapel pin with South Sudan's flag. But under the uniform he's worse for wear. Pursing his lips and putting dramatic emphasis on choice words, he explains, "When I *turn* down, when I *turn* down" the many illegitimate claims for payment that came across his desk, "then the word goes round—'this is a difficult guy.'" The emphatic pronunciation is a regular feature of Aggrey's delivery, as he identifies the main point in most every sentence he strings together. "*No-body* understands why Aggrey wants something done about the arrears," he says in the third person. Those who did understand his proposed prescriptions were reluctant to stick their necks out to support him. Aggrey had been confronted by a powerful tide. His effort to steer his country's economy away from the rocks was ultimately futile, undermined by both corruption and a dearth of professional technocrats.

Aggrey revisits some of the corruption schemes that blasted holes in South Sudan's financial system for years, but then turns to the feeding frenzy that began only after the conflict erupted in late 2013. The powerful men feeding were principally those of Bahr al Ghazal, the influential network of shadowy elders that had aggressively closed ranks around the president amid the unfolding war. Locking down ethno-regional control of key industries and lucrative projects, they were simply going to eat as much as they could for as long as they could, until the bottom fell out. When Aggrey refused to produce the cash for their off-budget payments or denied their bogus contracts, they paid him a visit. "You will not last," they warned, "whether you like it or not, you will not last." Recalling this, he laughs the kind of laugh that can easily morph into tears.

But the former finance chief confronted a problem rooted even deeper than corruption: a dearth of experience. To illustrate his point, he speaks of the vultures who came to South Sudan to prey on the limited capacity of some of the men in his government. "You have these people who come and dangle the possibility of financing, *fake* people!" He poses a hypothetical. "Say you are the minister of roads. A Chinese or Indian or Arab or Nigerian comes and offers to build your roads, and he tells you, 'If you can persuade the minister of finance, I can give you five billion dollars.'" The minister would then bring the proposal to Aggrey, and argue, "We have no money, and this guy is ready to bring billions. Let us do it." Aggrey shakes his head, explaining that a simple Google search showed that these financiers were con men, sometimes representing companies that didn't exist. "The next day it's the minister of education, then the minister of health, then the state governors."

The problem wasn't only that former SPLA guerrillas were awarded jobs in the new government for which they were not qualified. Starting in the 1950s and moving forward to the present, Aggrey explains the challenges faced even by Southerners who were fortunate enough to graduate from university and land jobs as technocrats in national institutions in Sudan. They found work in Khartoum's "central bank and the finance ministry and what-what," he explains. "*But!*" Aggrey punctuates his own narrative, "they were *never* placed in the policy sections of these institutions." Because Southerners were so flagrantly marginalized in Sudan, they got jobs as clerks, tellers, or deputies, but were almost never placed in departments where fiscal and monetary policies were developed. So when independence came, and these bureaucrats came south to staff up fledgling institutions in Juba, "Nobody had a clue as to how macroeconomics are done... You get my point?"

Faced with hyperinflation and dwindling foreign reserves, Aggrey recommended emergency measures, but the government just kept digging. Oil Minister Stephen Dhieu telephoned Khartoum in January 2015 to plead for a re-negotiation of oil transit arrangements. With production suppressed, and oil prices dipping to their lowest point in a decade, Khartoum was now earning more in fees on every barrel of South Sudanese oil than was Juba. The rebels watched closely, hoping that the government's own negligence and economic woes would cause it to implode. Soon the Chinese-led consortium was no longer making profits on oil extraction in South Sudan. In fact, they started losing money. Chinese officials confided privately that they resisted walking away for purely political reasons—"our contribution," one explained, to stability and the peace process.

Aggrey's replacement at the Finance Ministry, David Deng, hopped a plane to European capitals and the World Bank pleading for budgetary support, but he was rebuffed. Foreign diplomats grilled the parties with increasing intensity, arguing that they were driving their country past the point of no return, and there would soon be nothing left to fight over. Continuing its steady deterioration over the course of 2015, Juba's economic death spiral would ultimately force the government to alter its calculations at the negotiating table.

The widening economic crisis, mounting frustration over the conflict, and the lack of clear leadership also led some senior figures to consider taking matters into their own hands. Though there had been no coup in December 2013, senior security types began quietly considering whether a real one was now necessary to salvage what remained of the state. These entrepreneurial inquisitors included the deposed army chief of staff and other senior army brass—just the kind of clique necessary to orchestrate a putsch.

Several of them embarked on a regional tour, testing the waters in surreptitious meetings with regional intelligence and military chiefs, as well as Western diplomats. In euphemistic terms, they asked questions like, "What would be your reaction to a 'stable security takeover?'" Stunned by the ask and shuddering at the thought of more uncontrolled chaos, most Western diplomats responded with unequivocal discouragement.

Rumors of coup-plotting persisted throughout 2014 and into 2015, as some inside the government—most notably new army chief Paul Malong—appeared to join the mix. In hushed backroom discussions, names circulated as to who might lead an orderly transition. But it was no sure thing, and just as many winced at the notion of a more ruthless and partisan villain like Malong taking Salva's place.

Ultimately, no such surprise action materialized, but Salva's life and position remained under near-constant threat.

Riek remained in Addis Ababa with his own internal dissent to manage. A guest of the Ethiopian government, the former vice president was first accommodated in a luxurious Sheraton villa, and later a two-story house in a residential neighborhood across town. Each site bustled with body guards, negotiators, relatives, errand boys, tea ladies, and visiting commanders and chiefs.

Riek did not participate directly in the peace talks, but aides came to him with updates and returned with his instructions. This allowed the mediators and their diplomatic reinforcements to engage him directly when necessary. But it also shortened the leash of Taban and his negotiators, as ever smaller decisions were referred to the boss. And in time Riek's cantankerous manner would irritate Seyoum and his Ethiopian hosts, who had gone out of their way to accommodate him.

Riek was difficult in part because he was attempting to herd cats, and the impossibility of his task was evident in the first meeting Special Envoy Booth and I had with him upon arriving in Addis Ababa. We made our way down to his Sheraton villa, and found Riek at a backyard table accompanied by nearly a dozen members of his negotiating team. Those flanking him represented the smorgasbord of individuals and interests that comprised his loose rebel coalition. Some were interested in negotiating a deal. Others sought only military victory. All of them wanted justice for the massacres of Nuer civilians in Juba. While few of these men cared about Riek's own political future, they were all intent on riding his wave.

Attempting to juggle their objectives and his own, Riek put on a performance. As he responded to our diplomatic entreaties, it became clear that he was speaking not to us, but through us to those on his side of the table. They needed his political gravitas, and he needed their battlefield muscle. Their hardline positions would prove unrealistic in the long run, but he had to speak convincingly to their demands for now, lest the fragile "movement" shatter before him. It was a precarious game.

After a handful of these performances, I suggested to Riek that we would find a two-on-two format more constructive for future meetings. Relieved to blame us for the downsized meetings, Riek was an entirely different presence on his own—constructive, relaxed, reasonable. We found ways to seek out the views of the other rebel constituencies, but in a way that didn't invite Riek's public theatre.

No longer party to these smaller meetings, Riek's wife Angelina generously took to serving us tea. By no means a "conventional" wife, she soon made a practice of this traditional duty. "Would you like milk? How many sugars?" As we debated political and security issues with her husband, Angelina would enter the room and pour tea in curiously slow fashion. Sometimes she would return in short order to offer refills. Other times she would finish serving, quietly sit down, and then insert her own arguments into the discussion. It was one small hint of the increasing role she would come to play in shaping the politics of the rebellion. In time, she would become one of its most outspoken hardliners.

Six more months of talks yielded additional highs and lows, but 2014 ended with little to show. The credibility of the process steadily weakened, as the parties repeatedly tested the mediators, and were repeatedly met with little or no resistance. Despite high hopes for the chosen mediators, tactical and strategic mistakes occurred almost daily, on display for all to see. Seyoum came under criticism for being too flexible with hardened Southern negotiators. Foreign diplomats—and even some Southern negotiators—complained that he needed to show more backbone, to draw a line in the sand when necessary.

Sumbeiywo's mistakes and crotchety demeanor left seasoned observers wondering what had happened to the man they had worked with in the past. Though agreeable and supportive at the start, he became embittered by Seyoum's leadership style and by the complexity of a process that challenged his own diminished energies. Occasionally, Sumbeiywo's decisiveness and black-and-white approach provided a helpful contrast to Seyoum's style. But more often, Sumbeiywo was a singular manifestation of Kenyan-Ethiopian tensions. In time he would become gruff with the Ethiopians, then with the Americans and other Western supporters, and then with South Sudanese delegates. Worst of all, months into the process, speculation arose that Sumbeiywo was secretly colluding with Salva's government; colleagues worried he was leaking documents, offering inside information, and maneuvering to undercut the rebels.

Tensions between the two mediators also proved disastrous, a personal animus which precluded necessary planning, divided their staffs, and confused the process. While we and other diplomats had once had a constructive conduit through which to offer support, the feuding mediators and Sumbeiywo's stubbornness had all but closed that channel.

But the mediators were not solely to blame. Their bosses—the IGAD heads of state—failed to give them sufficient political backing or room to maneuver. Over the course of the peace process, IGAD leaders convened seven summits on the crisis in South Sudan. The chaos of each exemplified the process more broadly. Heads of state contradicted their own mediators, reopened issues already settled after months of painstaking negotiations, and rarely emerged with a common understanding of what had been agreed.

But their tough talk proved most damning. Five times the leaders threatened punitive action, but not once did they follow through. Soon the halls of IGAD summits were full of caustic jokes about paper tigers. Absent credible threats, the warring parties continued to fight, neglect their commitments, and slow-roll the peace process without consequence.

Yet for all the regional dysfunction, the warring parties were themselves most culpable. Neither Nhial's nor Taban's team articulated a political vision or an endgame, and so each looked to IGAD to define the substance and deliver it to them. Moreover, countless chances arose for each side to gain control of the political narrative, improve their positions domestically and internationally, and translate these into leverage at the negotiating table. But neither side missed an opportunity to miss an opportunity. And with each passing week, thousands more were hurt, driven from their homes, or killed.

Nhial and Taban did eventually succeed in one joint campaign: to exclude others from the table. The government intimidated or co-opted some invited participants while blatantly preventing others from even boarding a plane to Addis Ababa. But the mediators chose to proceed. Later, the leader of the civil society delegation, Deng Athui, criticized the SPLM and the government delegation for their elitism and lack of compassion, asking them to raise their hands if any of their own children remained inside South Sudan. (No hands were raised.) Upon returning to Juba, Athui was not so coincidentally shot by an unidentified assailant. Though he survived, he would never return to the negotiations. But the talks went ahead anyway.

Desperate to keep the process alive, Seyoum and Sumbeiywo seemed not to appreciate that their repeated concessions meant they were forfeiting any chance of success. Frustrated by the task of managing a multi-stakeholder process and deprived of needed chutzpah from their bosses, the mediators acquiesced. Increasingly cranky and unimaginative, Sumbeiywo rationalized the defeat in late 2014, admitting privately that an "inclusive process" was just "too difficult."

By the end of 2014, the multi-stakeholder peace process had been reduced to a three-faction SPLM affair. It seemed the re-making of South Sudan would belong to those of Salva and those of Riek, with a minor role for the eleven detainees. Those who had been pushed to the margins were losing hope.

————

It was time to begin seriously considering a "Plan B." As the calendar closed in on a full year of conflict, it was clear the IGAD talks were not going to succeed. If they didn't collapse altogether, we feared an equally bad outcome—that war and parallel negotiations would simply drag on indefinitely. At Special Envoy Booth's direction, I drew up preliminary plans to assert a greater American role in the process, including moving the negotiations to Washington, D.C.

A change of venue could help shake up a stagnant process. Moreover, hosting the talks on American soil would force Washington to invest greater political capital in their success. Those who "own" a process are more inclined to see it succeed, and given South Sudan's long-time champions in America, a second chance for them to help right past mistakes might amplify that effect.

In the preceding months, more than a few regional diplomats and South Sudanese negotiators had quietly urged us to take the reins, citing regional divisions and America's historic role in South Sudan. Plan B might present an opportunity to reset the terms of a soured process. But we had no intention of going it alone or breaking the rule against forum shopping. Strong regional involvement would remain a necessary ingredient. If IGAD states objected to our hosting talks, Plan B and anything it produced would be dead in the water. Diplomatic advance work would be required to bring all regional and international partners around a clear game plan. We would also invite a wider group of South Sudanese participants, given the perils of a deal struck only between Salva, Riek, and the SPLM elite.

We identified several suitable locations in the greater Washington area, each isolated enough to prevent distraction but close enough to Washington to call in heavyweights as needed—including President Obama, Secretary Kerry, Susan Rice, and members of Congress. We also identified a high-profile U.S. lead negotiator and devised a support architecture that drew on all diplomatic partners, including Seyoum and Sumbeiywo. A mediation support unit would coordinate technical input, as well as oversee protocol, communications, and logistics teams.

Twenty years earlier, American diplomat Richard Holbrooke had brokered the "Dayton Accords," which put an end to three years of war between Bosniaks, Croats, and Serbs in Bosnia. On behalf of Bill Clinton's administration, Holbrooke had sought to alter dynamics by sequestering the parties on a remote American military base outside Dayton, Ohio. The 1995 Dayton process had likewise built upon failed earlier efforts, and it, too, had brought a broader group of international players around the table. Bosnia's war had unique characteristics, it had taken place at a unique geopolitical moment, and it had garnered greater international attention than South Sudan. But it was a familiar model from which lessons could be drawn.

After Rice and Kerry notionally endorsed Plan B in late 2014, we needed to quietly gauge regional support before putting the plan in motion. Despite the encouragement from officials in the region, none of them were going to stand up and publicly ask Washington to take over a failing process. Regional co-ownership of Plan B would improve its chances for success and could allow the region a face-saving way out of its internal squabbles.

The IGAD talks had switched direction several times, confusing the parties and preventing South Sudanese or international partners from coalescing around core tenets of a peace deal. Rather than starting from scratch, Plan B could begin by synthesizing nine months of discussions, ideas, and inputs from South Sudanese parties, and building consensus around a single draft text. Talks would be time-limited and focus on carrying an advanced plan across the finish line.

The plan provided no guarantee of success; the realities of the country's deep internal divisions and poor leadership were unavoidable. But it was hard to imagine a reinvigorated effort yielding something worse than what could come of the tainted IGAD process. Conceivably it could halt a senseless war, set the terms of a political transition, and invest a wider swathe of Southern Sudanese and international actors in ensuring its success. Beyond that, a viable and peaceful South Sudan would be a generational endeavor, and one that would have to be driven from within. International friends could offer a great deal of help, though they need not look deep into Sudan's history to appreciate the limits of what could be imposed from the outside.

But as the next round of talks in Addis began, Plan B was put on ice. Some in Washington doubted the chances for regional support. Others were reluctant to "own" the problem and thought the U.S. should maintain its distance. It was a momentous decision, as the opportunity would not present itself again. What would have transpired is hard to say. But the choice to shy away from a bold move proved disappointing to those who feared the ongoing talks were destined to fail.

21

HOUSES DIVIDED

"Uneasy lies the head that wears a crown."
—William Shakespeare, *Henry IV, Part 2*

ADDIS ABABA / JUBA / PAGAK, JANUARY–AUGUST 2015

I f you make me do this," Salva told his peers, "you will have to keep me here." The presidents of neighboring countries were sitting with Salva for the umpteenth time, pressing him to compromise with Riek. The war was eating South Sudan from the inside, and several months of talks had passed with little to show. Some kind of bold move was necessary to escape a seemingly unending doom loop. But the president didn't see how he could cut a deal. Swallowing his pride, and wearing a grave expression, he continued, "If I do, and I go back, they will kill me."

Salva's plea was a convenient excuse, and one he made to his fellow heads of state on more than one occasion. But that did not mean it wasn't true. For Salva Kiir and Riek Machar, their greatest challenges would arise from within their own divided houses. Despite all the threats from outside, the pressure each man would encounter over the summer of 2015 from within their own camps seemed more immediate and existential than anything foreign actors could throw at them.

Pressure from the outside world surely weighed on Salva: the unrelenting entreaties from global powers, the damaging loss of legitimacy abroad, the prospect of criminal prosecution, travel bans and asset freezes, the warnings about economic collapse—not to mention his persistent paranoia about a foreign regime-change agenda. It was a formidable cocktail. But nothing felt more menacing to Salva than the domestic threats then tightening around him like a noose. Survival was the first order of business.

Powerful Dinka elders demanded he take steps to preserve Bahr al Ghazal's grip on power. Hardliners pressed him toward ever more uncompromising policies. And strongmen inside the regime were again contemplating his assassination. Salva also worried about the damage to his own legacy if he were to concede power to Riek, an outcome so many had deemed totally unacceptable.

Under the right circumstances, Salva might have been happy to rid himself of these burdens altogether. If only there were a certain path to give up his job, escape to a quiet farm, and leave this incredible stress to someone else. The accidental president surely wondered how life might have been different had he passed the baton to a successor in 2011, having delivered the South's independence. He could have retired the revered father of a nation. But this was now a mere fantasy, an alternate path disappearing in the rearview mirror. Instead, Salva was now at the center of a vortex, incapable of finding his way out.

Meanwhile, unbeknownst to many foreigners, a bitter battle continued inside Riek's rebel coalition. The prophetic son had a tenuous hold on the mostly Nuer rebellion, and the gap between him and his already disenchanted lieutenants was widening. "Maybe it's time for new leadership," some of his commanders vented, openly contemplating his ouster.

As peace talks wore on, and the military tide turned against the rebels, Riek knew that it was time to deal. He had long hoped Salva's government might collapse from within, but now it seemed that fate might instead be his own. He calculated that a power-sharing government—including a seat for himself, with access to the levers of power—was his last best chance to preserve a path to the presidency he so coveted.

But Riek's personal agenda was of little interest to his rebellion's rank and file. Not only did many resent his undemocratic leadership, they also harbored more hardline demands. They hated his courtship of the SPLM hierarchy and his insistence on labeling the rebel movement "SPLM-In-Opposition." They had little interest in the party that had never represented them, and whose elite had selfishly plunged the country back into war.

Riek needed this fractious coalition to project power, but for all their frustration, they needed him too. Though sometimes resentful of their leader, Nuer elders knew that an internal split could weaken their overall position and further marginalize them from central government power. Mindful of past failures and a painful stereotype—that the Nuer were prone to infighting and division—the inclination for clan unity mitigated against an open break. It was, at least in part, a marriage of convenience. Only Riek was capable of unifying Nuer clans. Only he had the national profile and political skill to go toe-to-toe with the government, and only he had the connections to build a broader anti-government alliance. Only Riek enjoyed entrée with African governments abroad, and only he could procure the kind of cash and arms needed to sustain the fight.

In mobilizing the predominantly Nuer resistance in the early days of the conflict, Riek and his men had summoned ethnic hatreds and stoked fears about genocide. He had inflated the facts about initial massacres in Juba, and fueled an already visceral narrative of revenge. Responding to popular demands for justice, he made accountability his rallying cry, and had called for Salva to be removed.

But by the summer of 2015, when Riek was ready to deal, the majority of his rebel forces wanted to continue the war. Riek had climbed up a tree, promising justice and Salva's head on a platter, and was now having a very hard time climbing down. Signing his name to a peace deal that didn't ostensibly deliver either was not going to be well received. In fact, some of the rebels might simply continue the war without him.

Operations were also a point of contention, and the rebel commanders bristled at Riek's presumptive supremacy and top-down approach. Despite the façade of a command structure and a consultative leadership arrangement, the reality was that decisions and resources remained solely in the hands of two men. Riek and his second-in-command, Taban Deng, controlled ammunition supply chains, circumvented chains of command, and manipulated subordinates so as to maintain a firm grip. There was a certain irony in Riek's style of leadership—the complaints about him sounded eerily similar to those a 38-year-old Riek had once leveled against his own rebel commander, John Garang.

Hoping to release the steam building up inside his movement, Riek convened rebel conferences in December 2014 and March 2015. These bush conventions drew hundreds of Nuer fighters, chiefs, community elders, and negotiators together in Pagak—a rural outpost straddling the South Sudan-Ethiopia border. Delegates came on foot from across the Nuer heartland, by bus from regional capitals, and a handful by airplane from Europe, Australia, and the United States. Hundreds of other ordinary Nuer showed up simply to get a glimpse of Riek, the Nuer messiah. But they had to wait, as Riek was late to the party.

As the numbers swelled at the second convention in Pagak, the middle-of-nowhere village was soon overwhelmed. Heavy weapons were in good supply, as were crates of ammunition stamped by Eastern-Bloc manufacturers. But food and water were not. Accommodation was also scarce, and thick brown muck and giant pools of rainwater made for increasingly sloppy terrain. Long rainy days were spent waiting for their belated leader to arrive. Outside one straw-roofed hut, a teenager in military fatigues shined Taban's boots and prepared his meal. At another, Riek's wife, Angelina—"the first lady," as detractors were now calling her—considered tactics. Top military commanders huddled to discuss their collective frustration with Riek and his team of politicians. Even the tracksuit-clad Nuer prophet, Dak Kueth, arrived, greeting scores of wide-eyed followers.

After a week, Riek arrived and processed around Pagak, waving to cheering warriors and singing choruses from the bed of a pickup truck. But the popular fanfare belied an equal and opposite undercurrent of resentment.

Commanders in army fatigues and green berets joined men in suit jackets and African prints, all squashing into makeshift tents, each eager to assert his importance and ideas. At the muddy edges, younger delegates strained to hear the day's speakers, who addressed the crowd via handheld megaphones. When these larger gatherings broke up, contentious debates ensued in smaller circles, where commanders aired complaints about Riek's and Taban's leadership and their comparatively moderate aims. However unrealistic a prospect by 2015, some delegates at Pagak still hoped to conquer Juba and run up their flag. So acrimonious were the deliberations that Taban opted to move about the conference grounds surrounded by bodyguards after the notorious commander Peter Gadet threatened to kill him.

Riek weathered each of the stormy conferences, maintaining both his position and tacit support for a negotiated end to the war. But the rebel powwows reflected deep internal differences. For Riek, negotiating within his own camp would continue to be at least as difficult as any negotiations with the government, and his survival was no sure thing.

Riek, like Salva, suffered physically from the immense pressure. The toll was evident in both men's appearances, in their body language, and in the medical attention they sought. (Salva more than once traveled abroad for medical treatment, while Riek underwent eye surgeries and battled a ballooning waistline.) Though neither man experienced the physical and emotional suffering his decisions had forced upon ordinary citizens, it was remarkable nonetheless that neither died while at the center of this highly personalized war.

⁘

Salva and Riek finally met for face-to-face talks in March 2015. Their agenda: how to share power, how to structure a new government, and how to organize their security forces. Locked in a room in a cavernous

Addis Ababa event hall, the adversaries talked while negotiators, diplomats, mediators, and journalists paced outside. It had become clear that only these two men were empowered to strike a deal, and yet paradoxically neither man could afford to compromise. When the doors opened and the two men emerged with nothing to show, the IGAD mediators knew the game was up. Strained for more than a year, the peace process had bent to a breaking point.

In an unusually frank memo to the leaders of IGAD, Seyoum wrote of agreements dishonored, deadlines missed, and of two men who were "prisoners to their own constituencies." He lamented the South Sudanese negotiators' tendency to "assign blame to everyone but themselves," and their "wanton disregard for the humanitarian disaster they have brought on their compatriots." Many of the delegates at the negotiating table in Addis Ababa were people "whose interests— assets, families, residences" were not bound to South Sudan. And if they failed in negotiations, Seyoum wrote, they had the luxury to simply "pursue their lives elsewhere."

Seyoum's scathing memo did not spare self-criticism, either. IGAD, he admitted, was in a state of "paralysis." Salva's and Riek's factions could see that the competing interests, empty threats, and contradictory signals sent by Kenya, Uganda, Ethiopia, and Sudan meant that they did not have to deal. They had "called IGAD's bluff."

The normally even-keeled Ethiopian prime minister, Hailemariam, was as frustrated as I had ever seen him. After thinking seriously about declaring the peace talks dead, he gathered his composure and instead responded by issuing a public "Message to the People of South Sudan."

"I regret to inform you that the talks did not produce the necessary breakthrough," the message read. "The consequences of inaction are the continued suffering of you, the people of South Sudan, and the prolonging of a senseless war in your country. This is unacceptable, both morally and politically." He apologized on behalf of the region and asked them not to lose hope. "My dear brothers and sisters... Leadership is never easy," he acknowledged, before hinting that Salva and Riek had no choice but to overcome the "individuals on both sides who continue to beat the drums of war." Continuing the conflict, he said, was "an abdication of the most sacred duty leaders have to you, their people: to deliver peace, prosperity, and stability."

⁂

Days later, in Washington, White House officials announced that President Obama would undertake his fourth and final visit to Africa in July. Stops would include Ethiopia and Kenya, his father's home-land. The visit presented an opportunity to harness the power of the American presidency to help end the war. After eighteen frustrating months of a disorganized and all-but-compromised regional peace process, many believed it time for the U.S.—widely seen as responsible for helping birth the country—to assert greater diplomatic leadership. "Plan B"—the idea of moving peace talks to American soil—had not come to fruition, but now the administration had another opportunity to shake up the status quo.

Frustration with the two sides was widespread, and the hyper-personalization of the conflict had reached a zenith. Neither South Sudanese leader had been able to lift his country out of the mess they had together created, while those Southerners ready to discuss creative solutions had been sidelined. And so Washington's tone toward the belligerents continued to harden, especially toward the government.

In early March, we penned a statement for Secretary Kerry that gar-nered considerable attention in Juba. "Legitimacy is not a presumed right of any government," it read. "It is conferred by the people, and it is sustained only by demonstrating leadership to protect and serve all citizens—responsibilities the government has neglected." Susan Rice underscored the tough messaging in July, as plans for the Obama trip were finalized: "Over the past 19 months, the government has abdicated its responsibilities, failed to protect its citizens, and squan-dered its legitimacy." The days of unflinching American support for the men in Juba were history.

Meanwhile the wheels churned in Washington; how might Presi-dent Obama reinvigorate the ailing process and catalyze meaningful progress? Drawing lessons from other post-conflict states, and a range of South Sudanese actors, all options were on the table. Experts, diplomats, and Southern Sudanese were then discussing a range of alternative governance models, each involving more sweeping changes than the power-sharing option already on the table: a caretaker government made up of technocrats, an ethnically diverse "council of the wise," even a pseudo-protectorate under UN or AU administration. Each imagined a political future without Salva and Riek.

After all, anyone paying attention was asking the same questions: could a power-sharing partnership between these two lightning rods realistically usher in a meaningful transition, or would it simply set the table for a repeat? Could they be encouraged or forced to step aside? It was an option that more than a few South Sudanese had urged both IGAD and the Americans to consider. But it required careful examination. Would their departure allow for a more stable future, or simply create a vacuum leading to further disintegration? Could the South Sudanese agree on successors, or would hardliners fill the void? And even if the notion was broadly supported by Southern Sudanese, how would the two strongmen be forced out?

The questions were not unique to South Sudan, and carried wider meaning in a geopolitical era that had been shaped by the messy consequences of regime change. America's standing in the world had been badly tarnished on account of its debacle in Iraq, and Barack Obama had been elected on a promise to walk back his predecessor's over-reach. He was skeptical of America's capacity to remake states, valued close consideration of unintended consequences, and was averse to the kinds of ideology and fervor that had gotten the United States in so deep with South Sudan in the first place.

An outright demand for Salva's and Riek's departure could expose President Obama to all-too-familiar risks. In response to the Syrian civil war in 2011, the world watched as Obama announced that it was time for President Bashar al-Assad to go. But a defiant Assad had survived, bruising American credibility on the global stage and rendering the episode a major White House foreign policy misfire. Would the unique circumstances of the South Sudanese context, including America's undisputed role as its chief patron, make such a pronouncement different in these circumstances? Would Washington invest the capital to make it stick, and could it?

Syria wasn't the only recent memory for the Obama White House to consider. In 2011, Obama had green-lit a military intervention in Libya that toppled long-time President Muammar Qaddafi and ultimately led to his bloody demise. The action had arguably saved thousands of civilian lives in imminent danger, and was for Obama, "the right thing to do." But when the ensuing chaos plunged Libya into sectarian war, Obama called "failing to plan for the day after" the "worst mistake" of his presidency.

The viability of any bold move from President Obama on South Sudan would depend on regional support and burden-sharing. But even then there could be no guarantees.

POTUS agreed to host a summit of regional heads of state during his stop in Addis Ababa. Its aims were two. One, confront the elephant in the room: regional divisions were poisoning the peace process and possibly preventing a deal. Two, bring visibility to the flagging process and create some new momentum. South Sudan's warring parties would not be invited. Though there was no intent to decide their country's future without them, surely a meeting from which they were excluded would prompt some anxiety and send a clear signal of American displeasure with all sides.

In the early afternoon hours of July 27, heads of state began arriving at the Sheraton Hotel, where a ballroom had been arranged to host a sort of Knights-of-East-Africa Round Table. Dozens of security types, handlers, and advisers filtered in on red carpets through the wood-paneled corridor, then one-by-one, President Kenyatta, Prime Minister Hailemariam, African Union Chairperson Dlamini-Zuma, and Sudanese Foreign Minister Ibrahim Ghandour. In characteristic fashion, President Museveni of Uganda arrived last—a subtle reminder of the elder statesman's seniority.

Museveni then delayed the meeting further by asking President Kenyatta to join him outside, and the two men retreated 50 paces back down the corridor to an anteroom. White House protocol staff, waiting to cue Obama and unaccustomed to "Africa time," looked as though they might tear their hair out. Though the Kenyan and Ugandan presidents were out of earshot, Museveni seemed to be informing his "younger brother" of his desired outcome for the meeting that was about to begin.

When all the presidents had settled in their seats, Obama opened proceedings, flanked by National Security Adviser Susan Rice and Special Envoy Booth. Looking across the white tablecloth and a centerpiece of red and pink roses, Obama thanked each party for their contributions to date and framed his objective for the meeting. "As a consequence of this discussion, our hope is that we can actually bring about the kind of peace that the people of South Sudan so desperately need." Then he got down to business.

There would be no peace in South Sudan, he suggested, until the region overcame its divisions and agreed on a common approach. Hinting at the partisan engagement of both Kampala and Khartoum, he challenged the IGAD leaders to instead use their respective influence to end the senseless war. Obama then turned attention to South Sudan's belligerents, to concrete measures that might alter their calculations, and to the mediators' most recent deadline for a peace deal—August 17. If yet another deadline came and went, things would have to change. And to this end, Obama signaled his readiness to back a political transition without Salva and Riek. He was prepared to isolate the two men, if necessary, but such a decision would require a united front from those now sitting around the table.

Hailemariam notionally endorsed the idea, but the other presidents waffled, offering uncertain degrees of support and hesitation. Though unanimity was not in the cards, the American president's appeal was not in vain. Not only did it send a clear signal to those in the room, but the message would also find its way back to the camps of Salva and Riek.

Museveni was, unsurprisingly, the least constructive participant, frustrating those who were tired of his eccentricities and his partisan intervention in South Sudan. Seeking to curtail the discussion and maintain his influence over the situation, M7 suggested that rather than air their dirty laundry in front of the Americans, the regional leaders should convene once more on their own to iron out their differences and agree a way forward. Obama agreed but insisted that they not leave the process open-ended. And so the leaders announced that they expected the parties to finalize a peace deal in three weeks' time, and that UNSC action, including punitive measures, would ensue if the deadline was missed.

The following day Obama delivered a historic speech at the impressive new headquarters of the African Union, the first by an American president, and a son of Africa no less. He addressed broad themes and strategic priorities in Africa, but reserved special mention for South Sudan. "I was there," he lamented of 2011, "when we held up South Sudan as the *promise* of a new beginning." Looking out over the stadium-like auditorium—three tiers packed with African leaders and diplomats—he then turned to the present. "Neither Mr. Kiir nor Mr. Machar have shown any interest in sparing their people from this suffering or in reaching a political solution." Given the urgency of the situation, he announced his and IGAD's affirmation of the August 17 deadline for a peace deal. If the two men failed, he added, "I believe the international community must raise the costs of their intransigence."

For nearly two years a peace process had tacked one direction and then another, sometimes losing speed and simply drifting in the wind. Now, the man who had helped deliver the country's independence had put its two most powerful men on notice. External threats had thus far failed to move the warring parties or its leaders, but Obama's intervention would prove harder to ignore. An American president had come to Africa and signaled his readiness to support a political rebirth that did not include them.

—

Soon after the summit, Seyoum delivered a draft comprehensive peace plan to Salva, Riek, and the other South Sudanese delegates for their review. The 72-page document, again titled "Agreement for the Resolution of the Conflict in South Sudan," drew upon two years of negotiations and inserted connective tissue where talks had thus far stalled. The plan set forth a new government under which Salva and Riek would share power: Salva would get 53 percent of government seats, Riek the vice presidency and 33 percent of seats. The remainder would be divided among the SPLM former detainees and other political parties. The deal codified a permanent ceasefire, economic reforms, and a new constitutional process, while mandating both a truth-telling commission and a court to investigate war crimes and try those responsible—including Salva and Riek.

Despite the deal's comprehensive nature, we had serious reservations about it. It was based in part on a draft deal we had assembled for "Plan B," but with some fundamental differences: it remained too narrow a governing arrangement and lacked a strong enough oversight mechanism to ensure implementation. After one final and problematic intervention from President Museveni, it was also too ambiguous on matters of security and de-mobilization. But it was too late to make wholesale changes. And despite notable flaws, the deal outlined a plan to end the fighting, frame a political transition, and initiate critical reforms. It was leadership, and the two sides' willingness to make peace, that would make or break any agreement.

The situation presented a classic policy dilemma—a choice between imperfect options. It was also a reflection of the limits of Washington's reach. With some skittish about "owning" the process, the U.S. had decided against asserting control of the peace process at an earlier juncture. Unless it was now willing to run roughshod over the region and commit to a greater political, economic—and maybe military—investment in re-making South Sudan, its only choice was to support the solution tabled by the country's African neighbors. The United States' boldest gesture to date—Obama's proposal for Salva and Riek to step aside—had failed to garner regional support. And so Washington joined the Europeans, the Chinese, and African states in urging the parties to commit to the deal now on the table.

Over the ensuing three weeks, more attention would be paid to South Sudan than at any time since the war's beginning. As Obama's deadline approached, it became clear that such an opportunity would not come again. Juba and regional capitals were abuzz with telephone calls, backchannel discussions, and round-the-clock shuttle diplomacy, all aimed at bridging gaps and delivering by August 17.

A last-ditch summit of regional presidents was organized for deadline day, ideally to witness the end of the process. As the clock ticked, diplomats scrambled to help the mediators plug holes, incorporate demands from IGAD states, and broker final compromises. While the action remained with the region, Obama's intervention had helped catalyze one final push toward a settlement.

High drama unfolded in both Salva's and Riek's camps. As the prospect of a deal loomed, each side endured incredible strain on account of internal divisions. And just a week before deadline day, the cleavages in the opposition ranks finally gave way. "We denounce and disown Dr. Riek Machar," read an August 10 missive from Peter Gadet and a group of disgruntled Nuer commanders. Both Salva and Riek had become "symbols of hate," they said. Riek was no longer their leader, they announced, and any peace deal he signed would be refused.

Riek dismissed the mutineers, and an emergency dialogue between him and frustrated Nuer elders failed to patch things up. Riek still maintained control of the majority of the movement, but the government smelled blood. They dispatched operatives on secret missions to solicit rebel commanders with suitcases of cash and promises of positions. If they could precipitate the collapse of Riek's rebellion, there would be no reason to sign a deal, and no opponent with whom to share power.

As plans for the 17th were finalized, another rebel domino fell. Gabriel Changson announced another round of defections and the formation of his own anti-government faction. Changson and his fellow departed understood the gravity of the decision: leaving could undermine the Nuer community as a whole, and it might not yield them a better outcome. But this peace deal, he believed, would not better the lot of the Nuer masses.

Changson and I spoke by phone, and in a characteristically impassioned tenor, he argued that he could not countenance an agreement that served Riek's personal ambitions but failed to heed fundamental Nuer grievances, especially a deal that vested so much power back in the old SPLM guard. Changson's departure turned up the heat further, and government hardliners flocked to the media to ponder, sarcastically, why the president should even show up on deadline day: "With whom are we going to negotiate?" Riek was weakened by the fissures, but as on so many occasions over the years, he survived. At least for the moment.

The acrimony in Salva's house, meanwhile, was no less vicious. As the president prepared to travel to Addis Ababa on deadline day, those in his cabinet most threatened by compromise pulled out all the stops. They waged a campaign of fear, threats, and misinformation in an attempt to ward off a deal. During one cabinet meeting, a participant reported, hardliners had "whipped up a frenzy of resistance, making it impossible for anyone to speak in favor of peace." One minister argued that Salva would be "taken hostage" if he went to Ethiopia—an elaborate plot he claimed was supported by Washington. Another manufactured a report that the U.S. Marines were "preparing to invade" South Sudan. Secretary of State John Kerry was among those who attempted to reach Salva and offer encouragement, but the president's office was refusing telephone calls.

The politicians hoping to dissuade the president from even boarding a plane for Addis Ababa were bolstered when they learned that army chief Paul Malong had weighed in: "If Salva goes to Addis, he should not plan on returning." The president's office floated a test balloon on August 15, suggesting his team would participate but that he would not show. But the half-measure was met with a firm response: a no-show would trigger a move for international sanctions against his government. The following day, as speculation mounted about deliberations inside Salva's government, foreign diplomats placed spotters at the airport to report on the verdict. Would he fly or not?

Salva's convoy eventually arrived on the tarmac. The president ascended his plane's steps, juggling opposing pressures from the region, the international community, and two groups at home: the hawks in his cabinet, and a new constituency now whispering in his ear—those who wanted Salva to sign the deal. To whom the accidental president would listen was anyone's guess.

In a secluded ante room at the Addis Ababa conference hall, Kenyatta, Hailemariam, Museveni, and Bashir sat waiting for Salva to arrive. The room was quiet, and the air stale. The buzz of fluorescent ceiling lights seemed deafening. It was the eve of deadline day, and the men were eager to be done with South Sudan's disaster.

When Salva arrived, they walked him through the elements of the deal, and encouraged him to sign. The president nodded and signaled his readiness, noting casually that he would run the decision by his cabinet and return for signature tomorrow. Riek waited in a similar ante room in another wing of the hall, surrounded by a dozen advisers. He had already hinted at his intent to sign, recognizing that it was the best—maybe the only—option that remained available to him.

The following morning, Salva returned to the venue for the much-awaited summit and signing ceremony. Inside the main hall, South Sudanese delegates and buoyant foreign diplomats chirped with rare optimism as they sensed the end of a grueling 20-month saga. But upon convening once more in the ante room, the regional heads of state learned that Salva, ever the prevaricator, had backtracked overnight.

Seyoum walked out of the backroom discussion, his fatigue and disbelief combining to yield a moment of visible detachment. "This Salva Kiir," he said with a blank expression, pacing back and forth, "This Salva Kiir is not a person in a position to make a decision." The words had just come out, a kind of reflexive verbalization of frustrated emotions rather than a conscious statement. But they had captured one of the fundamental challenges at the heart of the entire peace process. The hardliners had gotten to Salva, again. And true to form, he had agreed with the last person in the room.

Several hours of cajoling ensued, in which the IGAD heads—now beside themselves—were finally united in their approach. Even Salva's old enemy, Sudan's President Bashir, spoke encouragingly about leadership in overcoming domestic opposition. But Salva was unmoved. Surrounded by his top negotiators and the kind of mobile human cocoon spun only around presidents and A-list celebrities, Salva exited the wall of glass doors at the conference center's entrance, climbed into his black SUV, and sped away, reportedly en route to the airport. It seemed that the peace plan, copies of which had been printed just hours before, would remain an unsigned draft, a historical footnote to what might have been.

Presidents Bashir and Museveni left the country, while Kenyatta and Hailemariam remained, trying to overcome the impasse. They reached Salva before he left the country, and coaxed him back to the venue once more. The dramatic optics of his return offered one of the most shocking images of the entire peace process—a physical manifestation of the larger challenge he confronted.

As Salva's armored black SUV pulled up to the same spot from whence it had only recently departed, a throng of government supporters flocked to the vehicle. Aides opened the president's rear passenger door, in a panic about what their capitulator-in-chief might agree to once back inside. Upon disembarking, several senior members of the government delegation tried to physically block their president from re-entering. A vigorous exchange ensued outside the car door, as the cocoon rocked back and forth between the vehicle and the entryway, its energy mimicking the passion of the conversation at its core.

Government ministers—literally blocking Salva's path to the entry—implored the president not to re-engage but to proceed instead to the airport. Inside the wall of glass doors, mouths hung wide open. A handful of stunned onlookers stood stone still, barely able to grasp the spectacle unfolding before their eyes.

The president would prevail, but he was visibly shaken by the intensity of the bizarre moment. His last-chance exchange with Hailemariam and Kenyatta would be brief and futile, however, and he would depart again in short order having made no progress.

Ninety minutes of chaos ensued, as heads of state, mediators, diplomats, negotiators, and aides zig-zagged about the corridors, trying to salvage deadline day or, in many cases, just to find out what the hell was going on. With no clear pecking order and no clear plan, Kenyan and Ethiopian ministers, mediators, and support staff rushed to and fro, pursuing competing orders or looking for someone who could provide authoritative ones. Racing in and out of ante rooms, one mediator proposed a solution, while another hatched a different plan in the next room. At one point, a visibly irritated Kenyatta emerged from still another room, eyes bulging, and shouted at his staff to get him a copy of the agreement. Frustrated and strung out, Hailemariam once again contemplated announcing the end of the peace process.

The remainder of the diplomatic corps sat buttoned-up in the main hall, awaiting a signing ceremony and unaware of the mayhem in the adjacent corridor. When they were alerted that Nhial Deng, the government's lead negotiator, was proposing half-measures to avoid international opprobrium, the diplomats rushed across the hall and into the corridor. They urged Seyoum and Sumbeiywo not to fold again. "You cannot give the government another easy out."

Special Envoy Booth and I urged the mediators to proceed with the signing ceremony—let all the other parties and witnesses, who were already assembled in the main hall, sign the document and publicly isolate the government. Doing so would leave no doubt that Salva's government was the obstructing party. As this plan was being choreographed, an IGAD staffer burst in to the room to announce that Hailemariam and Kenyatta had devised their own plan and were making their way to the stage for a signing ceremony.

We hurried back into the main hall, where murmurs and exaggerated glances indicated widespread confusion. Copies of the agreement were delivered to those sitting on stage; Riek Machar signed for the rebels, and Pagan Amum for the eleven former detainees, followed by other stakeholders, all amid outbursts of excitement, tears, and ululations. Some led impromptu remonstrations against the government—the lone holdout—whose delegates looked on uncomfortably from the front row.

Having engineered this public signal, the pressure was now on Salva and his men. But President Kenyatta announced—to the dismay of most everyone in the room—that Salva's government would be afforded 15 additional days to return to Juba, consult internally, and then sign the document. More stunned glances. "Why?!" someone shouted, one of numerous objections from the crowd. No one knew what exactly Kenyatta meant: Why more time? And was the agreement "closed," or were they suggesting the government would be allowed to negotiate further changes? The scene was so confused that contradictory media reports materialized online, filed by journalists sitting elbow-to-elbow in the same auditorium.

⁂

Salva returned to Juba to face his toughest sell yet. As soon as he landed back home, doves in his government pleaded that it was time for peace, while hawks drummed up another round of virulent antagonism.

In New York, U.S. diplomats circulated a draft resolution to members of the UN Security Council. It was time to follow through on President Obama's pledge to "raise the cost of intransigence." Many old allies—in South Sudan, in the region, and in the West—had tried repeatedly to help Salva correct course, but when that proved futile, they resorted to pressure. The draft UN resolution authorized an arms embargo against South Sudan and sanctions against government spoilers if the new fifteen-day deadline was not met. Rumors swirled that Salva and his top ministers were named on a secret sanctions list accompanying the resolution. After months of empty warnings and toothless ultimatums, the move surprised some in Juba. It appeared they were now faced with a credible threat.

The new U.S. Ambassador to South Sudan, Molly Phee, had taken up her post in Juba just a month earlier. It was a baptism of fire, and included a front row seat to the extraordinary tumult inside Salva's government. She had a series of one-on-one conversations with him during the period, during which his increasing paranoia was also on display. "The guy was hysterical about the idea that we favored Riek," she recalled.

"You know Mr. President, I've heard a lot of speculation about U.S. policy," she'd said to him, "and I thought I might discuss the rumors with you and offer you the truth." Phee dispensed with wild stories about U.S. ground forces invading Juba to remove him and install Riek. She attempted to dissuade him of such outlandish notions, reassuring him that she was there to work with him, and encouraging him to sign the deal. "I listen to Obama, and he says no boots on the ground, and I believe that," Salva had replied. "But he will use a drone to get me."

Following nine days of government debate, Ambassador Phee suddenly received an invitation from the office of the president. A signing ceremony would be convened in Juba the following morning, it announced—August 26, at 10am. Marked "VERY URGENT," the invite noted that regional heads of state would be joining for the event, where the government "is expected to sign [the] proposed agreement."

Opponents had been lobbying against the deal and mobilizing public opinion for days, including making plans for a mass rally to oppose what they labeled the international community's "conspiracy to re-colonize South Sudan." Government insiders would relay details of the "vicious fight" that unfolded in the final 36 hours, but on the morning of the ceremony, word on the street was that Salva had come down on the side of signature. The leaders of Ethiopia, Kenya, and Uganda arrived in Juba and made their way to the long, white, rectangular tent known as Freedom Hall.

When 10am rolled around, there was no sign of Salva. Inside the hall, Phee sat waiting with government ministers, foreign diplomats, journalists, and invited citizens. It was hot. Fans and air conditioning units hummed, but struggled to keep up. An hour had passed when Ambassador Phee received a call from a frantic government minister. "The hawks" are in overdrive, the harried caller told her. "Everything is falling apart." General Paul Malong and others had leaned on the president into the wee hours of the morning, once again talking him out of signature. By sunrise, word had spread, and doves from the pro-peace camp had rushed to the palace to salvage the deal.

Five tense hours of tug-of-war ensued. Phee paced in the back of the cavernous tent, dialing government insiders and regional officials on her cell phone, hoping their presidents might extract Salva from the morass. His vacillation, Phee said, represented "exactly what was happening more broadly in the government. It's paralyzed... good guys on one side, tired of this fight, and on the other side, those fighting to hang on to their position and keep feeding at the trough."

Finally, at 4:00pm, Salva's motorcade arrived at Freedom Hall, where the packed house had been uncomfortably passing the hours. Salva entered and took the chair center stage, framed by a backdrop draped in red, green, blue, black, and yellow. Flanking him left and right were the regional heads of state, annoyed that they had surrendered an entire day but glad that the finish line was now (hopefully) in sight.

Riek remained in Addis Ababa, but his spotters in Juba sat with cell phones in hand, their batteries fully charged, ready to relay the news from Freedom Hall. As the ceremony commenced, everyone—maybe including Salva himself—wondered whether he would make use of the ceremonial pen that lay before him, or announce a rejection of the deal.

Nearly one million refugees had fled the country, thousands of lives had been lost, and South Sudan's communities were more polarized than at any point in their turbulent history. Nyakueth's children had fallen ill from the dreadful conditions inside the UN protection camp, and her husband was dead. Simon remained there too; he hadn't seen his mother in more than two years. Ayen remained out of work and her family, still squatting on Juba's west side after "coming home" from Sudan, were being harassed by police officers who had not been paid in months. Their fate, and that of their young country, boiled down to Salva and this one moment.

Salva took to the podium. "We have only the option of an imposed peace, or the option of a continued war," he began, reading from prepared remarks. His delivery was characteristically slow, and for some time, many in the crowd couldn't discern whether he was announcing his acceptance of the deal or not.

Gradually, it became clear he would sign the deal, and he eventually asked the regional leaders seated on stage to support its implementation. But, he qualified, "We have our deep and indeed serious reservations," and then began outlining a specific list of qualifications. Diplomats in the crowd turned to one another and murmured, trying to make sense of the bizarre twist. Salva's government would sign the deal, it seemed, but only with a series of detailed objections attached.

With a faction of his government refusing to capitulate, Salva had conceded to at least including their reservations. It was a strange maneuver, as the addendum paradoxically demanded that portions of the agreement Salva was about to officially endorse should later be deleted or revamped. Once international attention waned, antagonists might use this loophole simply to ignore parts of the agreement.

When Salva finished, government aides then asked regional leaders to endorse the reservations. They refused, and hardliner Makwei—the presumed author of the "reservations"—stormed out of the hall. "He just stood up abruptly and strode out the back," Ambassador Phee recalled, making a show of his contempt. "In our country, walking out on your president, you would be fired." Given the reservations' potential to undermine the shaky peace, Susan Rice would later issue a statement reinforcing the regional consensus, signaling that the United States did "not recognize any reservations or addendums to the agreement."

The region's presidents then rose to confront the mixed feelings in the room, and to signal unconditional support for the peace plan. "You cannot live in the past," President Kenyatta told the crowd, his words intended for government hardliners. "I know it is a difficult time for you," he said, but the desire for the "perfect" agreement could not be the enemy of an overdue peace. Museveni took to the podium next. Ever enigmatic, he cited former U.S. General Omar Bradley, calling South Sudan's conflict "the wrong war at the wrong time in the wrong place." After characteristic meandering, he concluded, "Sign it. Make peace. And we will support you."

At nearly 5:00pm, the heads of state—looking conspicuously drained—stood behind Salva as he took the pen and opened the document. They formed a half circle around him, as if to block out any more interference. Salva signed each page of the agreement and—finally—it was done.

The mood on stage lightened, as congratulations and laughs of exasperated relief were exchanged. Implementation would be a battle all its own, and the disquiet on both sides was hard to ignore. But now, it seemed, there was a blueprint to end the war. The peace process was finally complete.

22

LOVE LOST

"You can become close to someone but still be a tough friend . . . we were never a tough friend."
—Longtime American supporter of the SPLM

JUBA / WASHINGTON, JUNE 2016

Across the vast, lazy waterway moving right to left before us, the trees and thick green grasses on the opposite bank are drenched in a golden hue. Until an hour ago, the harsh white light of the afternoon sun had washed out the scene before us, robbing the set and its characters of nuance and detail and depth. But as the shadows of the mango trees drooping over us grow longer, the view from the riverside patio comes into sharper relief. Light and shadow work in tandem, revealing each thoughtful stroke a man in a wooden canoe makes with his paddle. In the shallows farther downriver, lanky figures soap themselves with routine movement, others kneel over wash basins.

It's that time of day when afternoon subtly becomes late afternoon, and the temperature outside becomes bearable enough to sit and talk without constantly wiping sweat from one's forehead. Two green bottles of beer clink together as a waitress moves them from her tray to our table with one hand. She pops off the caps, and Alier (*AH-LEE-ehr*) takes a swig. Exhaling a sigh of quenched relief, Alier looks across at me and says, "Let me cast."

The slightly awkward man in the short-sleeved, checkered shirt stands up, grabs his fishing rod, and sends his baited hook careening out into the yellow light, his head following its flight path until it plops unheard into the dark currents below. This is Alier's favorite fishing spot, and in years past we met here several times to talk. Warm, engaging, and unattached to any particular political agenda, he's always been a thoughtful conversant. Alier is a Dinka and a mid-level government bureaucrat; he is competent and plugged in, yet would always opt for an afternoon fishing over politics if you made him choose.

But things are different now. South Sudan is polarized, the war having driven even the most moderate and amiable citizens toward those poles. Per the terms of the August 2015 peace agreement, Riek Machar has recently returned to take up his post as vice president, accompanied by his negotiators and an agreed number of forces. Tensions are high, and the two sides—still hot under the collar—are feeling each other out. And so just fifteen minutes into our conversation, when an unfamiliar tone emerges, it's hard to believe the man sitting across the table is the same Alier I've known for years.

Like so many others in this war, he suggests that blame rests almost wholly with the other side. He denies or minimizes the actions of his government while suggesting the war, the destruction of towns, and the indiscriminate killings were all "the work of the rebels." I can hardly believe my ears when he suggests the massacre of Nuer civilians in Juba was in fact something of an elaborate ruse, undertaken by Nuer soldiers, and then "blamed on the government."

I flash Alier a conspicuous frown. "It's hard for me to comprehend that there could be such an intense war... all the killing, all the violence... that it could take place on just one side," I say. But Alier is undeterred.

He gets up to check his fishing pole, and I use the opportunity to turn our conversation to the now-completed peace process and the wider international efforts to help stop the war. Satisfied with the location of his bait, he collapses back into his chair. "Clearly there was a conspiracy," he says, echoing the besieged paranoia that has infected his government. "It was obvious from the beginning." The U.S., the UN, and regional countries, he explains, were working with the rebels to topple Salva and his government. "They would rather do business with Riek than with Salva," he says, regurgitating one of the many catchphrases that has taken root with those who want to point the finger at the international community.

The "mastermind of the whole thing," Alier says obliquely, was responsible for the rejection of the *coup d'état* allegations, and for creating a peace process that was deliberately stacked against his government. The mastermind to whom he is referring is the U.S. government. Though he has so far spoken in euphemisms, it becomes increasingly clear that Alier believes Washington is to blame for—well—everything.

I ask about the region's role in driving the peace talks and pressuring his government to make peace. "He who pays the piper calls the tune," Alier responds, suggesting that the Ethiopians, Kenyans, and Ugandans were simply doing as America told them. "Obama was using these people to serve his agenda." Even when it comes to Riek's mobilization of the Nuer fighters, he suggests a shadowy foreign hand. "The idea of [using] ethnicity to mobilize was not originally from the rebels either," he says, finally casting a look in my direction.

As Alier's rationalizations get more and more fantastical, I fight the urge to tell my trusted old contact just how ridiculous it all sounds. I try what I hope is a more respectful tack, asking questions that expose holes in his elaborate tale, and introducing information corroborated by independent sources. But I also refrain from fully attempting to change his mind, because I want to understand this point of view, one that permeates his government right up to its highest echelons. Alier is surely shading his remarks in talking to a foreigner—an American and former U.S. diplomat no less—but he is not out to spin me. Like so many of his government colleagues, he has come to believe the core elements of the narrative he's just presented.

Dueling narratives emerged during the first months of the conflict and solidified over the course of the war. By 2016, in talking to either side, one is confronted with solid granite. Both sides have regurgitated the narratives, passing them up and down their respective ranks, often times resulting in common language and slogans that surface in discussion after discussion, argument after argument. But neither that phenomenon, nor the fixation with America, is unique to Alier and his government.

⸻

"America should have done better. America should not have made us go back to a government under Salva Kiir," says Vanang, with no reservations or qualifications. It's one day after my conversation with Alier. With a familiar forthrightness I've grown to appreciate among many South Sudanese, the man now unabashedly sharing his political views wandered over to my table moments ago and struck up a conversation. I'm the only *khawaja* sitting on the back patio of this Juba hotel, my skin color a novelty that invites above-average interest. Vanang introduces himself, and I invite him to pull up another plastic chair. He has a narrow face and a goatee, and wears jeans, a T-shirt, and plastic sandals. I order us each a bottle of water.

When he finds out who I am and that I was involved in the peace process, he jumps immediately into insider politics. Vanang is a member of Riek's rebel opposition, a journalist by trade, and is university educated—a fact that distinguishes him from probably 99 percent of the men fighting the war. As with Alier, he pursues a well-worn narrative of complaints which focus not on homegrown issues or solutions, but on why Washington and the wider international community are to blame for the war. Where Alier told me yesterday that the U.S. masterminded a *coup d'état*, Vanang believes precisely the opposite. The Americans, he says, bankrolled the Ugandan intervention against his rebels and propped up Salva's government.

"America should have let us go all the way to Juba," he says, referring to the January 2014 rebel assault that came within striking distance of the capital. He insists that if Riek and the rebels had displaced Salva and assumed power, "there would have been peace."

"Really?" I ask with obvious skepticism. "I think there could have been yet another massacre." I suggest that, as elsewhere, a cycle of violence would have ensued as each faction traded Juba back and forth, civilians on all sides suffering as the one semi-developed urban center was decimated. He isn't willing to consider this, and leans forward with a pointed finger raised, ready to deploy his rebuttal. "There would have been peace," he repeats, before again blaming America for the current state of affairs.

"Could I ask why you see it as America's place to decide such matters?" I inquire, for the second time. And for a second time, he doesn't entertain the question, instead moving on to suggest the U.S. should have sent in its army to remove Salva. "If it didn't want to send its own troops, it could have done it through the region. America gives the money. So when they say, 'You do this,' it is done."

Here we go again, I think to myself. "I wish, Vanang," I say, disabusing him of such fantasies, and explaining the many constraints on American diplomacy in the region. "Trust me, those of Washington do not wake up and hold a secret meeting each morning to decide the fate of the world."

Also like Alier, my tablemate is convinced that the U.S. must be out to get his country's oil. "Are you familiar with the North Dakota oil boom?" I ask, attempting to puncture his conspiracy theory by hinting at revolutionary changes in the U.S. energy landscape. Vanang avoids the issue, pivoting instead to geopolitics on the continent. "The U.S. is out to counter China."

Each side fingers America for what they perceive as an unjust outcome. Surely this is the case for the world's predominant power in many corners of the world. But it is particularly pronounced in South Sudan, a legacy of America's hugely consequential interventions over the course of nearly three decades. For so long Southern leaders looked to America, to Europe, and to friends in the region to protect SPLM interests and advance the Southern cause. First humanitarian support and political advocacy, then weapons and financial resources, then pressure on Khartoum to end the war, and finally facilitation of the referendum on self-determination and independence. Today, the United States remains on the lips of many South Sudanese; but now they speak of how the Americans have failed them.

The South Sudan peace process and the accord signed in the summer of 2015 drew considerable criticism, and rightly so. The deal left much to be desired. Some criticism was rightly directed at the United States. But many also had inflated perceptions of America's role in what was essentially a regional process, and in its ability to engineer ideal outcomes. Given Washington's leading role in the CPA process a decade earlier, and in midwifing Southern independence, the view was understandable. But things had changed.

President Obama had arrived in office in 2009 amid an economic crisis that had no precedent. That global trauma, one White House adviser said, "had shaken world order to its core, more so than 9/11." The nature of U.S. foreign policy was meanwhile evolving; hard questions about the limits of American reach were revisited as Washington juggled conflicts in Syria, Iraq, Afghanistan, Egypt, Ukraine, and Libya. The tumultuous events of the so-called Arab Spring were not yet in the rearview mirror, a Sunni-Shia cold war in the Middle East was warming fast, and President Obama went all in on a nuclear deal with Iran. A historic opening with Cuba was also in the making, while Russian expansionism kept strategists awake at night. Meanwhile, just as South Sudan began to unravel, the so-called Islamic State (ISIS) burst onto the international stage, casting the "war on terror" in a new light and leaving a surprised administration scrambling to catch up.

President Obama had helped usher through Southern independence during his first term, the culmination of two decades of bipartisan American support. But Obama had neither the kind of historical investment in South Sudan, nor the ideological worldview, that was going to again prompt outsize American involvement. The era when expansive notions of state-building were en vogue was over. This was a president elected in part on his rejection of America's debacle in Iraq, and he was deeply skeptical about Washington's ability to remake foreign countries. So in the wake of the country's civil war, Obama's objectives were characteristically modest. Silencing the guns was one thing, engineering democracy or remaking the state was quite another.

It is not unusual for Washington to be consumed by a full menu of foreign policy challenges, but two other factors served to curtail American involvement. First, the overwhelming docket of global crises was eating up the bandwidth of the officials most historically associated with South Sudan's struggle. National Security Adviser Susan Rice and other longtime backers were now in leading roles in the Obama White House. Though they worked hard to stop the violence and salvage a legacy they had helped script, they were also busy with matters of far greater national security concern, and were not in a position to commit resources and attention commensurate with the past. The Sudanese civil war and North-South tensions had once carried modest strategic implications, as an expanding regional war would have had considerable ripple effects. But a civil war inside South Sudan? Almost none. (This also helps to explain the comparatively meager attention paid to South Sudan during its years of post-independence infancy.)

Second, the cause was no longer a "winner." Washington's darlings in the SPLM had taken their gift-wrapped opportunity and promptly squandered it. This was no longer a righteous battle for freedom and the liberation of an oppressed people; it was—or seemed—a senseless tale of greed, predation, and failure. South Sudan had become a case of damage control, and there wasn't a clear answer for how to fix it. There was simply "less time and political capital invested in its 'remaking,'" admitted one U.S. official. Others in the American coalition, stunned by the failure of a cause they had so fervently backed, opted to fade into the shadows.

The religious and activist communities that had catalyzed America's initial involvement had meanwhile moved on, lending their voices to other humanitarian causes. Aid groups did valiant work in blunting the daily impacts of the war, but with so many desperate crises around the world, it was consistently difficult to drum up support for this kind of man-made disaster.

The American investment in the making of South Sudan was, in some ways, unprecedented. U.S. engagement had historically been a product of the values-based currents of American foreign policy, as opposed to more realist calculations of national security interest. Driven by a handful of policymakers with Africa and human-rights credentials, a wave of interest groups, and a bi-partisan coalition, the cause was a worthy one. Despite failings along the way, these groups had achieved outsize impact in helping end Sudan's war and deliver the South its independence. But by the time the new Republic collapsed, the global environment had changed, its constituencies had moved on, and its champions were now otherwise occupied. The United States would commit billions in humanitarian aid and extend considerable diplomatic efforts to restore peace. But it wasn't again going to move mountains.

Just two weeks after my conversations with Alier and Vanang, a series of violent episodes would symbolize just how fundamentally the relationship between the United States and South Sudan had changed. Not only had the world's newest state faded from America's list of priorities, and relations deteriorated over the course of a brutal war, but what had once seemed an unbreakable bond would all but shatter in July 2016.

After dark on Thursday, July 7, seven American diplomats, most of them thirty-somethings, headed home from a jovial farewell gathering for a colleague at a local restaurant in Juba. The mood on the streets outside, however, was very different. Riek Machar was back in Juba. But tensions between his soldiers and those of Salva's government had been escalating in recent days.

The two armored Toyota SUVs carrying the Americans were stopped by SPLA soldiers at a checkpoint near the president's residence. One soldier knocked on the bulletproof glass window, but the Americans—per normal diplomatic protocol—signaled that they were not to open their doors. Unsatisfied, the soldier grabbed the door handle and attempted to open the door anyway. The embassy driver hit the gas pedal, and the SUV sped away. "My adrenaline went through the roof," recalled one of the Americans. The soldier and his colleagues aimed their weapons and opened fire, unloading a torrent of AK-47 fire on the escaping vehicles. "Shit, it was really scary," the American continued, "I mean, what would have happened if he'd gotten our door open?"

As the vehicles turned and raced toward the embassy, two more groups of soldiers unloaded their weapons on the speeding SUVs. Embassy radios squawked with frenzied chatter between the cars and personnel back at the U.S. compound. A U.S. Marine rapid response team was dispatched and ushered the group back to the embassy. While no one was injured, security personnel were dumbfounded as they saw the vehicles roll in, tattooed with nearly 100 rounds of ammunition.

Furious, U.S. Ambassador Molly Phee took a photo of the bullet-ridden vehicles to President Salva and SPLA generals the following morning and read them the riot act. The incident was neither premeditated nor ordered from on high, but that was no consolation. Some believed it a reflection of the ill-disciplined soldiers over whom Salva had too little control. Others were convinced it reflected the dangerous anti-American sentiment then permeating government circles. Just four days later, a second event would lend credence to this more worrisome explanation.

Riek Machar had returned to the capital in April 2016, but three months later, implementation of the peace deal was lagging. Riek arrived at the presidential compound, as he and Salva were meant to hash out details over how the transitional government would operate. But as they sat inside the palace, a gunfight erupted outside between their respective forces.

Four days of urban fighting followed, in what seemed a particularly painful episode of déjà vu. Hundreds were killed, tens of thousands of civilians again ran to UN bases, and SPLA helicopter gunships circled above the city, firing on Riek's forces.

On July 11, after government forces had flushed Riek's recently returned rebels out of the city, the buoyant soldiers turned their guns on a popular expat compound. Nearly 100 uniformed men poured onto the property after breaching its gate and began beating, taunting, and raping those inside—most of them foreigners. The *Associated Press* later published a detailed account of the four-hour attack, including horrifying accounts from several American survivors. Pointing a Kalashnikov rifle at one female aid worker, one of the assailants offered her an ultimatum. "Either you have sex with me, or we make every man here rape you and then we shoot you in the head."

She wasn't alone. "He kept hitting me with an AK-47," reported another American, after a soldier had forced her into a room. "Open your legs," he'd shouted at her. "I'm going to kill you if you don't open your legs." One local journalist was executed in front of the group, and at least two other aid workers were gang-raped, while a dozen more squeezed into a bathroom and locked the door. They, too, were eventually dragged out.

According to victims' accounts, the soldiers—some of them visibly drunk—appeared to be targeting Americans. Some expressed contempt for foreigners, with a particular focus on the United States, "You messed up this country. You're helping the rebels," they ranted. After beating one American with belts and the butts of their guns, they sent him away with a message: "You tell your embassy how we treated you."

Like the assault on American staffers days earlier, it's unlikely that the brutal attack was sanctioned by South Sudanese authorities. But the soldiers' anti-American attitudes had surely trickled down from above. Their commander-in-chief was refusing to meet the American ambassador or accept phone calls from Washington. His ministers, meanwhile, spouted anti-American rhetoric in public and were aggressive with U.S. officials in private. American Navy SEALS had been seriously wounded in the aborted helicopter rescue mission at the onset of the crisis, and the U.S. Embassy—again on high alert—was now crawling with extra security.

Just five years after independence, when the friendship between the two countries had reached a high-water mark, Americans were now being ruthlessly attacked in the capital city—by a government the United States had helped to create. Shocking administration officials, Congress, and many friends in America, the back-to-back events showed just how badly the relationship had soured. The war itself, the increasingly unfriendly interactions, the government's rhetoric and disregard for American diplomatic appeals had startled, and disappointed, many in Washington. But the targeting of Americans was another story altogether, adding an especially painful sting to those who had so long championed the Southern cause. This was hardly the fairytale ending envisioned in 2011.

"I don't know," said U.S. Ambassador Phee, when asked if July 2016 represented a low point in the relationship between the United States and South Sudan. "There've been so many low points. It is really hard to identify one." Phee had taken up her post only after a once tightly-knit relationship had been ripped nearly to shreds. She had a rare vantage point on the dangers of Washington's romanticized relationship with the SPLM, and an experience unlike that of her predecessors. "It's very hard to preside over the collapse of our bilateral relationship. It's deeply dispiriting given how much we [the United States] put into it. We worked so hard... Now they blame us for everything."

"It was so exciting, and so emotional," Frank Wolf's staffer remembers with a proud smile. "You know, everyone there recognized him." On the day of South Sudan's referendum in January 2011, U.S. Congressman Wolf and two staff members left their offices on Capitol Hill and drove to a polling site in Northern Virginia, one of many set up so that South Sudanese diaspora in America could vote.

Wolf shook hands with dozens of excited voters, some of whom he'd met before, others who had heard his spitfire speeches in Congressional hearings. Six months later, his longtime collaborator Donald Payne would travel to Juba for Independence Day festivities with a sizable American delegation. Though Wolf was unable to make the trip, one can imagine that the culmination of more than two decades of work made for a memorable day.

But before the country's first anniversary, Wolf says, he "started to worry." He didn't take action then, but acknowledges, "That's when the whistle should have been blown."

Across the conference table in his third-floor Virginia office, just across the Potomac River from Washington, the long-time crusader leans back in his chair. We've been talking for an hour on this sticky afternoon in August 2016. As the conversation turns from the historical relationship with South Sudan to the country's unraveling in recent years, the retired Congressman becomes frustrated. "I don't know, I don't know that I can answer that," he mumbles defensively, when I ask if a sentimental attachment to the rebels led American supporters to turn a blind eye to the worrying trends in South Sudan.

After a tense pause, Wolf pivots, as he's done once already, to what seems his main thesis about the unraveling. "I still believe that had [Garang] not died, the situation would be totally different." Wolf had been the first member of Congress to meet John Garang, and was shocked when he heard the news of the rebel leader's 2005 helicopter crash. Wolf is right; things may well have been different had the country's visionary icon survived, but it is not clear how, and it is by no means certain that South Sudan would have escaped its 2013 collapse. The charismatic rebel was a larger-than-life figure to many, but it is too easy a rationalization to use his death to explain away what happened, or to justify America's deep and uncritical attachment to the Southern rebels.

When I ask what hooked him then on the cause of Garang's SPLM, Wolf says without a beat, "The poorness, the suffering... my heart went out to the people of the South." But he then interrupts himself, and changes course in dislocating fashion. Turning the focus to just how bad Khartoum was by comparison, he says, "All the terrorist activity that has taken place in the West? That all really began in Sudan." This is an overstatement, a reflection of a sometimes hyperbolic narrative that SPLM representatives became skilled at peddling when making the rounds among friends in Washington. But amid recent news of further deterioration in Juba—the attacks on American diplomats and aid workers occurred just weeks before our meeting—Wolf's pivot seems an awkward attempt to justify two decades of unflinching support for the men now wreaking havoc in the new state. He's distinguishing the bad in Juba from the even worse in Khartoum.

"Is it possible America's champions got too close to the SPLM," I ask again, "mistaking interests for friendships?" Wolf concedes halfheartedly but changes course again—this time blaming Democrats. He suggests, as he has several times since the war began, that former Bush administration officials should get involved. But, he adds, "I don't think they wanted to hear from a Republican." These redirects seem misplaced, and betray the real frustration—the loss of American influence. Dispatching officials of different political stripes won't regain that influence. "You'll recall that President Bush placed a call to President Salva Kiir in the early days of the crisis," I remind him, when a disinterested Salva cut short the call with his once kindred spirit. Emphasizing the bipartisan nature of Washington's long friendship with South Sudan's leaders, I try once more, but Wolf interrupts me. "You know, bin Laden lived there for a time."

Critical reflection on 25 years of a firmly held policy is not something the veteran congressman is ready to entertain, at least not with me. Wolf wraps up a conversation he is finding increasingly unpalatable, punctuating his move for the door with a last word. "I cared about the people, my initial involvement was with the suffering people." I believe him, but it's hard to know if he's trying to convince me of his right intentions, or himself. I close my notebook, thank him and his staff, and return to the parking lot to wrestle with what I've just heard.

I unlock my car and toss my notebook on the passenger's seat, next to my copy of Wolf's book, *Prisoner of Conscience*. I rest my hands on the steering wheel and stare back at the office building I've just exited. I can't discern if Wolf is a politician simply shirking responsibility for a project gone bad, or if he's an honest do-gooder, disillusioned about having been fed a simple narrative for 30 years that was clean and true and righteous—until it wasn't.

More than one diplomat used the term "fanatic" in describing Wolf's engagement on Sudan. Fanatical maybe, but Wolf is anything but malign. His interest in the issue is genuine, and while his spirited campaigning may bolster his reputation as a moral crusader, it is hardly a career-making endeavor in the world of Washington politics. Given his sometimes simplistic reductionism of the players and their motivations, one wonders whether Wolf's grasp of the situation in Sudan was more superficial than the many letters and resolutions penned in his name suggest. Was his shortcoming that of naiveté? Righteous zeal and hard-charging policy demands but without a comparable level of comprehension?

Success has many fathers, but failure is an orphan. While many in Washington were happy to ride the bandwagon through independence, today, few are interested in engaging or being associated with what appears to many as a failed project. To his credit, Wolf has continued to pursue ideas about how to end the violence in South Sudan. But his effort lacks the gusto of years past; even for Wolf, the idealism seems punctured by a losing prospect.

Ahead of South Sudan's 2011 referendum on self-determination, long-time SPLM supporters inside and outside the Obama administration would become laser-focused on securing Southern independence and a peaceful separation. And their case was justifiable. But firmly in the corner of the "good guys," many wilfully ignored the deeply worrisome trends that had taken root in South Sudan's emergent capital.

"There wasn't a lot of critical thinking," says one U.S. official, reflecting on the contrast between the complexity on the ground in 2011 and the policy environment extant in Washington. "You just sort of knew this was the way it was, and assumed the environment was not going to change. This ridiculous narrative, it was immovable." The die was already cast.

Many SPLM supporters failed to grasp the consequences of adopting their cause with such singularity and zeal. In time, the rebel vanguard became accountable not to the South Sudanese people, but to a constituency of Western supporters apparently willing to back them at any price. Over more than two decades, this uncritical embrace, a simple moral narrative, and a sentimental attachment created a moral hazard.

"We lost objectivity," one repentant champion of the partnership told me in 2016. "You can become close to someone but still be a tough friend... we were never a tough friend."

23

KOANG'S DILEMMA

"The strongest heart is the heart that can forgive . . . It will never stop. Someone, somewhere has to take the toughest decision."

—Koang

WAAT, JUNE 2016

Whoosh... *whoosh-whoosh*. The giant rotor blades of the Ukrainian-built Mi-8 helicopter turn faster and faster overhead, until the whooshing turns into a high-pitched hum. The silver-haired man in the tan jumpsuit hands me a set of noise-canceling headphones. Like the other members of his flight crew, he sports a buzz cut and gold necklace, and his uniform is clean and well-fitted. His movements are nonchalant, but they do not disguise the seriousness and honor with which he does his job. Piloting is a prestigious profession back home in Ukraine, and these guys have been around the block. Flight crews and airframes from the former Soviet Union have been flying all across Africa for decades, a legacy of Moscow's huge spending on military aviation during the Cold War.

The Mi-8 is a military transport helicopter by design. Its rudimentary metal benches and clunky seatbelt buckles are meant to accommodate two dozen soldiers, and its rear cargo bay could hold a small car. But this chopper has been painted white and emblazoned with two giant black letters— "UN" —and its mission in South Sudan includes ferrying civilian passengers and UN cargo. At rest, its rotor blades, spanning 70 feet from end to end, droop nearly halfway to the tarmac. Now they are straight and ripping through the air, creating a strobe light effect inside the cabin. Peering out across the runway through one of its round porthole windows, I see an endless parade of humanitarian planes employed by the UN, the Red Cross, and Western aid groups. The single-prop fixed-wing caravans are likewise a fixture of this part of the world.

I feel the rotor reach top speed, and put on the headset as air rushes through the portholes. The Mi-8 stretches itself upright and lifts gently off the tarmac. The pilot then dips its nose aggressively and thrusts forward and up. Leaving Juba airport behind, we head north, the flying behemoth lifting higher and higher. Fading away are the heat and dust and smells of the street—the sweet stench of rubbish, the frying *mandazi*, the choking vehicle exhaust. Gone too, as we ascend, are the hum of diesel-fueled generators, the honking horns, and the shouting *boda boda* boys.

The bustle and sweat and confines of urban life give way to nature, and to the vast and untouched expanses that blanket this country. Beige and brown and black are replaced by a spectrum of green: emerald, hunter, lime. A giant feathered quill has scripted the River Nile like calligraphy on a boundless green parchment, its waters bending and curving infinitely into the distance. Shining tributaries snake in parallel, illuminated by sunbeams penetrating the cloud cover overhead.

Below there are no more buildings, no settlements, and no roads. Solid earth gives way to marshland. Round pools and oval lakes mirror the sky above, each dotted with islands like ink blots. Connected by more seasonal tributaries, the network of waterways look like an ancient language written into lush carpet. Two large white birds cut a diagonal flight path across the color wheel below. And to our left, the chocolate-colored *jebels* are silhouetted in the afternoon haze.

This ascent never gets old. The two Southerners pressing their foreheads on the windows next to me are likewise transfixed by the awesome beauty below. Also fading away are the messy politics of conflict—the angst and arguments and divisions that have enveloped the capital city behind us. We're humming north along the eastern bank of the river toward Waat, farther and farther from the warped politics of Juba, which are often mistaken to represent the whole of South Sudan.

I've decided to go and visit Koang (*KONG*), a young man I met seven years earlier when we were both in our late twenties. I haven't spoken with him since, and am looking forward to our conversation. Koang has "come of age" in the interim, and I am confident he'll offer a different perspective of where his country has been, and where it is going.

———

The steady whir of the chopper's rotor lulls me nearly to sleep, and I lean my head back against the metal fuselage and close my eyes. I think back to the first time I met Koang Rambeng, in Malakal, the capital of Upper Nile State. It was 2009 and I was doing research on local armed conflicts. He was doing what the most educated and capable youth did—working for a UN agency or international NGO. "He's a diamond in the rough," his UN supervisor had told me, "just go have a chat with him."

Koang and I convened one evening outside a local shack of a restaurant and ordered sodas as the sun set behind a grove of thorn trees. He eased into a discussion about inter-communal violence—the breakdown of traditional authority, the proliferation of weapons, the ways young men thought about their roles in the community. Animating his analysis with angular hand gestures, he placed these issues in a larger context, discussing the kinds of social changes he thought would enable his community to overcome the past and prepare itself for an independent future.

I scribbled in a tattered leather-back notebook as fast as I could. It was so dark I could no longer see Koang sitting in his opposing plastic lawn chair, nor the lined pages of my notebook, but I kept on writing, hoping my notes would be legible in the morning. The conversation was more creative and wide-ranging than any I'd had in recent weeks—most of them with individuals two and three times Koang's age. I lifted my pen only to slap at my bleeding shins, as I was also being devoured by mosquitoes. But so intrigued by my interlocutor, I suppressed both the inclination to move and the recollection that I was taking no malaria medication.

After more sodas and more pages of notes, I asked Koang how he might turn these ideas into political action. "Why not run for county commissioner or a seat in the state legislature?" Wearing a slightly pained smile, he dismissed the notion before I could finish my question. "It's not yet my turn." Two hours of ideas and enthusiasm seemed suddenly blunted by an unimpeachable deference to the so-called "liberation generation." Salva, Riek, and the SPLA commanders who had led the fight against Khartoum, and then secured the peace in 2005, were a venerated class. Many accepted that they were entitled to authority and government perks as payback for "the struggle." But while some liberation-era commanders had made successful transitions to minister, governor, or commissioner, many others had not. They ran their constituencies as militarized personal fiefdoms or simply phoned it in.

The demands of the future meant Southern Sudan couldn't sustain itself simply on the fumes of the past. This deference to a military elite was an understandable legacy, and one that could not be fully appreciated by an outsider. But it was also crippling the country. Wasted were those who had skills but had not been on the front lines, and constrained were a class of new movers and shakers like Koang, whose ideas and entrepreneurship were arguably a better fit for the task ahead. "They're treated like kids," Koang's former supervisor scoffed, describing the dismissive attitude veterans sometimes showed toward promising youth. "Koang, he's the perfect example of both the promise, and the wasted opportunity, of a generation."

Koang is more assertive and self-assured than most, but even he spoke of this deference as an established reality. It was not something open for debate. And so the only recourse was to await generational change, when the aging commanders would die or go of their own choosing. In the coming years, I was fortunate to meet and learn from many such youthful stars, who honored the struggle but whose minds were trained on the next set of challenges. One could imagine this crowd working, debating, and building institutions in these critical formative years, save for these complicated notions of entitlement and debts owed.

Five years after that buggy evening, when I had finished my work as a research analyst and begun work as a U.S. diplomat, I was delighted to learn that Koang had been appointed county commissioner in his native Akobo. Some of his constituents were pleased to see such a young person named to the post, as many commissioners were more than twice Koang's age. I wondered whether subsequent opportunities had thrust the able Koang into this role, or whether he had been playing his cards close to his chest that night, conscious that his odds were best if he didn't advertise his ambitions.

But by 2014, even the most promising and forward-thinking leaders had become embroiled in a divisive war, their communities forced to choose sides. Whether of his own accord, or under pressure from his Akobo County constituents, Koang had thrown his lot in with Riek's rebellion. Shortly thereafter, Salva dismissed him from his commissioner post. Though he had no official role in mid-2016, Koang remained in an informal leadership position in nearby Waat. Huge swathes of Nuer territory remained outside Juba's control, their citizens estranged from a government they did not trust. Koang, appointed by Riek, remained their representative.

Our chopper zeroes in on a small patch of exposed rust-colored earth in an otherwise green expanse. We're approaching Waat. An impromptu welcoming party has materialized in the swirling grasses below, several dozen children eager to see the Ukrainian flying machine make its weekly visit. The three other passengers and I disembark and grab our packs while the rotor spins overhead. It sucks a rush of cool air up and out, seeming to lift us almost off our toes.

The arrivals and the parade of junior hosts form a giant centipede, navigating pools of rainwater and pits of sludgy black mud, with bags and belongings carried overhead. Each foot searches for a tuft of grass that has anchored some resilient earth around it. The girls' dresses and *taubs* whip in the wind as the helicopter lifts off behind us. It is rainy season in Waat, and the temperature is pleasantly bearable, far cooler than in Juba. The sky is two-tone—a faint gray topped by a layer of spearmint blue—and it suggests showers are imminent. I breathe fresh cool air deep into my lungs, and it reaches depths that city air could never achieve.

"I'm here to meet Koang," I say upon arriving at a local NGO compound. "Could you tell me where I might find him?" As in towns across this country, that is all the information required. Everyone knows the leader and where to find him. Proud to undertake such important business, several young men assert that they will take me to him. "My name is Michael," says one, shaking my hand with an air of formality and writing his name for me on a piece of yellow legal paper. He states his role in the community and assures me that he is fit to assume the role of Koang's envoy. I thank him and we set off on foot, the others tagging along.

My escorts aren't alone in affiliating themselves with Koang. It's encouraging to learn how much the people here have come to respect him, just as those back in Akobo. I think of Simon, the young student who ran for his life amid the violence in Juba, and who found his brother lifeless. He too is an Akobo native, and when I mentioned Koang's name during a recent visit with Simon, his face lit up. "You know Koang?" he asked, with the pride of possession.

We pass through mini "compounds" of two, three, and four *tukuls*, their bronze thatch elegant and symmetrically woven. Across a muddy patch and on to a main dirt path, we tread into a sleepy market. Men and women chat, goats and stray dogs pick at discarded rubbish, and children play on the exposed engine block of an overturned yellow two-ton truck, which hasn't fired its pistons in at least a decade. It is one of several vehicle carcasses around Waat, stripped of tires and other usable parts, lying prominently in repose.

Passing us on foot in the other direction are women, twenty-somethings, in eye-catching colors—electric blue, hot pink, and a busy-patterned jade. Each is straight-backed, carrying substantial cargo on her head: bone-colored branches, long brown grasses, and giant, hollowed-out gourds. Coffee mugs dangle from the gourd spouts, ready to nourish hungry travelers with a road-side drink of the warm cow's milk inside.

We turn right, jump a few puddles, and cut through more *tukuls*, where I nod and greet the families in the Nuer language. "*Mah-lay*," I say, and they respond in kind, "*Mahlay mi goa*." Two young girls grinding sorghum stop and cackle like geese at the *khawaja*'s linguistic foibles. We veer around a large compound fenced with branches, and my guide hollers over its gate. A smiling teenager in shorts and T-shirt, with an AK-47 strapped over his shoulder, swings open the gate and welcomes us inside.

Inside is a giant thatched hut, maybe 50 feet in diameter, and two more rotting vehicle carcasses. I greet the group of five men and women sitting beneath the giant cone, while a guard goes into a smaller hut to inform its occupant of my arrival. We make small talk about the weather, as cool drops begin plopping on the hard-packed earth outside.

"Jeck," a voice says from inside the hut. I recognize the pronunciation of my name—close enough—and the gravelly-nasal mix of the voice. "My friend, Jeck," the man says again. Ducking through the *tukul* door and emerging erect is a handsome face atop a large angular frame. Koang is all frame; he has broad shoulders and long arms, and stands six feet eight inches tall. He's got a strong brow and a smile so wide it could span the Nile. He looks like a movie star or famous athlete emerging from the back of a limousine. We slap shoulders and then hands eagerly, in the Sudanese way, and then embrace.

"It's been what, seven years?" I say.

"Yes, long time Jeck," he says, laughing. "We were together then in *Mal-a-kal*," he says, in the speeding way that only locals can pronounce the name of that town. Slapping palms again, he says, "You have been *so* lost"—an expression used widely in South Sudan when you have not seen someone in a long time. "But now you are found."

After Koang has taken care of the day's business, and I have settled my accommodations back at the NGO compound, we reconvene at his temporary home. His mud hut is well-built but not tall enough to stand upright in, and not much wider than my wingspan. Koang sits against the back of the *tukul*, and the light coming through the open doorway projects a perfect shadow on the wall behind him. Outside, women prepare food and hang garments on a clothesline. A child with inquisitive eyes, maybe twelve years old, cares for a younger sibling perched on her hip. Koang's bodyguards sit on the ground with their Kalashnikovs, elbows resting on bent knees, and pass around a yellow jerry can of water. Behind them is a dirt bike caked in dried mud and sporting a sticker: "Purchased by US Agency for International Development."

Koang pours himself Johnny Walker whiskey in a tin cup. He offers me one, but I'm not much of a whiskey fan. Koang didn't imbibe the fashionable whiskey either the last time we met, and it's something that sticks with me throughout my visit. Drinking Johnny Walker is what the "big men" of Juba do. As with flashy accessories and expensive liquors anywhere in the world, it is a symbol of status and power. I can't help thinking that Koang is, at least in part, demonstrating that he too is a figure of authority.

We have a lot to catch up on. We talk about the war, the peace process, and where to go from here. But we also talk as peers about Koang, his own future, and the decisions now making his gut churn.

Koang says he was born "sometime in 1978," in Akobo, about 60 miles east of here. He is the eldest of six children, a position that meant increased familial responsibility when his father was killed in 1993 during Sudan's civil war. After several years being trained as a child soldier in the SPLA's youth wing, Koang was lucky to hook up with a group heading south to a refugee camp in Kenya. He left soldiering behind.

He continued to Nairobi, where he studied law and earned certifications in humanitarian operations and project planning. Along the way, he impressed Southern Sudanese development professionals and international aid workers, and when he returned home, one offered him a job with a United Nations program in Malakal. "I was struck by how mature he was for his age," says the former UN official who snatched him up, "by how articulate and how poised he was. He was something special."

Koang spent six years working for the UN and earning a salary that exceeded most in the country. He also married a young Dinka woman from a prominent local family, with whom he had two children. In 2009, some suggested Koang for Akobo county commissioner—the kind of opportunity that people don't turn down. But having just turned 30, Koang was very young for the job, and he demurred. "Yes, I wanted to be involved in politics at some point, to be part of decision-making, to help in correcting things," he says. But it was not yet his time.

"If you are in a position of power, you are almost a god," Koang says, leaning forward and digressing momentarily on the warped politics of privilege in his country. "You believe you do not have to work hard for yourself, and the people believe that everything is yours." He chafes at the notion, complaining of greed, nepotism, and "a dependency syndrome" that is crippling his country. "If I am in a position of power, you know, I can change that belief."

Koang's uncle was a powerful national minister, and politicians from Juba regularly meddled in local politics. He had the kind of pull to get Koang appointed to the commissioner post, but Koang was of two minds about it, and was probably fortunate to be passed over given the highly politicized jostling that ensued. "I was not yet established financially," Koang says, articulating his more principled concerns. He wanted to see that his brothers and sisters were first "set in their education." The UN job was better paid, and might position him to assume a commissioner post in the future. "If I am not first settled, economically and in my family responsibilities, I would end up using the government salary, looting public resources, to settle myself."

We both know that few others would be so discerning. "Why are you different? Why do you think differently than most?" I ask. Koang says his education abroad gave him a strong sense of duty, and after a youth spent navigating a society shredded by war, he found his moral compass during his time away. But as with so many young Dinka and Nuer men and women I know, there is a second and more fundamental answer: exposure. During Koang's time training as a child soldier, and later when he received a scholarship to study, he was living alongside Dinkas, Equatorians, and many others from across South Sudan. "We became one family. And I saw that we are all just the same… That was the first thing that made me interested in politics. I was convinced we could do the same back home."

I spend nearly an hour walking Koang through the ups and downs of the IGAD peace process, and he listens intently. Even Koang, who is savvy and well connected, knows only the broad outlines of what happened in Addis Ababa. We share our concerns that there were not enough Southerners around the negotiating table. Like many of his educated and politically active peers, Koang wishes the peace talks had yielded a "technocratic government."

"You see people here, they have seen no primary education, no basic health system. Nobody seems to be talking about that," he says, pretending to look around in search of it. "We are talking only of political positions and power-sharing." His concern is not only about the terms of the deal, but the kind of signal it sends more broadly. "If we want just to enrich ourselves as politicians, and then leave the general public the way they are…" he trails off, shaking his head. Without more fundamental changes, he says, picking up pace again "everyone has to keep struggling until they reach the status." I summarize the status game he's describing: "everyone aims for the V8"—a reference to the luxury SUVs equipped with eight-cylinder engines that have become the status symbol of government elites. "Everyone aims for the V8," he parrots the words back to me in affirmation. After a long pause, he adds, "not sustainable."

A gun is fired just outside the compound, but Koang pays it no attention. "Down here," he continues, referring to rural communities like this one, "people are still neglected. There is need to transform the whole country if we are to move somewhere." Koang is particularly concerned about nepotism and a lack of necessary competencies when jobs are overwhelmingly filled through family and tribal connections.

"Listen now, we need a transformation of *all* the civil service," he says. "And it needs to be done by people who are wholly blank of the past... neutral." He rests his elbows on his plastic chair and interlocks his fingers. "*Technical* people in the areas of finance, *technical* people in the area of judiciary, and so on, and they come and do screening from the director-general down to the last civil servant."

Koang excuses himself to take another in a series of phone calls from somewhere in the greater Nuer region. As he engages in a few rapid-fire exchanges in his native tongue, I focus on the afternoon's supporting soundtrack—the aggressive flies buzzing about the *tukul*, the cows mooing in baritone, the rise and fall of the men's conversation outside, and the crows of one unrelenting rooster that makes an occasional appearance in the doorway. Koang puts down the phone. "Yeah Kayanga!" he yells in an ear-splitting pitch to an assistant outside, and a young man comes in dutifully, offering a salute. Koang dispatches orders to the assistant, dismisses him, and then picks up our conversation. The business of local quasi-government never stops.

When the war began in late 2013, Koang was attending a meeting in Bor, the state capital, some 150 miles across Jonglei from Akobo.

The army, and the population, were suddenly fracturing. He worked with government colleagues, both Dinka and Nuer, to try to contain the situation, but the genie had already left the bottle.

The president ordered Jonglei state officials to report to Juba at once, but Koang had received news of the targeted massacres that had already taken place there. He worried that he might be detained or otherwise neutralized if he went to Juba, and his gut told him to return instead to his Akobo constituency. "I should be where my people are," he recalls thinking, "so that if I am to make a decision, I do so informed by the feeling of my community." When a government helicopter arrived from Juba to collect him and the others, Koang did not get on board.

"Did that feel like a big decision?" I ask. Koang sits back in his chair and exhales, staring out through the door into the middle distance. After a long pause, "*Yes!*" he says loudly, as if to exorcise some lingering unease. Koang was torn, and still is. He wanted to protect his community, but also wishes he could have remained in government and helped to broker a solution from within rather than be party to institutional breakdown. But Koang was forced to choose.

"He came under incredible pressure," says his former boss and mentor, who spoke with him in the hours before he made the decision. "He saw it as a rabbit hole. He saw the stakes and wanted to be part of the solution, not just part of a Nuer-only rebellion." But there was no middle ground. Koang met up with Riek Machar's entourage as it retreated into the Nuer heartland, and he informed Riek that he would join the emergent resistance.

Adopting a slightly defensive tone, Koang wants me to know just how difficult it was to make that choice. "The pastor from my home, Akobo, was among the first killed in Juba," he says, adding, "killed while wearing his collar. Shot, just like that." Koang says he otherwise had no political connection to Riek, but asks rhetorically, "My own people being killed by the very government that I am representing? I cannot accommodate that."

But neither is he comfortable with what happened thereafter in his own community, where fellow Nuer took justice into their own hands by retaliating against innocent Dinkas. "Any revenge is inappropriate," he says, the frustration evident in his voice. "I condemned the killings of Dinka." Koang was still in Bor, and says the killings would not have happened had he been back to Akobo in time—an assertion that hangs in the air in the space between hope and a matter of fact.

He wishes the few senior Nuer who remained in the Juba government would have publicly condemned the killings in Juba. Such a pronouncement would have afforded space for local leaders like Koang to follow suit, maybe even to remain working for the government. But there was no middle ground, and Koang wasn't established enough to do it himself.

While this time was surely different, violence between Koang's Nuer and other tribes was not new. The divergent paths before him had long been a source of tension. While he was better than most, one UN official explained, he was still "less than objective" during times of tension with the Dinka. Once in 2007, while working on various UN peacebuilding initiatives, fighting broke out between his community and the SPLA, which was attempting to forcibly disarm them. "He turned up at the office in military uniform," his supervisor recalled with surprise and dismay, "and I was like, what the hell are you doing?"

Koang is still finding his way, but he's more confident now of his own views. "The strongest heart is the heart that can forgive," he says, speaking of the cycles of violence and revenge killings that have plagued his home state for years, and have now engulfed the nation. "It will never stop. Someone, somewhere, has to take the toughest decision."

Moving on to South Sudan's larger predicament, Koang says he is convinced that "what is needed, above all, is leadership that can facilitate reconciliation." Not in words, but in practice. He's not certain, however, that the two men that have so defined his country's divisions are right for the task. "If Salva and Riek cannot meet in Juba, how am I to reconcile the population on the ground?" The ministers? No better. "Michael Makwei says this, Taban Deng says the other thing?" Koang asks rhetorically, turning up his palms.

"Signals have to come from the top," Koang continues. Salva and Riek, he says, "must travel around the country and say, 'We killed you people, for no reason. I am sorry… Forgive us. We are brothers and must work together.'" If the two men can do that, Koang says, and show the people an agenda for where they can take the country? "They will be forgiven." Koang is talking faster now, the speed born of conviction. "But let me tell you," he says, raising a finger, "for as long as there is a clique around Salva facilitating Dinka interests, there will always be a clique around Riek who will do the same."

He speaks from experience, having tried to foster inter-ethnic dialogue at a local level. His attempts to be a voice of reconciliation have drawn hostility—from his own quarters. Following vicious attacks on social media earlier in the year, Koang was forced to issue a statement establishing his bona fides and rebutting assertions that he was an agent of Salva's government.

"The thing that makes me sad," Koang's friend and former supervisor tells me, "is that he can say, 'Now I want to find a middle way.' But as soon as he tries, it's, 'You're a traitor, you're trying to sell us out.'" If he goes to speak to the government, or to the Dinka in his home state, she explains, "It's, 'Come back here and prove your loyalty, or you're dead to us.'"

The heaviness Koang feels about his decision to join the rebellion was not only political, it was personal. When he chose to return to Akobo, his wife knew well what that would mean. They argued. "If you go there, you are rebelling," she told him, upset. He did not want to rebel, he told her, "but I wanted to resist the killing of Nuer." His voice slows in pace, and lowers in volume, quivering on occasion. I know the feeling, he doesn't have to say it. The rising star of Akobo is heartbroken.

"She took a decision, and began to pull away from our relationship," he says, picking up the story again. Their circumstances were further complicated because his wife, then in Juba, was from a well-connected Dinka family. But for Koang, more painful still is that, despite being on opposite sides of a growing ethnic and political chasm, his wife's family supported their staying together. I ask why she decided to leave.

"Well, probably she... I think she does not see the end of this. She does not see it ending anytime soon. And she does not want to be stuck... in darkness like that, living without her husband, not knowing whether I would survive the war." He pauses again. Koang is mourning the loss of his wife, but it's symbolic of something larger; the high-minded ideals and hopeful future for his young country have, for now, been swallowed up by the realities of tribalism and mistrust. But pulling himself out before he spirals down any further, Koang the optimist switches tune. He emphasizes the good relations he maintains with his wife's family, holding out hope that, one day, the couple may re-unite again. Then he clears his throat and returns to politics.

"I am not fighting for Riek Machar," he says, metaphorically, of his allegiances, "I am fighting for an objective." He believed the killing had to stop and the government had to be transformed. "If Riek can go back and execute such changes, ok. If he cannot, I must be working to change him also. But not through the barrel of a gun." This all sounds nice, but I push him further. "These guys are in control. How is this new arrangement going to be any different than December 2013? How do you avoid a repeat?"

I return to the conversation Koang and I began seven years ago, over sodas, about generational change. "Are you going to wait? Are you, and the people like you, going to wait?" I outline the options I sense are already on his mind: "One, you're going to leave. Two, you're going to be co-opted into a corrupted system. Or three, you're going to find a third way. To change it." Pouring himself another cup of Johnny Walker, Koang jumps in, "Exactly, this is it, you are right." He concedes that if he stays, and does nothing, he will very soon become part of the problem that he has so clearly articulated. I interrupt him in jest, "I mean, you already drink Johnny Walker." We share a laugh, a momentary break in what has been several hours of intense conversation.

After moving our two plastic chairs outside, Koang picks up the conversation again. "There are other young people in South Sudan that have influence now in their communities. People who also think things must be done differently." He explains that this generation of common minds must find a way to link up. "It can be done. But I am here now sitting alone, in Jonglei, thinking about ideas, scratching my mind." He continues, scratching his head theatrically. "Let me know those in Duk, in Warrap, in Juba, who think like me."

He's right, there are others like him. And he thinks they may be growing in number, as the war has finally opened a crack in the generational ceiling. Koang mimics the conversation he envisions having with them: "Now, young people of South Sudan, what is the way forward? What do we do? How do we organize for elections? Do we form a mass movement of civilians for change? How do we sell our ideas?"

Another hour passes, and though Koang hasn't moved from his seat an arm's length away, we are now totally enveloped by darkness. Only two voices remain, complemented by the ferocious buzz of swarming flies. We wrap up our conversation for the day, and he descends into his *tukul*, asking me to wait a moment, adding, "I want to be free." I understand only when he emerges, having traded his shirt, pants, socks and shoes for sandals and a traditional white *jalabiya*.

Koang makes a few more phone calls and then insists on escorting me back to the NGO compound where I'll spend the night. His ramshackle security detail—a handful of his friends, brothers really—lead the way in plastic sandals. We retrace the route back through town and across the dirt road at the edge of the village. Illuminated by the glow of a nearly full moon, it's a comical scene, as these men with guns tiptoe carefully through muddy ditches, each slipping occasionally and sinking knee deep in muck. Koang holds the cloth of his *jalabiya* in one hand and balances himself with the other, as he and the others argue playfully in their native tongue about the best path across.

We have a hearty laugh as one of them turns back to help me out of a sinkhole. I withdraw a muddied leg, but before continuing, I pause to stare up at the stars above. It's a different celestial landscape here than back home in the Northern hemisphere, and in a village with zero light pollution, the stars are brilliant.

Koang and his cohort leave me back at the compound, where I use a flashlight to find my way to my assigned *tukul*, and hang a mosquito net. Then to the outhouse, and to the clothesline to retrieve the shirt and socks I'd hand-washed earlier. As I traverse the camp, the young woman acting as my host reminds me to keep watch for snakes and scorpions. She also invites me to join the handful of local aid workers who have convened in the main tent to pass the evening hours.

I help myself to some beans and rice in the main tent, take a seat, and shoo away a lizard that's just approached my dinner plate. Suddenly the group erupts with a cheer and the tent is bathed in fluorescent blue. "*Heyyy-ooooh!*" The television had been without power, but it has just come back to life, and a favorite European soccer match is satellite-beamed into the tent.

The camp's diesel-powered generator has been broken since this morning, but the man who just fixed it is now a hero. The WiFi internet also returns, and I begin exchanging text messages via the web with a friend who is hurtling between London and Brussels aboard a Eurostar train. The others check Facebook on their phones. There are no paved roads here, no toilets, no electricity, no running water. But the WiFi connection on my iPhone seems as fast as any in Silicon Valley.

Outside of Juba and the oil fields, UN agencies and NGOs like this one are sometimes the only entities doing business of any kind. Oxfam, Save the Children, Tearfund, Concern, and Doctors Without Borders are among the many aid groups digging wells and latrines, administering vaccinations, grading roads, and training teachers. Their rural outposts are equipped with fuel, batteries, generators, 4x4 vehicles, telecommunications equipment, tools, medical supplies, and internet routers. Their programs often present prime job opportunities for the local best and brightest. Ubiquitous in South Sudan are these aid groups' T-shirts, hats, vests, and other paraphernalia, each emblazoned with their logos and mission statements.

Aid agencies show up in war-torn countries to provide much-needed emergency relief, and their stays are theoretically temporary. But after decades of war, hunger, and underdevelopment, they have become a fixture of Southern Sudanese society. Their resources, staff, and security have fused with local government authorities and communities.

I relied on the generosity of a great many of them during my years doing research across the country. Flying in their own supplies on a regular basis, they don't rely on the state for anything. In fact, the state often relies on them. Koang will be pleased to hear the internet is back on. He comes to the compound every few days to check his email and make internet-based phone calls to Juba.

In Juba, it's easy to think of South Sudan the "state." The concentration of government institutions, commerce, and men in blue police uniforms make for a convincing facade. But out here there is almost no evidence of a state. An occasional 4x4 vehicle hints at the presence of a local government official, but he probably has no office and little by way of a budget. A soldier in SPLA fatigues hints at the existence of national security institutions, but he isn't always paid, and half his divided unit is still fighting the government. Teachers convene daily lessons, but they too go months without paychecks, or are compensated by church networks and charities. You can't post mail here, or apply for a driver's license, or get a hearing with a formal judicial authority.

Out here is a long way—literally and figuratively—from Juba, and even farther from Addis Ababa and the re-making of South Sudan. Even if Salva's and Riek's competing factions manage to get along and can implement the peace deal, the question remains: how long before positive impacts trickle down to places like Waat?

Just two years into South Sudan's fledgling experiment in democracy, politics had degenerated into violence. The immediate challenge for the Southern Sudanese and their international partners was to push competition back into the realm of politics.

Ending the horrible slaughter here, or anywhere else, is a moral imperative. It's also a political one, as international actors can no more "stand by" in the face of such atrocities. But the urgency of this impulse can sometimes work against the kind of transformative changes needed for a lasting peace. As Albert Einstein once said, "Peace is not merely the absence of war but the presence of justice, of law, of order."

South Sudan's 2015 peace accord was based on the notion that Salva and Riek would share power—a prospect some thought doomed from the beginning. The two were most capable of stopping the violence, but as Koang had wondered aloud, were these old dogs capable of reconciling their people and transforming their broken state into a nation of "justice, law, and order?"

It was a worthy debate in its own right, hotly contested during two years of acrimonious peace talks. But one had to wonder whether a more fundamental question was being lost in the shuffle: What exactly were the Southern Sudanese and their international friends attempting to re-make?

Like so many peace accords around the globe today, the attempt to put South Sudan back together was based on the model of a "liberal democratic state," with institutions to regulate political activity, a separation of powers, popular elections, and a market economy. But for many in villages like Koang's, a more basic ingredient—a social contract—was missing. Most Southerners had little or no experience of a government that delivered services, provided security, or promoted the general welfare. For them, it was alien.

During their late-19th-century "Scramble for Africa," Europe's colonial powers convened in Berlin, in 1884, to carved up a map of the continent. They drew arbitrary borders around territories of interest, often with little regard for the people living there, their heritage, or their interests. They imposed European systems and institutions that neither enjoyed popular support among ordinary citizens, nor promoted their general welfare.

By the late 1950s, the jig was up. Nationalist movements and a changing international environment together prompted the decolonization of Africa. Britain, France, Belgium, and other European colonizers retreated from the continent, and independence celebrations heralded dozens of newly sovereign states. Many of the new states faced common challenges, and their roads to state formation would be rocky and violent. For some, uphill battles yet remain, but by the end of the 20th century, Africa and its leading lights were showcasing remarkable growth and dynamism on a global stage.

South Sudan's independence, by contrast, came a half-century later. It was a historical outlier. Having escaped oppressive rule only in 2011, it faced many of the same pitfalls its neighbors had at the time of decolonization—only in a region and a world that had long since moved on. The language of liberation had exhausted its cachet, and the era of Cold War patronage and realpolitik was over. This was a smaller, more open, more connected world—a liberal international order that had taken a greater interest in promoting universal values. New global norms and standards had emerged in "human rights," "development," and "governance," as had an explosion of treaties, reports, and institutions through which they were measured. The world's newest state was eager to join the rest of the world. But South Sudan had more ground to make up, and less time in which to do it.

The problem was not the development of universal norms, as these reflected human progress. The problem was one of expectations. Presenting the Southern Sudanese with a liberal-democratic-state-in-a-box, complete with requisite handbooks and tools, and expecting them to simply assemble it was unrealistic.

The next morning Koang and I convene again for our second and last discussion. I thank my NGO hosts and leave behind my mosquito net for the camp manager, who is delighted to replace her own, which is starting to resemble Swiss cheese. Later I will catch a ride to the next village, about an hour's drive away, where another UN helicopter will make a brief stop. I keep an eye on the skies, as I must make it there before the coming rains turn the adjoining road into a river. The UN chopper comes just once a week.

Koang and I revisit the peace talks again, and he asks about the specific contributions of some of the big men at the negotiating table. He's keen to understand how they performed, as well as how they were perceived. But in short order, he returns to ideas about flipping South Sudan's top-down power structure on its head.

"Now, we are waiting for the money from Juba, which means we are dependent on Juba, directed by Juba, listening to Juba," he says, his voice gathering pace again. From productivity incentives to tax collection to local resource management, he outlines a system that he believes could return some of the disproportionate focus on the capital to the states. "So that when it is me that is directing resources from here to Juba, Juba must listen to what I have to say." It's the kind of idea that few of the big men in Addis Ababa ever broached.

We speak of the risks of confronting Juba's old guard with transformative ideas, and of the climate of mistrust that persists in the wake of the war. Koang nods. "They will think: 'Why is he talking like that, who is he connected to... Does he have foreign support? Does he want to rebel?'"

Young people like Koang who are trying to break through to the next level are in a precarious position. Outside of government, there are few livelihoods, opportunities for advancement, or platforms for civic participation. If he pushes an agenda that challenges the status quo, the powers that be will simply shuffle him out of government. And so many of his generation are simply beholden.

"It is difficult, a sacrifice, you know? You will live in a *tukul* like this," he says, pointing with a raise of his brow to his modest mud hut, "while some of your colleagues are building more stories on to their houses." Some of his friends in government have been co-opted. They have chosen to suppress their feelings about what they know is wrong, Koang says, in exchange for personal gain.

Koang has no doubt toyed with the idea of selling out himself. Being driven around in a flashy V8, enjoying the outsize respect and privileges afforded to a "big man," these are fantasies he's surely entertained. He explains that such temptations are compounded by expectations from one's community. "Can you pay for my grandfather's medical procedure? And what about my daughter's school fees?" The de facto system of patronage means Koang will come under pressure to deliver money and other opportunities—from local chiefs, uncles, cousins, colleagues, friends, really anyone from his community in need. In a stateless society, when things break down, family and tribe are all that remain.

His speaking aloud now about the choice feels a way to affirm his decision to himself, and maybe to create some accountability by saying it to another. "This is all you have," he points again to the *tukul*, "but you are genuinely believing in yourself. It gives you the space to speak the truth… so that is something."

"Look, he's done amazing things with the hand he's been dealt," Koang's former supervisor told me. But she wishes he could have finished law school and avoided the toxic political atmosphere that has compromised so much since 2013. Despite the principles he holds dear, Koang is nonetheless becoming increasingly enveloped in the partisan mess. "I'd like to see what could've happened if he hadn't been forced to take a side, if he hadn't been dragged back to the bush." The two have stayed in touch for more than a decade, and while she remains hopeful about him, she also believes "his story is a good indicator of how this place has eaten people up and spit them out."

As Koang and I continue talking, he vacillates between principled government official and peer in search of a sounding board. "I am caught between," he says, unconsciously gesturing to his gut, where the churning manifests itself physically. Stay and help to bind his country's wounds or simply pick up and leave altogether? He wonders aloud. If there is a constructive role offered to him in the coming transitional government, one "where I can contribute, then surely I will stay." But he's understandably skeptical about that possibility. "Maybe I will go and continue my studies instead," he says, positing aloud what another hiatus in Kenya, Ethiopia, or further afield might look like. He could wait out the current generation of leaders and then return to national politics with even greater credentials. There's a logic in this plan. But he also knows that some who go never come back.

As he's outlined during our hours of conversation, leadership is arguably the most important ingredient in his young country's success. Who is he, then, if he picks up and leaves now? It's a matter of identity. Leaving, he believes, would be a kind of betrayal of both his people and his ideals. "But," he admits uncomfortably, "my internal debate is telling me that I am giving up... that I am resigning."

Though his cohort of contemporaries here would do anything for Koang, none have the same education, experience, or broad perspective. It's not a conversation he can have with them, at least not fully. I try to imagine myself in Koang's shoes. It's hard to think I've just dropped in on him, and will be departing again in a few hours just as casually as I arrived. When I leave, Koang will remain here, where the days are slow, the opportunities limited, and the decisions more consequential than any I face.

I want Koang to stay, but it's hardly my place to convince him. We explore all the ways he might maximize his potential, and I offer as much encouragement as I can. But our time has run out. After sitting in silence for a while, I fumble to try to say something meaningful to conclude. "I... I can only imagine how difficult your internal struggle must be. I admire your commitment and hope that you can stay strong."

"You remember your last statement," Koang replies without a beat, "when we met at Malakal?" It has been seven years. "You told me, 'You have to get involved in politics somehow.'"

"Yes," I reply, "I told you I would vote for you." I remember after that trip telling colleagues about Koang, and how rising stars like him could mean a brighter future for South Sudan.

"At that time, it looked to me like you were just saying something," he says, emphasizing the casual nature of the exchange, "just... just forecasting the future. But a few years later, it happened. So if you're telling me now, 'You stay strong,' it can happen."

He pauses, and says again to himself, "It can happen."

EPILOGUE

"Our country survives only in words, not as anything of substance. We have lost it all. We have only ourselves to blame."
— Cicero, *The Fallen State*, 52–43 BC

"We have nothing. We are nothing, the South Sudanese . . . We have no pride, no dignity, no honor. We were not this way before. It's all gone."
— South Sudanese female activist, 2015

When the pace of South Sudan's civil war slowed from its initial zenith in early 2014, and protracted negotiations supplanted the headline-grabbing violence, a broader realization began to set in: the country's internationally celebrated birth had given way to disaster—one of the world's worst—in less than three years. The making and unmaking of South Sudan warranted critical review, a hard look at where national and international actors had gone wrong, for surely they had.

But some critics and commentators took the argument a step too far. They went beyond criticizing failures to suggest the conflict was evidence that South Sudan should never have become independent in the first place. This was a lazy argument, and failed to appreciate the history, context, and likely alternative to secession in 2011.

Southern Sudan was already among the most neglected places on earth—denied political representation, economic opportunity, and social justice for generations. It had resisted forcible attempts to supplant its cultural identity with a purely Islamic state, and lost millions of its people to war, starvation, and flight. The question of self-determination—which for many Southerners was a euphemism for independence—was not new, but had been debated since before London turned the state over to Northerners in 1956. Fifty years of turmoil ensued before the 2005 peace deal secured their right to self-determination.

Had the citizens of Southern Sudan been denied their hard-won referendum in 2011, a new and larger war with Khartoum would most likely have ensued. With two armies on high alert, each far better armed than they had been a decade earlier, yet another civil war would have come at horrific human cost. And it might well have drawn neighboring states into a protracted battle with devastating consequences for the entire region.

But there was more to consider than the immediate circumstances of 2011. More broadly, didn't Southern independence represent the righting of a clear historical wrong? The community of nations had enshrined the right of all peoples "to determine their own destiny." After generations of political exclusion and violent subjugation, Southern Sudan seemed to present as clear a case as any of a people being denied a chance to choose their own political destiny.

It was hard to see the rationale for forcing Southerners to remain together with their oppressors inside one giant and constantly tumultuous state. International borders had been largely sacrosanct since the Second World War, a means of curbing aggression and maintaining order. But in the old Sudan, the primacy of borders was undermining domestic and regional stability, not maintaining it. South Sudan's transition to self-government would inevitably be rocky, and too little attention was paid to questions of the state's viability. Nonetheless, separation seemed to offer a better oppor-tunity than another half-century of violence in a country that had never treated Southerners as citizens. On these grounds, international support for South Sudan's independence was justified.

Did South Sudan's liberation class fail to make good on this golden opportunity, squandering both international goodwill and the kind of oil revenues many states would kill for? Yes. Did the country's African and Western backers need to engage in some serious soul-searching, having helped deliver independence, only to leave the fragile project dangerously unfinished? Yes. But to suggest that South Sudan would have been better off remaining within an unreformed Sudan? Or to suggest that violent collapse in South Sudan was inevitable? This is narrow thinking.

Independence was not *inherently* a mistake. The more pertinent critiques are those of expectations, and of execution. With so much focus consumed in securing sovereignty itself, the territory's leaders—and their international backers—did too little to prepare the political, social, and economic foundations for a *viable* state.

Political theorists have for centuries debated the sources of "state formation"—roughly speaking, the gradual processes by which central governments exert authority over a territory and "states" are made. In this they often take a special interest in the role of violence. Does war signal a breakdown of political order, they ask, or is it a central element in forming—even maintaining—a state?

Almost a hundred years after America's independence from England, its own Civil War threatened the very existence of its state. But the Union's decisive victory also empowered the national government and solidified a set of political, economic, and social norms that have grounded a stable democracy ever since. It raises the question for South Sudan: just two years after its inception, was the violence that caused so much suffering part of its unmaking, or will it ultimately prove an awful but formative part of its becoming a viable state?

South Sudan's post-independence government was weak, its army still a fragile amalgam of ethnic militias. Neither the state, nor any single ethnic group, enjoyed what the social scientist Max Weber called a "monopoly of violence." Suggesting that a single dominant majority might have made governance more manageable, one observer opined, "There are too many Dinkas in South Sudan—and not enough Dinkas." Some thus see the country's post-independence war as a crude but inevitable "sorting out" process that, if world history is any guide, will continue until one party achieves dominance. In this way, the violence did not represent the collapse of an established order; instead, it was a fight to capture an entity still up for grabs.

Barbarous wars for dominance, however, are less tolerated today. "Whether in South Sudan or Syria or wherever, we're not going to just sit around and let them fight it out for a hundred years," said one of my colleagues, a veteran scholar of state formation, when I put the question to her. But where there is understandably—maybe fortunately—no tolerance, there are also no easy solutions. "We are committed to a course of action based on an assumption that we can do state-building," the scholar resolved. "And we can't. A whole industry that has been built up around the notion of state-building... and it's just nonsense."

Skeptics took aim at the folly of international state-builders in South Sudan, and at the grandiosity of their enterprise—the technical jargon, the patronizing tenor, the mountains of wasted cash. There was no drinking water in South Sudan, but the state-builders demanded Southerners ratify obscure protocols and conventions governing international law. Adoption of the country's 411-page development plan, which included sections such as "Building capacity to build capacity," had been a hoop-jumping exercise designed to meet international donor regulations and keep the aid spigots flowing. Southern elites went through the motions to satisfy the state-builders while running a shadow system out the back door.

Critics argued that the state-building efforts, however generous and well-intentioned, were too often detached from reality. The quixotic expectations and unrealistic time horizons ignored the reality that nation-states mature over generations, not overnight.

Southern Sudan had long been deliberately under-developed by administrations in Khartoum. Its people were largely illiterate, and nearly all of them—including the emergent country's leaders—had experienced deep and lasting trauma. The Southern regional government had existed for just six years before it raised a flag in 2011, and the independent government had less than three under its belt when things came undone in 2013. In other words, South Sudan was not even a decade into its transition from brutal war to free and peaceful self-government. This historical perspective was sometimes lost on foreign diplomats and donor officials, who showed up on short-term assignments with clipboards and checklists, ticking off South Sudan's progress against the benchmarks of a modern liberal democracy.

The implicit expectation was not only that South Sudan's path to state formation was determined, but that it should simply short-circuit the kind of violence and protracted turmoil that characterized the formation of states elsewhere, including in Europe and America. Drawing lessons from generations of human and societal experience was one thing—leapfrogging it altogether was quite another.

Economics and social cohesion also feature in debates about the making of states, and South Sudan faced obstacles on both fronts.

Theorists argue that an economic engine is necessary to drive state formation, but South Sudan didn't have one—it wasn't producing anything. For those in Washington who had wrestled with the question of viability, the emergent country's oil revenue was the answer. But while oil provided billions in revenue, it wasn't clear those dollars were stabilizing the new nation. Poor spending and corruption aside, the oil industry was purely extractive, involved few workers, and did little to catalyze wider industrial development. Juba had little reason to bother taxing the population, and thus did little to develop any relationship with them at all.

Farming was the economy of the future, an industry that had figured prominently in the development of many modern states. But with no infrastructure to link South Sudan's diffuse population or transport goods, an agricultural revolution would require political vision and huge investments. And who was going to champion that as long as the fat oil paychecks kept rolling in?

The politics of oil would also shape what kind of state emerged. The Southern regional government had been mandated to allocate money to the states, but when Juba's coffers first began swelling with petrodollars in 2005, the money did not trickle down. Politics soon became a zero-sum battle for control of the capital city and its booty. At the time of independence, latent tension existed between South Sudan's regions and tribes over how to divvy up revenues going forward. But the matter was deferred for later, and so there was no agreement in 2011 about how the new republic's wealth would be shared.

Upon the country's unraveling, critics rightly pointed to the problem of resources and power concentrated in a volatile center—the prize over which competing factions might continue to fight. They criticized the 2015 peace agreement for failing to radically restructure the country's governance arrangement. And though their alternatives sometimes sounded good on paper, they weren't always politically realistic, nor did they necessarily solve the underlying problems.

Diffusing power through various kinds of enhanced federalism was surely sensible, but some foreigners suggested political partition: simply divide the tribes into three separate and semi-autonomous regions. Yet this didn't guarantee better security in any of the regions, nor was it clear that the regions would be more viable economic units on their own. Those of Upper Nile—home to all the country's oil— would surely question what incentive they had to share profits with a separate region of Equatoria, which had too little to offer in return. Dividing the country into parts seemed more a strategy of apartheid than it did a means to institutional, economic, or human advancement. And given the aspirations for a pluralist and democratic society voiced by many Southern Sudanese, was it not prejudiced for Westerners to suggest they simply weren't capable?

States also coalesce around organizing principles and shared ideas—the glue that binds citizens together and informs what it means to think of oneself as "South Sudanese." But when the realization of independence meant attention could finally focus on matters at home, the ruling SPLM had no vision for the future, no program to deliver on its promises, and no plan to cultivate a national identity. Southerners' collective contempt for Khartoum was not enough to forge a nation. Where other states had come out of wars by drawing on common historical foundations, South Sudan's ethnic communities had no shared symbols, ideas, or language on which to fall back.

South Sudan faced other unique obstacles, too. Unlike African states that had built upon and adapted colonial institutions, the Southern Sudanese "backwater" had been left largely untouched by the British. And because of the region's near perpetual state of war and suffering in the half-century since, the lines defining any normal "emergency" response had been blurred. Southern Sudan had become a kind of forever-crisis, perennially kept afloat by the international community.

For decades, food and basic services had been provided by the United Nations and Western aid groups. And in 2005, the UN peace-keeping mission asserted a greater role in the functions of government, from budgeting to police training to protecting government institutions. Its interventions had saved many lives, and done a great deal of good, but its presence had also reinforced a kind of external dependency, warped power dynamics, and clouded notions of sovereignty even before the country was born. "So little about this place has been organic," one observer said.

Nowhere were these synthetic peculiarities better captured than in the lives of the country's super-elite. Political classes elsewhere in post-colonial Africa had connections in, and access to, their former colonial capitals in London, Paris, or Brussels. But Salva, Riek, Pagan, Deng, and the rest of the SPLM vanguard had access to all of them, and to Washington, and to modern and flourishing African centers in Nairobi, Lagos, and Pretoria. As they navigated political circles on behalf of the cause, they also built homes, schooled their children, and scored business deals abroad. They joined an international class and became increasingly detached from the ordinary lived experience of their fellow citizens; increasingly removed from places like Waat.

Taken together, it was a daunting prospect: South Sudan was beset by a resource curse, lacked an alternative economic engine, and had no national consciousness (beyond a shared contempt for Northern governments). Its own government was internationally recognized, but weak at home and short on political legitimacy. It faced many of the problems that had confronted other new states—from social divisions to rising inequality to over-centralization—but it faced them all at once. Visionary leadership might have been a game-changer, but John Garang was dead and the deep rifts in his movement meant his successors were busy battling for supremacy or feeding at the trough. The South's international backers had propped up the SPLM and delivered a temporary peace, but misjudged both the movement and the enormity of the task that would follow once it stood on its own two feet. In retrospect, it seemed painfully evident that the deck was stacked against the new Republic.

There are no easy answers in South Sudan. It is hard—and in many ways, too early—to make conclusions about the country's ultimate fate. More may be gleaned, however, about American foreign policy and the international community's continuing struggle with the challenge of nation-building.

South Sudan realized independence at a time when traditional institutions, including the "state" itself, seemed in jeopardy. In 2011, states across the fractious Middle East and North Africa were being torn apart, and the so-called Islamic State was attempting to supplant two states with a 7th-century caliphate. Drug cartels in Latin America wielded more power than government institutions, while *Wikileaks* and cyber-security attacks were posing dangerous new threats to even the strongest of nation-states. Globalization had manifest economic, technological, and information revolutions that had altered power dynamics across the planet and were casting doubts upon the continuing primacy of the nation-state.

This raised a second question: should the world's attempts to make peace, whether in South Sudan or other fractured societies, continue to be based on the "state" as the traditional building block of international order? Or were there other, more fitting models for the country's particular circumstances? The question wasn't about to be answered amid South Sudan's rapidly unfolding crisis—a drastically different model wasn't going to materialize on the fly. Nor was a country like South Sudan, with no strategic value to major powers, likely to prompt such a fundamental rethink. That would require a wider lens, and deeper scrutiny about the very nature of state-making in the 21st century.

Much like U.S. interventions in Iraq, Afghanistan, and Libya, Washington's political intervention in South Sudan began with idealistic aspirations but ended in malaise and withdrawal. It was another painful episode in the continuing search for balance between America's power and its principles. What did South Sudan mean for America's engagement abroad, its ability to remake troubled societies, and the fate of the global order over which it presided?

During my eight years working on South Sudan, I saw the country through the lens of an analyst, assessing political developments and identifying worrisome trends as they unfolded. I saw it through the lens of policymaker and diplomat, confronting difficult choices in real time, choosing the least worst option, and doing everything possible to make it work. And in writing this book, I saw it through the lens of an historical observer, reflecting on events and choices made with the benefit of distance, hindsight, and thoughtful interlocutors. After these eight years, I can report that there exists no efficiently wrapped box of "lessons learned" about the making and unmaking of the world's newest state.

Nonetheless, I hope that many of the specific hazards and lessons of South Sudan's story have revealed themselves in the preceding pages—issues that are worthy of consideration as international actors respond to civil wars and political transitions elsewhere in the world.

For example, South Sudan's predicament of having to simultaneously pursue two possible futures between 2005 and 2011: on the one hand, Juba was supposed to give unity with Sudan a fair chance; on the other, it was to quietly ready itself for the enormous responsibility of independence—an eventuality about which the 2005 peace agreement said very little. In some sense, this left just six months in which the South could manifestly prepare itself to stand on its own, a period characterized by uncertainty, militarization, and unresolved tension with Khartoum. In retrospect, a more detailed gameplan in the event of a secession vote, including a longer window of dedicated preparation, could, *arguably*, have contributed to greater stability. It might also have allowed for a much-needed reorientation of relations between Juba and its foreign patrons.

But beyond these specific considerations, a more general set of principles have made themselves evident, which I also hope emerge herein: Recognize that individuals matter, but should not be lionized or unduly relied upon—they can die in helicopter crashes. Be modest in attempting to forge or remake states from the outside, and realistic about what it takes to achieve political and economic viability. Be mindful of getting too close, lest interests be mistaken for friendships. When it comes to expectations, and to measuring success, assess whether the appropriate metric for post-conflict transformation is years, or decades. Appreciate the limitations of what can be engineered from the outside and the dangers of inflated expectations. Pay due diligence to the law of unintended consequences, and be conscious of the awesome responsibility that accompanies such interventions.

For a variety of reasons, Southern leaders and their foreign partners paid too little attention to the making of a *viable* state, both before and after independence day. This task will continue, even though the country is now far worse off than it was on the occasion of its euphoric birth. But that doesn't mean that popular self-determination, and the realization of the country's independence, were mistakes in and of themselves. The story of South Sudan is one of triumph, and one of despair; but above all, it is an unfinished story, and one that need not end in tragedy.

"Do you have any hope?" I asked Koang, in the spring of 2018, upon reaching him on his satellite telephone. South Sudan remained atop the list of the world's most fragile states. Its conflict had evolved but persisted, and the prospects for peaceful transition remained in doubt. Koang himself was further embroiled in the messy politics of war that he had hoped to avoid.

The telephone line was scratchy, but after missing his first few words, I heard Koang's voice come through again. "The people of South Sudan went through a struggle for real and meaningful independence... All of us," he said. "That things have fallen apart is not the end of everything. All this will end, and we shall pick these things up to move our country forward."

NOTES

PROLOGUE

p. 6   "…'few forces on earth… and united in sacrifice.' Emphasizing the special relationship…'My country too was born amid struggle… welcomes the world's newest state.'" Rice, Susan E. "Remarks by Ambassador Susan E. Rice At a Ceremony Marking the Independence of the Republic of South Sudan, Juba, South Sudan." United States Mission to the United Nations, 9 Jul. 2011. 2009-2017-usun.state.gov/remarks/5102.

p. 8   "Men and women… described being forced to drink the blood of slaughtered family members, others to eat the burned flesh of decaying corpses." Author Interviews, Juba, Jun. 2016; *African Union*. "Final Report of the African Union Commission of Inquiry on South Sudan." 15 Oct. 2014. www.peaceau.org/en/article/final-report-of-the-african-union-commission-of-inquiry-on-south-sudan.

p. 9   "At a police compound on Juba's west side…" Accounts of the event at the Gudele police facility were widely reported, and later documented by the AU Commission of Inquiry and Human Rights Watch. See: *Human Rights Watch*. "South Sudan's New War: Abuses by Government and Opposition Forces." Aug. 2014. www.hrw.org/report/2014/08/07/south-sudans-new-warabuses-government-and-opposition-forces.

CHAPTER 1

p. 22   "Estimates put Juba's 2009 population at a few hundred thousand … seven years later, credible guesses had doubled and tripled that figure." South Sudan National Bureau of Statistics. *Population Projections for South Sudan by County 2015–2020*. Mar. 2015, p. 18. www.ssnbss.org/sites/default/files/2016-08/population_projections_for_south_sudan_by_county_2015_2020.pdf.

p. 23   "More than two million people have been displaced… one-third of the country's entire population, are facing a potential famine." United Nations Office for the Coordination of Humanitarian Affairs. *2016 Humanitarian Needs Overview: South*

Sudan. Nov. 2015. reliefweb.int/sites/reliefweb.int/files/resources/2016_HNO _South%20Sudan.pdf.

p. 29 "The price tag on these monster SUVs … was north of $50,000, triple the annual salary of an SPLA general." The maximum annual salary in 2009 for the highest-ranking officers active at that time (Lieutenant General) was 41,400 Sudanese pounds (less than $15,000). SPLA Payscales 2009, Obtained by Author.

CHAPTER 2

p. 34 "It is a fever-stricken wilderness… The *Sudd*, he wrote, was, 'a heaven for mosquitoes and a damp hell for man.'" Baker, Samuel. *The Albert N'yanza; great basin of the Nile, and explorations of the Nile sources*. London: MacMillan, 1888. Chapter 1, Entry for 25 December 1862.

p. 35 "And so racial and cultural subjugation of Southern black Africans also became more pronounced, just as the modern state was forged." Johnson, Douglas. *The Root Causes of Sudan's Civil Wars*. Bloomington: Indiana University Press, 2003. pp. 2–7.

p. 36 "And so the South, like Sudan's other outlying regions, remained isolated, under-developed, and poorly understood." Johnson, *Root Causes*.

p. 36 "… while the rest of the country remained, in the words of one notable historian, 'relegated to an exotic periphery.'" Johnson, *Root Causes*. p. xiv.

p. 37 "Though huge chasms existed as a result of decades of 'administrative segregation'…" Johnson, *Root Causes*. p. xiv.

p. 37 "… Jaden, then a district commissioner, was fired by his Khartoum bosses after he refused to play the new national anthem in his district or hoist the country's new flag." Kuyok, Kuyok A. *South Sudan: The Notable Firsts*. AuthorHouse, 2015.

p. 37 "In short order, the British were gone from Sudan… a new foreign overlord had simply taken their place." Deng, Francis. *War of Visions: Conflict of Identities in the Sudan*. The Brookings Institution, 1995.

p. 37 "'Of the 800 posts taken over from British Administration, only 4 junior posts were offered to Southerners,' it read. 'It therefore became clear… that we in the South were going simply to exchange masters.'" Sudan African Closed Districts National Union. "Petition to United Nations by Sudan African Closed Districts National Union (SACDNU), South Sudan." 1963.

p. 38 "… the Arab and Islamic character of the dominant elite would infuse Sudan's conflicts with complicated notions of power and identity." Some argue that the complicated self-perceptions of Arabs in the North has informed their discrimination toward other Sudanese in the South and other peripheries. For example, see: Deng, Francis. *Sudan at the Brink: Self-Determination and National Unity*. Fordham University Press, 2010.

p. 38 "… Sudan's wars, as one historian noted, would be difficult not only to resolve, but even to explain." Johnson, *Root Causes*.

p. 39 "While the South… a bubble of economic and political superiority was preserved at the center, in Khartoum." For a more detailed discussion of center-periphery dynamics and the nature of Sudan's political instability see: De Waal, Alex. *War in Darfur and the Search for Peace.* Global Equity Initiative Harvard University, 2007.

p. 39 "'It is now clear beyond any reasonable doubt that the war between the Southern Sudan and the Northern Sudan can never be won by your country.'" Jaden, Aggrey. "Independence for the Southern Sudan Now." Letter to Prime Minister Sayed Mohamed Ahmed Mahgoub, 5 Dec. 1965.

p. 40 "First, oil was discovered by American oil giant Chevron in the late 1970s…" A detailed account of Chevron's oil exploration and subsequent development of the industry can be found in: Patey, Luke. *The New Kings of Crude: China, India, and the Global Struggle for Oil in Sudan and South Sudan.* London: Hurst & Company, 2014.

p. 40 "Former U.S. President George H.W. Bush… visited Khartoum to alert the Sudanese to oil deposits and facilitate introductions to American companies." Khalid, Mansour. *Nimeiri and the Revolution of Dis-May.* London: KPI, 1985. pp. 305–6.

p. 40 "Shortly thereafter, Nimeri's government attempted to re-draw borders along the North-South frontier, so as to keep the newly discovered oilfields 'away from any Southern regional government and firmly under Khartoum's control.'" Vertin, Zach. "Compounding Instability in Unity State." *International Crisis Group,* Africa Report no. 179, 17 Oct. 2011. www.crisisgroup.org/africa/horn-africa/south-sudan /south-sudan-compounding-instability-unity-state.

p. 41 "'Because of the oneness of the Sudanese people,' Garang proclaimed in his first major speech in the spring of 1984…" Garang, John. *John Garang Speaks.* Edited by Mansour Khalid. London: KPI Limited, 1987. p. 23.

p. 43 "More than two million lives … lost in the space of a generation…" "Sudan: The Quick and the Terrible." *Frontline World,* Jan. 2005. www.pbs.org.

CHAPTER 3

p. 46 "A self-described 'follower of Jesus,' the Congressman has stated that his personal mission, even as a retiree, is to protect 'human rights and religious freedom—both domestic and international.'" Pershing, Ben. "Frank Wolf to retire after 17 terms in Congress; N.Va. seat will be a prime battleground in 2014." *Washington Post,* 17 Dec. 2013.

p. 46 "'I was interested because of my faith,'" Wolf tells me, as we take seats across a wide conference table." Author Interview with retired Congressman Frank Wolf, Falls Church, Virginia, 16 Aug. 2016.

p. 48 "'This is a *fundamentally evil* government… evil… these are evil people!'" "Rep. Frank Wolf (R-VA) Condemns the Government of Sudan." *YouTube,* uploaded by CSPAN. House Foreign Affairs Subcommittee on Africa, Global Health, and Human Rights. U.S. House of Representatives. 4 Aug. 2011. www.youtube.com /watch?v=LOpcYhHAaBc.

p. 49 "'Frank was often the first guy to jump on a plane… well, let's say he did not always have the best judgement.'"Author Interview, retired senior U.S. diplomat, Washington, D.C., Aug. 2016.

p. 51 "But Garang's affiliation with the Eastern bloc garnered him no support in Washington, where many distrusted his new movement as 'a bunch of Marxists.'"

Collins, Robert. *A History of Modern Sudan*. Cambridge: Cambridge University Press, 2008. p. 143; Author Interviews, Washington, D.C.

p. 51 "'In time, Frank Wolf was no longer doing it for Garang; it was now *his* cause.'" Author Interview, Pagan Amum, Denver, Colorado, May 2016.

p. 51 "Wolf and Payne... remarked two decades later on the extraordinary bipartisanship that sustained their odd-couple coalition's influence..." Boswell, Alan. "The Failed State Lobby." *Foreign Policy*, 9 Jul. 2013. foreignpolicy.com/2012/07/09/the-failed -state-lobby/.

p. 52 "'They know that the only hope for their nation is the Lord Jesus Christ,' Graham wrote, announcing plans to convene tens of thousands of Southern converts in Juba for an 'evangelistic Crusade.'" Graham, Franklin. "We can't say no." *Billy Graham Evangelistic Society*, 24 Aug. 2012. billygraham.org/story/we-cant-say-no /comment-page-6/.

p. 52 "'He tailored his remarks and the Bible verses he quoted'...'They were hanging on his every word.'" Author Interview, Washington, D.C., Sept. 2016.

p. 53 "... the group met for discreet strategy sessions... and even gave themselves nicknames: the 'Emperor,' the 'Spear Carrier,' and the like." Hamilton, Rebecca. "Special Report: The wonks who sold Washington on South Sudan." *Reuters*, 11 Jul. 2012. www.reuters.com/article/us-south-sudan-midwives- idUSBRE86A0GC20120711. The Reuters report was the first to publicly profile the work of the so-called "Council," which was otherwise well known only to Africa policy watchers. Additional "Council" members included Brian D'Silva, one of Southern Sudan's earliest advocates in Washington and a fellow student of John Garang, and Francis Deng, a prominent South Sudanese scholar and diplomat. The article notes that Susan Rice also "became an informal member of the Council."

p. 53 "As founding member Roger Winter once summarized it, in Sudan, 'there's a good guy and a bad guy.'" Griswold, Eliza. "The Man for a New Sudan." *The New York Times Magazine*, 15 Jun. 2008. www.nytimes.com/2008/06/15/ magazine/15SUDAN-t.html?pagewanted=all&_r=0.

p. 54 "... Winter suggested he wasn't interested in engagement with Khartoum, and thought neutrality 'morally bankrupt.' 'I'm an evangelist,' he told the reporter, 'I preach the gospel of Sudan.'" Griswold, "The Man for a New Sudan."

p. 54 "The two reportedly spoke almost daily by phone... reportedly referred to Dagne as his 'nephew.'" Hamilton, "The Wonks who Sold Washington"; Author Interviews, Juba, Jun. 2016.

p. 55 "'He was all over it... nothing happened in Congress without Ted, and without checking with Ted.'" Author Interview, Washington, D.C., Sept. 2016.

p. 55 "I swore to myself that if I ever faced such a crisis... going down in flames if that was required." Massimo Calabresi, "Susan Rice: A Voice for Intervention." *TIME*, 24 Mar. 2011.

p. 56 "They started with a 1993 resolution—drafted by Dagne—recognizing a right to self-determination for Southern Sudan, a move that sent a clear signal of support to the liberation fighters and put Congress well out in front of the Clinton administration." Author Interviews, Washington, D.C., Aug., Sept. 2016.

p. 56   "They also called on the Clinton administration to ratchet up pressures against the North and provide political and material support, as well as food and humanitarian assistance, directly to the SPLA and its allies." H. R. Con. Res. 75, 106th Cong., 1999.

p. 57   "'Sweet lord. New leaders of Africa?' one recalls, slapping his forehead in mock disbelief. 'Unbelievable… none of these scalawags were democrats.'"Author Interview, former official, State Department Africa Bureau, Washington, D.C., Sept. 2016.

p. 57   "All three 'frontline states'… even donning SPLA uniforms." Vertin, Zach. "Sudan: Regional Perspectives on the Prospect of Southern Independence." *International Crisis Group*, Africa Report no. 159, 6 May 2010. www.crisisgroup.org/africa/horn-africa /sudan/sudan-regional-perspectives-prospect-southern-independence; *Human Rights Watch*. "Global Trade, Local Impact: Arms Transfers to all sides in the Civil War in Sudan." Aug. 1998. www.hrw.org/sites/default/files/reports/ sudan0898%20Report.pdf.

p. 58   "'There was no logic to our policy,' the American ambassador in Khartoum later lamented, no logic 'beyond punishing Khartoum and supporting the rebellion in South Sudan.'" Cohen, Roger. "The Rice Question." *New York Times*, 4 Dec. 2012. www .nytimes.com/2012/12/05/opinion/roger-cohen-The-Rice-Question.html?_r=0.

p. 59   "'You couldn't criticize them… It was *their* issue.'"Author Interview, Washington, D.C., Aug. 2016.

p. 59   "It was easy; when things were black and white… it was 'harder to sustain interest' after South Sudan's collapse in 2013, when the situation became, 'murkier… when it wasn't so black-and-white, or so easy in terms of solutions.'" Author Interview, Congressional staffer, Washington, D.C., Sept. 2016.

p. 60   "Reflecting the gathering steam of the activist movement, the legislation formally fingered Khartoum for genocide, appropriated an eye-popping $300 million of new support for rebel-held territories in the South, and demanded the U.S. government throw its full weight into ending the war, including by using 'all means of pressure'" necessary. Sudan Peace Act. Pub. L. 107–245. 116 Stat. 1504– 1510. 21 Oct. 2002. www.congress.gov/107/plaws/publ245/PLAW-107publ245. pdf. Initial legislation was first introduced on the Senate floor in 1999.

p. 60   "… Danforth was a three-term Senator and had been on the short list to become Bush's vice president." Bush, George W. *Decision Points*. New York: Crown, 2010. p. 67.

p. 60   "The president… was 'committed to bringing stability to the Sudan, so that many loving Americans, non-governmental organizations, will be able to perform their duties of love and compassion within that country.'" Office of the Press Secretary. "President Appoints Danforth as Special Envoy to the Sudan." The White House, 6 Sept. 2001. georgewbush-whitehouse.archives.gov/news /releases/2001/09/20010906-3.html.

p. 61   "'Either you're with us, or you're with the terrorists… Our enemy is a radical network of terrorists, and *any government that supports them.*'" "Address to the Joint Session of the 107th Congress, September 20, 2001." *Selected Speeches of President George W. Bush: 2001–2008*. Transcript. georgewbush-whitehouse.archives.gov/infocus/ bushrecord/documents/Selected_Speeches_George_W_Bush.pdf.

p. 61   "'American ground troops... 'the Sudanese thought Bush was nuts. They were absolutely convinced they would be next.'" Author Interviews, former U.S. diplomats, May, Aug. 2016.

p. 61   "'Clinton may have bombed an aspirin factory... try Bush,' he recalls telling them. 'They got the message.' ... 'they were in full punishment mode from the beginning.'" Author Interview, former senior State Department official, Telephone, May 2016.

p. 62   "...and Council member Eric Reeves penned a 2004 opinion in the *Washington Post*, titled simply "Regime Change in Sudan." Reeves, Eric. "Regime Change in Sudan." *Washington Post*. 23 Aug. 2004.

p. 63   "One long-time observer described the 'vindictive' manner in which some Council members 'went after anyone who questioned the narrative' or attempted to advance alternative solutions."Author Interview, May 2016.

CHAPTER 4

p. 64   "The ensuing events would both reshape the environment in which a "North-South" peace was eventually concluded..." For a fuller examination of the links between North-South peacemaking efforts and the emergent crisis in Darfur, see: Srinivasan, Sharath. "Negotiating Violence: Sudan's Peacemakers and the War in Darfur." *African Affairs*, vol. 113, no. 450 (2014): pp. 24–44.

p. 65   "By 2004, the United Nations said the ongoing events amounted to 'ethnic cleansing.'" "Press Briefing on Humanitarian Crisis In Darfur." United Nations Press Conference, 2 Apr. 2004. https://www.un.org/press/en/2004/egelandbrf.DOC.htm

p. 66   "'In September 2004... State Colin Powell announced the State Department's conclusion that 'genocide had been committed.'" Powell, Colin L. "The Crisis in Darfur." Testimony before the Senate Foreign Relations Committee, 9 Sept. 2004. 2001–2009.state.gov/secretary/former/powell/remarks/36042.htm.

p. 67   "... too often reflecting an inclination to 'act before seeking to understand'..." Mamdani, Mahmood. *Saviors and Survivors: Darfur, Politics, and the War on Terror*. Doubleday, 2009. p. 3.

p. 67   "Its tactics, message, and prescribed solutions... have adverse effects on peacemaking efforts and on the crisis itself." This draws on a thoughtful assessment of the Darfur advocacy campaign: Hamilton, Rebecca. *Fighting for Darfur: Public Action and the Struggle to Stop Genocide*. New York: Palgrave Macmillan, 2011. Chapter 14.

p. 69   "they were going to a Darfur rally in the U.S... 'they didn't know Darfur was in Sudan.'" Author Interview, Nairobi, Kenya, Fall 2009.

p. 69   "Complaining directly to its leaders, one aid representative wrote, 'I am deeply concerned by the inability of Save Darfur to be informed by realities on the ground and to understand the consequences of your proposed actions.' He fingered the movement for 'misstating facts,' spending millions on unhelpful activities, and even falsely claiming ties to groups delivering life-saving services on the ground. He also expressed concern about unintended consequences, arguing the movement's ill-informed policies 'could easily result in the deaths of hundreds of thousands of individuals.'" Strom, Stephanie and Lydia Polgreen. "Darfur Advocacy Group Undergoes a Shake-Up." *New York Times*, 2 Jun. 2007. www.nytimes.com/2007/06/02/world/africa/02darfur.html.

p. 70   "Darfur, one critic argued, had become, 'a place without history and without politics.' Instead, it had become a cause which offered the average American a chance to feel like a 'powerful savior.'" Mamdani, *Saviors and Survivors*. p. 62.

p. 70   "Another complained of policies 'driven, very often, by activists who have never been' to Darfur, and who 'perceive the war as a simple morality tale in which the forces of 'evil' can be defeated only by outside saviors.' Darfur, she argued, had become 'not a place with a complex history; it's a moral high ground. Darfurians are no longer real human beings who laugh and love and care for their children; they are one-dimensional images of suffering.'" Flint, Julie. "Darfur, Saving Itself." *Washington Post*, 3 Jun. 2007. www .washingtonpost.com/wp-dyn/content/article/2007/06/01/AR2007060101850.html.

p. 70   "It wasn't a 'serious' national security... one journalist aptly called 'culturally hip do -goodism'?" Boswell, "The Failed State Lobby."

p. 70   "It was *easy*... and it was *gratifying* to have such a righteous cause." Author Interview, retired senior U.S. diplomat, Washington, D.C., Aug. 2016.

p. 71   "A top Bush administration diplomat went further, rebuking the movement and explaining that it had chosen to deliberately 'mischaracterize the situation in order to keep their followers motivated'—an approach he argued had aided Khartoum and 'made it much more difficult' to end the tragedy. Natsios, Andrew. *Sudan, South Sudan, and Darfur: What Everyone Needs to Know*. New York: Oxford University Press, 2012. p. 155.

p. 71   "She concluded that its demand to 'do something' had prompted politicians to undertake quick and visible actions over those best suited to resolving the crisis ... That desire for 'quick wins,'... did not improve the situation for the voiceless people it purported to represent." Hamilton, Rebecca. *Fighting for Darfur: Public Action and the Struggle to Stop Genocide*. Palgrave Macmillan, 2011. p. 194.

p. 71   "... rebels sometimes mistook... 'for real political and military commitments to topple President Bashir's regime...'" Cockett, Richard. *Sudan: Darfur and the failure of an African State*, New Haven: Yale University Press, 2010. p. 236.

p. 72   "Sudan's National Congress Party (NCP) government was among the world's worst." Note: The National Congress Party (NCP) was originally known as the National Islamic Front.

p. 73   "It's not enough to criticize. It may make you feel better, but people are still suffering." Griswold, "The Man for a New Sudan."

p. 73   "the SPLM 'made no secret of its readiness to mobilize its 'friends' in the United States or threaten to do so,' when it disliked Washington's official positions." Lyman, Princeton. "The United States and South Sudan: A Relationship Under Pressure." *The Ambassadors REVIEW*, Fall 2013.

p. 73   "And I got the message. It's not open for debate, and I think that hurt us in the end... but it doesn't make for good policy." Author Interview, Princeton Lyman, Washington D.C. Aug. 2016.

CHAPTER 5

p. 75   "Our four meetings with the president were matched by four hammering phone calls from Secretary of State John Kerry." The Office of the State Department

Spokesperson outlined the Secretary's outreach: "The Secretary has spoken with South Sudan President Kiir and former South Sudan Vice President Machar, both of them on Saturday, December 28th; both of them on Thursday, December 26th; both of them on Tuesday, December 24th. He spoke with President Kiir as well on December 23rd, 21st, and 20th." "Daily Press Briefing," U.S. Department of State, 30 Dec. 2013. https://2009-2017.state.gov/r/pa/prs/dpb/2013/12/219160.htm. Additional call readouts followed, for example, "Daily Press Briefing," U.S. Department of State, 7 Jan. 2014. https://2009-2017.state.gov/r/pa/prs/dpb/2014/01/219433.htm

p. 80   "…'this African military officer from a faraway land' was not only 'brilliant,' but that people in Ames, Iowa, had quickly 'thought him one of us.'" Author Interview, Washington, D.C., Sept. 2016.

p. 81   "Garang would ask himself, 'If the United States could fashion a free, secular, democratic, and united society' from its own multi-ethnic, multi-religious, multi-cultural society, 'why not Sudan?'" Collins, Robert O. *A History of Modern Sudan.* p. 141.

p. 85   "It is one of those events, like the Kennedy assassination, that becomes a historical enigma…" Author Interview. Telephone. Pagan Amum, Spring 2016.

p. 87   "'Nothing could be more precious than our unity,' recalls one senior military man at the heart of the impromptu deliberations." Author Interview, Juba, Jun. 2016.

p. 89   "'Cataclysmic… The truth is, we didnt know anyone else.'" Author Interview, Cameron Hudson, Washington, D.C., Dec. 2016.

p. 90   "'I accept that God has come to collect him…'It is just my husband who has died. His vision is still alive.'" "Sudan clashes continue after death of rebel leader." *New York Times,* 2 Aug. 2005. www.nytimes.com/2005/08/02/world/africa/sudan-clashes-continue-after-death-of-rebel-leader.html.

p. 91   "'We never had a democratic culture… And that,' says the critic, was South Sudan's 'original sin.'" Author Interview, Lam Akol, Juba, Jun. 2016.

p. 93   "Who told you that? You're the *president*!" "You do this…you do that." "Salva Kiir and Riek Machar: South Sudan's shaky peace | Talk to Al Jazeera." *YouTube*, uploaded by Al Jazeera English, 9 Jul. 2016. https://www.youtube.com/watch?v=uB0kf_liEQ4&t=657s.

p. 94   "Though more comfortable in Arabic and Dinka, the job meant Salva had to conduct most public business in English." Dinka would not have been appropriate for national affairs. Arabic was often used and more widely spoken, but its usage contradicted Juba's desire to distance itself from Sudan and its Arabizing impositions.

p. 96   "Such a hopeful disbelief… just more skilled at distancing himself from the unpleasantness." The phenomen is set forth in Wrong, Michela. *It's Our Turn to Eat.* HarperCollins, 2009. pp. 172, 235.

CHAPTER 6

p. 99   "According to an investigation by Amnesty International…" *Amnesty International.* "Sudan: A Continuing Human Rights Crisis." 14 Apr. 1992. www.amnesty.org/en/documents/afr54/003/1992/en/.

p. 99 "'I would like to take this opportunity, tonight, to apologize... I should take squarely the responsibility for the events of 1991.' The crowd began to stir, stunned by a moment they thought would never come. 'I was shocked!' Rebecca said." Author Interview, Rebecca Garang, Telephone, May 2017.

p. 99 "One newspaper reported that the vice president 'broke down and wept, to the point where he nearly collapsed.'" "Riek Machar in tears as he admits to 1991 Bor massacres." *The London Evening Post*, 16 Aug. 2011. www.thelondoneveningpost.com /riek-machar-breaks-down-in-tears-as-he-admits-to-1991-bor-massacres/.

p. 100 "We want Southerners to forget all the bitterness..." Ngor, Mading. "Bor MPs cautiously laud Riek Apology about 1991 Massacre, Ask him to Extend it to Grassroots." *The New Sudan Vision*. 11 Aug. 2011.

p. 100 "'We didn't want Dr. Riek to apologize... it shouldn't have been a one way thing.'" Author Interview, May 2017.

p. 101 "Riek's 'honeyed purr of a voice,' as one adroit observer called it..." Scroggins, Deborah. *Emma's War*. Pantheon Books, 2002, p. 166. *Emma's War* is one important source of biographical and other information for this book.

p. 107 "Prophetic traditions remain an important component... life today." For a comprehensive study of Nuer prophetic history and religion, see: Johnson, Douglas. *Nuer Prophets, A History of Prophecy from the Upper Nile in the Nineteenth and Twentieth Centuries*. Oxford: Oxford University Press, 1997.

p. 108 "Eleven years!... the liberation struggle is united today!" "Dr. Riek Machar Teny." *YouTube*, uploaded by Komach Dey. 1 Sept. 2011. https://www.youtube.com /watch?v=DEpJxWGKE9I

p. 108 "'He was a firefighter,' one close observer remarked, 'he did everything.'" Author Interview, May 2016.

CHAPTER 7

p. 116 "The Dinka... comprising more than 35 percent of the population..." While the percentages used here (Dinka 35%, Nuer 15%) are commonly referenced, reliable ethnographic data for Southern Sudan has always been elusive, due in part to conflict and logistical and political obstacles to data collection. Doubt has also been cast as result of allegations of politcally-motivated manipulation of census data by central governments in Khartoum.

p. 116 "a point intellectual Francis Deng ascribed to his tribe's intense 'pride and ethnocentrism.'" Deng, Francis. *The Dinka of the Sudan*. Waveland Press, 1984. p. 2.

p. 117 "Evans-Pritchard, the renowned British anthropologist, himself assessed the Nuer to be a 'turbulent people,' who are 'easily roused to violence'..." Evans-Pritchard, E.E. *The Nuer, a description of the modes of livelihood and political institutions of a Nilotic people*. Oxford: At the Clarendon Press, 1940.

p. 117 "As one South Sudanese social critic lampooned, 'they wake up in the morning, they wash their faces, and they go to war.'" Jok, Jok Madut. Lecture. Sudan & South Sudan Course, *Rift Valley Institute*, Entebbe, Uganda, Jun. 2016.

p. 118 "'They are cowards,' the same South Sudanese social critic says...'They are not nationalists... so when there is trouble, they run to Uganda.'" Jok, Sudan & South Sudan Course.

p. 119 "indigenous religions continue to 'inform ideas about ethical behavior, the moral community, and political action'..." Johnson, *Root Causes*. p. xvi.

p. 119 "South Sudanese culture... is a strikingly hard to define thing.'" Tong, Nyuol, ed. *There Is a Country: New Fiction from the New Nation of South Sudan.* McSweeney's, 2013. p. 8.

p. 119 "ethnic and regional identities—tribes—remain far stronger than any national consciousness." Vertin, Zach. "Jonglei's Tribal Conflicts: Countering Insecurity in South Sudan." *International Crisis Group*, Africa Report no. 154, 23 Dec. 2009. www.crisisgroup.org/africa/horn-africa/south-sudan/jonglei-s-tribal-conflicts-countering-insecurity-south-sudan.

CHAPTER 8

p. 126 "'The walkout was mishandled,'...'We were just being activist, only protesting, not governing. Like school boys... with big egos.'" Author Interview, Washington, D.C., Dec. 2016.

p. 127 "As Washington's top diplomat at the time wrote, 'Transformation would have to wait.'" Lyman, Princeton. "Sudan and South Sudan: The Tragic Denouement of the Comprehensive Peace Agreement." *Africa in World Politics: Constructing Political and Economic Order, 6th ed*. Edited by John Harbeson and Donald Rothchild, Westview Press, 2016.

p. 128 "Successive U.S. ambassadors in Southern Sudan were 'treated like rock stars.... Honestly, we could just come and go anytime without an appointment,' one US diplomat explained... 'no one else had that kind of VIP access.'" Author Interview, U.S. diplomat, Telephone, Jun. 2017. [NB: The chief American diplomat posted in Southern Sudan was technically a charge d'affaires, not an ambassador, as South Sudan was not yet a country. The difference meant little in practice, however].

p. 128 "According to one White House official, the first meeting between the two men was 'a fucking train wreck.'" Author Interview, Washington, D.C., 2016.

p. 133 "In a country accustomed to turbulence and changing circumstances, one would not waste a chance to get ahead during their turn at the feeding trough." Author Michela Wrong explores this phenomenon in her excellent book about politics and corruption in neighboring Kenya: *It's Our Turn to Eat*. New York: HarperCollins, 2009.

p. 136 "It was a core tenet of his SPLM manifesto, which mandated a shift *away* from an 'urban-based and centre-focused development paradigm.'" Garang, John. "TEXT: Garang's speech at the signing ceremony of S. Sudan peace deal." *Sudan Tribune*, 9 Jan. 2005. www.sudantribune.com/spip.php?article7476.

CHAPTER 9

p. 152 "The SPLM had a history of maintaining cohesion by relying on 'force rather than persuasion,' wrote one notable historian of Sudan's wars." Johnson, *Nuer Prophets*. p. 91.

p. 153 "Some of the SPLM's unpopular incumbents even intercepted telephone calls of opponents and manipulated communication signals to advance their campaigns." Author Interview, May 2016.

p. 154 "Standing in a voting center alongside Salva Kiir, U.S. Congressmen Donald Payne… 'a great day for democracy.'" United Nations Audio Visual Library. "Sudan / Salva Kiir Voting," shortlist. 11 Apr. 2010. https://www.unmultimedia.org/avlibrary/asset/U100/U100411d/.

p. 154 "But the moment referendum ballots were cast, 'they went back on their word'…" Author Interview, Onyoti Adigo, Juba, Jul. 2016.

p. 156 "The SPLM would need to get its own house in order… risk recreating the kind of hyper-centralized and unstable state from which South Sudan had finally managed to extricate itself." This section draws on a report by the author: Vertin, Zach. "Politics and Transition in the New South Sudan." *International Crisis Group*, Africa Report no. 172, 4 Apr. 2011. www.crisisgroup.org/africa/horn-africa/south-sudan /politics-and-transition-new-south-sudan.

p. 157 "'There were assassinations left and right' one former American diplomat tells me… 'All of that violence, he was part of all of it.'" Author Interview, Washington, D.C., Oct. 2016.

p. 158 "Another outspoken critic later wrote that decision-making structures under Dr. John were a 'glittering façade' behind which he would direct the movement 'alone and unquestioned… while at the same time hoodwinking the world' into believing it was a democratic operation. Akol, Lam. *SPLM / SPLA: Inside an African Revolution*. Khartoum: Khartoum University Printing Press, 2011. Lam Akol was a senior SPLA commander who partnered with Riek Machar in the 1991 attempt to oust John Garang.

p. 158 "As power became concentrated almost entirely in his hands, Garang would become increasingly unaccountable and 'surrounded by sycophants.'" Collins, Robert. *A History of Modern Sudan*. Cambridge University Press, 2008. p. 203.

p. 158 "Many began to bristle at his authoritarianism, but Garang managed to evade a reckoning; he diluted demands for reform while keeping attention on the external enemy in Khartoum." Young, John. *The Fate of Sudan: the Origins and Consequences of a Flawed Peace Process*. London: Zed Books, 2012. pp. 76–78.

p. 158 "'Democracy will not just fall from heaven,' the critic complains, 'like we'll suddenly become democratic overnight? This is our biggest problem. We never had a democratic culture. We think that the gun is everything.'" Author Interview, Lam Akol, Juba, Jun. 2016.

p. 158 "Even some of Dr. John's closest supporters now cop to his 'dictatorial' ways, ascribing their party's ultimate failure, in part, to the ethos of the movement he built." Author Interviews, Senior SPLM figures, Juba, Jun. 2016.

p. 159 "'We were not self-reliant. We were spoiled—we had everything we needed form the start; guns, food, supporters,'…'so we never had a relationship with the people.'" Author Interview, senior SPLM figure, Juba, Jun. 2016.

p. 160 "…'every now and then we would run to the Americans for help when things were stuck; 'please mediate, and oh by the way don't forget this is our position.'" Author Interview, Lam Akol, Juba, Jun. 2016.

p. 164 "'In ten days of meetings… spent arguing who should or should not be removed from his party leadership position.'" Akol, Lam. "Statement on the Launching of Sudan People's Liberation Movement-Democratic Change." 6 Jun. 2009. www

.oesterreichisch-sudanesische-gesellschaft.org/images/Statement%20on%20
the%20launching%20of%20SPLM-DC.doc?PHPSESSID=202474abb5ae013b
f4f0e9d2261d8e92.

CHAPTER 10

p. 166 "… ultimately amounting to an estimated $12 billion in revenue over six years (estimates vary widely)." Email correspondence with Norwegian Oil Expert, August 2018. For a variety of reasons, exact revenue figures are not available. This high-end estimate is based on interviews with oil industry experts, budgets from the ministry of finance, limited reporting to the CPA's Assessment and Evaluation Commission, and other research conducted on South Sudan's industry. For example, see: Shankleman, Jill. "Oil and State Building in South Sudan." U.S. Institute of Peace, Special Report No. 282, Jul. 2011.

p. 166 "Like 70 percent of their fellow citizens, the goat herder and his wife remained illiterate…" *The World Bank*. "The World Bank in South Sudan: Economic Overview." 20 Oct. 2016. www.worldbank.org/en/country/southsudan/overview.

p. 167 "Later, it quietly introduced legislation intended to re-draw state borders and annex the valuable new oil fields to the North." Shinn, David H. "Addis Ababa Agreement: Was it Destined to Fail and Are There Lessons for The Current Sudan Peace Process?" *Annales d'Ethiopie*, vol. 20, no. 20, 2005: p. 252. www.persee.fr/doc /ethio_0066-2127_2004_num_20_1_1077.

p. 167 "… the companies developing the fields—the Chinese consortium, but also major Western firms—were later accused of complicity in war crimes and crimes against humanity." "Unpaid Debt: The Legacy of Lundin, Petronas and OMV in Block 5A, Sudan 1997–2003." *European Coalition on Oil in Sudan*. Jun. 2010. www.ecosonline.org /reports/2010/UNPAID_DEBT_fullreportweb.pdf.

p. 168 "… GDP per capita was $1,600 in 2010, better than two-thirds of other African countries—better even than India. "GDP per capita: South Sudan." *The World Bank*, 2017. data.worldbank.org/indicator/NY.GDP.PCAP.CD?locations=SS.

p. 173 "One ministry withdrew an astonishing $30 million dollars for 'office equipment' … purchase of some four hundred Toyota SUVs." South Sudan National Audit Chamber. "The Report of the Auditor General on the Financial Statements of the Government of South Sudan: For the Financial Year Ended 31st December 2008." Jun. 2012. www .auditchamber-ss.org/reports/nac-ag-report-financial-statements-2008.pdf, Author Interviews.

p. 173 "Some transactions cited dubious line items, others were shamelessly explicit in their personal nature—one letter authorized $50,000 for a cousin's medical treatment…" Author Interviews, Washington, D.C., Mar. 2015, Nairobi, Jun. 2016.

p. 174 "One such shareholder, with a 25 percent stake in 'Combined Holding Limited,' was the twelve-year-old son of President Salva Kiir. The youngster's passport listed his occupation as 'Son of the President.' Author discussions with independent researchers examining illicit financial activity in South Sudan, Washington, D.C., Spring, 2016. Cited also in: "War Crimes Shouldn't Pay: Stopping the looting and destruction in South Sudan."

The Sentry, Sept. 2016. cdn.thesentry.org/wp-content/uploads/2016/09/Sentry_WCSP_Finalx.pdf.

p. 176 "South Sudan was no Saudi Arabia, with its 10 million per day. It wasn't Iran (4 million) or even Nigeria (2.5 million). U.S. Energy Information Agency." "Total Petroleum and Other Liquids Production 2011." www.eia.gov/beta/international/rankings/#?prodact=53-1&cy=2011&pid=53&aid=1&tl_id=1-A&tl_type=a.

p. 177 "Small deposits might be found near already producing fields... better technology could increase recovery yields." Author Interview, Anders Hannevik, Norwegian petroleum expert, Telephone, Jan. 2011.

p. 178 "President Vladimir Putin... not 'fall asleep under the warm blanket of petrodollars.'" Author Interview and email exchange with Russia expert, Washington, D.C., Spring 2017.

p. 180 "(One shows a young woman posing in the sunroof of a BMW on a coastal highway in Australia.)" "War Crimes Shouldn't Pay: Stopping the looting and destruction in South Sudan." *The Sentry*, Sept. 2016.

p. 182 "There was a kind of 'moral licensing" at play—an idea popular in social psychology, in which a past deed of good moral behavior makes people more likely to do immoral things 'without worrying about feeling or appearing immoral.'" Merrit, Effron. "Moral Self-Licensing: When Being Good Frees Us to Be Bad." *Social and Personality Psychology Compass,* May 2010: pp. 344–57 Accessed: www.compassionate.center

p. 183 "'Our cow has delivered; let us divide and drink the milk among ourselves.'" Author Interviews, senior SPLM and non-SPLM figures, Juba, Jun. 2016.

p. 185 "'An estimated $4 billion are unaccounted for... Once we got to power, we forgot what we fought for and began to enrich ourselves at the expense of our people.'" Letter from the President of the Republic of South Sudan, Salva Kiir, to undisclosed recipients. 3 May 2012. Copy obtained by the Author.

p. 186 "Working quietly from inside Salva's office, Dagne had been intimately involved in the corruption investigation." Author Interviews, South Sudanese and U.S. government officials, senior UN officials, Jan. 2012.

p. 186 "Fairly or not, some thought him interested in playing politics... Others alleged he was somehow out to make money for himself." Author Interviews, Juba, Jun. 2016, Jul. 2016.

p. 186 "Dagne was reportedly forced to flee the country for his own safety." "Foreign advisor to South Sudan's president flees Juba after disclosure of corruption letter." *Sudan Tribune.* Aug. 20 2012. www.sudantribune.com

CHAPTER 11

p. 188 "'We can have this whole country with fields extending to indefinite end,' he thought to himself. 'It will be possible for us to be very rich.'" Author Interviews, Pagan Amum, Denver, Colorado. May 2016.

p. 193 "They would negotiate 'in good faith to promote the common interests of the people... regardless of the outcome of the referendum.'" "Guiding Principles on Post 2011 Referendum Arrangements Negotiations." Juba, 20 Jul. 2010. Obtained by Author.

p. 196 "... South African President Thabo Mbeki, who had been appointed by the African Union to support the process." After leading a 2009 African Union assessment on the conflict in Darfur, the AU expanded the mandate of Mbeki's panel to support North-South dialogue on the completion of the CPA and post-referendum arrangements.

p. 196 "'It was important that Khartoum not feel that Africans were conspiring with the West to dismember Sudan.'" Author Interview, African Union diplomat, New York, Sept. 2016.

p. 197 "Culling the CPA's slogan to 'make unity attractive,' he argued that it was now time to 'make separation attractive.' Author Interviews, Khartoum, Sept. 2010, Juba, Jun. 2016.

p. 197 "'There are rising calls that the South... knows that nothing could be further from the truth.'" "Keynote Address on the Occasion of the Congressional Black Caucus Foundation 40th Annual Conference Foreign Affairs Brain Trust Event at the Washington Convention Center by Gen Salva Kiir Mayardit, First Vice President of the Republic of Sudan and President of the Government of Southern Sudan." *AllAfrica.com,* 17 Sept. 2010. Accessed: www.allafrica.com/stories/201009170967.html.

p. 198 "The best way to clear a path to the referendum... on the thorny post-referendum agenda." This section draws on a report by the author: Vertin, Zach. "Negotiating Sudan's North-South Future." *International Crisis Group,* Africa Briefing no. 76, 23 Nov. 2010.

p. 200 "'They didn't give a shit... They didn't give a shit about the little man.'" Author Interview, May 2016.

p. 201 "'will not enjoy citizenship rights, jobs or benefits; they will not be allowed to buy or sell in Khartoum market... we will not even give them a needle in the hospital.'" "Referendum raises expulsion fears." *IRIN News,* 27 Sept. 2010. www.irinnews.org/fr/node/249330.

p. 201 "The Speaker... warning Southerners they would soon be 'second class citizens.'" Vertin, *ICG,* "Negotiating Sudan's North-South Future."

p. 201 "It was critical to 'show that the world is united,' she said, and to 'ensure that the referendum goes off on time and peacefully.'" "Salva Kiir: Southern Sudan Vote Delay Could Risk War." International Peace Institute, 22 Sept. 2010. www.ipinst.org / 2010/09/salva-kiir-southern-sudan-vote-delay-could-risk-war

p. 203 "The two-page document—the product of a bitter inter-agency fight in Washington... and ease some sanctions." The roadmap's North-South provisions were complicated enough to begin with, but an additional set of American asks—the source of a bitter inter-agency fight in Washington—were tacked on before Kerry delivered it to Khartoum. Full termination of economic sanctions, as well as multilateral debt relief—the most important "carrots," in diplomatic speak—would also be contingent upon a series of improvements to the situation in Darfur. The additional elements showed the Sudanese the long-term path to complete normalization with the United States, but many involved in the fraught policy process worried about confusing an already long list of demands. After a bloody battle at the National Security Council, one participant explained the Darfur conditions remained "for one reason, and her name is Susan Rice."

p. 203 "It also hinted, vaguely, at the possibility of debt relief... and military de-escalation." "Sudan's Path to a Changed Relationship with the United States" (aka "the roadmap"). Nov. 4 2010. Obtained by the Author.

p. 204 "Though they continued to harbor doubts, they agreed to the American roadmap." Following the Southern referendum, a dispute did arise between Khartoum and Washington over promises made and promises broken, which took an already troubled bilateral relationship from bad to worse. Khartoum initiated a new conflict in another of its marginalized regions, and though it did not pertain directly to the roadmap, the Americans would find it politically impossible to grant Khartoum relief and benefits while it waged another war. Senior American officials would fly to Khartoum with a follow-on offer, attempting to patch up the tattered roadmap and silence the guns. But the damage was done. Furious, Khartoum believed it had been taken for a ride, again, by an American government intent on its demise. The episode would deepen a hole from which the two sides have yet to climb.

CHAPTER 12

p. 209 "President Obama called the exercise an 'inspiration to the world,'..." The White House. "Statement by the President on the intent to recognize southern Sudan." 7 Feb. 2011.

p. 209 "... Secretary of State Hillary Clinton lauded the 'compelling statement' made by the people of Southern Sudan." U.S. Department of State. "Congratulating Sudan on the Results of the Southern Sudan Referendum." Secretary of State Hillary Rodham Clinton, 7 Feb. 2011. 2009–2017.state.gov/secretary/20092013 clinton /rm/2011/02/156107.htm.

p. 209 "Sudanese President Omar al-Bashir appeared on national television and announced that he would 'accept and welcome these results because they represent the will of the Southern people.'" McDoom, Opheera. "South Sudan in landslide vote for independence." *Reuters*, 7 Feb. 2011. af.reuters.com/article/topNews /idAFJOE7160CW20110207.

p. 210 "'After the darkness of war, the light of a new dawn is possible...'" The White House, Office of the Press Secretary. "Statement of President Barack Obama on the Recognition of the Republic of South Sudan." 9 Jul. 2011.

p. 213 "By the end of 2012, almost two million refugees..." United Nations Office for the Coordination of Humanitarian Affairs. "Humanitarian Bulletin: South Sudan 31 December – 6 Jan. 2013." 6 Jan. 2013. https://reliefweb.int.

p. 215 *"My government will stand with ... member of the international community."* Rice, Susan E. "Remarks by Ambassador Susan E. Rice At a Ceremony Marking the Independence of the Republic of South Sudan, Juba, South Sudan."

p. 216 "'Our country, as it stands today, is a four-legged animal,' South Sudanese intellectual Jok Madut Jok remarked, 'but the legs are broken.'" *Sudan: The break-up.* Prod. Jamie Doran. *Al-Jazeera,* 12 Jul. 2011.

p. 216 "Nine out of ten people lived on less than a dollar per day." United Nations Children's Fund. "Children in South Sudan." 9 Jul. 2011. www.unicef.org.

p. 218 "'People's first entity of affiliation... What is the glue that binds us together?'" "South Sudan as the search for its Soul: Jok Madut Jok at TEDxJuba." *YouTube*, uploaded by TEDx Talks. 5 Aug. 2012. https://www.youtube.com/watch?v=KXGu1aOPaJs

p. 220 "... one year the finance ministry... exceeded its own budget by an astonishing 1900 percent." Southern Sudan Audit Chamber. "The Report of the Auditor General on the Financial Statements of the Government of Southern Sudan: For the Financial Year Ended 31st December 2006." 2007. Web. 15 Nov. 2016.

CHAPTER 13

p. 226 "The loss of some 60 percent of Sudan's total revenue (and more than 90 percent of exports)..." Hannevik, Anders. "Sudan Petroleum Sector - Post Secession Options." Lecture at Economic Dialogue, Addis Ababa, 1 Mar. 2011. Obtained by Author.

p. 226 "... one proposal was floated for a 50-50 'wealth-sharing' deal." Author Interview, Princeton Lyman, Washington, D.C., Aug. 2016.

p. 229 "... Juba's oil exports 'would be halted at port until a settlement is reached.'" Khartoum calculated its earnings owned on the basis of a unilaterally stipulated fee of $35—its starting position in negotiations and a figure no one deemed reasonable.

p. 229 "'The council of ministers decided today'... instructed to begin 'a complete shutdown of oil production.'" "South Sudan orders oil production shutdown within 2 weeks deepening row with Khartoum." *Al-Arabiya*, 20 Jan. 2012. www.alarabiya.net/articles/ 2012/01/20/189465.html.

p. 230 "'What the fuck?' That was the response of one American... 'People in DC were irate'..."Author Interview, Washington, D.C., Aug. 2016.

p. 232 "Bashir again pressed Salva to replace Juba's brash pointman, calling him a 'warlord who has no interest in peace'... Another Sudanese official echoed the president's disdain, blasting Pagan's 'notorious hostility towards the North and the Arabs.'" "Why Is Khartoum Calling for the Dismissal of Pagan Amum as the Head of South Sudan's Delegation to the Addis Ababa Talks?" *South Sudan News Agency*, 4 Mar. 2012.

p. 233 "'Grossly naïve... It was: 'just surge funds to the SPLA and we'll be at the gates of Khartoum in no time.'" Author Interview, Skype, Oct. 2017.

p. 234 "'Nobody saw it coming'... and it freaked everyone out.'"Author Interview, Washington, D.C., Oct. 2016.

p. 234 "'I call on South Sudan to immediately withdraw... and a clearly illegal act.'" Nichols, Michelle. "U.N. chief says South Sudan infringing on Sudan sovereignty." *Reuters*, 19 Apr. 2012.

p. 236 "I was in every one of those meetings, and there was no such loan discussed." Author discussions with senior Chinese official, Dec. 2015.

p. 237 "'A percentage of something is better than a percentage of nothing' Clinton said at a joint press conference in Juba...'You've made your point' about '*your* rights to *your* resources.'" U.S. Department of State. "Press Availability With South Sudanese Foreign Minister Nhial Deng." Secretary of State Hillary Rodham Clinton, 3 Aug. 2012. 2009–2017.state.gov/secretary/20092013clinton/rm/2012/08/196050.htm.

p. 237 "'It is true… the negotiating team, including myself personally as a chief negotiator were subjected to extreme pressure from the Americans, British, the Norwegians'…'They were forcing us to give away the resources of South Sudan.'" "S. Sudan, AU panel suffered 'extreme' pressure to reach deal, Pagan." *Sudan Tribune,* 8 Aug. 2012. www.sudantribune.com/spip.php?article43500.

p. 238 "'I really like Pagan, he has a vision, and there is an innocence underneath it all'… 'someone is going to checkmate you.'" Author Interview, New York, Sept. 2016.

CHAPTER 14

p. 243 "During one firefight in Gadet's Mayom County… destroying more than 7,000 tukuls." Vertin, Zach, "Compounding Instability in Unity State." *Crisis Group.*

p. 243 "… rebel supporters showed me videos." The videos had been shot across the border in Sudan, where the rebels were receiving materiel support from Khartoum—just as they had during the civil war.

p. 247 "This guy is a professional…" Author Interview, Bentiu, Aug. 2011.

p. 249 "'Don't lie to the president…'" Author Interview, Washington, D.C., Dec. 2011.

p. 250 "We nearly fell off our chairs!'…'it was difficult to enlist Obama's help'…" Author Interview, Princeton Lyman, Aug. 2016.

p. 252 "… UN patrols snapped startling aerial photos of some 8,000 young men." "Briefing on Jonglei violence." *IRIN News,* 10 Feb. 2012. www.irinnews.org/news/2012/02/10 /briefing-jonglei-violence.

p. 253 "'You have the Wild West in your country'… well, this is the Wild East.'" Author Interview, Telephone, Nov. 2016.

p. 253 "Such feuds were not uncommon, as the centrality of cattle to all aspects of Nilotic life made them a trigger for confrontation between communities." Vertin, Zach "Jonglei's Tribal Conflicts: Countering Insecurity in South Sudan." *International Crisis Group*, Africa Report no. 154, 23 Dec. 2009. www.crisisgroup.org/africa/ horn-africa/south-sudan/jonglei-s-tribal-conflicts-countering-insecurity-south-sudan. Pp. 170-79 draw further detail from this report.

p. 255 "No education, no health, no water, no roads, and no positions in government!" Author Interview, Murle community leader, Juba, Fall 2009.

p. 257 "… he was brought back to the fold with an attractive package: military rank, house, car, and cash." Copnall, James. *A Poisonous Thorn in Our Hearts: Sudan and South Sudan's Bitter and Incomplete Divorce*. London: Hurst & Company, 2014, p. 165.

p. 257 "…'it wasn't really on our radar'…" Author Interview, Washington, Spring 2017.

p. 258 "There wasn't really an understanding… targeting its own citizens.'" Author Interview, State Department official, Telephone, Spring 2017.

CHAPTER 15

p. 260 "The world is watching… much of its past.'" "Readout of Call with South Sudan President Salva Kiir Mayardit." Press Statement, Secretary of State John Kerry, 27 Jul. 2013.

p. 264 "Born 'around 1951' in a disputed border territory called Abyei..." Author Interview, Deng Alor, Juba, Jun. 2016.

p. 270 "'A simple case of character assassination; nothing more'... 'Salva is out to undermine his rivals.'" Author Interview, Juba, Jun. 2016.

p. 271 "'What is happening now is a crisis in the ruling party... It is not the state itself that is sick. The sickness is in the party.'" Tisdall, Simon. "South Sudan: two years old but nothing to celebrate." *The Guardian*, 4 Jul. 2013.

p. 272 'I went to the bush not (for) myself..." "Speeches for the 2nd anniversary celebration of South Sudan Independence 9th, July 2013 as it happen." *Youtube*, uploaded by Robert atomic. 11 July 2013. Recording from Radio Miraya. https://www.youtube.com/watch?v=0igt0sjGoqY. 'Quotation smoothed for clarity.'

p. 273 "'To avoid authoritarianism and dictatorship, it is better to change... I have been serving under Salva Kiir... I think it is time for a change now.'" Tisdall, "South Sudan: two years old..."

p. 273 "'We were an independent state... We did. We did discuss it... There was no other way.'" Author Interview, Riek Machar, Juba, Jun. 2016.

p. 274 "Please remain calm... this is how we're going to continue." BigEye.ug. "South Sudan Former VP's Status Update." *Facebook*, 24 Jul. 2013. www.facebook.com/bigeye.ug/posts/558333084226591.

p. 274 "We didn't see it coming... and had not much beyond phone calls and prayers to throw at it." Author Interview, Washington, D.C., Jan. 2017

p. 275 "Rejecting the calls to arms, Riek... he urged the army to maintain its neutrality." "Machar renews calls for calm, reaffirming Kiir's right to remove him." *Sudan Tribune*, 29 Jul. 2013. www.sudantribune.com/spip.php?article47465.

p. 276 "Government dissolution is one thing. But the party is a red line... there will be violence... no question." Author discussions with Deng Alor, Juba, Sept. 2013.

p. 276 "Do you think that today the [party] structures still have the legitimacy to continue functioning?" *South Sudan's President Kiir Dissolves SPLM Structures Apart from Chairmanship*. Prod. Sudan Tribune. *AudioBoom.com*. 16 Nov. 2013. audioboom.com/posts/1734011-south-sudan-s-president-kiir-dissolves-splm-structures-apart-from-chairmanship.

p. 277 "We, the SPLM leaders... the internal crisis that has engulfed the SPLM and paralyzed the government." "South Sudan Politics in Juba." *YouTube*, uploaded by Ally Ngethi. 10 Dec. 2013. www.youtube.com/watch?v=bCIrmgBO6VY.

p. 281 "'They took their positions for granted, they got spoiled by the luxuries of office and forgot that we are servants of the people...'I must warn,' he continued, 'that this behavior is tantamount to indiscipline which will take us back to the days of the 1991 split... I am not prepared to allow this to happen again.'" "National Conference of SPLA Board – President's Salva Kiir Speech." *YouTube*, uploaded by South Sudan Online. 15 Dec. 2013. www.youtube.com/watch?v=5y3bp6Oehis.

p. 281 "'*Anguen thou wen kuan janub!*' It was an old war song from Bahr al Ghazal... which proclaimed it better to fight and die than to be humiliated." Translation, Dinka. "Song of SPLA Fourth Division Mourmour-Wolf Battalion, 1984." Obtained by Author.

CHAPTER 16

p. 286 "Twenty-four hours later, the number surged past 16,000." @tobylanzer. "Numbers of civilians seeking protection at #UNMISS fell before Noon but just surged again as the day starts to wind down: 16,000 & counting." *Twitter.com,* 17 Dec. 2013, 5:27 AM. twitter.com/tobylanzer/status/412937140939399169.

p. 288 "The purpose of this press statement..." Salva Kiir's remarks and ensuing answers to questions from the press were delivered part in English, and part in Arabic. Translation obtained by Author. "President Salva Kiir announced foil a coup attempt led by Riek Machar." *YouTube,* uploaded by South Sudan Online. 16 Dec. 2013. https://www.youtube.com/watch?v=boLU20O5JDI

p. 290 "But collecting litter, they explained, had been a pretext for the new force to conduct reconnaissance and map Nuer areas for later targeting." Author Interviews, Juba, Jun. 2016; *AU,* "Final Report of the African Union Commission."

p. 295 "... One of the first assessments by international observers found some Nuer neighborhoods 'totally depopulated.' They were barred by government forces ... including "prepared meals left untouched in homes." "Protection Monitoring Assessment." Conducted by UN agencies and partner NGOs, Juba 19 Dec. 2013. Obtained by Author.

p. 295 "... Some Nuer civilians were tied up and burned alive inside their homes; others were forced to drink the blood of murdered family members." *AU,* "Final Report of the African Union Commission."

p. 296 "In 1963, political theorist Hannah Arendt... introduced the notion of the 'banality of evil.'" Arendt, Hannah. *Eichmann in Jerusalem: A Report on the Banality of Evil.* Penguin: New York, 1994.

p. 296 "... African Union's 2014 investigation... 'widespread or systematic nature,' and carried out 'in furtherance of a state policy.'" *AU,* "Final Report of the African Union Commission." p. 225.

p. 296 "... legendary mound of the most famous Nuer prophet of the nineteenth century, the hallowed ground where he performed ceremonial rites, dispensed advice, and sang songs that allegedly foretold of South Sudan's violent reckoning." Johnson, Douglas. "The fate of Ngungdeng's dang." *Rift Valley Review,* 29 Aug. 2014. riftvalley.net/news/fate-ngungdeng%E2%80%99s-dang.

p. 300 "One soldier present said Gadet had... shot him at point blank range." Author Interview, soldier, Juba, Jun. 2016.

p. 301 "Dozens of decaying bodies soon lay in the streets of Bor... survivors would bury hundreds of family members and neighbors in mass graves." *Human Rights Watch.* "South Sudan's New War: Abuses by Government and Opposition Forces."

p. 302 "During their second occupation of Bor, Nuer fighters murdered fourteen elderly women... Some reports suggested the women were subjected to sexual violence." United Nations Mission in South Sudan. "Interim Report on Human Rights: Crisis in South Sudan." 21 Feb. 2014.unmiss.unmissions.org/sites/default/files/hrd_interim_report_on_crisis_2014-02-21.pdf.

CHAPTER 17

p. 307 "Tonight there is a new crisis spot for the world... and there's growing fear there of an all-out war." "Dec. 23: Nightly News Monday broadcast." *NBC.* 23 Dec. 2013. www.nbcnews.com/watch/nightly-news-netcast/dec-23-nightly-news-monday -broadcast-99062851900.

p. 308 "We knew there were tensions... I think nobody could have expected." Johnson, Hilde. "Press Conference on the Situation in South Sudan." United Nations Mission in South Sudan, 26 Dec. 2013. Transcript. www.un.org/en/peacekeeping/missions/unmiss /documents/SRSG_PRESS_CONFERENCE_26%20December_2013.pdf.

p. 308 "'Let me be absolutely clear. The world is watching all sides in South Sudan'...." UN Secretary General. "Opening remarks at press conference in New York following visit to the Philippines." 23 Dec. 2013. https://www.un.org/sg/en/content/sg/speeches/2013-12-23 /opening-remarks-press-conference-new-york-following-visit-philippines.

p. 308 "'Stop the violence...no time to lose.'" UN Secretary General. "Secretary-General's press encounter following the Security Council's adoption of resolution on crisis in South Sudan." 24 Dec. 2013. https://www.un.org/sg/en/content/sg/press-encounter /2013-12-24/secretary-generals-press-encounter-following-security-councils.

p. 308 "'We pray for social harmony in South Sudan... where current tensions have already caused too many victims.'... threat to 'peaceful coexistence in that young state.'" The Vatican. "Urbi Et Orbi Message of Pope Francis: Christmas 2013." *Vatican. va,* 25 Dec. 2013. w2.vatican.va/content/francesco/en/messages/urbi/documents /papa-francesco_20131225_urbi-et-orbi-natale.html.

p. 309 "... for an emergency 'principals committee' meeting. The government's highest-level decision-making body had been convened... assessments were being briefed to President Obama." Office of the Press Secretary, The White House. "Readout of Obama's Updates On South Sudan." Dec. 21 2013.

p. 309 "The U.S. Embassy in Juba had already suspended normal operations and evacuated nearly 700 Americans and other foreign nationals." U.S. Department of State. Office of Press Relations. "U.S. Citizen Evacuation in South Sudan." 22 Dec. 2013. 2009-2017.state.gov/r/pa/prs/ps/2013/219057.htm.

p. 310 "Air Force Major Ryan Mittelstet piloted 'Rooster 73,' the lead Osprey... SEALs checked their gear and readied to extract the stranded Americans." This account comes almost entirely from: Whittle, Richard. "MacKay Trophy For AFSOC Osprey Crews: A Tale of Bullet Riddled Planes." *BreakingDefense.com,* 3 Nov. 2014. breakingdefense.com/2014/11/mackay -trophy-for-afsoc-osprey-crews-a-tale-of-bullet-riddled-planes/.

p. 310 "'Taking fire!' Mittelstet shouted into the radio seconds later, 'Go around! Go around!' More than 100 rounds of AK-47 and .50 caliber rifle fire riddled the Ospreys' fuselage... the barrage of unexpected fire wounding four SEALS." Whittle, "MacKay Trophy For AFSOC Osprey Crews."

p. 311 "After round-the-clock deliberations, Obama's National Security team decided to draw down the number of personnel at the embassy... Only the Ambassador and a skeleton staff would remain, and emergency security squads would be flown in to protect them." "Drawdown of Diplomatic Personnel at the U.S. Embassy in Juba, South Sudan." Press Statement, U.S. Department of State, 3 Jan. 2014; U.S.

Africa Command. "Marines Evacuate Embassy in South Sudan." 4 Jan. 2013. www.africom.mil.

p. 315 "... Over the next week... each meeting buttressed by calls from Secretary Kerry." "Daily Press Briefing," U.S. Department of State. 30 Dec. 2013

p. 316 "In a speech to parliament days later, the president called for restraint and dialogue while expressing sadness at the 'despicable atrocities' committed... blaming the "power thirsty" coup plotters for destroying the country." "Speech of President Salva Kiir in the National Legislative Conference." *YouTube,* uploaded by South Sudan Online. 23 Dec. 2013. www.youtube.com/watch?v=-FlK07rCRBU.

p. 321 "Recalling the 'hope for freedom, justice, and prosperity...'" Communique of the 23rd Extra-Ordinary Session of the IGAD Assembly of Heads of State and Government on the Situation in South Sudan, State House, Nairobi, 27 Dec. 2013.

p. 323 "... we shall have to go for him, all of us... defeat him." Aaron Maasho and Carl Odera, "Uganda says region ready to take on, defeat South Sudan rebel leader." *Reuters,* 30 Dec. 2013.

p. 324 "It happened so fast... Ugandan airplanes and bombs... it seemed to us that this had been a coordinated attack on the Nuer, something planned in advance." Author Interview, Skype, Mar. 2016.

p. 324 "'While the conflict that has engulfed the ...giving support, military and otherwise, to their ethnic leaders.'" Dr. Jok Madut Jok "Testimony before the U.S. Senate Committee on Foreign Relations." 20 Sept. 2016.

CHAPTER 18

p. 327 For a more detailed assessment of the South Sudan peace process, the mediation context, and lessons learned, see: Vertin, Zach, "A Poisoned Well: Lessons in Mediation from South Sudan's Troubled Peace Process." International Peace Institute, New York, Apr. 2018. Some analysis and quotations from chapters 18–21 were synthesized for use in the IPI publication, as identified therein.

p. 327 "Prominent hotels have been a unique part of post-colonial history across much of Africa; as author Michela Wrong wrote, they are often 'microcosms of their countries' tumultuous histories.'" Wrong, Michela. *In the Footsteps of Mr. Kurtz.* New York: HarperCollins, 2001. p. 16.

p. 334 "... $2,000 daily stipend..." "South Sudanese chief negotiator paid 'allowance' of $2,000 per day." *Radio Tamazuj,* 5 Dec. 2014.

p. 337 "Excellencies, Ladies and Gentlemen,' Seyoum began...'The signing of the agreements mark an important milestone... a thousand miles begins with one step.'" "South Sudan Government and Rebels Ceasefire Agreement – Addis Ababa." *YouTube,* uploaded by South Sudan Online. 25 Jan. 2015. www.youtube.com /watch?v=dUNn7Y7BOK0&t=8s.

p. 338 "... President Obama welcomed the 'critical first step toward building a lasting peace.'... he urged the parties to immediately 'start an inclusive political dialogue to resolve the underlying causes of the conflict.'" The White House, Office of the Press Secretary. "Statement by the President on South Sudan." 23 Jan. 2014. obamawhitehouse.archives.gov /the-press-office/2014/01/23/statement-president-south-sudan.

CHAPTER 19

p. 341 "'African states and the West share a common interest in ending conflicts,' Booth later reflected in a speech... challenges—which, if not carefully managed, can complicate peace processes or compromise outcomes.'" Booth, Donald. "South Sudan's Peace Process: Reinvigorating the Transition." *Chatham House*, 9 Feb. 2016. www.chathamhouse.org/sites/fileschathamhouse/events/2016-02-09-south-sudan -peace-process-reinvigorating-transition-transcript.pdf.

p. 342 "Now that's one promise broken, Mr. Minister." "South Sudan Information Minister Michael Makuei – Interview." *YouTube*, uploaded by South Sudan Online. 3 Jul. 2014. https://www.youtube.com/watch?v=ii4d0iWE2gE&t=5s.

p. 346 "'We feel we have a contribution to give... People talk about a military coup, there was no coup... that's why we are here." "South Sudan's 7 Former Political Detainees to Join Peace Talks." *YouTube*, uploaded by CGTN Africa. 16 Feb. 2014. www.youtube.com /watch?v=kTsx3y87a1c.

p. 348 "But... 'the very first issue they wanted to discuss was getting someone to pay for their laundry bills!' the diplomat spouted, shaking his head. 'It was appalling.'" Author Interview, European diplomat, Washington, D.C. Feb. 2017.

p. 349 "And so 'following a request by SPLM Chairman, President Salva Kiir,' the Tanzanians established the alternative process..." The United Republic of Tanzania, Directorate of Presidential Communications "Statement on SPLM Agreement in Arusha." Jan. 21 2015.

p. 350 "*Everything* is always focused on them. As if *we* have nothing to offer?" Author Interview, Skype, Jun. 2017.

p. 352 "... Nuer commanders took to the radio waves, telling Dinka civilians they would be hunted, and calling on their supporters to rape Dinka women. Barbash, Fred. "An 'abomination:' Slaughter in the mosques and churches of Bentiu, South Sudan." *The Washington Post,* 23 Apr. 2014. www.washingtonpost.com/news /morning-mix/wp/2014/ 04/23/an-abomination-slaughter-in-the-mosques-and -churches-of-bentiu-south-sudan.

p. 352 "Some 250 bodies were moved out of town in the middle of the night and dumped in a drainage ditch." United Nations Mission in the Republic of South Sudan. "Attacks on Civilians in Bentiu & Bor April 2014." 9 Jan. 2015. www.ohchr.org/Documents /Countries/SS/UNMISS_HRDJanuary2015.pdf.

p. 352 "'We are horrified... Images and accounts of the attacks shock the conscience.'" The White House, Office of the Press Secretary. "Statement by the Press Secretary on South Sudan." 22 Apr. 2014. obamawhitehouse.archives.gov /the-press-office/2014/04/22/statement-press-secretary-south-sudan.

p. 352 "'*President Obama!... Vice President Biden!...* This is happening on your watch!'... 'in South Sudan and the potential for the recent violence to spiral into genocide.'" Statement of Rep. Frank R. Wolf, U.S. House of Representatives Session, 1 May 2014. C-SPAN. https://www.c-span.org/video/?319051-1/us -house-general-speeches&start=15568.

p. 356 "... raining cluster bombs over rebel-held territory was quite another." Evidence of cluster bomb use was reported by the United Nations: United Nations Mission in the Republic of South Sudan. "Conflict in South Sudan: A Human Rights Report." 8 May

2014. unmiss.unmissions.org/sites/default/files/unmiss_conflict_in_south_sudan_-_a_human_rights_report.pdf.

p. 356 "... State Department, we warned of 'the serious consequences which could result from any regionalization of this conflict,' and reiterated the need for a 'withdrawal of foreign forces.'" U.S. Department of State, Office of Press Relations. "U.S. Concern About Violations of Cessation of Hostilities in South Sudan." 8 Feb. 2014. 2009-2017.state.gov/r/pa/prs/ps/2014/02/221487.htm.

p. 356 "What if violence rolls back... will the US be there to help?" @defenceuganda. "What if violence rolls back into Bor, Juba after UPDF withdraw, will the US be there to help?" *Twitter.com,* 10 Feb. 2014. twitter.com/defenceuganda/status/432863024798781440.

p. 358 "His army had also deployed around the region to plunder timber, coltan, diamonds, and other valuable resources." For example, see: United Nations Security Council. "Final report of the Panel of Experts on the Illegal Exploitation of Natural Resources and Other Forms of Wealth of the Democratic Republic of the Congo." S/2002/1146, 16 Oct. 2002. www.un.org/en/sc/documents/letters/2002.shtml.

p. 359 "Obama's order authorized travel bans and asset freezes for anyone disrupting peace talks, committing atrocities, or interfering with life-saving humanitarian aid." The White House, Office of the Press Secretary. "Executive Order-Blocking Property of Certain Persons With Respect to South Sudan." 3 Apr. 2014. obamawhitehouse.archives.gov/the-press-office/2014/04/03/executive-order-blocking-property-certain-persons-respect-south-sudan.

p. 359 "The United States will not stand by... expected their leaders to be statesmen, not strongmen." The White House, Office of the Press Secretary. "Press Statement from the White House Regarding South Sudan." 3 Apr. 2014. obamawhitehouse.archives.gov/the-press-office/2014/04/03/statement-press-secretary-south-sudan.

p. 359 "In a rendezvous the next morning with IGAD, AU, and UN leaders, Kerry ... to impose sanctions if immediate progress was not made." See: "Press Availability in Addis Ababa" and "Remarks With Ethiopian Foreign Minister Tedros Adhanom, Kenyan Foreign Minister Amina Chawahir Mohamed, And Ugandan Foreign Minister Sam Kutesa After Their Meeting." Secretary John Kerry, 1 May 2014. https://2009-2017.state.gov/secretary/remarks/2014/05/index.htm.

p. 360 "The secretary's 757 would not fly the next leg of the trip to Juba, but was swapped out for a C-17 U.S. military transport aircraft... ascending stairs to a VIP seat in the cockpit." Department of State. "Secretary Kerry Chats with Pilots of C-17 Flying him to South Sudan." May 2 2014. www.flickr.com/photos/statephotos.

p. 361 "Jogging up red-carpeted stairs... flanked by two rows of advisers." Department of State. "Secretary Kerry, South Sudanese President Prepare for Meeting in Juba." May 2 2014. For more visuals from Kerry's trip, see: www.flickr.com/photos/statephotos.

p. 361 "'I just completed an in-depth, very frank, and thorough discussion with President Kiir,' Kerry began... Before the promise of South Sudan's future is soaked in more blood," he continued, the two sides must take steps to end the violence, lest they "completely destroy what they are fighting to inherit." For Secretary Kerry's detailed account of the meeting with Salva Kiir, see: U.S. Department of State.

"Press Availability in South Sudan." Secretary of State John Kerry, 2 May 2014. 2009-2017.state.gov/secretary/remarks/2014/05/225531.htm.

CHAPTER 20

p. 373 "... Olony is a towering physical presence who once proclaimed to a public rally that he had a "Ph.D. in war-fighting." Copnall, James. "Upper Nile diary: atrocities, federalism and the Shilluk." *Africanarguments.org*, 6 Oct. 2014. http://africanarguments.org /2014/10/06/upper-nile-diary-atrocities-federalism-and-the-shilluk-by-james-copnall/.

p. 377 "By the end of the year, the price of oil had dropped by 50 percent—from more than $110 per barrel to roughly $55. A year later, it had plummeted below $40." "Year in Review: Crude Oil Prices 2014"; U.S. Energy Information Administration. "Daily Crude Spot Oil Prices, 2015." www.eia.gov

p. 384 "...speculation arose that Sumbeiywo was secretly colluding with Salva's government; colleagues worried he was leaking documents, offering inside information, and maneuvering to undercut the rebels." Author discussions, and subsequent interviews with, IGAD secretariat staff, January 2018.

CHAPTER 21

p. 391 "Riek and his second-in-command, Taban Deng, controlled ammunition supply chains, circumvented chains of command, and manipulated subordinates so as to maintain a firm grip." Author discussions with John Young, as well as unpublished research on the SPLM-In-Opposition conducted by Young, 2014–2015.

p. 391 "As the numbers swelled at the second convention in Pagak, the middle-of-nowhere village was soon overwhelmed." Details of the events at the Pagak from author discussions and interviews with those present, both participants and foreign observers.

p. 393 "In an unusually frank memo... Seyoum wrote of agreements dishonored, deadlines missed, and of two men who were 'prisoners to their own constituencies.'" Intergovernmental Authority on Development Special Envoys for South Sudan. "Developments in the IGAD-led South Sudan Peace Process, challenges and recommendations for the way forward." Memo to H.E. Hailemariam Desalegn, Prime Minister of the FDRE and Chair of the IGAD Assembly of Heads of State and Government. Mar. 5 2015. Obtained by Author.

p. 393 "I regret to inform you that the talks did not produce the necessary breakthrough... abdication of the most sacred duty leaders have to you, their people: to deliver peace, prosperity and stability." Intergovernmental Authority On Development Secretariat. "Message From H.E. Hailemariam Desalegn, Prime Minister of the Federal Democratic Republic of Ethiopia and Chairperson of the IGAD Assembly to the People of South Sudan." 6 Mar. 2015.

p. 394 "Legitimacy is not a presumed right of any government... It is conferred by the people, and it is sustained only by demonstrating leadership to protect and serve all citizens—responsibilities the government has neglected." U.S. Department of State. "Secretary Kerry on South Sudan Negotiations." Secretary of State John Kerry, 2 Mar. 2015. 2009-2017.state.gov/secretary/remarks/2015/03/238106.htm.

p. 394 "Susan Rice underscored the tough messaging... 'Over the past 19 months, the government has abdicated its responsibilities, failed to protect its citizens, and squandered its legitimacy." The White House, Office of the Press Secretary. "Statement by National Security Advisor Susan E. Rice on South Sudan Independence Day." 9 Jul. 2015. obamawhitehouse.archives.gov/the-pressoffice/2015/07/09 /statement-national-security-advisor-susan-e-rice-south-sudan.

p. 396 "The action had arguably saved thousands... and was for Obama 'the right thing to do.' ... Obama called failing to plan for the day after the 'worst mistake of his presidency.'" "President Obama: Libya aftermath 'worst mistake' of presidency." BBC, 11 Apr. 2016. https://www.bbc.com/news/ world-us-canada-36013703.

p. 397 "'As a consequence of this discussion... the kind of peace that the people of South Sudan so desperately need.'" Addis Ababa, The White House. "The President holds a Multilateral Meeting on South Sudan and Counterterrorism." 27 July 2015. https:// obamawhitehouse.archives.gov/photos-and-video/video/2015/07/27/president -holds-multilateral-meeting-south-sudan-and-counterterror.

p. 398 "Obama then turned attention to South Sudan's belligerent parties... a transition without Salva and Riek... a clear signal to those in the room, but the message would also find its way back to the camps of Salva and Riek." On the margins of the summit, senior administration officials also informed reporters of the desire for a transitional government that would "not necessarily include the current players." (Kosinski, Michelle. "Obama, African leaders meet to end South Sudan's civil war." CNN, 27 Jul. 2015.) A week later, citing his summit with IGAD leaders and the expectation that Salva and Riek form a transitional government, Obama again signaled his readiness to pursue an endgame without the two men, if necessary: "If they miss that target, then I think... it's going to be necessary for us to move forward with a different plan and recognize that those leaders are incapable of creating the peace that's required." "President Obama with Secretary General Ban Ki-Moon." 4 C-SPAN, August 2015. https://www.c-span.org/video/?327463-1 /president-obama-meeting-un-secretary-general-ban-ki-moon

p. 398 "And so the leaders announced that they expected the parties to finalize a peace deal in three weeks' time, and that UNSC action, including punitive measures, would ensue if the deadline was missed.'" Accounts of this meeting draw on author interviews with U.S. and non-U.S. individuals with primary and secondary knowledge of the meeting's events. Juba, Jun. 2016; New York, Sept. 2016; Addis Ababa, Jan. 2018; Telephone and Skype, Jun. 2017, Aug. 2018; Participating U.S. officials also briefed reporters before and after the summit. See: Peter Baker and Marc Santora, "Obama Gathers Leaders in Effort to End South Sudan War." *New York Times*, 27 July 2015.

p. 398 "'I was there... when we held up South Sudan as the promise of a new beginning.'" Office of the Press Secretary, The White House. "Remarks by President Obama to the People of Africa." 28 Jul. 2015.

p. 400 "'We denounce and disown Dr. Riek Machar,' read an August 10 missive from Peter Gadet..." Letter from General Peter Gadet, Deputy Chief of General Staff for Operations, SPLA In Opposition, 10 Aug. 2015. Copy obtained by Author.

p. 405 "In New York, U.S. diplomats circulated a draft resolution..." UN Security Council. "US proposes UN arms embargo on South Sudan." *Al Jazeera*, 20 Aug. 2015.

p. 406 "The guy was hysterical about the idea that we favored Riek." Author Interview, Molly Phee, Telephone, 2017.

p. 408 "... Susan Rice would later issue a statement... that the United States did 'not recognize any reservations or addendums to the agreement.'" The White House. "Statement by the National Security Advisor Susan E. Rice on the South Sudan Peace Agreement." Aug. 25 2016.

CHAPTER 22

p. 415 "That global trauma... more so than 9/11.'" Author Interview, former White House National Security Council official, Washington, D.C., Jun. 2017.

p. 416 "There was simply 'less time and political capital invested in its 'remaking'..." Author Interview, Washington, D.C., Oct. 2016.

p. 418 "'My adrenaline went through the roof'..." Author Interview, Washington, D.C., Oct. 2017. Accounts of the 7 July events draw on Author Interviews with U.S. embassy and other government officials in the Fall of 2017, as well as media reports, see: Lynch, Colum. "Dinner, Drinks, and a Near-Fatal Ambush for U.S. Diplomats." *Foreign Policy*, 6 Sept. 2016.

p. 419 "The *Associated Press* later published a detailed account of the four-hour attack... 'You tell your embassy how we treated you.'" While author discussions with individuals in Juba and Washington D.C. in 2016 and 2017 corroborated the general events, the detailed account of this attack (and the quotations herein) draw almost exclusively on the *Associated Press* report: Patinkin, Jason. "Rampaging South Sudan troops raped foreigners, killed local." *Associated Press,* 16 Aug. 2016. apnews.com/52f948f476874cbda6277492a4f8468e/rampaging-south-sudan-troops-raped-foreigners-killed-local.

p. 423 "There wasn't a lot of critical thinking," says one U.S. official... 'You just sort of knew this was the way it was, and assumed the environment was not going to change. This ridiculous narrative, it was immovable." Author Interview, Washington, D.C., Aug. 2016.

p. 423 "Many SPLM supporters failed to grasp the consequences of adopting their cause with such singularity and zeal." This paragraph draws upon an opinion article penned by the author in 2016. Vertin, Zach. "George Clooney and the Rot in South Sudan." *Washington Post*, 23 Sept. 2016.

p. 424 "'We lost objectivity'... we were never a tough friend.'" Author Interview, Washington, D.C., Fall 2016.

CHAPTER 23

p. 428 "'They're treated like kids'...the promise, and the wasted opportunity, of a generation." Author Interview, Nairobi, Jun. 2016.

p. 438 "... Koang was forced to issue a statement establishing his bona fides and rebutting assertions that he was an agent of Salva's government." Chol, Koang Rambang. "Bieh State Deputy Governor Gen. Koang Rambang: 'I Will Never Defect.'" *Nyamilepedia*, 18 Aug. 2016. nyamile.com/2016/08/18bieh-state-deputy-governor-gen-koang-rambang-i-will-never-defect/.

ACKNOWLEDGMENTS

I am forever grateful to the many people who helped me complete this book. Atop the list are the countless Sudanese and South Sudanese interlocutors who educated me—in many different ways—over the course of more than eight years; they are far too many to name here. Additionally, I am indebted to the following people for their ideas, edits, and encouragement throughout what was by turns a rewarding, challenging, and educational process: Aly Verjee, Karen Bulthuis, Joe Sharkey, Allison Lombardo, David Mozersky, Goi Yol, Bob Templer, Greg Puley, Kim Taylor, Katherine Ratledge, Nikki Haan, Nicola Reindorp, Victoria Brereton, David Mitchell, Maya Mailer, Dan Vexler, Michela Wrong, Alex Cuadros, Finbarr O'Reilly, Bart Gellman, Jason Stearns, Andy Burnett, Will Echols, Endre Stiansen, Susan Stigant, Douglas Johnson, Robin Miller, Nealin Parker, Alex Bick, and Megan McGuire. An extra special thanks to my tireless and good-spirited research assistants, Melanie Kent and Abraham Tall, without whom there would be no book. Thanks also to Jessica Case at Pegasus Books and to the team at Amberley Publishing for shepherding this project to the finish, and to the brilliant Jen McDonald, whose editing skill and intuition and energy I could not have done without.

Sincere thanks also to the following institutions for their support for this project, including great spaces to think and write: the Carey Institute for Global Good (including Josh Friedman, Carol Ash, Tom Jennings, and the entire Carey team), and the Woodrow Wilson International Center for Scholars (Rob Litwak, Kim Conner, and the Wilson staff). I am especially grateful to Ambassador Donald Booth and to my many colleagues in the Office of the Special Envoy, the Obama Administration, and at the International Crisis Group.

To Ambassador Princeton Lyman, a diplomatic giant and tireless public servant who elevated those around him, and whose leadership and humility will live on in those he mentored. To the many young South Sudanese men and women who were taken too soon, but whose energy and optimism for their country will likewise outlive them. Among them was Koang Rambeng, who passed away, unexpectedly, in 2018 after this manuscript was completed. To my professor Rene McGraw, who has been mentor, friend, and honest human for fifteen years. And to my friend Susan Linnee, who introduced me to ideas and books and ways to live, and who read the first half of this book, but sadly was not able to see it finished. She will be forever missed. Lastly, and most importantly, I am grateful to my mother and father, Maggie and Stephen, for teaching me about the world, and to the many other family members who have supported me along the way.

INDEX

INDEX